CONTAMINATED COUNTRY

Weyerhaeuser Environmental Books

Paul S. Sutter, Editor

CONTAMINATED COUNTRY

Nuclear Colonialism and Aboriginal Resistance in Australia

Jessica Urwin

University of Washington Press
Seattle

Contaminated Country is published with the assistance of a grant from the Weyerhaeuser Environmental Books Endowment, established by the Weyerhaeuser Company Foundation, members of the Weyerhaeuser family, and Janet and Jack Creighton.

This publication was also supported by a grant from the Australian Academy of the Humanities.

Design by Mindy Basinger Hill / Composed in Minion Pro

UNIVERSITY OF WASHINGTON PRESS *uwapress.uw.edu*

LIBRARY OF CONGRESS CATALOGING-IN-PUBLICATION DATA
Names: Urwin, Jessica, 1995– author
Title: Contaminated country : nuclear colonialism and Aboriginal resistance in Australia / Jessica Urwin.
Other titles: Nuclear colonialism and Aboriginal resistance in Australia
Description: Seattle : University of Washington Press, [2025] | Series: Weyerhaeuser environmental books | Includes bibliographical references and index.
Identifiers: LCCN 2025009790 (print) | LCCN 2025009791 (ebook) | ISBN 9780295753782 hardcover | ISBN 9780295753799 paperback | ISBN 9780295753805 ebook
Subjects: LCSH: Nuclear weapons—Australia—History | Nuclear weapons—Government policy—Australia | Nuclear weapons—Testing—Environmental aspects—Australia | Aboriginal Australians, Treatment of—Australia | Nuclear weapons—Great Britain—Testing | Antinuclear movement—Australia
Classification: LCC UA870 .U78 2025 (print) | LCC UA870 (ebook) | DDC 355.8/251190994—dc23/eng/20250512
LC record available at https://lccn.loc.gov/2025009790
LC ebook record available at https://lccn.loc.gov/2025009791

♾ This paper meets the requirements of ANSI/NISO Z39.48-1992 (Permanence of Paper).

To all those who have resisted and continue to resist.

CONTENTS

FOREWORD The Curious Case of Australian Nuclear Colonialism, by Paul S. Sutter *ix*

ACKNOWLEDGMENTS *xv*

NOTE TO THE READER *xix*

INTRODUCTION Fission and Fusion *1*

ONE Radioactive Riches *15*

TWO Fields of Thunder *41*

THREE Australia in the "Nuclear Playground" *68*

FOUR Paving the "Yellowcake Road" *92*

FIVE Unearthing the Hidden Histories of the Tests *125*

SIX Finding a Seat at the Table *154*

SEVEN Irati Wanti *184*

CONCLUSION Fallout *211*

NOTES *219*

BIBLIOGRAPHY *265*

INDEX *291*

FOREWORD

The Curious Case of Australian Nuclear Colonialism

Paul S. Sutter

It is easy to see the dawn of the nuclear age as a moment of rupture in world history, for the bomb unlocked the elemental energy of the atom in ways that required humans to rethink their relationships to nature and each other. From an environmental standpoint, the bomb raised all sorts of questions about Promethean powers and sin. "For the first time in some two million years of human history," the environmental historian Donald Worster lamented in *Nature's Economy*, "there existed a force capable of destroying the entire fabric of life on the planet." For Worster, the detonation of the first bomb marked the beginning of the "Age of Ecology," a transformative event that produced both profound environmental anxieties and modern ecological concern. More recently, the members of the International Commission of Stratigraphy's Anthropocene Working Group recommended locating the beginnings of the Anthropocene—a proposed new epoch in the Earth's geological history characterized by pervasive human influence—in the middle of the twentieth century because of the stratigraphic signals produced by fallout from nuclear weapons testing. To environmental thinkers, the atomic age has appeared to be something new under the sun. From the standpoint of human relations, the dawn of the nuclear age has also seemed a point of profound change, particularly in the international arena. While the United States emerged from World War II with a nuclear monopoly, soon there were several other nuclear weapon states that made claims to geopolitical power on the basis of their nuclear capacities. The bomb thus seemed to shift international relations away from fading colonial regimes, with their civilizational logics, and toward a new international order in which nuclear modernity was the salient dividing line.

Recent scholars have troubled these arguments for nuclear exceptionalism. As Gabrielle Hecht argues in *Being Nuclear*, her study of Africa's role in providing fissionable materials to nuclear weapon states, colonialism is alive and well in this new nuclear order, though the fictive category of "nuclearity"—of what does and does not count as "nuclear"—obscures such colonial relations. In the North American context, scholars such as Traci Brynne Voyles, Lianne Leddy, and Myrriah Gómez have written compellingly about the nuclear order's impacts on Indigenous lands and peoples. Together these scholars suggest that nuclear colonialism, although new in some of its dimensions, is best seen as a continuation of long-standing imperial and settler-colonial dynamics. They also draw our attention away from the universalizing logic of the threats posed to "humanity" and "life on earth" by nuclear weapons and toward the persistent environmental injustices of the modern nuclear order. Worster's "Age of Ecology," they suggest, was also an age of nuclear inequality whose origins predate the first mushroom cloud.

As Jessica Urwin writes in *Contaminated Country*, her groundbreaking history of nuclear colonialism, Australia provides a curious case study, for it is "one of the only historical examples of an independent non-nuclear weapon state offering up its own sovereign territory for the testing of another state's nuclear weapons." Urwin is not the first historian to attend to the fact that Australians allowed the British to conduct a dozen nuclear tests in their territorial lands and waters between 1952 and 1963. But others have focused mostly on how Australia's continuing colonial relations to the British explain their strange history as a testing ground. Conventional wisdom has largely understood Australia to have been a victim of nuclear colonialism rather than its perpetrator, and this, Urwin argues, has allowed settler Australians to ignore their own complicity in the nuclear colonialism experienced by Australia's Aboriginal peoples. *Contaminated Country* is a bold effort to correct that misapprehension, a study that rejects the exceptionalism of the nuclear age and insists that we see nuclear colonialism in Australia as part of a longer history of settler colonialism on the continent.

At the heart of Urwin's analysis is the Aboriginal concept of Country. Country not only encompasses the more-than-human world of lands, waters, skies, and other beings, but it also speaks to origins, kinship, and ancestral connections to these elements, to traditional knowledge, the sacred, sovereignty, and relationships of care and reciprocity. As her title suggests, Urwin asks readers to imagine how the various manifestations of nuclear colonialism in Australia contaminated Country in all of its layered complexity, and in doing so she demonstrates some of the limitations and dangers of using Western concepts of "nature" and "environment" for making sense of this history. Country takes us beyond questions about how radioactivity contaminated the environment and human bodies, or how the nuclear order dispossessed Aboriginal peoples, though these are all vital themes in the book that follows. The Aboriginal perspectives that Urwin foregrounds ask us to see a kind of cultural violence that sits at the heart of nuclear colonialism.

Urwin locates the beginnings of Australian nuclear colonialism in the early twentieth century, when scientists and prospectors discovered radioactive metals in the Australian interior. As in the United States, mining was critical to settler colonialism in Australia, as gold rushes brought settlers deep into Aboriginal territories in search of quick wealth. The story was similar for radioactive metals such as radium, which was immensely valuable for medical and other uses in the pre-atomic era. The success of such prospecting relied on appropriating Aboriginal lands and exploiting Aboriginal knowledge and labor, though sources from the period rarely acknowledge the roles that Aboriginal peoples played in this initial chapter of Australia's nuclear history. That erasure was symptomatic, Urwin argues, of a settler imaginary that viewed Australia's red heart as hostile and empty, its resources available for the taking. But as mid-century approached, nuclear colonialism's prospector phase gave way to the British search for an "Empire" supply of uranium and the Australian government's decision to earmark their uranium for Crown use. Even before the first detonation of an atomic bomb, Urwin argues, the layered nature of nuclear colonialism in Australia was apparent.

After World War II, nuclear colonialism's hunger for supposedly empty lands revealed itself in another way. As the British searched for places to test their nuclear weapons, they hit upon the maritime and desert territories of Australia as ideal sites. While the British conducted a few tests on the Monte Bello Islands off the coast of Western Australia, most occurred at two sites in South Australia, Emu Field and Maralinga. Australian antinuclear activists would later criticize the imperious British for exploiting Australian territory to advance their nuclear ambitions, and the Australian politicians who went along with the plan. But, as Urwin makes clear, these tests occurred on lands belonging to the Kokatha, Barngarla, Arabunna, Pitjantjatjara, Yankunytjatjara, and Antakirinja peoples, and the government in Canberra was deeply implicated in these acts of nuclear colonialism. Decades of missionary activity and government policies had already sought to manage the lives and movement of Aboriginal peoples across the central deserts. The dispossession that came with nuclear testing, then, continued settler-colonial processes that were well underway.

Ironically, it was the proximity of French nuclear testing in the South Pacific in the 1960s that finally raised substantial opposition among Australians to nuclear testing, linking Australian activists with others around the world who were growing concerned about the impacts of such testing on colonized peoples. But much of this new Australian consciousness was focused outward and neglected Australia's own history of testing and its impacts on Aboriginal peoples. Only with the growth of Aboriginal activism did settler Australians finally face what Urwin calls "the persistence of the Australian public's ignorance toward its own country's role in perpetuating nuclear injustices against Aboriginal peoples."

By the late 1970s, a new front in Australian nuclear colonialism had opened with the commencement of large-scale uranium exploration and mining in the Northern Territory and South Australia. South Australia's proposed Olympic Dam mine was, and remains, the largest known uranium deposit in the world. But it also sits within Kokatha Country, and the rise of both the environmental and Aboriginal rights movements meant that the mine became a flashpoint. In the end, the economic downturn of the 1970s meant that many Australians supported the mine's development, favoring economic growth over Aboriginal rights or environmental concerns, another venerable settler colonial pattern. Indeed, even as South Australia passed landmark legislation that granted Aboriginal rights to a huge swath of territory and pledged to protect Aboriginal sacred sites, mining companies and their political supporters ran roughshod over Country in their efforts to get the Olympic Dam mine up and running.

But the politics of dispossession and contamination were changing by the 1980s. Under considerable pressure, the Australian government formed the Royal Commission into British Nuclear Tests in Australia to investigate British conduct during their weapons testing program. While the purpose of the Royal Commission was to heap blame on the British for subjecting their former colony to nuclear contamination, Urwin shows how Aboriginal peoples both insisted on meaningful involvement in the inquiry and, through their powerful testimony, began shifting the narrative toward Australian complicity. While, in the end, the Royal Commission maintained a narrow focus, the settler narrative's grip was slipping. Indeed, the 1980s and 1990s would see the international mobilization of Aboriginal activists, who built powerful transnational connections and ultimately convinced both the British and Australian governments to undertake major remediation efforts of former testing grounds and provide Aboriginal peoples with substantial compensation for the dispossession and contamination they had endured and continue to endure.

As a structure, settler colonialism can be difficult to dislodge, a fact made abundantly clear by the Australian government's remarkable decision in the 1990s to establish a national radioactive waste repository in a remote part of South Australia known as Billa Kalina. Aboriginal peoples had already been subject to uranium mining and nuclear testing, and now they faced the possibility of long-term storage of nuclear waste on their lands. Nuclear colonialism had many faces in Australia. In response, a group called the Kupa Piti Kungka Tjuta, or Coober Pedy Senior Women, organized to fight the waste dump. Aboriginal women have important roles in caring for Country, and, remarkably, they stopped the repository plans in their tracks. In 2003, Yankunytjatjara and Antakirinja woman Eileen Kampakuta Brown AM and Kokatha woman Eileen Wani Wingfield received the Goldman Environmental Prize, widely known as the Green Nobel, on behalf of the Kupa Piti Kungka Tjuta, a fitting recognition of the remarkable Aboriginal resistance to nuclear colonialism that is one of Urwin's essential themes.

Contaminated Country beautifully embodies a new generation of environmental history scholarship characterized by a commitment to social justice, the centering of alternative and often subaltern epistemologies and ontologies, and the embrace of more-than-human approaches. It is a brand of environmental history that Australian scholars have been particularly influential in developing. *Contaminated Country* thus demands our attention as an innovative Australian history with broad implications for our understanding of nuclear colonialism and Indigenous environmental justice all over the world. As nations flirt anew with nuclear power as a potential energy solution in a warming world, this is a history that we all must know.

ACKNOWLEDGMENTS

I am extremely privileged to have lived and worked on the unceded lands of the Ngunnawal and Ngambri peoples while writing this book. And although the majority of *Contaminated Country* was completed on these lands, I want to acknowledge the other lands on which this book's content was researched, or about which this book is written, including those of the Pitjantjatjara, Yankunytjatjara, Arabunna, Kokatha, Barngarla, Maralinga Tjarutja, Antakirinja, Gadigal, Yuin, Nukunu, Kaurna, and Adnyamathanha peoples. This book would not have been possible without the generosity and continued custodianship demonstrated by these communities and many others.

The individuals with whom I spoke for this research shared their stories with incredible grace, and for that I will be eternally grateful. Karina Lester shared generously about her late father, Yankunytjatjara man Yami Lester, and grandmother, prominent Kupa Piti Kungka Tjuta and Senior Yankunytjatjara and Antakirinja woman Eileen Kampakuta Brown. Janice Wingfield, Lynette Allen, Sonja Gaston, Tania Wingfield, and Ian Wingfield told stories of the knowledge shared with them by Kokatha woman (and their mother, aunty, and grandmother) Eileen Wani Wingfield. Michele Madigan met with me on the side of a windy highway halfway between Port Augusta and Adelaide to detail her involvement in the Irati Wanti campaign. Andrew Collett, Maggie Brady, and Heather Goodall have been both invaluable interviewees and sounding boards from this project's start to its end. And while my plans to visit Maralinga in 2020 were unceremoniously interrupted, the Maralinga Tjarutja Council, through their general manager, Sharon Yendall, and the chair of the Maralinga Tjarutja Trust, Jeremy LeBois, endorsed this research irrespective of the extensive strains on their time and resources.

The intellectual development of this work would have been impossible without those listed above, but it would also have been greatly impoverished without the brilliance and generosity of many mentors, colleagues, and friends. Angela Woollacott, Carrol Pursell, Maria Nugent, Ramesh Thakur, Martin Thomas, Michelle Staff, Joshua Black, and Emily Gallagher have seen this work develop from the very beginning. Ruth Morgan, Ben Silverstein, and Heather Goodall read this book in its entirety at various stages in its development, offering invaluable advice and guidance. Countless others have read chapters or extracts, provided words of encouragement, and asked formative questions along the way. Though I do not have the space to individually acknowledge everyone who has influenced this research, the formative fingerprints of dozens of fantastic scholars are all over this book.

Alongside the oral history interviews I conducted, this research drew on a wealth of archival collections. I want to thank the National Archives of Australia (NAA), National Library of Australia (NLA), Adolph Basser Library, Noel Butlin Archives Centre, Mawson Centre, State Library of South Australia, South Australian Museum, State Records of South Australia, Flinders University Special Collections, Hawke Prime Ministerial Library, State Library of New South Wales, Australian Institute of Aboriginal and Torres Strait Islander Studies, and National Archives, London, for access to their collections. Each of these repositories relies on the passion and hard work of knowledgeable and generous librarians and archivists, and I had all my research requests handled with great enthusiasm. My ability to travel to many of these repositories was made possible by generous funding from several organizations, including the National Museum of Australia, Australian Academy of Science, Australian Historical Association, History Council of New South Wales, Australian National University, and American Society of Environmental History.

In addition to their written records, the pictorial collections of the NAA, NLA, and Mawson Centre are represented among *Contaminated Country*'s illustrations. Glen Wingfield, Janice Wingfield, Maggie Brady, Kingsley Palmer, and Barry O'Malley provided further photographs from their own private collections. I am so grateful for their willingness to have these images included. These photographs are accompanied by several fabulous maps and a meticulously prepared index. The maps were created by Karina Pelling of CartoGIS at the Australian National University, and the index was compiled by Rani Kerin.

The passionate Weyerhaeuser Environmental Books team at the University of Washington Press guided *Contaminated Country* through to publication with enthusiasm and generosity. Paul S. Sutter, Mike Baccam, Justine Sargent, Dandi Meng, Jennifer Comeau, and Jane M. Lichty were an absolute dream to work with. They offered support, encouragement, and vital feedback on this book, handling it with care.

Contaminated Country was a labor of love enabled by the unwavering support of my nearest and dearest over many, many years. In particular, my parents, Lesley and Tony Urwin, have long fostered my curiosity and supported my passions, as have my grandparents. My grandmother Christine Urwin has inquired in dozens of letters and during many phone calls about the book's progress and I look forward to sharing it with her. My friends offered laughter and escape. My canine companion, Dingo, provided endless hours of company on often long days at the desk. And my partner, Andrew Palm, has been a perpetual source of positivity, laughter, love, and adventure over the course of this project. His untiring support, generosity, intellect, and quick wit have aided the process of writing this book immensely.

NOTE TO THE READER

Throughout *Contaminated Country*, I have endeavored to be as specific with my terminology as possible. As in the book's title, where I refer to "Country"—a word used by Aboriginal communities to capture the complex relationships between the earth, waters, skies and stars, flora and fauna, ancestral pasts, presents and futures, and unceded sovereignty of Aboriginal peoples and their lands—the term is capitalized. When used outside of this context, it is lowercased.

For the most part, I use "Indigenous" to refer more generally to Indigenous peoples the world over and "Aboriginal" to refer to the Indigenous peoples of Australia. I have used the specific language group of Indigenous and Aboriginal individuals wherever possible in accordance with the Australian Institute of Aboriginal and Torres Strait Islander Studies' agreed Indigenous naming practices.

Though the deserts within—and extending beyond—the borders of the contemporary South Australian state have specific ecological and cultural boundaries, I refer to them generally in this book as the "central desert region" or "central deserts." "Aṉangu" is the Pitjantjatjara word for "people" and is commonly used to refer collectively to the Aboriginal people of this region. It is used as such at various points throughout *Contaminated Country*.

As this book is concerned with shifting Aboriginal and settler politics and these changes are often reflected in language, I have retained the terminology and capitalization used by others when I quote historical material. For readability, except where there are genuine spelling errors, I have not used "*sic*" in instances where other authors have used alternative terminology or capitalization when referring to Aboriginal or Indigenous peoples. As such, I acknowledge that there may be terms quoted within the pages of this book that are considered offensive today. Their inclusion is purely illustrative.

Please note that this book refers to and contains images of Aboriginal people who are now deceased.

CONTAMINATED COUNTRY

INTRODUCTION

Fission and Fusion

In 2023 Karina Lester, an Aboriginal woman of the Yankunytjatjara people of northwestern South Australia, addressed the United Nations as a second-generation survivor of Britain's nuclear tests in Australia.[1] She began her address by introducing her father, Yami Lester, who was only twelve years old in 1953 when Britain's first inland nuclear test—Totem I—ripped through his traditional lands in the South Australian central desert region.[2] In heart-wrenching detail, she described her father's experience of encountering a "black mist," a roiling, oily cloud that swept across his lands following Totem I's detonation, making the old people sick and, in some cases, leading to their deaths. Over the following four years, Yami slowly lost his sight. He was entirely blind by age sixteen.

Karina Lester's grandmother, Yankunytjatjara and Antakirinja Elder Eileen Kampakuta Brown, also bore witness to the nuclear tests. Lester explained to the UN General Assembly that she and other Aboriginal Elders "were the ones there at the time when the ground shook and the black mist rolled and illness fell over our community." In the decades afterward, these Elders advocated strongly for their lands and their people, imploring the Australian government to acknowledge the disproportionate burdens borne by Indigenous people subjected to nuclear testing, uranium mining, and waste disposal. "We know our lands are poisoned," Lester told the United Nations; "we know the fallout contaminated our Country, our traditional lands, but also our families and our people who moved through those traditional lands."[3]

The concept of Country mentioned here by Lester is one powerfully evoked by Aboriginal peoples across Australia. Individuals use it to encapsulate the interconnections between the earth, water, skies, flora, fauna, ancestors, stories, and unceded sovereignty of their communities' ancestral lands. All of this is Country. Thus, to care for Country is to care for the environment, the plants and animals that rely on it, oneself, one's community, one's ancestors, one's culture, and future generations. As nuclear survivor and Kokatha woman Sue Coleman-Haseldine articulated it to the UN in 2017, "Aboriginal people have the oldest living culture on the planet and have cared for th[eir] lands continuously." Aboriginal peoples' protection of the environment from nuclear impositions is therefore intimately tied up in the protection and preservation of Country for past, present, and future generations. "Animals and plants, which are also harmed by radiation can't speak for themselves and are ignored and left to die," Coleman-Haseldine explained.[4] Resisting the contamination of Country is a cultural obligation.

Lester's and Coleman-Haseldine's speeches, and their invocation of Country, reveal the increased scrutiny placed on the global nuclear order in recent years, not least by nuclear survivors. In 2017, following extensive negotiations and amid what some have dubbed a "nuclear renaissance," 122 states voted in favor of the Treaty on the Prohibition of Nuclear Weapons (TPNW). Underpinning this treaty are the humanitarian consequences of nuclear weapons, including those experienced by Indigenous peoples the world over. During negotiations in March, June, and July 2017, members of the UN General Assembly heard the personal stories of those affected by nuclear weapons and their production. Such stories—including those of Lester and Coleman-Haseldine—encouraged decision-makers to reckon with the global nuclear order's imposition on Indigenous peoples and lands for over nearly a century.[5] The TPNW's preamble has enshrined this acknowledgment in law by including the phrase "*Recognizing* the disproportionate impact of nuclear-weapon activities on indigenous peoples."[6] This book seeks to grapple with these disproportionate impacts in an Australian context.

By centering the environmental justice concept of "nuclear colonialism," *Contaminated Country* explores the historical interplay between nuclear processes, colonialism, and Aboriginal resistance in Australia. What is revealed is the intimate relationship between Australia's nuclear past and the nation's settler-colonial underpinnings. Australian authorities have historically drawn inspiration from settler-colonial visions of their island continent's utility to dispossess, silence, and contaminate its Aboriginal peoples in pursuit of nuclear development. As a result, not only have Aboriginal peoples borne the brunt of nuclear-weapons activities, but these communities and their lands have been subjected to both small- and large-scale radioactive mineral extraction and nuclear waste disposal. The concept of nuclear colonialism offers a lens through which to interrogate this subjection and its impacts while viewing the concurrent progression and adaptation of Australian settler colonialism leading up to and during the so-called nuclear age. Often these adaptations occurred in the face of anticolonial challenge.

The history of nuclear colonialism is also a story rich in examples of Aboriginal resistance. While those interested in nuclear colonialism often focus on the infliction of nuclear harms on Indigenous lands and peoples, *Contaminated Country* demonstrates that communities have both experienced incalculable physical, spiritual, and cultural harm *and* vehemently refused nuclear colonialism, challenging it time and again. In Australia, this challenge—or refusal—began as survival. But as the twentieth century progressed, it transformed into active resistance, the reclamation of Country, and demands for reparations. As Coleman-Haseldine powerfully explained to the United Nations, "Despite attempts to annihilate, assimilate and suppress us, we remain committed to looking after our people, cultural knowledge, lands and waters."[7] By accounting for both Aboriginal experiences of and resistance to nuclear colonialism in Australia, *Contaminated Country* interrogates the historical tensions between radium and uranium extraction, nuclear weapons testing, radioactive waste disposal, and colonialism across the course of the twentieth century.

Australia's Nuclear Past (and Future)

When prompted to think about global nuclear history, few think of Australia. In fact, even Australians fail to think of Australia. Unlike its closest allies, the United States and the United Kingdom, Australia has never developed or possessed its own nuclear weapons. It has never developed or relied on nuclear power. It is not what one would typically class as a nuclear state. Nevertheless, it has a remarkably complex nuclear past (see map 1), existing as a globally pertinent example of the need for contemporary nuclear scholarship to expand its geographical remit.

From the first decade of the twentieth century, Australians were involved

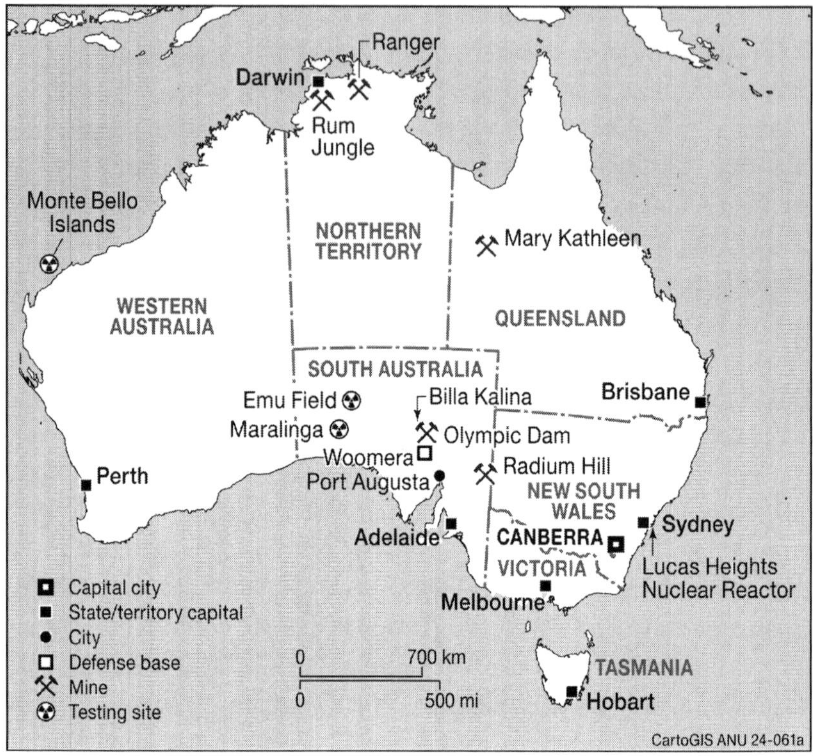

MAP 1. Australia has been subjected to both inland and offshore nuclear weapons tests, is home to some of the world's largest uranium deposits, and has set aside large swathes of land for the defense facilities of its allies. This map details the locations of these various sites across the country. Map provided by CartoGIS Services, Australian National University, Canberra.

in the global hunt for radioactive minerals (see chapter 1). The 1898 scientific discovery of radium by Marie and Pierre Curie prompted prospectors to hope that somewhere in Australia, radioactive minerals abounded. Those settlers who ventured into Australia's inland in search of radium were not wrong to speculate that the continent was brimming with radioactive riches; however, early searches yielded insufficient evidence of radium's abundance in nature. Individuals and firms struggled to justify the cost of continued exploration, and Australia's radioactive minerals market went stagnant for several decades.[8]

However, government interest in radioactive minerals increased exponentially in the 1940s when radioactivity's military applications were realized by scientists across the world. The British government encouraged its Australian counterpart to invest in exploration, armed with evidence that radioactive minerals did appear to occur in Australia. As part of the Combined Development Agency's attempts to secure global uranium supplies, British- and American-supported uranium mines sprang up in the Australian states of South Australia, Queensland, and the Northern Territory, their meager supplies fueling Britain's and the United States' nuclear weapons programs.[9] By 1950, not only was Australia supplying the uranium necessary for Britain to build its nuclear weapons, but it had been picked as the potential future site for their testing.

Though Australia does not possess, nor has it ever possessed, nuclear weapons, its lands have been subject to nuclear testing. In fact, Australia exists as one of the only historical examples of an independent non–nuclear weapon state offering up its own sovereign territory for the testing of another state's nuclear weapons. In 1951, Australia's Prime Minister Robert Menzies agreed to host a series of British nuclear weapons trials off the coast of Western Australia. Within the decade, Australia had conceded two further proving grounds in its arid interior. Between 1952 and 1963, Australia's offshore marine and inland desert environments were subjected to twelve nuclear detonations and hundreds of accompanying experiments involving radioactive substances (see chapter 2).[10]

Australian officials in Canberra hoped that in exchange for their provision of nuclear testing facilities, the British government at Whitehall would provide the scientific knowledge and technology Australia required to develop its own nuclear energy program. While several historians maintain that Prime Minister Menzies envisioned this program to be military in nature, there is also ample evidence to demonstrate that Australia had hopes of developing nuclear power.[11] While nuclear power never got off the ground in Australia—plagued by its immense financial cost and the division of state and federal power—Whitehall did agree to supply Canberra with a research reactor based on the heavy water reactors developed for the Atomic Energy Research Establishment's use at Harwell in Oxfordshire. Australia's sole research reactor, sited near Sydney at Lucas Heights, began its operations in 1958.[12] It remained Australia's only research reactor until it was decommissioned in 2007 and replaced with a new open-pool Australian light-water reactor (OPAL).

Less than a decade after Australia's first reactor went critical, the French government decided to conduct atmospheric nuclear tests in its Pacific territories. This decision coincided with a significant global surge in protest, reflected in the transnational proliferation of environmental, moratorium, peace, and antinuclear movements, among others (see chapter 3). Australians took to the streets in the thousands, imploring Canberra to boycott French goods and impose sanctions on the state. At the same time, however, several multinational mining corporations "discovered" and prepared to exploit numerous large uranium deposits across Australia (see chapter 4). From 1977 onward, Australia was a major exporter of uranium, including to France.[13]

The proceeding decades of Australia's nuclear history are punctuated by public agitation against the industry. Protesters chained themselves to the gates of uranium mines in the Northern Territory and South Australia on numerous occasions, organizing successfully against the expansion of uranium mining operations across the country. A federal inquiry conducted a thorough public investigation into the British nuclear tests in Australia (see chapter 5).[14] France's renewed Pacific nuclear tests in the 1990s were greeted with vehement opposition by the Australian public, unions, and businesses. And community lobbying halted government plans to establish a nuclear waste storage facility in the desert (see chapter 7). For a nation that had once been willing to host nuclear weapons trials, Australia had become decidedly hostile to nuclear imposition by the century's end, all the while greatly benefiting financially from uranium extraction.

Australia's nuclear future is set to be as controversial as its past, however. In 2021, former Prime Minister Scott Morrison announced AUKUS, a trilateral partnership between Australia, the United Kingdom, and the United States. Under AUKUS, Australia is set to receive a fleet of nuclear-powered submarines developed with British and American technology; the high-level nuclear fuel from the submarines will need to be disposed of in Australia.[15] Complicating this matter is the unavoidable reality that previous attempts to dispose of nuclear waste in Australia have proved messy (see chapter 7). In addition to AUKUS, several notable Australian politicians and public figures have reignited the nuclear power debate. As the nation seeks to reach zero emissions by 2030, conservative politicians and think tanks have rallied once again around the benefits of nuclear energy as an alternative to Australia's reliance on coal-fired power. Irrespective of AUKUS and potential power debates, Australia continues to rely on radionuclides for medicine and research, ensuring that the nuclear past and present are here to stay.

Going into the nuclear future, Australians first need to grapple with their nuclear past. What is absent from the above overview of Australia's nuclear history—one modeled on the accepted narrative popularized in Australia—is any mention of those whom these processes impacted or the colonial mechanisms that justified their pursuit. To understand the experiences of Australia's nuclear survivors, including those described in *Contaminated Country*'s opening pages, it is vital to acknowledge the settler-colonial visions that have underpinned, enabled, and justified Australia's nuclear ambitions since the beginning of the twentieth century. Nuclear colonialism allows us to access such visions.

Australian Nuclear Colonialism in Global Perspective

Nuclear colonialism is a phenomenon that perpetuates environmental injustice. Scholars can agree on this. However, what constitutes nuclear colonialism is still up for debate. For some, it is a modern manifestation of what might be considered a standard form of colonialism—a practice of domination of one group over another—and defined as the historical top-down process that involved states targeting Indigenous lands for their nuclear weapons tests or other nuclear processes in the twentieth century.[16] For others, it is the mentality that continues to justify the contamination of people of color living within proximity to nuclear facilities.[17] For others still, it is a markedly modern phenomenon that replaced the influence of empires following the Second World War, better understood as nuclear imperialism.[18] This lack of consensus should not be read as evidence of significant disagreement across the scholarship. Rather, it reflects nuclear colonialism's fluidity, its multiple manifestations, the way it differs across temporal and geographical scales, and the varying experiences of this phenomenon from nation to nation. In response to the ambiguity that surrounds our understanding of nuclear colonialism, especially outside of North American contexts, *Contaminated Country* takes this phenomenon and considers what its historical manifestation in Australia might offer to contemporary understandings of environmental injustice and justice.

Environmental justice scholars assert that the relationships inherent in nuclear colonialism are both facilitated by and constitutive of blatant environmental racism, be it conscious or unconscious.[19] As North American scholars and activists have argued since the 1980s, people of color are disproportionately and often deliberately targeted by the state for the siting of polluting or contaminating industries.[20] Recent developments in environmental justice scholarship have demonstrated the extent to which nuclear powers have forced marginalized communities within their own states, as well as others, to bear the world's extensive nuclear burdens.[21] States inflict irradiation and environmental contamination on those communities most ill-equipped to deal with their consequences for socioeconomic reasons tied intimately to racial prejudice, class inequality, remoteness, or financial insecurity.[22] Nuclear processes, by the same token, further the marginalization of otherwise already subjugated communities. But what form does nuclear colonial marginalization take in a state like Australia, which is still intimately bound to its settler-colonial past?

Many historians have characterized nuclear colonialism *not* as a product of settler colonialism, but rather as a neocolonial product of the contemporary "nuclear age." They consider the phenomenon as characteristic of a new epoch of "nuclear imperialism," a phase of new imperialism that several scholars purport replaced the old order. It is therefore defined by the technological advancement and rapid militarization of numerous world powers after 1945.[23] Central to this particular iteration of nuclear colonialism is the notion that nuclear weapons presented a *new* form of military imperialism that capitalized on, but ultimately replaced, the empires that had existed prior to 1945.[24] For example, Britain's and France's apparent pivot away from the maintenance of empire and toward nuclear weapons as the ultimate demonstration of their power from the 1940s onward has facilitated the perception that nuclear weapons represented something different from previous forms of imperial control, something exceptional.[25] Abiding by this logic of nuclear exceptionalism, several Australian historians have argued that Britain subjected Australia to nuclear colonialism when it tested its weapons on its soil. However, a more complex picture emerges if we consider nuclear colonialism as the historian Gabrielle Hecht does: as a phenomenon that did not overthrow colonial structures but rather appropriated them.[26]

Nuclear colonialism in Australia has been historically predicated on settlers' long-held assumption that land was, and continues to be, there for the taking. Since the continent's systematic colonization by Anglo-Europeans starting in 1788, white settlers in Australia have been legally recognized as the nation's property owners. Land possession (and thus Indigenous *dis*possession) and the denial of Indigenous sovereignty have been mainstays of the patriarchal settler sovereignty that underpins the contemporary nation-state.[27] As a result, and as Goenpul scholar Aileen Moreton-Robinson pithily observes, "signs of white possession are embedded everywhere in the landscape."[28] Signs of settler-colonial possession are ubiquitous in Australia. The nation cannot get away from its settler-colonial past. And the same goes for Australia's nuclear industry, not least because the rapid technological development that characterized the nuclear age capitalized on extant settler logics to succeed.

Rather than represent a rupture in Australia's colonial history, the logics of dispossession that underpin nuclear colonialism echo the type of rhetoric mobilized by settlers during invasion and since. This includes the settler notion that Aboriginal peoples' sovereign territories constituted land available for the taking.[29] Settler-colonial pursuits, including pastoralism, made use of lands deemed otherwise unused. The state's justifications for pursuing nuclear development appear eerily similar. Radioactive resources offered individual settlers and the Australian state the promise of material and territorial riches.[30] Nuclear weapons testing violently laid claim to Australia's central desert region as a site of modern utility. And multinational mining corporations invested in mining Australian uranium—among other minerals—on lands they maintained had long-held importance to pastoralists and other settlers, rather than Aboriginal peoples.

For those within proximity to radioactive resources, processes, and facilities, then, nuclear colonial violence has been inflicted on them since the moment settlers identified radioactive resources for exploitation. The mining of radioactive minerals, weapons testing, and radioactive waste disposal have exposed communities to, and have required them to understand and counteract, nuclear contamination.[31] But communities are exposed not only to contaminants by these processes. Just as Hecht has shown for Niger and other uranium-rich countries on the African continent, Traci Brynne Voyles for the Navajo Nation, Myrriah Gómez for Nuevo México, and Lianne Leddy for Serpent River First Nation, in Australia the extraction of radioactive minerals facilitated and necessitated the spread of colonial control and capital into areas that had largely defied traditional colonial settlement.[32] As with other forms of colonial resource extraction, nuclear processes have been historically dependent on the co-optation of Indigenous land. Often, this was land settlers labeled as empty.

The use of language to elide Indigenous connections to land has been essential to the historical enactment of nuclear colonialism. Numerous scholars have explored the ways in which colonial and imperial authorities discursively unpeopled desert spaces across the globe through their assurance that such environments were sparsely inhabited and of little worth.[33] In Australia, government officials and news outlets consistently described the continent's arid central desert region as inhospitable, barren, and cruel. However, with the dawn of the nuclear age came settlers' realization that nuclear testing could catapult the central deserts out of the backwardness of the "stone age" and into a new, decidedly modern, epoch.[34] This kind of logic underpins what Voyles has termed "wastelanding," a process of discursively constructing lands as useless or practically empty, demarcating them as able to be polluted.[35] Through the process of wastelanding Aboriginal lands for the testing of nuclear weapons in particular, government authorities in Australia and Britain leaned into the common nuclear colonial refrain that inflicting harm on the few is reasonable—necessary, in fact—for the benefit of the many.[36]

Each of the nuclear colonial episodes discussed throughout *Contaminated Country* relied on settlers' dispossession and denial of Country to succeed. Nuclear colonialism is thus best understood as an intersection of colonial logics, mechanisms, and assumptions that have shaped, and continue to shape, the industry globally. In Australia, the phenomenon exists as a colonial manifestation of an increasingly capitalist and neoliberal global context, whereby nuclearization and militarization cemented decades of structural violence for those already subject to settler colonialism. Given the island continent's relationship with its key allies—namely, Britain and the United States—it is a phenomenon that was historically responsive to the imperial and colonial ambitions of Australia's "great and powerful friends," intersecting with other equally oppressive forces (including settler colonialism and imperialism) to bear down on Aboriginal peoples.[37] However, as *Contaminated Country* explores at length, nuclear colonialism has had to fight hard to maintain its logics of (dis)possession, thanks in no small part to the tireless resistance of Indigenous people globally.[38]

Contaminating Whose Country?

Nuclear colonialism's insidious forces have impacted a significant number of Aboriginal communities in myriad ways, but few more so than those in South Australia. Admonished as Australia's "nuclear state" by environmentalists and antinuclear activists, South Australia is undoubtedly the center of Australia's nuclear past, present, and potential future. Prospectors discovered the nation's earliest radioactive deposits within the state. Its ecologically rich deserts were chosen by Britain and Australia to host nuclear weapons. It is home to Australia's largest extant uranium mine, which boasts the biggest known uranium deposit in the world. And it has been the battleground for two national debates about nuclear waste. As a result, the Country of many of the communities whose histories are explored throughout *Contaminated Country*, including those who contributed their oral histories to this research, is within the bounds of the contemporary South Australian state.

For the various Aboriginal nations contemporarily referred to as the Adnyamathanha, whose Country encompasses the greater Flinders Ranges area on the eastern side of the state, their exposure to Australia's earliest iterations of nuclear colonialism was enabled by radium prospecting.[39] Well before the beginning of the nuclear age, settler prospectors feverishly searched Australia's mineral-rich regions for any evidence of radium-bearing ore. As chapter 1 explores, their efforts, alongside those of geologically trained scientific explorers, assisted the settler state in identifying minerals and other potential natural resources in regions as yet unclaimed by traditional colonial settlement. In the Adnyamathanha's rock Country, the communities' knowledge, labor, and land were claimed by settlers on the hunt for radioactive riches. Settlers' vision of Adnyamathanha Country and its resources as ripe for the picking dictated Australia's early nuclear industry, justifying the state's dispossession of Aboriginal peoples in pursuit of economic wealth, development, and prestige.

Similar visions underpinned the Australian government's decision to host Britain's nuclear weapons tests across Pitjantjatjara, Yankunytjatjara, Kokatha, Barngarla, Arabunna, and Antakirinja lands in the central desert region. These tests—at least for the British and Australian authorities involved in organizing them—necessitated large swathes of unoccupied, or at the very least *sparsely* populated, lands. Conveniently for the Australian government, Aṉangu (Pitjantjatjara for "people" and a term Aboriginal peoples living across the South Australian central deserts use to refer to themselves) were already subject to considerable state control by the mid-twentieth century, enabling authorities to monitor and manipulate Aṉangu movements around the testing sites. As chapter 2 details, the nuclear colonialism embodied by Britain's nuclear tests was enabled by existing colonial practices and mechanisms that dispossessed and silenced those whose Country was subjected to the nuclear ambitions of both Britain and Australia.

In the decades after Britain's tests, the Australian public began to extol the links between nuclear weapons testing and imperialism across the Pacific. Student groups and emergent social movements condemned France's tests in the Algerian Sahara (1960–66) and their early program in the South Pacific (1966–74), demanding that the Australian government take a stand against French imperialism. Nevertheless, as highlighted in chapter 3, most Australians remained silent on the topic of their own government's involvement in similar nuclear injustices. This silence would not persist, however, as Aboriginal politics developed apace in the 1960s and 1970s, exposing the role of the Australian state and people in dispossessing, silencing, and subjugating Aboriginal peoples.

This increased momentum in Aboriginal politics challenged the emergence of large-scale uranium mining across Australia during the 1970s and 1980s. The deposit at Olympic Dam, Australia's only remaining operational uranium mine, was discovered by mine geologists on Kokatha Country in the mid-1970s. Chapter 4 demonstrates the empowerment felt by the Kokatha to demand greater control over their Country, enabled by several pieces of land rights legislation assented to by the South Australian and Northern Territory governments over the course of the 1960s. While settlers continued to uphold their own right to develop the deposits, for the apparent betterment of all, the Kokatha asserted their specific Aboriginal right to the land, as custodians.

The success of the Aboriginal land rights movement also reignited interest in Britain's nuclear testing program, precipitating the initiation of a federal inquiry into the tests. As chapter 5 explores, during this inquiry—the Royal Commission into British Nuclear Tests in Australia (1984–85)—both British and Australian government authorities attempted to maintain distance between themselves and the colonial consequences of the tests. Aboriginal witnesses had other ideas. The testimonies of Aboriginal survivors centered dispossession and displacement from Country as one of the greatest tragedies of the tests. Neither Britain nor Australia was exempt from blame for this explosive episode of nuclear colonialism.

As Australia's nuclear colonial secrets unraveled, dispossessed communities began to demand compensation for their contaminated Country. Maralinga Tjarutja—formerly the Southern Pitjantjatjara—had been removed from their Country to make way for the nuclear tests, and now that their story was public, they demanded reparations. Chapter 6 details how Maralinga Tjarutja reckoned with their dispossession by participating in scientific studies on their Country, connecting transnationally with other nuclear survivors, and seeking compensation directly from the British government. Maralinga Tjarutja asserted themselves as experts in their land—their Country—finding a seat at the negotiating table after half a century of silence.

Having built steadily across the twentieth century, nuclear colonial resistance in Australia climaxed in the 1990s. In 1998, the Australian government announced a proposal to establish a nuclear waste repository on the lands of Aṉangu previously subjected to weapons testing. A group of Elders, the Kupa Piti Kungka Tjuta (Coober Pedy Senior Women), protested the further destruction of their Country by nuclear contaminants, kick-starting their Irati Wanti (The Poison, Leave It) campaign. Chapter 7 tells the story of this campaign, from its initiation through to its end.

The narrative of nuclear colonial history woven throughout *Contaminated Country* does not focus solely on harm. Interwoven among stories of dislocation, dispossession, and contamination are messages of hope, insight into the intricacies of living on and with Country, and the centrality of caring for Country, contaminated or not. What *Contaminated Country* shows is that while nuclear survivors' experiences of nuclear colonialism have differed across temporal and geographical spaces, their collective mobilization has shaped—and continues to shape—the ways many understand, acknowledge, and attempt to remediate nuclear harms. Taken together, the case studies explored throughout *Contaminated Country* demonstrate how nuclear colonialism has developed in response to various historical influences and challenges, from the Cold War nuclear ambitions of various so-called great powers to the rise of decolonial rhetoric and the global Indigenous rights movement. Understanding and reckoning with this history is vital if Australia—or any state—is to have a just nuclear future.

ONE

Radioactive Riches

While now associated with the explosive development of nuclear weaponry, radioactive metals such as radium and uranium were once mere scientific curiosities. In 1906, soon-to-be-famed Antarctic explorer Douglas Mawson provided readers of Adelaide's newspaper *The Register* several tips on how to identify the world's latest "marvel of science," the rare earth metal radium.[1] Capable of emitting energy in the form of heat and light and able to cure ailments ranging from birthmarks to cancer, radium was hotly discussed by reporters in the national press, many of whom speculated that great sums were to be made by its discovery in Australia.

"In searching for ores likely to contain radium," Mawson advised, "the prospector is specially warned to be on the lookout for heavy, black, homogenous minerals."[2] This was likely to indicate the presence of uraninite, a mineral from which the highly radioactive elements radium and uranium could be isolated.[3] "Besides the dark-coloured varieties," Mawson continued, "a series of yellowish minerals also constitutes an important source of the element." These minerals included carnotite, an "altered form" of uraninite with the potential to yield radium, although only in small amounts. In a third description, Mawson advised prospectors to be on the lookout for "shining green flakes," characteristic of uranium-mica. These indicators were all signs to the judicious prospector that "payable pitchblende may eventually be found in the same district."[4] From pitchblende, radium could be extracted in notable quantities. And with radium valued at up to £750,000 per ounce in 1906, many prospectors sought any ore of a uraniferous nature.[5]

In the same year, the settler-prospector Arthur Smith began searching for tin near Olary, 250 miles (400 kilometers) northeast of Adelaide in South Australia's Flinders Ranges. After stumbling across an unfamiliar ore while prospecting in the rugged mountain range, Smith wrote to the South Australian Department of Mines in search of answers. On receiving Smith's letter, the department sought the expertise of Mawson, recently employed as a lecturer of petrology and mineralogy at the University of Adelaide. Drawing on his familiarity with radioactive minerals, he confirmed the sample was carnotite, the radium-bearing mineral whose recent discovery in Colorado had sparked great interest among geologists internationally.[6] There was a buzz of excitement in the local press as reporters, geologists, prospectors, and scientists speculated as to the significance of Australia's discovery of radioactive minerals.[7] "A mineral discovery that may prove valuable has just been made at Olary," *The Register* announced with delight.[8] "Is it radium?" several other papers wondered.[9]

The cataclysmic emergence of the nuclear age, demarcated by the first detonation of a nuclear weapon in 1945, has overshadowed the history of early radioactive mineral discoveries across the world. This is certainly the case in Australia. But as this chapter reveals, long before the purported beginning of the nuclear age, settler-nationalist ambitions for wealth, scientific discovery, and development supported and encouraged radioactive mineral exploitation. As such, explorer-scientists and settler prospectors in early twentieth-century Australia were driven by the draw of discovery and capital, engaging in and influencing processes that should be understood as early manifestations of nuclear colonialism. Mawson's pursuit of radium fits this pattern.

Settler-colonial ambitions, echoed and encouraged by the Australian state, underpinned Mawson's geological training and his exploitation of radium in the Flinders Ranges during the early decades of the twentieth century. These were ambitions realized by Mawson's employment of an Aboriginal tracker, prospector, and cameleer—"Claypan George"—whose dispossession, labor, and knowledge were essential to Mawson's exploitation of radium. However, Mawson's lack of acknowledgment of George's contributions reflects the colonial dimensions of mining during this period, reliant as it was on the extraction of land, ore, *and* knowledge. This colonial contradiction, involving the dual elision of and reliance on Aboriginal people, was central to many settlers' pursuit of minerals in the early decades of the twentieth century. Mawson's ambition to find and exploit radioactive minerals in the Flinders Ranges was no different, at least until the 1920s, when a fundamental shift in the value of such ores occurred.

Through the 1930s, 1940s, and 1950s, the medicinal and potential military applications of radioactive minerals drew increased attention from various governments, not least those in Britain, Australia, and the United States. The increasingly relevant imperial and geopolitical benefits of radioactive materials engendered a shift in the relationship between radioactive mineral exploitation and colonialism worldwide. As the Second World War loomed, the era of the lone explorer-scientist such as Mawson gave way to a more systematized, state-based form of mineral exploration, dictated by British imperial influence in Australia. The centrality of nuclear technology's development to the geopolitical power of individual states in the mid-twentieth century justified both Britain's attempts to acquire an "empire supply" of radium and uranium from Australia *and* Australia's decision to contribute radioactive minerals to civilian and military nuclear programs in Britain and the United States.

In the first half of the twentieth century, radium and uranium transformed from speculative "wonder" metals to vital imperial resources. In Australia, the exploitation of radioactive ores relied on the usurpation of Aboriginal lands, co-optation of Aboriginal labor, and exploitation of Aboriginal knowledge. As such, the feverish hunt that many Australians undertook in pursuit of radioactive ores across those decades inaugurated a set of colonial processes that would enable the dispossession of Aboriginal peoples over the remainder of the twentieth century. In fact, fulfilling a nuclear future of radioactive riches would be contingent on such dispossession.

Early Explorations for Radium

By the turn of the twentieth century, settlers across the six Australian colonies had been reliant for decades on the wealth accrued through mineral extraction. From the 1850s onward, gold rushes in New South Wales and Victoria facilitated the expansion of the capital, population, infrastructure, and general prosperity of both colonies.[10] In the 1890s, long after the rushes in the eastern colonies had come to an end, prospectors struck gold in Western Australia, kick-starting a mineral economy that is, today, unmatched by any other Australian state.[11] However, South

Australia's comparably small goldfields never yielded the mineral wealth of its neighbors' prospects. As a result, by the end of the nineteenth century, and in the face of an emerging economic crisis, many South Australian politicians were anxious to enjoy "the adventitious prosperity which so suddenly lifted" Australia's other colonies "into eminence."[12]

In pursuit of mineral wealth, the South Australian colonial government designed legislation that encouraged its citizens to prospect for exciting new minerals through various inducements. First, the cost of purchasing a Miner's Right was minimal in South Australia, allowing holders to prospect for minerals cheaply on land held by the Crown.[13] In fact, of all the states, the Australian Radium Corporation noted, "the Mining Laws and Regulations under the Government of South Australia are of the simplest, and offer every inducement for the development of the fields."[14] Second, the government offered financial incentives to successful prospectors. The South Australian Mining Act of 1893 stipulated that handsome rewards would be paid to "the first actual discoverer of any new mineral district or of any new and valuable deposits."[15] Such economic encouragement led thousands of settlers to try their hands at prospecting, precipitating the creation of tens of thousands of ephemeral land claims clustered around sites of reported mineral discoveries. The exploitation of these claims by prospectors was, for the most part, sporadic, unregulated, and undertaken with little professional knowledge. In their feverish pursuit of minerals, prospectors doubled up as opportunistic and transient explorers, charting the colony for riches.

The aridity of Australia's inland had made its initial settlement by colonists difficult.[16] The continent's desert lands seemed, at least to many urban-dwelling settlers, to be hostile to human life, especially when contrasted with the comparably temperate area colonized along the continent's southeast coast. Those who did settle in Australia's remotest regions have been historically valorized by folklorists and popular writers for their demonstration of the triumph of Anglo-European settlers over a hostile environment, extolled as leading protagonists in the history of a nation seemingly anxious about its occupation of an unfamiliar landscape.[17] The development of the science of geology and the incentivization of mining, however, transformed settlers' relationship to Australia's arid interior at the end of the nineteenth century. For explorer-scientists, geology assisted in appraising the inland for its untapped promise, including its potential possession of commercially, imperially, and colonially important resources.[18]

The discovery of rich mineral resources played an integral role in the garnering of both wealth and pride across the Australian colonies. Such discoveries were assisted by scientific expeditions, which proliferated in the 1890s. Several of Australia's most notable expeditions in this period were sponsored by individuals with interests in the mining industry, and all involved myriad explorers with expertise ranging from geology to meteorology to anthropology.[19] In nineteenth- and twentieth-century Australia—as elsewhere—scientific exploration assisted in the commercial appraisal of nature, overlaying Aboriginal occupation with colonial ambitions for the exploitation of potential commodities. Scientific expeditions provided settlers with the opportunity to fill in the "last blank spaces on the map" by accounting for the continent's valuable resources.[20] As the historian Erika Bsumek observes in the American southwest, "explorer-scientists" employed Indigenous experts, collected data, and wrote reports "that revealed not only how the government crafted its long-term vision for the land" settlers had occupied "but also the underlying racial structure within those visions."[21] A similar process unfolded in South Australia's interior—its "red heart"—a frontier of untapped colonial potential that continued to beckon to settlers in the early twentieth century.[22]

The knowledge accrued by scientific expeditions gave settlers a greater understanding of the exploitable aspects of the continent's expansive, and seemingly impenetrable, inland. Explorer-scientists were thus vital to the claiming of the entire Australian continent. In 1914, when the British Association for the Advancement of Science visited Adelaide, the authors of an accompanying handbook told delegates that Australians owed "a big debt to the men who filled in the map of our island continent," for "not a year goes by—scarcely a day—without an addition to the map of some range of hills, lakes, a tract of country suitable for the raising of live stock, or an auriferous belt where the prospector may with advantage follow up the success of the road-breaking legion."[23] "The roll call of South Australian explorers contains many honored names of men who," the association was told, "nobly did their duty" in "letting light into 'Darkest Australia,'" facilitating the apparently "peaceful occupation of the country."[24] This account of South Australia's revered explorers gave the geologist and proclaimed hero Douglas Mawson and his recent Antarctic explorations pride of place.

Likening Mawson to those pioneers who forged a path of "light" into a dark interior, popular writers have represented his two Antarctic expeditions as examples of the masculinist bravery embodied by Australia's explorers at the beginning of the twentieth century.[25] Central to Mawson's perceived heroism was his expertise as a geologist, honed prior to, during, and following his expeditions to Antarctica. By the time Mawson embarked on the Australasian Antarctic Expedition in 1911, the classic expeditionary drive to chart the apparently "blank spaces" left on the map had been replaced by a scientific imperative.[26] Expedition leaders were redirecting their focus toward understanding, categorizing, and claiming the plants, animals, geography, and geology of spaces that had thus far defied extensive settlement due to their extremeness.[27] As the historian Tom Griffiths has explained it, "For adventurous and scientific Australians of the early twentieth century, two frontiers beckoned: the white ice and the red heart, the far south and the immediate north."[28] And while the relationship between "the ice and the inland" may seem somewhat abstract, for settlers both sites offered the potential for adventure, scientific discovery, physical and mental challenge, and a place in history.[29]

Mawson and the "Marvel of Science"

Mawson's contribution to the exploration of Australia's southern frontier is well-founded, but the tales of his forays into the ice often obscure his role in "knowing" Australia's inland.[30] Born in England, Mawson studied mining engineering at the University of Sydney between 1899 and 1901, before his mentor T. Edgeworth David encouraged him to pursue geology. In 1903, Mawson took off to the French and British colony of the New Hebrides (Vanuatu) for fieldwork. The geological research he undertook there was characteristic of that embarked on by many explorer-scientists in the same period. Not only did he go in search of a land he considered "*Terra Incognita*," according to his reports from the trip, but his work (and survival) was reliant on Indigenous peoples' knowledge and labor, and his field diaries record the many samples, photographs, and curios—including pottery, masks, baskets, spears, bows, and arrows—he collected and later donated to the South Australian Museum.[31] Upon his return from the Pacific, Mawson was offered a job as a lecturer of petrology and mineralogy at the University of Adelaide in 1905. Moving from Sydney to Adelaide brought him into contact with Ernest Shackleton, facilitating Mawson's first Antarctic expedition in 1907.[32] Mawson is now renowned for that expedition, but upon returning from Antarctica in 1909, he continued in his role at the university, traveling frequently into remote South Australia to satiate his hunger for geological discovery.

This passion drove Mawson's involvement in the scientific appraisal of Australia's radioactive resources from their discovery onward. As early as 1904, only a year after Marie and Pierre Curie accepted the Nobel Prize in Physics for their discovery of radium, Mawson collaborated with University of Sydney physics student Thomas Laby on an article titled "Preliminary Observations on Radio-Activity and the Occurrence of Radium in Australian Minerals."[33] Mawson and Laby speculated that traces of radioactivity occurring in mineral samples they had acquired from across New South Wales were an indication of the existence of a variety of radium-bearing ores in Australia. While the article's findings were inconsequential, it nevertheless marked the first of Mawson's attempts to align himself with scientists involved in pioneering the study of radioactivity all over the world, a pursuit that would preoccupy him until his death in 1958. In an interview with *The Register* in 1906, Mawson referred to this article as evidence of his and Laby's critical involvement in the "discovery" of radium in Australia.[34]

Mawson's self-promotion as an expert on radioactive metals placed him in a burgeoning international network of scientists with comparable expertise. In fact, a student of Mawson's—the geologist Reg Sprigg—speculated that Mawson's ability to visually identify radioactive minerals had originated from advice given to him by his friend and fellow scientist Marie Curie. Having received her doctorate in 1903 for discovering how to isolate radium from pitchblende, Curie had supposedly advised Mawson: "If you ever come across bright green or yellow minerals which you cannot identify, suspect the new element, Uranium—the mother of wonder element

Radium."[35] This tip would have certainly assisted Mawson in identifying rare radioactive metals occurring in nature, ensuring he was among the first geologists consulted by the South Australian government following radium's suspected discovery in Australia in 1906. By the end of the first decade of the twentieth century, Mawson had cemented himself as an expert in radioactive metals, the scientific exploration of which had led radiation scientists to speculate publicly that these metals were a significant source of energy, a reliable treatment for dermatological ailments, and a potential cure for cancer.

Medical practitioners were especially interested in the potential health applications of radiation, which many ventured could be miraculous. The Australian press seemed particularly interested in radium's ability to cure cancer, with newspapers frequently discussing the results of medical experiments taking place across the globe. In 1909, Émile Roux at the Pasteur Institute in Paris sewed a vial containing traces of radium into the stomach of a female patient suffering with cancer. "If the case is successful," the Sydney *Evening News* told its readers, "the great curative value of this stuff will be assured."[36] In the same year, King Edward VII opened London's Radium Institute, heralded in the Australian press as an important opportunity to develop "a definitive answer to the much disputed question of the curative value of radium."[37] Yet accompanying this hopeful coverage, some scientists encouraged the public to exercise restraint, warning that radium's miracle properties were—at this point—merely speculative and that radium's use as a treatment for any ailment required "caution and exact empirical knowledge."[38] The pioneering Australian dermatologist Herman Lawrence declared in a 1911 treatise not only that it was "capable of curing, removing or delaying the progress of the lesions of a great number of skin affections" (including from lupus, psoriasis, eczema, verrucae and warts, acne, herpes, and syphilis) but that the "cumulative effect of radium treatment" could create "a bad cosmetic result," such as a burn or an ulcer, which would cause "the patient . . . [to] prefer the disease to the cure."[39] Such warnings reflected both radium's healing properties and the potential harm it could induce. Its dichotomous properties nevertheless remained a source of intrigue, described by reporters as a "marvel of science" and indicative of scientists' emergence as "the romancers of the twentieth century."[40]

In addition to radium's medicinal uses, newspapers in the decades following its discovery advertised the numerous domestic applications of the metal, including its potential as a source of energy. "Radium manure" was attributed with having the effect of encouraging rapid plant growth: "six times the ordinary"![41] A new multipurpose product—Radium Spray—promised to save users "labour, time, and money" as a "liquid cleanser and polisher, a dust layer, disinfectant, deodoriser and killer of vermin."[42] Radium paint applied to clock dials and watches allowed users to tell the time day and night due to radium's luminosity.[43] And some scientists speculated as early as 1906 that radium harbored energy levels "perhaps millions of times more powerful than dynamite," which would be useful for military, mining, and economic applications.[44] Though society is now aware of the dangers of radioactivity, such that many of these domestic products seem inconceivable today, scientists were correct about radium's energy-producing potential. But irrespective of the public's hopes for radium, its seemingly wonderous applications would never be realized if new sources of the metal were not found.

Radium is exceptionally rare and was even more so in the first decade of the twentieth century. Few known deposits of the metal existed. As such, the Curies and other scientists depended heavily on the small amounts of radium they could purchase from one of the world's only established sources at the time: the silver mines of Jáchymov, Bohemia (now in the Czech Republic).[45] As radium does not occur in isolation and requires extraction from radium-bearing ores, such as carnotite or pitchblende, it was—and remains—necessary to refine a very large quantity of such ore to reap any notable amount of radium metal. Consequently, even tiny samples of the metal remained prohibitively expensive throughout the early twentieth century, and the minimal amount of radium available to scientists slowed the rate at which its properties could be explored, understood, and widely applied. A front-page article in Victoria's newspaper the *Ballarat Star* lamented in 1904 that radium would be "impossible to put into popular use" until it came "somewhere within a measurable distance of a popular price."[46] Rather than cause a loss of faith, however, radium's rarity (and immense value) increased the fervor with which Australian prospectors sought it out. Surely Australia, a country known for its mineral wealth, possessed deposits containing this coveted metal.

Newspapers contributed to the feverish pursuit of radium across the continent by speculating wildly about the astronomical sums prospectors sought to gain if they could identify a source of the metal in Australia. The *Ballarat Star* noted that radium sold for "fabulous sums," fetching "from £40,000 to £75,000" for a single ounce.[47] The *Cairns Post* of Queensland published a higher figure, valuing radium at "£4 per milligramme (equivalent to £164,000 per ounce)," while Sydney's *Evening News* recorded "absurd prices" as high as £750,000 an ounce.[48] These were—and still are—exorbitant sums, and they played a significant role in encouraging prospectors to try their hand at finding traces of this wonder metal.

Given its value, the discovery of radium-bearing carnotite at Olary in South Australia's Flinders Ranges in 1906 brought prospectors to the region. The race to mine the wealth there was swift but short-lived. Testing of ore samples by the University of Adelaide's Nobel Prize–winning physicist, chemist, and mathematician William Bragg—a colleague and friend of Mawson's—confirmed that the concentration of radium in the carnotite at Olary was far too low to be of any significant value either to individuals or to mining syndicates.[49] He suggested that prospectors were better off searching for pitchblende, a mineral commonly referred to as uraninite and from which uranium can be extracted.[50] Despite Bragg's assessment, Mawson wrote to an acquaintance in September 1906 about Australia's possession of "uraniferous" ore, detailing a business deal he had struck with an unidentified firm in Paris: "I have an offer (private) from a Paris firm for uranium ores . . . at 500 francs per unit."[51] It is possible that Mawson overestimated the commercial value of the carnotite found at Olary, but it is equally likely that his enthusiasm aimed to create overseas interest in Australian radioactive minerals so as to secure funds for further exploration.

Regardless, Mawson later admitted that the ore found at Olary possessed too little radium to be economically significant. As historians have noted in relation to carnotite mining in Colorado in the same period, "faith out distanced the reality."[52] The knowledge that carnotite in the United States was only yielding low levels of radium, coupled with geological analyses publicized by Bragg, forced Mawson to consider the likelihood that the deposit identified by Smith would ultimately come to nothing. "With regard to the ore from Olary [I] am becoming much discouraged after detailed analytical work," he wrote in a letter dated September 1906.[53] Within the year, most prospectors had abandoned their search for radioactive ore in the northern Flinders Ranges. But that did not dampen Mawson's desire to contribute to the evolving field. Persisting with the pursuit of radioactive minerals in South Australia, Mawson continued to explore seemingly "uncharted" landscapes in the name of scientific discovery, development, and, later, national interest.

Radium in the Flinders Ranges

The northern Flinders Ranges "is an eerie landscape," wrote Reg Sprigg in 1984. It is a landscape "slashed by deep rocky gorges, some that cradle cool deep waterholes and the hideouts of the colourfully marked Yellow-footed Rock Wallaby."[54] But for many, thirst-quenching waterholes and ring-tailed marsupials did not define this landscape. Rather, the Flinders offered an abundance of mineral curiosities to prospectors and explorers. The increased exploitation of such curiosities by settlers in the early twentieth century brought the worlds of geologists and prospectors into direct contact with those of the region's Aboriginal communities, not least as the pursuits of the former became entwined with the labor and long-held knowledge of the latter.[55]

Aboriginal extraction, use, and trading of various minerals did not commence with the European invasion of their lands. Minerals such as ocher and flint (or chert) were integral to traditional ceremonies, economies, and diplomacy between many Aboriginal communities prior to colonization. The remains of ocher quarries, ethnohistorical accounts from contemporary Aboriginal peoples, and the writings of early colonists indicate that the use of ocher in ceremonies (for painting the body) and its exchange between communities was widespread.[56] In fact, it was not uncommon for single deposits to hold unique and varied significance for numerous communities, as in the case of the Flinders Ranges' red ocher deposits that were—and remain—of vital importance to the unique traditions of the Kuyani, Diyari, Yangruwantha, Yawarrawarrka, Ngameni, Wailpi, Pirnkarla and Wangkangurru peoples, some of whom traveled up to 300 miles (500 kilometers) to access the mineral.[57] Similarly, arrowheads and spear tips made from flint have been found notable distances from their geological origin, indicating significant and complex trade routes among communities.

The familiarity of Aboriginal peoples with minerals ensured their knowledge was invaluable to explorers like Mawson. Recent scholarship has sought to account for the neglected histories of Aboriginal prospectors who proved integral to the discovery of important mineral deposits, later exploited by settler Australians.[58] The result has been the acknowledgment by historians that Aboriginal people were not mere ancillary workers for settler prospectors, but they themselves identified minerals such as alluvial gold and tin, sparking rushes. In many cases, Aboriginal miners utilized their superior identification of minerals to gain greater independence from colonial authorities and exercise some semblance of freedom on their Country.[59] This was likely the case for "Claypan George," an Aboriginal man of the Flinders Ranges who was described in colonial archives as a prospector, laborer, and cameleer.[60] Mawson's company—the Radium Extraction Company—employed George in 1910 to assist with the extraction of ore. George's involvement in Mawson's exploits both complicates the notion that Aboriginal people were mere background figures in Australian histories of mining and highlights the centrality of settler ambition and dispossession to radioactive mineral extraction.

In 1910, while scrambling across the top of a ridge in the northern Flinders Ranges, South Australian pastoralist and prospector William Bentley Greenwood and his son Gordon "Smiler" Greenwood spotted an ore seam that glinted yellow. Familiar with the mineralogical makeup of the region, William Greenwood suspected their discovery was important. Intent on confirming his suspicions, he sent samples to Mawson, who had recently returned from his first expedition to Antarctica. When Mawson received samples from Greenwood that demonstrated radioactive properties, he was determined to extract the lode as quickly as possible. Mawson established the Radium Extraction Company, a small business he registered with the South Australian government, and put the mechanisms in place to exploit South Australia's potential radium deposits.[61]

Accompanied by the Greenwoods, in October 1910 Mawson wound his way from the Mount Coffin Mine near Leigh Creek to Mount Painter to assess the Greenwoods' find for himself.[62] At the beginning of their journey, the party stopped at the Mount Serle government depot for camels and supplies, the former valued by prospectors for their strength and endurance and often accompanied by experienced camel handlers. They then forged on, Mawson taking notes as he went. He speculated on the character of certain lodes and whether they were "favourable for the presence of pitchblende."[63] On several occasions Mawson noted the potential presence of radium. In written accounts of his arrival at Radium Ridge—referred to as such by the Greenwoods following their "discovery"—one can sense Mawson's excitement as he considered the possible yield from this deposit: "The ore can be treated very inexpensively and this will offset the low grade character." "So far as I am aware this is the most extensive uraniferous lode formation in the world," he speculated.[64]

While Mawson's field notebooks are mostly devoid of description beyond those of a geological nature, he took dozens of photographs to accompany his observations. These images record geological phenomena; several show Smiler Greenwood seated in the foreground as a scale marker, demonstrating the sheer size of the mineral deposits housed by the Ranges (fig. 1). Others capture the journey itself, including photographs of the camels, led by Greenwood and his father, weighed down by the heft of equipment they bore. When viewing these photographs, one is struck by the beauty of the region, seemingly untouched by settlers save for the occasional abandoned mine shaft or pastoral run. For scientific explorers—geologists among them—photographs assisted in capturing data. But these photographs also obscure the settler-colonial interactions that made them possible, eliding any evidence of the region's Aboriginal communities, contemporarily known as the Adnyamathanha.[65] Given Mawson's reliance on Aboriginal labor later in the decade, and his quasi-anthropological 1926 publication "Relics of Aboriginal Occupation in the Olary District," which acknowledged Aboriginal presence (albeit rather paternalistically), this absence can be read as deliberate.[66] Mawson's pursuit of radioactive minerals fundamentally relied on the exploitation of Aboriginal peoples, their labor, and their knowledge, regardless of whether Mawson actively acknowledged it or not.

Mawson's attempts to sell radium to international buyers following this 1910 expedition to Radium Ridge further reflect the colonial adventurism

FIGURE 1. Mineral-rich regions such as the Flinders Ranges attracted many settlers keen to try their hands at prospecting. In this photograph, likely taken by Antarctic explorer and geologist Douglas Mawson in 1910, the son of pastoralist and prospector William Greenwood, Gordon "Smiler" Greenwood, sits in the scene's foreground as a size marker. Photograph courtesy of the Mawson Centre, South Australian Museum, Adelaide.

embedded in his scientific pursuits. Having seen the Greenwoods' find for himself, Mawson returned to Adelaide and oversaw his new company's operations from afar, all the while endeavoring to entice companies to purchase his radioactive wares. In one instance, Mawson wrote to Delta Metals Co. Ltd., a British firm operating from London and Birmingham, about the "huge ore body" he and the Greenwoods had discovered, such that he could "assure regular and large shipments" of radium to England.[67] His description of this ore body to local newspapers further contributed to the colonial vision pursued by explorer-scientists in this period, so much so that Adelaide's *The Register* reported that Mawson's "recent trip to the Far North does more than confirm faith in the latent mineral resources of South Australia. . . . Stretches of rough mountainous country useless for agriculture or pastoral pursuits offer the promise of yielding to the patient scientist and industrious miner rare and mysterious minerals of fabulous value."[68] However, while Mawson publicly received praise for his "discovery" of these "mysterious minerals," capable of transforming South Australia's fortunes, William Greenwood and a group of contractors worked tirelessly to physically extract the ore for sale.

The extraction of radium ore by prospectors was backbreaking work made increasingly difficult by the remote and rugged environment characteristic of the Flinders Ranges.[69] In December 1910, Greenwood wrote to reassure the secretary of the Radium Extraction Company that he and his son would do their best to extract the ore—the outcome of which would "be much to [the] company's advantage"—but that it was not an easy task.[70] Subsequent letters reveal the challenges faced by Mawson's prospectors on the ground. Greenwood details the difficulty of boring for water and traversing the rocky outcrops of Radium Ridge while leading camels laden with ore. It is likely that Mawson was more concerned with reading Greenwood's letters for glimpses of his promising mineral finds than with inquiring after the welfare of his men; references to "rich samples" are pitted throughout.[71]

Before long, these difficulties, along with the fact that "getting ore to camels entails a lot of heavy labor," encouraged Greenwood to employ the additional assistance of "Claypan George."[72] The employment of Aboriginal laborers by the Greenwood family was likely not unusual. In fact, a 1964 interview with Smiler Greenwood referenced his and his family's familiarity with Adnyamathanha in and around the Flinders Ranges. He told the interviewer that he, his brother, and his father "had quite a lot to do with the blacks there." They reportedly "intermingle[d] quite a lot in those days."[73] Still, on account of the usual silences imposed on Indigenous intermediaries, William Greenwood's first reference to the Radium Extraction Company's employment of an Aboriginal laborer is significant. On 23 May 1911, he wrote of a "Claypan George (Ab.)."[74] The employment of George, who was tasked with handling the camels the company hired from the Flinders Ranges' Mount Serle camel depot, highlights important interactions between settlers, prospectors, pastoralists, and Aboriginal people in the Ranges.[75] The Mount Serle camel depot was—often—the origin site of such interactions.

The history of Mount Serle predates its existence as a camel depot by many decades, reflecting the extent to which the colonial project was engrained in the lives of the Ranges' Aboriginal peoples by the beginning of the twentieth century.[76] Police reports from Corporal Alfred Burtt, based near the depot in the 1850s, indicate that violence between the pastoralists residing there and various Aboriginal groups was common.[77] According to Burtt, in June 1858 he received a report that "the natives to the number of about 40" attacked settlers at the Mount Serle pastoral station, burning their hut to the ground.[78] Following the initial bloodshed of invasion, ongoing conflict most frequently arose from Aboriginal people killing livestock and being murdered by pastoralists in reprisal.[79] In this instance, massacres of Aboriginal peoples were committed by settlers to purportedly "prevent" further "aggression" from Aboriginal groups around the area. Nevertheless, these clashes reflect the imposition of pastoralism on communities and their traditional ways of life. Pastoralism had destroyed many Aboriginal food sources as lands were monopolized by stock that compromised or destroyed water supplies and native plants, driving away fauna.[80] With a diminished capacity to produce or hunt for food, laboring for pastoralists became a more compelling option for many Aboriginal people.[81] State authorities provided pastoralists across settled regions of Australia with rations to be distributed to Aboriginal people in an attempt to reduce conflict between the surviving population and settlers.[82] However, rations—as we will see—assisted in controlling Aboriginal mobility and labor across Australia well into the twentieth century.

Given the station's provision of food, water and employment, Mount Serle proved an important gathering place for Aboriginal peoples from across the Flinders Ranges.[83] The rations distributed by settlers were of poor quality, consisting mainly of staples such as sugar, tea, and flour, along with the occasional provision of tobacco or rice.[84] No fresh food was handed out. Unsurprisingly, by the turn of the century there was increased public concern about malnutrition in the Aboriginal population in response to the higher number of deaths recorded at Mount Serle in the preceding years, no doubt exacerbated by a serious drought in the 1890s.[85] With social and environmental conditions restricting Aboriginal people's access to traditional food sources, Mount Serle proved a vital supply of food and employment not least because, by the 1890s, it was operating as a camel depot. It was in this capacity that the Greenwoods visited, looking to hire camels and engage Aboriginal cameleers to assist with their prospecting.

The introduction of camels to Australia revolutionized settlers' ability to explore the country's interior, facilitating the colonization of desert landscapes (fig. 2). These beasts and their South Asian drivers (colloquially referred to as "Afghan cameleers" by settlers) proliferated in the Australian colonies from the 1860s onward. Having arrived from British Indian ports, camels and cameleers created a vast transportation network throughout the interior, connecting remote settlements with goods across large swathes of Australia's inland.[86] Camels, well suited to the arid interior, facilitated settler access to the colonies' most remote regions, allowing for the colonization of lands previously deemed inhospitable to settlement.[87] In turn, camels integrally altered the socioeconomic and physical landscapes of Aboriginal peoples in early twentieth-century Australia.[88]

By the time Mawson was passing through the Mount Serle camel depot in 1910, many Afghan cameleers had been replaced by Aboriginal laborers. This transition from migrant labor to Indigenous labor in Australia's interior was partially facilitated during Australia's Federation by the creation of the Immigration Restriction Act in 1901 (more commonly known as the White Australia policy). This legislation both restricted non-white

FIGURE 2. Introduced camels were integral to the colonization of Australia's inland reaches. Their hardiness and ability to bear large loads made them ideal for eager prospectors such as Mawson and the Greenwoods, whose expedition to Mount Painter in 1910 is pictured here. Photograph courtesy of the Mawson Centre, South Australian Museum, Adelaide.

migration to Australia *and* facilitated the deportation of purportedly "undesirable" non-white migrants already living in the country.[89] Prejudicing against migrants, this legislation led to the deportation of many Afghan cameleers and created a vacuum in the industry that, in some cases, Aboriginal workers filled.[90] In the Flinders Ranges, for example, the adaptation of communities to the colonization of their Country—including the destruction of traditional water and food sources—involved many becoming entwined in the settler economy through cameleering and prospecting.[91] Living on Country and within proximity to the Mount Serle camel depot, the communities later referred to as the Adnyamathanha earned modest wages and rations by caring for the station's camels, guiding settlers through Country, locating waterholes and food, acting as translators and "go-betweens" for explorers, and trying their hands at prospecting.[92]

It was within this context that George was hired by William Greenwood to undertake myriad odd jobs for the Radium Extraction Company, contributing to the exploitation of potential radium-bearing ore in the rugged Flinders Ranges. The nature of George's work was briefly described by Greenwood in a series of letters written to the company's secretary throughout 1911. Greenwood first tasked George with relaying messages between scattered members of the company's workforce. But he later used George to extract and then transport ore by camel, such was George's skill with these unruly beasts. "No white man could have done better at double the pay," Greenwood wrote to the company's secretary; "so good with and to the camels too."[93] Greenwood described George as "a good man," "a reliable chap and good worker and prospector," later suggesting that the company keep him on the books, not least due to his skill with the camels.[94] While at first glance these letters appear mundane, their direct references to George are notable. Archival silences typically accompany settlers' employment of Aboriginal labor in Australia, but Greenwood clearly identifies George as Aboriginal in his letters. Corroborated by brief references to George in local newspapers, these letters exist as one of the few direct archival references to Aboriginal involvement in radium extraction in Australia.

While brief and fleeting, these mentions of George assist in subverting the archival silences often perpetuated by settler-colonial narratives, such as those that center Mawson's heroism and contribution to Australian science and development. Glimpsed through archival traces, George's relationship to Greenwood and the Radium Extraction Company reflects the interactions enabled (and often necessitated) by scientific discovery and mining on Australia's inland frontier. George's employment on his own land—on his own Country—facilitated his interaction with settler society's preoccupation with scientific modernity, an essential feature of Australian nationalism and one arguably embodied by Mawson. This historical episode also echoes broader trends in the colonial relations inherent in early settler mining practices in Australia, whereby Aboriginal knowledge and labor were harnessed by settlers to exploit Country for what lay within. However, as became the case in the Flinders Ranges, settlers were not always successful in their exploitation of such lands. Sometimes Country did not yield the desired results or resources.

Much to both Mawson's and Greenwood's disappointment, the deposit found at Radium Ridge proved only mildly radioactive. Its continued exploitation was subsequently deemed unprofitable by South Australia's government geologist L. Keith Ward, who lamented, "As often happens on such occasions, a mere promising discovery has shared the fate of those which are not so deserving of further attention."[95] The radioactive riches that newspapers and scientists alike had promised to the judicious "discoverers" of such minerals in Australia had not been forthcoming. And with no other deposits in sight, the Radium Extraction Company soon folded.[96] Nevertheless, the process of exploring for and exploiting potential radioactive minerals in the South Australian interior had assisted in satiating settlers' hunger to know and claim Australia's inland. And the colonization of these spaces would only accelerate as imperial powers increasingly recognized the military and civilian applications of radioactive minerals.

The Dawn of the Nuclear Age

The fever for radioactive minerals that had gripped many Australian prospectors following Smith's discovery at Olary certainly subsided in the proceeding decades, but never truly broke. Hope in the potential of radioactive ores simmered away, boosted in the wake of the First World War when the military application of radioactivity became apparent to the world's major powers and its medicinal properties highly sought-after.[97] Despite global dips in demand and price in the 1910s, by the 1920s there were medical, political, and military reasons for the Australian government (and Mawson) to reconsider the value of the ores in the Flinders Ranges, alongside other sources of radium-bearing ore previously deemed unprofitable.[98]

On 12 November 1923, A. C. Broughton—another geology student and previous employee of Mawson's—reiterated what Mawson had observed over a decade earlier. Broughton noted in a geological report that "radio-active minerals occur in [the] mountainous country" of the northern Flinders Ranges. However, "immature developments in the district" had left these radium lodes unexploited, the area having "not yet emerged from the prospecting stage."[99] Referencing Mawson and Greenwood's abandonment of their prospect, Broughton suggested that there was significant wealth yet to be reaped from the region. Companies made various attempts to repeg and further exploit areas that Mawson and others had previously identified as bearing radioactive metals, including at Olary and Radium Ridge.

Alongside renewed interest in Olary in the 1920s, several mining enterprises, including the Mount Painter Heights Syndicate, demonstrated their interest in exploiting the deposit Greenwood had identified as Radium Ridge (later known as the Mount Painter deposit). In 1926, a letter to the syndicate from the United States Department of Commerce acknowledged the "keen interest . . . being manifested in the radium deposits of South Australia" overseas, accompanied by a request for samples of the ore in question.[100] In a similar appeal, the manager of the United Mount Painter Radium Company asked Broughton and the syndicate for a "few good, showy samples for Sir Ernest Rutherford," who was then the director of the Cavendish Laboratory at the University of Cambridge.[101] All the while, Mawson maintained a close eye on the evolving situation throughout the 1920s and 1930s, filing away letters, brochures, newsletters, and articles relating to the development of radium deposits and nuclear technology all over the world. He savored information from fellow geologists about potential new finds, looking on with interest and ambition as radioactive ores were discovered in the United States, Papua, and Namibia, across the Belgian Congo, and at Canada's Great Bear Lake.[102]

By the end of the 1920s, Mawson was once again being consulted for his expertise in Australian radioactive minerals, this time by the British government. In February 1929, A. Bowler of the Australian Radium Corporation traveled to the metropole to discuss Australian radium with the British government's Committee of Civil Research. The committee had expressed interest in radium for use in British hospitals and medical facilities, and Bowler hoped that appealing directly to the British government would assist in funding his radioactive exploits. Bowler assured the committee that Australia possessed "every mineral in the world," including radium, and that Mawson himself had confirmed his suspicions by advising him where to strike.[103] The committee subsequently sent Bowler back to the Flinders Ranges empty-handed, save for the advice that he commission Mawson to draw up a formal report of Bowler's prospect. Mawson's services were then procured directly by the committee, which sought his advice about whether radium did indeed occur in notable concentration in Australia.

In a letter to Neville Chamberlain, then at the British Ministry of Health, British MP Lieutenant Commander Joseph Kenworthy conveyed Mawson's conclusion: "While there are considerable deposits of radium-bearing ore, the quality is doubtful, and unless some richer seams are discovered it may not be possible to exploit them commercially."[104] British interest in Australian radium waned, until radioactivity's potential military applications were fully realized over a decade later.

In the 1940s, the Australian government considered uranium sufficiently important to warrant directly funding a new round of exploitation for radioactive ores across the country. This renewed search coincided with a rumor spread via Australian nuclear physicist Mark Oliphant (who was also involved in the Manhattan Project) that Britain was working on its own atomic program. Oliphant actively fueled Britain's interest in Australian uranium, having consulted with Mawson in 1943 regarding the occurrence of radioactive ores in Australia. The physicist subsequently advised the British government to act quickly, encouraging officials to assess for themselves all of Australia's known deposits.[105] No longer were radium and uranium simply the passionate pursuit of the individual prospector, whose value to colonial consolidation was through the claiming of land and resources and dispossession of Aboriginal people. The advent of nuclear weapons ensured that radioactive minerals were central to the imperial and technopolitical futures of both the British Empire and the United States. As a result, their exploitation became highly regulated.

The centralization of radioactive mineral exploration occurred, in large part, as a response to the British search for an "empire" supply of uranium in Australia. When the British sought to supplement their meager uranium supplies with ore from their dominions, the potentially radium-rich ores previously identified by geologists such as Mawson seemed an obvious starting point.[106] The Australian government responded enthusiastically to Britain's interest, reserving all uranium deposits for Crown uses under the Atomic Energy (Control of Materials) Act of 1946.[107] Smiler Greenwood, having requested that Mawson test a sample of ocher he had acquired near his property in the northern Flinders Ranges, discovered in Mawson's reply the consequences of Australia's zeal to supply the empire.[108] Mawson wrote in February 1944 to inform Greenwood that while the ocher was of little value, the Australian government was eager to locate a national uranium deposit. Mawson correctly speculated that the government's decision to search for such a deposit was made "in view of the possibility that uranium [would] be of extreme value in post-war times as a source of atomic energy" and due to the "possibility of making an extremely powerful explosive from uranium."[109] The Australian government's search for a national ore deposit from which radium could be extracted looked to threaten Mawson's and Greenwood's personal ambitions to benefit financially from radioactive minerals in South Australia.

Supporting this assertion, in July 1944 Mawson told Greenwood that the Commonwealth was "very unfair" in closing the Mount Painter area and claiming all uranium in the region. Mawson argued, "You have for years interrogated these Ranges and made observations and discoveries the value of which under this arrangement will be denied to you."[110] He implored him to seek compensation from the government, expressing his opinion that it was "hardly fair on prospectors . . . to suddenly change regulations controlling mining."[111] Commencing his geology career under the colonial protections of the Mining Act of 1893, Mawson cherished the act's prioritization of discovery, the royalties for which—he believed—should be reaped by the finder. While his letters suggest that he held concern for Greenwood's claims, it is just as likely that Mawson feared that the Commonwealth's interest in uranium deposits would override his own involvement in and benefits from the discovery of this important mineral. Moreover, the interference of both the Australian and British governments threatened settler-colonial freedoms to prospecting established nearly a century earlier, further complicating the nuclear colonial dynamics at play in Australia.

Despite Mawson's umbrage at federal authorities interfering with South Australia's radium and uranium deposits, he remained a key consultant of the federal government. Letters between Mawson and Smiler Greenwood reveal that Mawson assisted the Commonwealth with determining the significance of the radioactivity present in the Mount Painter region. This, in turn, entitled him to certain insights. In August 1944, Mawson wrote "in great haste" to inform Greenwood that the claim he had pegged out in the east Painter region was of potentially great importance. "One of the party (Sullivan), a Commonwealth geologist, brought to me the set of specimens" taken from the region, Mawson wrote. "There are two radioactive minerals of importance in it," he continued.[112] Mawson also indicated that Australian government authorities had agreed to compensate Greenwood for the losses caused by the Commonwealth's seizing of his claims at Mount Painter.[113]

In addition to his involvement with the Commonwealth, Mawson recommenced publishing on radioactive minerals. In doing so, he sought to remind both Australian and international scientific and mining communities of his involvement in the discovery of radioactive minerals. In the introduction to his 1944 article "The Nature and Occurrence of Uraniferous Mineral Deposits in South Australia," Mawson told readers: "Now that there is a revival of interest in uranium it seems appropriate for me having been associated with the first publication on the radio-active minerals of Australia and later with the discovery and investigation of two of the most important uraniferous deposits in South Australia, to publish what information I have accumulated."[114] As the Australian government embarked on its exploration of the explosive power of radioactive elements, scientists contributing to the fledgling field of nuclear physics and its associated disciplines were increasingly consulted, employed, and revered by governments across the Anglophone world. These men (and they were exclusively men) held considerable political power. As such, Mawson was determined to be counted as a key player in the rapidly developing global nuclear industry, but British authorities derided his attempts. Mawson's 1944 article was dismissed by Charles Findlay Davidson, a geologist at the British Geological Survey and Museum and an official geological adviser to the British intelligence services during World War II, who described it as resulting "from a sense of offence to his scientific *amour propre*."[115] Beyond Australia, the industry was moving on without him.

This was an industry centered around an ore that, in a short period of time, had metamorphosed from a geological novelty with potential to enrich individuals into an invaluable political, military, and scientific resource. Consequently, scientists of international renown such as J. Robert Oppenheimer, Niels Bohr, William Penney, Philip Baxter, Mark Oliphant, and Ernest Titterton, all of whom had become central to the development of nuclear weapons in both the United States and Britain, are commonly remembered for their historical role in nuclear development.[116] Despite Mawson's efforts to associate himself with the discovery of radioactive minerals in Australia, he continues to be admired instead for his expeditions in the ice, as a pioneer of Antarctic exploration. Mawson's concern with his legacy is evident in a 1956 letter, written two years before his death, in which he scolded the Australian Department of Mines and Energy for crediting the prospector Arthur Smith with discovering carnotite at Olary. Mawson described this claim as "rather amusing," for "A. J. Smith had not the remotest knowledge of Uranium" and thus would have been unable to identify the ore without Mawson's help. "Evidently you have not known the full story of the Radium Hill discovery," he wrote to the department.[117] Mawson made it clear that he should have been credited with the discovery.

In the final years of his life, Mawson acknowledged that his exclusion from the nation's nuclear history, and the closing of the door to the public exploitation of deposits with which he had enjoyed a long association, left him "sore." This was especially so, he posited, "considering I was fundamental in establishing the presence of Uranium" in Australia.[118] While Mawson's laments over his exclusion are important for their demonstration of his own personal and professional ambitions, they also point to the ways that the arrival of the nuclear age was remaking state-based, federal, and global relationships between nuclear processes and those individuals, decision-makers, and corporations keen to engage in them.

Reaping the Riches

Where, in 1906, radium existed as a scientific marvel with the potential to make individual prospectors wealthy, by 1944 it had become a mineral of national and imperial significance, the power and devastation of which the world would soon witness.[119] This transition reflects the layered nature of settler colonialism and imperialism in Australia, such that settler prospectors actively exploited Aboriginal people and Country in pursuit of radioactive minerals while later experiencing the seeming injustice of having one's own rights to land taken away by the state. And while there is no comparing the violent dispossession experienced by Aboriginal people from 1788 onward and the rolling back of mining rights from settlers such as Mawson and Smiler Greenwood in the 1940s, these intersecting narratives demonstrate both the nuances of nuclear colonialism as a phenomenon and the overlapping influences of colonialism and imperialism in Australia during the mid-twentieth century.

As the narration of Mawson's relationship to radioactive resources in the early twentieth century makes clear, prospecting for radium assisted in furthering settler-nationalist ambitions to reveal the riches of an apparently barren land. This ambition would continue through the twentieth century, fundamentally shaping the historical relationship between Australia's pursuit of radioactive minerals and settler colonialism. Mawson's involvement in radium prospecting demonstrates that early enactments of nuclear colonialism in Australia (as elsewhere) predate the beginning of the nuclear age, entwined with extant colonial mechanisms enabled by and facilitated through scientific discovery and settler-nationalist ambition.

But as with many similar colonial interactions, these relationships constituted more than simply exploiting ore within a place of significance to the contemporary Adnyamathanha people. Individual laborers were involved in the process. To reap ore from the Flinders Ranges, Mawson had to engage with prospectors who—in turn—enlisted the labor of Aboriginal people living in the region, several of whom had established individual reputations as prospectors, trackers, and cameleers. As this pattern suggests, settler understandings of land's utility, the importance of Aboriginal knowledge and labor, and the primacy of nationalistic and imperialistic ambition have historically dictated the relationship between radioactive mineral extraction and colonialism in Australia. The complex interplay created by this relationship only deepened across the twentieth century as the geopolitical relevance of nuclear weapons surged in the 1950s and Australian settler colonialism and British nuclear imperialism became increasingly entangled.

TWO

Fields of Thunder

To date, Australia remains one of the only independent countries in the world to have offered up its sovereign lands for the testing of another state's nuclear weapons. Between 1952 and 1963, Britain conducted twelve major tests in the maritime and desert territories of its dominion Australia. British scientists and military personnel exploded nuclear weapons onboard ships near the Monte Bello Islands (off the Western Australian coast), atop towers at Emu Field (South Australia), and via airdrop and tied to balloons at Maralinga (South Australia). They also conducted hundreds of minor tests to determine the volatility of nuclear weapons by emulating accidents through the dropping, burning, and exploding of plutonium products.

These activities took place over a vast tract of desert Country belonging to the Kokatha, Barngarla, Arabunna, Pitjantjatjara, Yankunytjatjara, and Antakirinja peoples, who had been subject to the paternalistic welfare policies of Australian state and federal authorities for over a century. Through decades of missionary influence, the provision of rations, the creation of Aboriginal reserves, and the active removal of Aboriginal people from their Country, settler Australians had facilitated the systematic unpeopling of the central desert region. The perceived suitability of Australia's remote desert environment for nuclear testing only increased the pace of this process of Indigenous depopulation.

It is therefore too simplistic to argue, as others have, that Britain's testing program was colonial by virtue of having taken place on Aboriginal land. The nuclear colonialism at the heart of these tests runs far deeper than that, characterized by a convergence between the nuclear imperial ambitions of the British Empire and Australian government *and* the long-standing settler-colonial paternalism that Australian authorities deployed to govern Aboriginal lives. By integrating these two, usually distinct, threads of historical analysis, this chapter demonstrates how this mid-twentieth-century manifestation of nuclear colonialism constituted a merging of long-held colonial assumptions and structures on the ground and emergent imperial interests that were proliferating globally alongside nuclear weapons.

With the emergence of nuclear energy and its immense military and civilian possibilities, successive Australian governments recognized the benefits of becoming involved in the development of a British nuclear posture. Initially, Australian politicians considered collaboration with Britain on Commonwealth defense matters an opportunity for Australia to acquire guided missiles and nuclear energy. And although these ambitions did not come to fruition, the imperial and geopolitical promises—and influence—of such developments were nonetheless extensive in the late 1940s. Setting the direct acquisition of an Australian nuclear posture aside, many officials hoped that the involvement of Australian scientists and defense personnel in Britain's program would have profound impacts on Australia's geopolitical position in the Pacific, while also providing opportunities for the development of Australia's scientific experience and nuclear expertise. As it transpired, the most direct and obvious way for Canberra to secure its involvement in nuclear development was to provide the sites necessary for the testing of Britain's expanding military arsenal. In doing so, successive Australian prime ministers offered up large tracts of Country to Britain for both missile and nuclear testing. The systemic dispossession of Aboriginal communities from the purportedly "uninhabitable" lands surrounding these desert testing sites—at Woomera, Emu Field, and Maralinga—was thus inherently linked to both Whitehall's and Canberra's defense ambitions.

The perceived "problem" of arid Australia's Aboriginal populations, as authorities represented it, existed in direct opposition to the unparalleled modernity and military, scientific, and geopolitical promise of nuclear weapons. Those communities that remained in the central desert region in the 1950s had been subject to long-standing welfare policies that perpetuated the notion that Aboriginal people remained a political and social "problem" standing in the way of the nation's progress. Such assumptions underpinned settler efforts to manage Aboriginal communities living in the central deserts both prior to and during the tests. In fact, the approaches that various government authorities deployed to manipulate Aboriginal mobility within and around the Maralinga Prohibited Area aligned with, and were often facilitated by, extant paternalistic policies including segregation and assimilation. Aimed at "protecting" Aboriginal people from what many settlers perceived to be degeneracy, such policies assisted in dispossessing them of their Country.

Ultimately, Britain's nuclear tests in Australia were predicated on the newly developed belief that these weapons held great potential for the strategic future of the British Empire and Commonwealth. However, the active pursuit of both Britain's and Australia's nuclear ambitions was facilitated by long-standing forms of settler-colonial control with a history that runs deeper than the tests themselves. This episode of nuclear colonialism thus highlights the role of the British and Australian governments in the construction and perpetuation of perceptions of Aboriginal inferiority and dependence, which facilitated the infliction of significant harm on those communities dispossessed by Britain's nuclear tests. While many Australian histories have focused on British complicity in this process, this chapter offers new insight into Australia's role in the tests, demonstrating the multilayered nature of the nuclear colonialism enacted in the central deserts during the 1950s and 1960s.

An Imperial Arsenal

In 1950, British Prime Minister Clement Attlee approached his Australian counterpart, Prime Minister Robert Menzies, about hosting a series of British nuclear tests in Australia. Menzies, by most accounts, jumped at the opportunity to support Britain's program, circumventing his cabinet and offering up Australian soil to the British. Several historians popularly recall this as the moment that Australia first became subjected to British nuclear imperialism, a form of imperial subjugation enacted through weapons possession and testing, and in this instance enabled by Menzies's renowned Anglophilia.[1] Yet several earlier developments in British Commonwealth defense during the 1940s demonstrate that Australia's desire to be involved in the global nuclear order predated Menzies's government. While many scholars posit that the British nuclear tests in Australia's central desert region were colonial by virtue of having taken place on Aboriginal land, the nuclear colonialism at the heart of this historical episode is markedly more complex.[2] Rather, it is characterized by the co-optation, manipulation, and cementing of existent settler-colonial structures in the furtherance of Australia's (and Britain's) nuclear ambitions.

By the time the United States had tested its first nuclear weapon at Alamogordo, New Mexico, signaling the apparent dawn of the nuclear age, Australia was an independent nation in the British Commonwealth. It had been since 1901, when the six British colonies of New South Wales, Victoria, South Australia, Queensland, Western Australia, and Tasmania had federated to form the Commonwealth of Australia, adopting a constitutional monarchy as its system of government.[3] Under the 1931 Statute of Westminster, Britain's Parliament recognized Australia as a dominion of the British Empire and Commonwealth, capable of developing foreign policy ambitions independent of Whitehall.[4] British influence nevertheless remained strong in Australia and encouraged successive Australian governments to assist in imperial defense development during the 1940s and 1950s.[5] This close relationship included the development of an imperial arsenal of nuclear weapons.

Throughout the 1940s, consecutive Labor governments laid the groundwork for Australia's contribution to the nuclear future of the British Empire. Australia's shifting alliances during the Second World War have encouraged many to view Australian Prime Minister John Curtin's (1941–45) famed "turn toward the United States" as a sign that Australia's relationship with Britain was weakening.[6] But this so-called turn did not spell the end of Australia's commitment to the British Empire and Commonwealth. In reality, Curtin envisaged a future where Australia would actively contribute to improving the "machinery for Empire co-operation."[7] Such preoccupations similarly guided Prime Minister Ben Chifley's (1945–49) approach to nuclear development in the years after Curtin's death. Under the auspices of these two Labor leaders, Australia was to be proactively and comprehensively involved in the defense of the British Commonwealth, particularly through the development of guided weapons.

Guided ballistic missiles, which Germany had first deployed during the Second World War, marked a shift in military technology that nuclear weapons would soon embody. These missiles allowed an aggressor to "sit snugly at home and point his finger of force against another country."[8]

With the rapid development of nuclear technologies in the mid-1940s, it was not long before the world's powers—the United States, the Union of Soviet Socialist Republics (USSR), and Britain among them—realized that a long-range ballistic missile could and would be armed with a nuclear warhead. Whitehall quickly deduced that any nation able to combine these two emergent military technologies would have Britain "at its mercy."[9] Attlee's Labour government consequently decided that "the only hope was to deter an aggressor by the threat of swift and certain retribution."[10] Such a strategy required Britain to build nuclear weapons and guided ballistic missiles simultaneously.

To this end, between April and June 1946, Australian representatives participated in a series of informal conferences organized by the British government to discuss issues of imperial cooperation and defense science.[11] With the "application of science to offensive and defensive warfare" becoming "immense and revolutionary in character," the British government suggested to its dominions a coordinated Commonwealth strategy.[12] According to His Majesty's Government, "the resources of any one member of the Commonwealth alone" were "insufficient to cope" with global military developments. And, at the June conference, the British chemist and chair of the Defence Research Policy Committee, Sir Henry Tizard, assured representatives that his government was "in favour of the fullest co-operation with the Dominions in the field of defence Science and all that such co-operation implied."[13] What such cooperation implied for Australia was the use of its geographical advantage to host imperial defense facilities.[14]

A key outcome of these conferences was the determination that Australia was well suited to host the Commonwealth's new guided missile range due to its vast open spaces and geographic isolation away from the rest of the empire. At the initial Dominions Prime Ministers' Conference in April 1946, British representatives had insisted that the "Dominions . . . make available for joint use areas suitable for carrying out development trials of such new weapons as cannot adequately be tested in the United Kingdom, i.e. atomic weapons, long-range rockets and weapons connected with bacteriological and chemical warfare."[15] In light of this request, Australia's Prime Minister Chifley consented to Britain conducting a secret survey mission in Australia to search for a missile testing range of approximately

2,000 miles in length. Following this survey, Major General L. E. Beavis, leader of the Australian delegation to the June conference, "expressed Australia's keen interest in the project."[16] Both Canberra and Whitehall subsequently agreed that it would be "desirable to set up in Australia facilities for the full scale development and testing of guided and propelled missiles and projectiles."[17] Such commitment to Commonwealth defense was tied up with Australian self-interest.

Chifley, like his predecessor Curtin, recognized the benefits of assisting Britain with the development of armaments. A particular hope of Chifley's—and later of Menzies's—was that such assistance would facilitate Australia's own scientific development, a process that was critical if Australia was to obtain an independent arsenal of this "new generation of weapons for use in any future war."[18] As British representatives had made abundantly clear, this new generation of weapons would include nuclear technology.

Unpeopling the Central Deserts

In pursuit of the desire to make a contribution to Commonwealth defense, the Australian government set aside over 62,000 square miles (100,000 square kilometers) of the nation's desert "wilderness" for testing long-range missiles.[19] Government officials named the range "Woomera," appropriating the Dharug word for an Aboriginal spear-throwing device. Commenting on the juxtaposition exposed by this moniker, the Adelaide *Advertiser* reported: "Nothing could be more marked than the contrast between the simple woomera of our stone-age man and the wondrous rockets that will be the subject of experiment at the Woomera range-head of modern science."[20] What this commentator failed to recognize, however, was the bitter irony encapsulated by the name, a word taken from a then-extinct coastal dialect of Dharug from the area now known as Sydney and transplanted thousands of miles west in the desert. The purportedly "simple woomera" was not the relic of a "stone-age man," but rather the vital tool of a living culture concealed and elided by "Woomera."[21]

The establishment of Woomera accelerated the active "unpeopling" of the central deserts by Australian authorities, a colonizing process that later made way for nuclear testing. While the history of Australia's inland frontier is one of incremental emptying as surviving Aboriginal peoples either were forced off or migrated from their traditional lands toward sources of food and employment, these processes were both enabled and exacerbated by the rapid militarization of the central desert region.[22] This militarization was initially made possible by the seeming uninhabitability of desert spaces, many of which had defied active colonial settlement over the preceding century due to their aridity and hostility to settlers. Australian authorities justified the establishment of Woomera—and then later the Emu Field and Maralinga test sites—as an important use of Australia's "wide open spaces," unbothered by their habitation by remote Aboriginal communities.[23] In fact, the militarization of these spaces offered the Australian state and federal governments an opportunity to expedite the unpeopling of the central desert region in an attempt to assimilate Aboriginal people into what politicians and others deemed the Australian way of life.

In the 1950s, settlers still considered the central desert region uninhabitable, desolate, and cruel. While a select number of seemingly adventurous settlers traveled into these deserts in search of the country's "red heart," for many the center of Australia remained a site of vast loneliness, "a desolate wasteland punctuated by isolated homesteads and the bleached bones of swagmen and prospectors."[24] Writing in the early 1960s about the establishment of Woomera, the popular military writer Ivan Southall explained that this tract of desert country had been chosen because its "spirit had expired," as "man had arrived too late."[25] Despite this hardly being the case, historians and other scholars have identified similar settler characterizations of desert lands elsewhere, whereby lands of use to the nuclear imperial ambitions of various states have been "wastelanded," rendered rhetorically useless and thus ripe for the picking.[26] As the historian Traci Brynne Voyles evocatively describes it, "The 'wasteland' is a racial and a spatial signifier that renders an environment and the bodies that inhabit it pollutable."[27] While Voyles's focus was Navajo lands subject to uranium mining, settler framings of Australia's central desert region can be understood similarly.

By describing the arid inland as a veritable wilderness, detailing its harshness, heat, and lack of vegetation, Australian government representatives and the media alike were able to extoll the transformative effects of militarization in modernizing these lands. Woomera was described by the *Daily Telegraph* as an "oasis in the desert," "an Eden" by the *Sun News-Pictorial*, a place where "wonder grows" on account of its new amenities, running water, and representation of modern Australia.[28] "Australian scientists, soldiers and airmen," the Adelaide *Advertiser* detailed for its readers, "have turned this wild corner of South Australia into a gigantic open-air laboratory to test the weapons of the future."[29] These descriptions sit in stark contrast to the minister for defense's characterization of this region as "largely uninhabited" gibber country—or rock-littered desert—devoid of human habitation bar a few large-scale pastoral runs and the occasional Aboriginal camp.[30]

But these lands *were* inhabited. Not only did Aboriginal people live in these desert landscapes, and do still, but they also relied and continue to rely on the plants and animals that occupy them. These lifeways were not unknown to settlers at the time, as the line of fire from Woomera passed directly through the Central Aboriginal Reserve. A relic of Australia's lingering policy of segregation, this state reserve had been designed to protect Aboriginal people from the "degenerative" impacts of unmonitored contact with settlers by separating Aboriginal people from the broader population.[31] In announcing the government's decision to proceed with Woomera, the minister for defense addressed the presence of Aboriginal people in the reserve, arguing that their scarcity in numbers ensured that the "probability of a missile falling on them would be extremely remote." Although he assured the public that the risk to Aboriginal people was less than "the danger of an aircraft falling from the skies," the violation of the apparently inviolable Central Aboriginal Reserve became a topic of significant public debate.[32]

Members of the Australian public took on both sides of the discussion. Letters to the editors of various newspapers both questioned the rocket range's need to take over large swathes of the Central Aboriginal Reserve and lamented the degeneration of the reserve's people, welcoming its demise. One correspondent wrote to the editor of the Melbourne *Argus* in February 1947: "There is considerable public indignation that the last miserable retreat of our aborigines should be violated, and I share this intensely." The writer further acknowledged the range's connection to the potential development of nuclear weapons, arguing, "We prepare an unimaginable holocaust for our children."[33] Conversely, members of the Australian public questioned the reserve's effectiveness, with another correspondent writing to the editor of *The Advertiser* with the opinion that many of the stories told of the central deserts' "wild natives" did "not argue for healthy tribes within the reserve." As such, the author opined, "By all means let us protect the aborigines, but let us keep our heads, for mercy's sake!"[34]

Acknowledging the inevitable impact of the range on Aboriginal people in one way or another, Canberra tasked the recently formed Australian Committee on Guided Projectiles to address key issues relating to Aboriginal welfare within the range.[35] The committee consisted of representatives from across the armed forces, the Council for Scientific and Industrial Research, and state and federal departments charged with Aboriginal welfare.[36] Four "experts" on Aboriginal people were invited to contribute to discussions: the former chief protector of Aborigines in Western Australia, A. O. Neville; anthropologist A. P. Elkin; Presbyterian Aboriginal rights campaigner and missionary Charles Duguid; and anthropologist Donald Thomson.[37] The task of these men in particular was to address the potential impacts of the range on Aboriginal communities and formulate strategies to minimize the risks apparent to them. The inclusion of Duguid and Thomson is notable. Both were invited by the committee to contribute to discussions on account of their vehement, and incredibly public, opposition to the range.[38]

Duguid was the public face of opposition to Woomera even prior to its formal establishment. In various letters published in newspapers throughout 1946, the missionary actively condemned the United States' treatment of the Marshallese on Bikini Atoll, seeking to dispel the idea that the central desert region's Aboriginal populations could be dealt with "like the natives of Bikini," by simply removing them from their homelands.[39] This "shows ignorance of the aboriginal people and their ways," he maintained, for they "cannot be compensated for the loss of their tribal hunting grounds, and spirit lands."[40] Duguid therefore considered it abhorrent that the South Australian Aborigines Protection Board supported the range's use of the Central Aboriginal Reserve, resigning from the board in protest. Publicizing his resignation in a London newspaper, he justified his actions as in pursuit of peace: "If we are going to precipitate an atomic war, we are going to wipe out civilisation."[41] He begged the public's consideration: "Having driven [Aboriginal people] from all the good country are we now to sit back and allow them to be treated as human guinea-pigs in atomic tests?"[42] And while the rockets launched at Woomera were ballistic missiles, rather than nuclear weapons, Duguid's question remains a haunting prediction of what would unfold in the central deserts over the proceeding decades.

Another of Duguid's concerns lay in the danger presented by "the introduction into the Reserves of the personnel required to man the observation posts."[43] In other words, Duguid was anxious about the prospective impact that increased white presence in the Central Aboriginal Reserve would have on this vestige of "unadulterated" Aboriginal Country and its population.[44] He was especially worried about "detribalization," a term anthropologists and others used in the mid-twentieth century to refer to the supposedly deleterious transition undertaken by Aboriginal populations following unmanaged contact, whereby individuals were perceived to "lose" their culture and emerge "stranded."[45] Aboriginal people "deprived of their land, and their living, must in the course of time die," Duguid had warned the public during a radio broadcast in 1944.[46] With this concern front of mind, he told the Australian Committee on Guided Projectiles that while he was heartened by the Commonwealth government's concern for Aboriginal welfare, "the life of aborigines in the Reserves would be interfered with by contact," irrespective of measures taken by the government to ensure Aboriginal safety from dropping bombs.[47] Thomson, it was noted, supported Duguid.[48]

But the protestations of these men were not enough. The committee ultimately concluded, "De-tribalisation of the aborigine is inevitable," and thus "neither of these gentlemen had advanced any reason which precluded" the range's establishment.[49] This determination reflected a shift in Australian approaches to Aboriginal welfare in this period.[50] Under South Australia's conservative Premier Thomas Playford, the Aborigines Act Amendment Act of 1939 had replaced earlier policies of segregation with policies of assimilation, aimed at integrating Aboriginal peoples into the broader settler population, rather than separating communities from it.[51] Assimilationist policies purported to champion "wholesome" contact between settler Australians and Aboriginal communities through employment and education, enacted by state governments in pursuit of a future where Aboriginal people would (be forced to) adopt Anglo-European "social norms, values and deportment" and "could learn to be useful workers in colonial enterprise."[52] As such, the provisions put in place to protect populations during any missile (or later nuclear) tests would simply ease an already inevitable—and newly desirable—reality, "putting forward . . . the clock of de-tribalisation by possibly a generation" and speeding up the process of assimilation.[53]

Such paternalistic policies, enlisted to "guard" the rights of people who apparently could not "defend themselves," characterized this period and the nuclear tests more broadly.[54] So while Duguid believed that Woomera would engender "a state of utter 'bewilderment' and 'degradation'" among the Aboriginal communities of the central deserts, the committee disagreed. For many Australian government representatives, Woomera's establishment would only smooth the process of encouraging Aboriginal people to move out of the Central Aboriginal Reserve and toward white settlements, effectively unpeopling the central deserts and facilitating the lands' use for nuclear testing.[55]

Fields of Thunder

In agreeing to host Britain's guided missile range, Canberra had committed wholeheartedly to the development of imperial defense. By 1950, and in light of the USSR's first successful nuclear test in 1949, Whitehall had made it clear that obtaining an independent nuclear posture was strategically, militarily, and reputationally necessary. A British "uranium bomb" had been in the works for several years by this point, but Britain's fluctuating relationship with the United States had a significant impact on nuclear development. Congress's passing of the McMahon Act in 1946 had prohibited the United States' sharing of nuclear knowledge and technology, stifling cooperation with Britain.[56] Without Anglo-American cooperation, Britain's scientists set to work developing a "simple Nagasaki-style bomb" independently, but before long they were faced with the dilemma of where to test it.[57]

Australia was not Britain's first choice. Initially, British authorities approached the United States about the possibility of using the latter's test site at Eniwetok, citing their desire to use the atoll to measure the potential impact of an underwater nuclear detonation.[58] However, no immediate reply was forthcoming from Washington. In the meantime, and anticipating the United States' reluctance to freely share its Pacific proving ground, British officials considered several other possibilities suggested by their scientific experts. Among them were the Monte Bello Islands, an archipelago approximately 80 miles (130 kilometers) off the northwest coast of Western Australia. The Monte Bellos appeared ideal for several reasons, including Australia's dominion status, the lack of human inhabitants across the archipelago, and the suitability of the scattered islands for simulating a sea-based nuclear attack. In September 1950, while still awaiting word from Washington, the Ministry of Defence contacted the British High Commission in Canberra to inquire whether "first . . . the Australian Government would be prepared in principle to agree that the first United Kingdom atomic weapon should be tested in Australian territory" and, if so, "whether they would agree to [Britain's] experts making a detailed reconnaissance of the Monte Bello Islands."[59]

Canberra's response was agreeable. Menzies made it clear that "any special facilities which Australia might possess for this or similar purposes would of course be made available."[60] After considerable back-and-forth between British officials over the merits of waiting for the United States to make a formal decision on Eniwetok, Whitehall decided that it would be unwise to risk losing Australia's agreement by delaying the decision.[61] Thus, within a year of returning to power, Menzies had agreed to host a series of British nuclear tests in Australian territory. The three weapons tested on the Monte Bello Islands were accompanied by nine inland tests conducted in the central deserts at Emu Field and Maralinga.

Britain's inland tests have proved far more controversial than those on the Monte Bellos, not least due to the importance of this desert Country to numerous Aboriginal communities. The first inland test site at Emu Field facilitated Operation Totem, which comprised two weapons tests that took place in 1953.[62] Emu's remoteness made it difficult to access, and so a second, more permanent inland proving ground was established to the

FIGURE 3. The hundreds of "minor" tests undertaken by Britain in the central deserts during its nuclear testing program have been credited with spreading the most amount of contamination across the region. Protective clothing, such as that pictured, was used by *some* personnel during these experiments, but limited supply and the extremely hot desert conditions made adequate protection from contaminants difficult. Photograph courtesy of the National Archives of Australia, Canberra. NAA: A6257, P214.

south of Emu Field and closer to rail access. Having appropriated a Dharug word for Woomera, authorities once again took inspiration from the continent's original inhabitants and named the permanent site Maralinga, purportedly meaning "fields of thunder" in Pitjantjatjara.[63] Nine further nuclear tests took place there as part of Operation Buffalo in 1956 and Operation Antler in 1957. In addition to these operations, British scientists undertook hundreds of "minor" tests, largely to determine the impact of accidents on weapons (fig. 3). The explosions that ripped through the desert environment at these locations turned the sand to glass, flattened the desert's abundant spinifex grass, and spread immeasurable amounts of radioactive products, such as uranium, plutonium, beryllium, and cobalt-60, across the interior.

This was not barren land. The desert ecosystems at these sites were abundant. Pale claypans dotted the region, naturally forming shallow lakes following desert rainfall. Rock holes nourished the environment by holding water near the desert's surface, offering reprieve to birds, animals, Aboriginal people, and—after colonization—stock seeking to quench their thirst. The roots of small shrubby mulga trees and spiny spinifex grass held together the desert's vast red sandhills, offering shade and shelter. And abundant fauna—kangaroos, dingoes, lizards, snakes, and more—inhabited the region.

But much of what made this desert region abundant presented a physical obstacle for test infrastructure. Dense mulga trees initially provided endless difficulties for military vehicles making their way to the sites (fig. 4). Beyond the trees, red sands shifted under tires, bogging down heavy machinery and vehicles alike. The region's scarce water supply and considerable remoteness required personnel to construct roads and airstrips, clear swathes of vegetation to make way for buildings, and sink bores for water and sanitation. But perhaps most consequentially, the region's vastness, shady mulga trees, permanent rock holes, and provision of bush foods made monitoring Aboriginal movement across the test sites particularly difficult.

Missions, Rations, and Superstitions

Emu Field and Maralinga encountered issues similar to those at Woomera, namely, that they were peopled spaces. However, unlike in the case of ballistic missiles aimed to fire across the central deserts and into the ocean off the continent's west coast, the risk of nuclear weapons to the region's communities was undeniable. In an effort to avoid actively bombing communities, the Australian government employed a Native Patrol Officer to single-handedly monitor over 62,000 square miles (100,000 square kilometers) of desert, discouraging Aboriginal movements through Country. Walter MacDougall, the man hired for the job, encouraged Aboriginal people's congregation at missions and stations on the deserts' fringes by coordinating the distribution of rations, intercepting and turning around groups traveling across Country, employing young Aboriginal guides to

FIGURE 4. The scrubby spinifex and mulga of Emu Field and Maralinga is far from the oft-conjured image of rolling sandhills usually associated with desert landscapes. This low-growing but nonetheless dense scrub made traversing the landscape in military vehicles with materials for infrastructure tricky. This image, taken near Ooldea in 1953, shows some of the (natural) challenges faced by defense personnel. Photograph courtesy of the National Archives of Australia, Canberra. NAA: A6457, P302-516.

identify and dismantle totemic sites, and deploying Aboriginal understandings of *mamu*, or bad spirits, to foster fear among communities around the testing sites.[64] The prevailing influence of colonial paternalism in the central desert region, enacted through missions, rations, and superstitions, thus played an integral role in facilitating the nuclear tests.[65]

Missions are central to the history of colonialism in Australia. Countless missions were set up across the Australian colonies during the nineteenth century to "civilize" Aboriginal people through Christian conversion, education, and participation in the colonial labor force. In theory, the paternalism that underpinned these institutions aimed to "protect" Aboriginal people from their apparent (and expected) degeneration. In practice, this paternalism often entailed missionaries of various Christian denominations discouraging Aboriginal peoples' use of their traditional languages, restricting their movement, and facilitating their removal from Country and into employment for settlers.[66] Missions in Australia have historically been spaces within which issues of and with race have been mediated by settler-colonial authorities, and in the case of the nuclear tests, they became key mechanisms for the state's control of Aboriginal movement. As a result, many Aboriginal survivors' memories of the nuclear tests have been refracted through their experiences at various missions.

This is certainly the case for the Ooldea Mission on the southern fringes of the Maralinga Prohibited Area (map 2). Long before Ooldea was the site of a mission, it was a traditional meeting place for Aboriginal people from different communities who gathered at its natural soak, known as Yuldi by A<u>n</u>angu.[67] Yuldi was a fresh underground water source, nestled among red sandhills and accessed through digging in the sand. This permanent supply of water provided A<u>n</u>angu with fresh water in times of drought, offering refuge from the heat of the desert.[68] It was a natural meeting place, and many families journeyed for hundreds of miles to gather at its waters.

Yuldi, or Ooldea Soak, was a cultural and geographical touchstone for innumerable A<u>n</u>angu, but by the 1910s it had become a vital water source for settlers. Reflecting on Yuldi in her old age, Maralinga Tjarutja woman Alice Cox described how her family had frequently traversed the red-sanded spinifex Country of the central desert region via rock holes, all the way south to the soak.[69] But as the settler colonization of the central deserts ramped up in the early decades of the twentieth century, the soak became a popular destination for travelers, a source of water for the Trans-Australian Railway, and the site of a Lutheran mission. Hughie Windlass, who went to Ooldea as a young boy, described the gathering of a "big mob" that "came in, took rations and went out again for dingo scalps."[70] Windlass also recalled the influence of the mission on A<u>n</u>angu, such that they were "punished with no rations if [they] tried to run away."[71] Pitjantjatjara and Antakirinja woman Tjunmutja Watson described how her family's usual migration across the central deserts was interrupted in the 1930s when they were on a visit to her family members at Ooldea: "[The missionary] round us up and put us in a school."[72] She was no longer able to visit her Country. Watson was later moved to the Gerard Mission in South Austra-

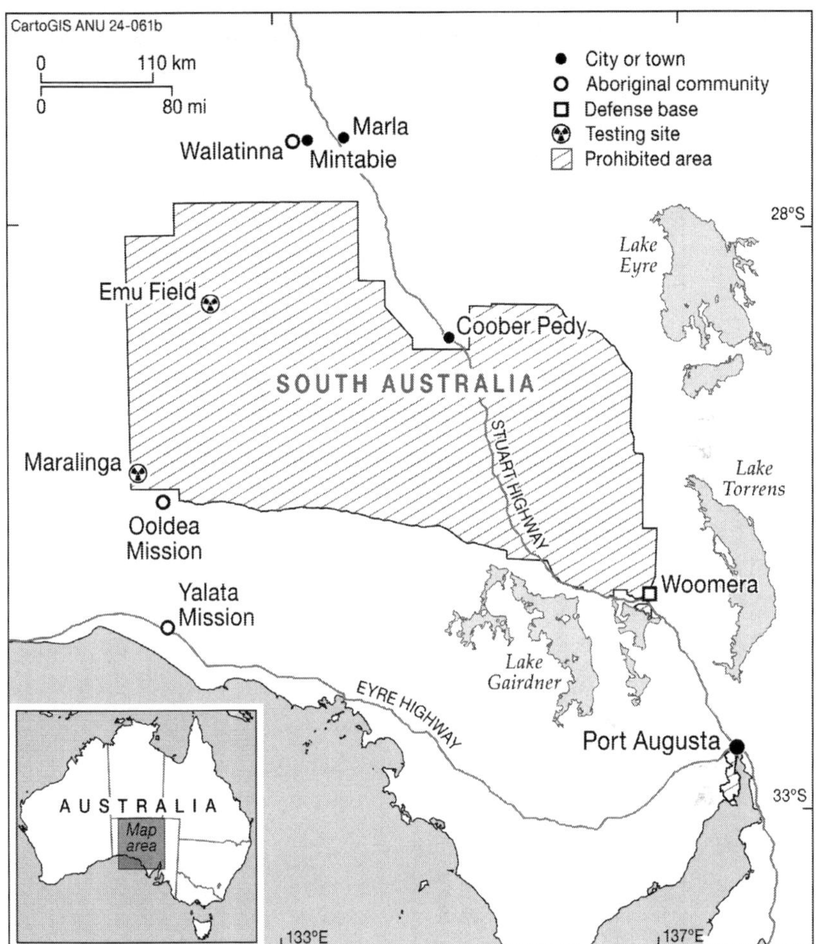

MAP 2. The Maralinga Prohibited Area and associated inland nuclear testing sites tracked across a large swathe of the South Australian state. Away from the state's capital, Adelaide, these sites instead cut across the Central Aboriginal Reserve and the lands of numerous Aboriginal communities, including the Pitjantjatjara, Yankunytjatjara, Antakirinja, Barngarla, Kokatha, and Arabunna peoples. Map provided by CartoGIS Services, Australian National University, Canberra.

lia's Riverland region to do domestic work, sent by missionaries over 600 miles (1,000 kilometers) east of her homelands. The Ooldea Mission closed in 1951, and Watson could not return to Country. Cox and Windlass had similar experiences. What was once a vibrant center of Aboriginal trade and initiation had become the site of colonial paternalism. It was soon to become the site of rampant nuclear colonialism.

By the commencement of the nuclear tests, the soak's natural waters had been devastatingly depleted by settlers. The United Aborigines Mission that ran Ooldea made the decision to move the hundreds of Aṉangu living around the mission's perimeter approximately 90 miles (140 kilometers) south to Yalata in search of a better water supply and meaningful employment. This timing, and Ooldea's proximity to the future Maralinga testing site, ensured that in the memories of many survivors the demise of the Ooldea Mission has become intimately wrapped up in the broader trauma of the testing program.[73] Aṉangu described Ooldea as *their* Country, but following the commencement of the tests, they said, "We were told we could not go back there."[74] This removal from Country created considerable anguish within communities, deepened by colonialism's destruction of desert water sources—such as the soak—which sustained communities physically and spiritually. Exacerbating this trauma were the various tactics authorities used to discourage communities from ever returning to their Country.

Early in the weapons testing period, MacDougall enlisted young Aṉangu to assist him in turning away Aboriginal people traveling into the testing region. William Wangati was just a "young fella" when MacDougall picked him up "out bush" and employed him to assist in "turn[ing] back all the blackfellas."[75] Wangati described "mustering up" other Aboriginal people like "bullocks." His memories include traveling with MacDougall from Emu Field through South Australia's northern sandhill Country in search of Aṉangu. On their travels, they came across large groups of Aṉangu hunting dingoes, the scalps of which formed a vital economy for Aṉangu due to the bounty that settlers placed on these native dogs. Wangati was instructed to tell the groups to move north, away from the testing sites.[76] He accompanied MacDougall on several occasions, sometimes joined by one or two other young men and his wife.

MacDougall also employed young men like Wangati to help identify and dismantle sacred sites in an effort to erase Aboriginal connections to their Country. Three years after Ooldea's residents had been moved south to Yalata, MacDougall reported to the Aborigines Protection Board that he had finally removed all sacred and ceremonial objects from north of Ooldea that might have encouraged Aboriginal migration back into the area.[77] At Paroo, he noted that "all totem poles and sacred objects" had been removed, and at Untinja, the area had ceased to be an important hunting ground, such that there was "no need for ceremonies."[78] North of Ooldea, MacDougall concluded, there was "no justifiable reason for retaining Reserve as such."[79] With MacDougall's assurance that "all significance [was] lost," the lands around Ooldea Soak underwent a metamorphosis, transformed from Country to future nuclear proving ground.[80]

This process had been supported by missionaries for decades. MacDougall noted in a 1954 report that prior to the removal of totemic objects, the "ceremonial value" of the area had already "ceased" as a direct result of a "lack of interest by the young people" perpetuated by "opposition" to custom "by the missionaries." "Young initiates," he continued, "refuse to be initiated, secure in the protection of missionaries and white man's law."[81] The patrol officer directly cited the effect of mission policies on Aboriginal pursuits of ceremony. "Owing to the policy of the Koonibba Mission authorities," he wrote, "any interest [in Country] will quickly die among the school age children."[82] Missionary opposition to Aboriginal ceremony in the Ooldea region led to there being "no practical or ceremonial benefit remain[ing] on the Ooldea Reserve." And while this was certainly not the case for those communities whose Country this was, MacDougall assured the superintendent of Woomera and the authorities at Maralinga that any Aboriginal movement in the area would likely be "as a means of access to work on stations." Monitoring such movement would not be too difficult according to MacDougall, as it would be linked directly to "white man activity."[83]

In conjunction with mission staff, those who owned and operated stations within and around the Maralinga Prohibited Area were enlisted by authorities to assist with the management of Aboriginal migration. Even prior to the nuclear tests there was a focus on providing employment for

Aboriginal people at pastoral stations, especially in South Australia and its bordering eastern colonies. Through labor, authorities attempted to introduce populations to "a more 'civilised' mode of existence," or, rather, facilitate their employment as shepherds and stock workers, partaking in sheep farming on the far west coast of the state.[84] In 1953, MacDougall reported ahead of the first nuclear test at Emu Field: "The tendency is for the Jangkuntjara [*sic*] to stay close to cattle properties where life is considerably easier." "Station personnel encourage them," he maintained.[85] In another 1953 letter, the test program's security officer wrote to assure the Department of Supply that station hands had been encouraged to assist with Aboriginal management: "They all expressed willingness to co-operate from a security point of view in advising . . . of any persons arriving at or passing through their properties. This of course includes movements of blacks."[86] Government authorities provided pastoral stations with rations for the express purpose of attracting Aboriginal people toward their properties.

Ration programs were vital (and highly paternalistic) management tools.[87] As at Mount Serle (see chapter 1), the provision of rations to Aboriginal people at stations and missions across the central desert region was integral to the function of the settler-colonial project in Australia throughout the late nineteenth and early twentieth centuries. In the Maralinga Prohibited Area, this included both the distribution *and* withholding of rations. In December 1954, MacDougall referenced the increased reliance of Aboriginal people on rations as one of the motivating factors for the growing disinterest of Aboriginal people in their traditional lands. "They all—young and old—have become dependent on Government rations," he wrote.[88] Commenting on this increased reliance, the Aborigines Protection Board in 1954 condemned the routine apparently adopted by communities of "moving from Station to Station for free food," for fear that it was creating "laziness, uselessness and a loss of self-respect in the population."[89] This condemnation strategically ignored the fact that settlers had been actively mobilizing such tactics to control the movement and management of Aboriginal populations for decades. It also ignored the fact that, for many, collecting rations from missions and stations only supplemented, rather than replaced, their reliance on Country. Many Aṉangu continued to move across their Country unhindered, as they had done for generations, occasionally capitalizing on the provision of rations by settlers and actively challenging authorities' insistence that the land was empty.

Much to the dismay of officials, in the months leading up to the first inland test at Emu Field in 1953, over fifty Aboriginal people from South Australia arrived at Cundeelee Mission in Western Australia as part of a corroboree, or ceremonial meeting. They had journeyed on foot for hundreds of miles across arid desert Country. The group, arriving at the mission "sick, half starved" and clearly "dependent" on mission assistance, sought food and shelter from staff. Authorities in Western Australia expressed their shock at the group's arrival given that missions had been encouraged to actively deter Aboriginal migration by withholding rations. "Irrespective of our policy to discourage inter-state migrations," authorities maintained, in this instance "to refuse them food . . . would be tantamount to murder."[90] The Aborigines Protection Board of South Australia was informed of the incident by Cundeelee staff and asked firmly to ensure the prevention of "future occurrences" of this nature. Authorities were shocked that the movement of this group had gone completely unnoticed. This incident both exposed the considerable flaws in the monitoring of populations within the Maralinga Prohibited Area and demonstrated the impossibility (and unreasonableness) of the task entrusted to MacDougall. Controlling individuals over such vast tracts of desert Country clearly required more creative interventions.

MacDougall's experience working with Aṉangu over several decades led him to believe that one way to control the movement of those living away from missions and stations was through the manipulation of their own epistemologies. He suggested to government officials that they could influence Yankunytjatjara movements around the northern boundaries of the testing range through the use of their own traditional knowledge. He detailed that "by using their own beliefs and fears of evil spirits and invisible avengers," he could "convince them" that the area was "no safe place for them."[91] MacDougall used Aṉangu's understanding of *mamu*, poison or malevolent spirits, to control their movements in and around the testing site. In one instance, MacDougall prevented a young Aboriginal man, Kunmanara, from traveling south from Ernabella (to the northeast of Mintabie) by warning him that "there was a poison there which was worse for Aṉangu than whites, and that was so strong it would kill people who breathed it."[92] This tactic yielded tangible results at the time, with MacDougall confidently reporting to the range superintendent in the lead-up to the tests at Emu Field that many Aṉangu avoided prohibited areas: "They are afraid of both the mythical and human occupants whom they believe still live in that area."[93] But even those who avoided traversing the central deserts were not necessarily out of harm's way.

Lallie Lennon was camped at Mabel Creek in 1953 when she first heard about the proposed inland nuclear tests at Emu Field. She was noodling for opal with her husband, Stanley, and two small children approximately 124 miles (200 kilometers) east of the testing site, when she recalled seeing "soldiers and trucks going past" accompanied by "a war tank, one war tank went through."[94] Several months later, Lallie and Stanley had moved north to the opal mining town of Mintabie, where she heard on the radio that a bomb test was imminent. Stanley recalled MacDougall telling the couple that they were fine to continue fossicking for opal as long as they did not travel south of Mintabie.[95] Reflecting on her experience of that first weapons test, Lallie noted that "it rumbled, the ground shook, it was frightening."[96] In her attempt to reconcile the experience, Lallie described the rumbling: "[Like] a big storm, you know, when it started off. Then it just went louder. Then it just vibrated." "I was scared," Lallie explained, such that she "did not really watch" the mushroom cloud ascend, as she "did not know what was going to happen next."[97] Lallie and her husband feared that "the ground was going to cave in."[98]

The test that Lallie experienced was Totem I, which took place in October 1953 and produced what Aboriginal survivors later referred to as the "black mist." The black mist was described by witnesses as a dark roiling cloud that swept across the desert landscape, low to the ground, enveloping everything in its path. Lallie was understandably terrified when she experienced this meteorological phenomenon in the wake of the ground rumbling. "We reckon it was poison and all that," she recalled. "I just didn't know what to do," "thought we was going to die."[99] After the cloud had passed through, Lallie and her husband inspected the trunks of nearby mulga trees. She would usually eat honey directly from the mulgas' branches, but the trees were covered in dust: "We would not touch it any more."[100] In the weeks that followed, she and her family fell sick. Lallie fed her children castor oil to stave off flu-like symptoms, and she developed sores on her skin.[101] She suffered from these psoriasis-like lesions for the remainder of her life, as did many others. However, due to British authorities' attempts to conceal this incident in what the historian Heather Goodall has described as an "example of official forgetting," many struggled to reconcile their experiences of this phenomenon until decades later, when the Australian government undertook a federal inquiry into the tests.[102] Until then, the experience of this unexplained black mist haunted many.

Over the following years, seven further weapons were detonated at Maralinga, and criticism of the authorities' treatment of Aboriginal communities mounted. For MacDougall, the continued expansion of the testing program and its accompanying infrastructure forced him to lament to the commissioner of Native affairs, "Almost all of the country that is of any value to human beings has been taken from the aborigines." While he had been intimately involved in the dispossession of Aboriginal people across the testing region, MacDougall maintained: "The policy of segregation is almost impossible to enforce and . . . no country, no matter how remote, can be kept for the sole use of aborigines if the white man finds some profit in it." MacDougall's comments offer a searing critique of both the central deserts' colonization and the impracticality of segregationist policies in the face of rampant colonial incursion into the deserts. Training Aboriginal people in meaningful work, MacDougall suggested, would enable the population to "earn what they want," and "avoid increasing numbers of displaced people wandering about existing by begging, stealing and on Government hand-outs."[103] For MacDougall, assimilation could offer a salve to the ailments of dispossession, the nature of which was destroying the lives of Aboriginal people across the region.

This correspondence was not the only time that MacDougall questioned the Australian government's dispossession of Aṉangu in pursuit of its nuclear ambitions. In January 1956, MacDougall wrote to the Department of Supply in relation to the government's construction of a meteorological station over the Western Australian border to service the testing sites. "The country under discussion belongs to the tribe," he told the minister of supply, "however, we propose to take it away from them and give nothing in return. We might as well declare war on them and make a job of it."[104] The government's response was swift. The department's chief scientist, William Butement, responded that MacDougall "should be made aware of his duty as a servant of the Commonwealth," condemning the "lamentable lack of balance" in MacDougall's outlook. Butement eviscerated MacDougall for "placing the affairs of a handful of natives above those of the British Commonwealth of Nations," encouraging him to instead "get on with the job within his sphere of activity" and "leave policy matters" to those who held these responsibilities.[105] According to Butement, it was MacDougall's job to keep the area clear of Aboriginal people, not advocate for their rights.

But MacDougall was not alone in his disdain for the treatment of the central deserts' Aboriginal communities. By 1957, reports reaching the United Kingdom detailed that Aboriginal people were "being driven from their hunting grounds by the establishment of the Maralinga atomic proving grounds."[106] A Save the Children campaign was started in Britain to raise funds for Aboriginal children who had been reportedly displaced by Woomera and the nuclear tests.[107] And British members of Parliament started to ask their more senior colleagues whether Her Majesty's Government had an obligation to protect Australia's Aboriginal populations from the impacts of testing. In response, Whitehall stated its position: "They are not *our* bomb testing grounds. They are part of Australia, under the sovereignty of Australia, and the problems therein must be dealt with by the Australian Government."[108] By arguing this line, Whitehall attempted to distance itself from the human consequences of the tests, insisting that Australia was to blame for any injury inflicted on the country's Aboriginal peoples.

Canberra's response to such deflections was to assert that no harm had befallen any Aboriginal people on account of the tests, therefore there really was no blame to ascribe to anyone. The minister of the Australian Department of Supply argued that accusations to the contrary were "absurd": "No Aborigines had been driven out of Maralinga or Woomera areas," and the poor "conditions of life of the Aborigines" as well as "the prevalence of malnutrition and disease among them have existed for centuries."[109] Arguing similarly, a member of the New South Wales Aborigines

Welfare Board wrote to Save the Children: "[Take] no notice of all those sentimental reports that you hear about aborigines being exploited, and cruelly treated," for all they really suffer from is "booze and apathy."[110] Developments in the central deserts, the Australian government maintained, "have made little or no difference to them," not least as the lands chosen for testing were "very arid . . . in fact, uninhabited." "No natives have been found there, therefore, none have been interfered with."[111] In their defense of the tests, Australian authorities were quick to deny the presence of Aboriginal people in the region. But that did not align with MacDougall's experience of having to turn around Aṉangu across the Maralinga Prohibited Area or with that of missionaries taking in people who had journeyed hundreds of miles across the region.

Approximately six months after the minister for supply had publicly declared that no Aboriginal people had been found in the vicinity of either inland testing site, a family was found camping near a bomb crater. Edie Milpuddie and her husband, Tjanyindi, along with their children, Henry and Milpadi (Rosie), and four dingoes, had been traveling by foot, moving from rock hole to rock hole for water as they journeyed south to the Ooldea Mission.[112] Unbeknownst to the Milpuddies, the mission had closed five years earlier and much of the Country they traveled through was now part of a military exclusion zone.[113] One warm evening in May 1957, Edie and her family found an impression in the sand to sleep in overnight. The following morning, military personnel discovered them, decontaminated them, shot their dingoes, and drove them hundreds of miles south to the Yalata Mission. They had been sleeping by the crater created by Marcoo, the second nuclear weapon detonated as part of Operation Buffalo at Maralinga less than a year prior.[114] What had happened to the family remained a secret for decades; while tales of sickness and poison were whispered among those at Yalata, they were actively concealed by the Australian government. Edie's experiences in 1957, and in the years afterward, later became integral to federal investigations undertaken into the tests in the 1980s.

Edie's story—alongside those of other Aṉangu displaced or irradiated during the tests—reveals the complexity of the nuclear colonialism at the center of Britain's testing program. The continued presence of Aboriginal peoples in this desert region points to communities' subversion of settler narratives. This was not an empty wasteland, nor was it uninhabitable. But as a result of both state and federal attempts to manipulate Aboriginal mobility and empty the testing areas, Aboriginal experiences of the tests became punctuated by confusing encounters with white authorities and military personnel, the increased presence of military jeeps and planes across their lands, their removal from Country, and an abject fear of what remained unexplained. Without their knowledge, Aboriginal communities across the central deserts had been subjected to Britain's imperial will, a will enacted by Australian authorities through colonial mechanisms that had been used to manage Aboriginal communities for decades. For all of those whose stories are woven throughout this chapter (among hundreds of others), this imposition resulted in their dispossession and separation from Country.

Official silences surrounding the tests ensured that Aboriginal experiences of this historical episode were not heard until the early 1980s. A confluence of new nationalism, anti-imperial sentiment, and Aboriginal political mobilization encouraged the Australian government and people to take a closer look at what went on in the central deserts during the 1950s (see chapter 5). What Aboriginal peoples' accounts of this history revealed has fundamentally shaped contemporary understandings of the tests as a potent act of nuclear colonialism. This episode was characterized not merely by nuclear weapons' use and contamination of Aboriginal lands. Rather, at the heart of the tests were deep-rooted colonial welfare policies, which when exercised by Australian authorities were fundamental to propping up nuclear weapons' supremacy in the central deserts.

Canberra's Complicity

The persistent falsehood peddled by Australian and British authorities about the central deserts' uninhabitability echoes the colonial assumptions that underpinned early radium and uranium mining. Aboriginal occupation of lands deemed useful to the settler-colonial project was elided by decision-makers to make way for the nuclear tests. But at the same time, the manipulation and control of Aboriginal communities for access to lands and the provision of labor vitally supported the facilitation of the tests.

Bringing the nuclear ambitions of Australia into conversation with the paternalistic approaches taken to Aboriginal affairs in the same period illuminates the nuclear weapons tests as a complex and important episode of nuclear colonialism. While the modern marvel that was nuclear weapons existed in stark juxtaposition to the supposed primitiveness of the deserts' Aboriginal communities, the mechanisms used to "protect" them were seriously wanting. As such, the nuclear tests conducted from 1952 to 1963 cannot and should not be considered a contained episode of nuclear colonialism from which Canberra was exempt from blame. Rather, these tests slotted into a broader historical context, defined in part by Australia's preoccupation with the pursuit of nuclear technology and a deeply paternalistic approach to Aboriginal affairs. This episode was representative of broader colonial politics, the nature of which was shifting and changing as the technological developments of the nuclear age took hold.

Australia's preoccupation with nuclear technology was decidedly geopolitical and represented the government's pursuit of a scientific and "modern" future. Assisting the British Empire and Commonwealth with its development of groundbreaking defense capabilities would have the effect of securing Australia's importance to imperial defense, while providing the training and technology necessary to develop the nation's own nuclear technologies. This was not a desire isolated to the "Anglophilic" Menzies, but rather a sustained and entrenched ambition of several governments from across the political spectrum.

As a result, Canberra was notably complicit in the subjugation of Aboriginal peoples during Britain's nuclear testing program. Yet many Australians failed to properly grapple with Australia's role in the global nuclear (colonial) past and present. As will be explored in chapter 3, large swathes of the Australian public vehemently opposed French nuclear testing in both Algeria and the Pacific from the 1960s onward. Many labeled the French nuclear imperialists, while politicians and the public alike left the tests at Maralinga and Emu Field unscrutinized. As with every case of nuclear colonialism explored in this book, Aboriginal people were certainly not absent from the debate around nuclear testing's morality in the 1960s and 1970s, but were notably sidelined by dominant settler narratives, prevailing geopolitical motivations, and Australia's inability (and unwillingness) to acknowledge its complicity in the emerging global nuclear order.

THREE

Australia in the "Nuclear Playground"

In 1953, the same year as Britain's first inland nuclear test in Australia and seven years after the United States' first Pacific test, the journalist George T. Eggleston wrote for the international readers of *Reader's Digest* that "in the midst of wars and tensions of the atomic age, the South Pacific . . . is still a beautiful and unspoiled paradise." He described "cocktail bars and dance floors," "an infinite capacity for . . . fun, at work and at play," "moonlit nights," and "native feast[s]."[1] For Eggleston, the paradisiacal landscape of the South Pacific was an oasis in a nuclear-crazed world.

By the beginning of the following decade, rumors were swirling that France had selected this "unspoiled paradise" as the host for its hydrogen bomb tests, rendering the South Pacific its "nuclear playground."[2] Irrespective of the Pacific's long history with nuclear testing—beginning as early as 1946 with Able, the United States' first test on Bikini Atoll in the Marshall Islands—many Australians were outraged at France's decision to test so close to home. Ignorant of their own historic connection to nuclear geopolitics, Australians deplored French "H-bomb[s] in paradise," fearing that the "world's dirtiest nuclear tests" were set to "'dust' Australia."[3]

In the two decades between 1954 and 1974, the number of Australians in vocal opposition to nuclear testing grew considerably, challenging the government's seeming ambivalence toward French nuclear imperialism in their immediate region and further afield. In its response to French nuclear testing in both Algeria and the South Pacific, Australian antinuclear sentiment converged with global discussions of imperialism, decolonization, Indigenous self-determination, and environmental degradation in the 1960s and 1970s. This was partly in response to the conservatism and antisocialist agenda of Prime Minister Robert Menzies and his successors, which engendered a shift in the Australian population toward more socially progressive policy demands. But it was similarly influenced by international debates about the morality and legality of nuclear testing in colonial territories and the development of numerous transnational social movements, including the antinuclear, environmental, and Aboriginal land rights movements. This wave of progression culminated in the election of Labor's Gough Whitlam (1972–75), whose first challenge as prime minister was to address the issue of French nuclear testing. In a move that marked a shift in Australia's geopolitical response to atmospheric testing in its immediate region, Whitlam took the French government to the International Court of Justice (ICJ) in 1973.

By the mid-1970s, the Australian government's involvement in nuclear geopolitics had shifted in character, reflecting the Australian public's own transition from blind trust and ignorance to increased defiance and conflict. Where prior to the 1970s the vast majority of Australians had been relatively ignorant of the impact of nuclear processes on Indigenous communities both at home and overseas, the visceral reactions elicited by France's decision to test nuclear weapons in the South Pacific signaled among the public a new consciousness of testing's colonial (and associated environmental) implications. While this new consciousness was initially trained outward, toward the Pacific, it would eventually turn inward in recognition of the very real impacts of Australia's own nuclear and colonial pasts.

French Nuclear Ambitions in the South Pacific

Nuclear weapons transformed the geopolitics of the postwar world for many formerly "great" empires. Some historians have characterized this transformation as the emergence of a unique form of imperialism, "nuclear imperialism," which one scholar has defined by its "capitalist formation, intervention and militarization of space . . . through nuclear means."[4] Embodying this definition, nuclear supremacy by the late 1950s was underpinned by the notion that one's geopolitical standing was directly related to the size of one's arsenal.[5] For states seeking some semblance of their former imperial glory, nuclear weapons, alongside other forms of nuclear technological development, were exceptionally enticing. As a result, according to the historian Gabreille Hecht, the atom bomb became the "ultimate fetish of our times."[6] But while some declared this "new" era the "atomic age" or "nuclear age," 1945 did not represent a death knell for empire.[7] Rather, nuclear weapons facilitated the recalibration of imperial power and politics, rather than their end.

Like Britain, France developed nuclear weapons in the early years of the Cold War, reinvigorating its waning empire at a time when it was being challenged internally and externally. The Second World War had engendered a crisis for the French Empire, as its wartime annexation by enemy forces had drawn into question its military power, cultural identity, and government structures.[8] Consequently, the French government sought something that could represent "the essence of a renewed France" in a world transformed by the geopolitical power of nuclear weapons and the decline of traditional forms of empire.[9] France's involvement in early nuclear science through Marie and Pierre Curies' groundbreaking discoveries and the maintenance of imperial territories in Algeria and the Pacific (ideal for testing) were cause for enthusiasm in the nuclear age.[10] This was a period in which political leaders at the helm of waning empires—such as the French Empire—recognized nuclear weapons' potential contribution to their states' technological prowess and geopolitical importance.[11]

This entanglement—and its dire human and environmental consequences—was demonstrated particularly starkly when the United States military tested its first thermonuclear weapon at Bikini Atoll in the Pacific in March 1954. Code-named Castle Bravo, its explosive force was one thousand times that of the weapon that decimated Hiroshima. Not only did the sheer size and destructive power of this test send coral dust into the atmosphere, irradiating the surrounding area for hundreds of miles, but it sent shockwaves throughout the world. The detonation of Castle Bravo occurred at a time when Australia was still subject to Britain's nuclear tests, and for many Australians it drove home the dangers of nuclear testing. It provided a glaring reminder that these tests were, after all, experiments.

Immediately following the detonation of Castle Bravo, Australia's minister for external affairs, Richard Casey, issued a public statement. Casey assured the public that the United States' possession of nuclear weapons was not of concern. "In truth the fears of the free world are not centred upon the possible misuse of atomic weapons by the Western Powers," he declared, but rather "upon aggression by Communist countries, using either atomic or conventional weapons that would precipitate a world war." In fact, Casey argued, the "atomic weapons possessed by the Western alliance redress the great preponderance of armed manpower . . . at present possessed by the Communist powers."[12] So while many Australians feared the potentially devastating consequences of nuclear development demonstrated by Castle Bravo, the Menzies government assured them that the United States' or United Kingdom's weapons were not to be feared. The West's possession of nuclear weapons was in fact a welcome protection against communist aggression.

This overt support of Western nuclear weapons did not extend to France, however, as the Australian government sought to limit the possession of nuclear weapons to the three existing nuclear weapons states—the United Kingdom, United States, and USSR—for several key strategic reasons. Of particular concern to Australian officials was that international debates surrounding the safety of a future French nuclear weapons program could potentially highlight the more questionable safety aspects of Britain's tests in Australia. This was clear in the Department of External Affairs' decision to abstain from voting in an Afro-Asian resolution in the UN's General Assembly during 1959, which sought to ban France's proposed tests in the Sahara. Put forward by representatives interested in pursuing Algeria's independence from France, the resolution was rumored to refer to the "'grave dangers' of fallout."[13] Australian officials understood that voting either for or against such a resolution would raise questions about fallout and the Maralinga and Emu Field tests. Abstention enabled Australian officials to withhold any definitive stance on the safety (or lack thereof) of fallout impacts on Australian populations. But it also allowed the Australian government to maintain its opposition to the emergence of new nuclear powers, most notably China.[14]

China's potential rise as a nuclear power in the 1960s significantly influenced Australia's position on nuclear proliferation, as perceived communist aggression was a threat that concerned Prime Minister Menzies in particular.[15] Menzies was reelected to the Australian prime ministership in 1949 on a decidedly antisocialist platform, which included banning the Communist Party of Australia. A year later, his government introduced the Communist Party Dissolution Act, which deemed the party unlawful. While a subsequent High Court ruling deemed the act unconstitutional,

Menzies's government maintained its anticommunist predilections, training it outward toward states such as China.[16] An Australian Joint Intelligence Committee report produced in 1960 plainly declared that the Australian government needed to be seen to resist France's emergence as a nuclear power, or it risked enabling countries such as China to continue their own nuclear development.[17] Catching wind of Australia's motivations for resisting France's nuclear ambitions, French officials claimed that Australia "was running a grave risk of disillusionment," arguing that the latter's preoccupation with preventing China's emergence as a nuclear power could—in this case—endanger the West by virtue of limiting the number of Western nuclear powers.[18] Furthermore, French officials viewed Australia's stance on a fourth nuclear power as an outright attack on France's continued control over Algeria, which was coming under increased scrutiny as decolonization took hold across the African continent.[19]

It is no secret that decolonization influenced numerous states' decision-making on French nuclear testing in Algeria, which remained a formal French colonial possession until 1962. Of relevance to Australian geopolitics was Britain's demonstrated desire to maintain stable relations with its remaining African colonies and independent Commonwealth nations on the African continent, many of which condemned France's tests in the Algerian Sahara.[20] In the face of increasing discontent from numerous newly independent African nations, Britain opted to abstain from voting in the United Nations' resolutions regarding the tests, hoping to appear somewhat neutral on the issue. Australian officials took a similar approach, inspired at least partially by the clear "resentment" expressed by numerous African nations "that a European country was using Africa as a testing ground." Following a particularly heated debate on the topic, Australia's delegation to the UN described the insistence of numerous states that "European powers had to get completely out of Africa."[21] For many, resistance against nuclear testing entwined intimately with arguments for decolonization and self-determination.

Given its own complicity in nuclear colonialism, Australia was placed in an uncomfortable position. While the government opposed France emerging as a nuclear power and condemned French testing in Algeria, it had supported British and US (nuclear) imperialism in their colonial possessions across the Pacific. In 1959, the Department of External Affairs anticipated that explicit Australian opposition to French tests would lead to charges of hypocrisy: "While we actively helped the U.K. to become a nuclear power we now want to stop France from becoming one."[22] This concern became only more acute as murmurs reached Australian officials that France's nuclear tests would be moving from the Sahara to France's Pacific and Southern Ocean territories.[23]

By 1963, France had confirmed that it planned to conduct a series of atmospheric nuclear tests in the South Pacific.[24] In the same year, Australia signed and ratified the Partial Test Ban Treaty, which prohibited the testing of nuclear weapons under water, in outer space, and in the atmosphere. In accordance with Australia's UN obligations as a signatory of this treaty, and in acknowledgment of the Australian government's reluctance to see the emergence of a fourth nuclear power, the Australian Embassy in Paris expressed its regret that France sought to proceed with a series of Pacific tests: "We much regretted a decision to test and had hoped it would not be felt necessary to make it." Australia "did not welcome the tests" or the "risks of fall-out and the precautions taken against it."[25] These were not exclusively health risks.

For the Australian government under conservative Prime Minister Robert Menzies, nuclear testing in the Pacific presented several challenges, both domestically and geopolitically. First, if the Australian government failed to outright condemn French nuclear tests in the Pacific, there was a chance that other states—namely, communist states—would take advantage of Australia's apparent ambivalence and also commence testing in the region. Second, nuclear tests taking place so close to home—and the conversations they would elicit—had the potential to jeopardize Australia's domestic situation by drawing the Australian public's attention to the potential dangers of Britain's nuclear tests in the previous decade. But, by the same token, British or American exertions of nuclear influence in the region had the potential to strengthen Australia's geopolitical position by curbing communist aggression and enabling Australia's involvement in the development of a Commonwealth nuclear posture. Australian officials also had interests in maintaining commercial relationships with France, not least through the potential export of Australian uranium to the state.

There was thus a concerted effort by the Australian government in the 1960s to draw a clear distinction between potential nuclear cooperation with France and the issue of its nuclear tests.[26]

But for many Australian citizens, it was impossible to distinguish between Australian nuclear cooperation with the French government and the condonement of nuclear testing. As a result, the global geopolitical tensions that stemmed from nuclear testing had significant local consequences. By July 1966, when the French exploded their first nuclear weapon at Mururoa, domestic protests in Australia and New Zealand were almost impossible to ignore. And what Australians were observing, they purported, was imperialism at work.

The Antinuclear Movement and Imperialism

In South Australia's capital city, Adelaide, thousands of protesters took to the street to oppose French nuclear testing in the Pacific (fig. 5). Youths in bell-bottoms hoisted banners emblazoned with "Stop French N-tests" above their heads. Alongside them marched older women, partaking in the chants of the swelling group. Evoking the terror of radioactive fallout, young men donned gas masks or covered their faces with bandanas, and several women shouldered coffins adorned with the words "the yet unborn." Organized by environmentalist groups including Friends of the Earth (FOE) and taking place in 1972, this march was the culmination of several years of tension between the conservative Australian government and a growing wave of radical constituents who sought to highlight public fears over radioactivity's insidious unknowns. But it was also a consequence of a growing environmental and social consciousness that flooded cities across the world in the 1970s. With this flood came the assurance that Australians would vehemently question the necessity, safety, and morality of French nuclear testing taking place in the South Pacific in the 1960s and 1970s.

The growth of social consciousness in the 1960s was aided substantially by the transnational flow of ideas, people, and politics. At the beginning of the decade, Australians were still suffering from what the University of New South Wales Student Union newspaper *Tharunka* described as "ap-

FIGURE 5. Following a boom in the environmental movement, groups such as Friends of the Earth organized demonstrations against French nuclear testing (such as this one, held in Adelaide in 1972). Australians from a variety of backgrounds marched against the tests, united in their concern for what these experiments would mean for the Australian environment and the country's Pacific neighbors. Photograph courtesy of Soc Hedditch and the National Library of Australia. NLA: PIC/6563/4.

athy" toward nuclear testing, but with increasingly radical ideas relating to social progress flowing across borders, many became inspired to rebel against the closed-minded conservatism of their respective governments.[27] As a 1968 US Central Intelligence Agency report titled "Restless Youth" detailed, "Because of the revolution in communications, the ease of travel, and the evolution of society everywhere, student behaviour never again will resemble what it was when education was reserved for the elite . . . student activism has caught the attention of the world."[28] This was no different in Australia. In an increasingly global context, Australia's anti-nuclear movement was undoubtedly influenced by intersecting international struggles, including the US civil rights movement, the global peace movement, the student movement, the moratorium movement, and the growth of environmentalism.[29] The transnational links between young activists in this period were, as the historian Frank Zelko put it, part of a "chain that stretched from Vancouver to Auckland."[30] That chain, for our purposes, should be extended to Adelaide, where the transnational radicalism gripping much of the Western world in the late 1960s played out just as vehemently.

Just as the nuclear age was proclaimed in the dust and debris of the United States' first nuclear weapons test in New Mexico in 1945, the beginning of Australia's transformative seventies coincided with France's first Pacific test—Aldébaran—on Mururoa Atoll in 1966.[31] Close to a decade of challenge and change exploded out of Aldébaran, precipitated by the electoral loss of the Australian Labor Party (ALP) in the same year.[32] Coupled with the sting of the recently reelected conservative government choosing to follow the United States into Vietnam, the ALP's defeat revolutionized many young Australians who had rested their hopes on Labor leader Arthur Calwell ending conservative rule in Australia.[33] Many young settler Australians identified as part of a New Left movement, advocating for reform, civil rights, and democracy while simultaneously condemning war, environmental degradation, and social inequality. This shifting tide in Australian politics led many to consider nuclear weapons as symptomatic of a broken system, accompanied by capital greed, rampant militarism, unadulterated imperialism, and severe inequality. Antinuclear activists reflected this in their call for an end to nuclear tests alongside the granting of independence to colonies subject to them.

Australian antinuclear activists linked France's use of Algeria as a nuclear testing site during the early years of the 1960s to broader debates regarding decolonization and self-determination. During this decade, many radical protest groups venerated "the heroic Third World freedom fighter."[34] In keeping with this trend, between 1960 and 1963, several Australian broadsheets published stories on Algeria's struggle for liberation from the French Empire. Much of the reportage detailed the major violence involved in the war between Algerians and their European colonizers, but some reports—mostly published in the Communist Party of Australia's *Tribune* newspaper—explicitly articulated the need for African liberation from "French imperialists."[35]

France's insistence on continuing to test its nuclear weapons in the Sahara only increased Australian support for Algerian liberation, especially among card-carrying members of Australia's Communist Party. Reflecting the party's animosity toward France for refusing to let go of its empire, the *Tribune* reported in 1961 that the World Peace Council had described France's latest nuclear test as existing "hand in hand with an intensification of the colonial war against the Algerian People."[36] Another report argued that "the latest French A-bomb explosion ha[d] sharpened the resistance of the Algerian people to continued French occupation" and predicted, "The anomaly of an Algeria under colonial control when the rest of Africa has, or is getting, its independence can't last much longer."[37] A third article detailed a "new stage in [the] African liberation struggle" against both the "remnants of colonialism" and "neo-colonialism," the latter of which the newspaper considered "a grave danger" to recently independent African nations.[38] Anti-imperial sentiment against France persisted in the *Tribune* for over a decade, only intensifying once France's tests had moved to the Pacific and the Vietnam War had begun.

It was in response to deafening calls for independence and decolonization in Africa, the *Tribune*'s reportage suggested, that France had moved its tests elsewhere.[39] In the days leading up to France's first tests in the Pacific in 1966, the *Tribune* asserted that, through their choice of testing site, "the French politicians were just as careful of their own voters" as they were "careless of the Polynesians and other inhabitants of the Pacific, including Australians."[40] By testing in the Pacific, *Tribune* reporters declared plainly, the French were making use of their colonial outposts to expand their defense arsenal, an arsenal they deemed too risky to test in France itself. Others followed suit, condemning what many perceived as an overt exercise in French imperialism.[41]

Even the more conservative national broadsheet, the *Canberra Times*, implied that France's actions in the Pacific were neocolonial in nature. In 1965, under the headline "Tidying Up the Colonial Backyard," the *Canberra Times* reporter A. J. Fitzgerald observed: "The French . . . are more active in a . . . colonial sense today in the Pacific than they have ever been. In French Polynesia they are spending millions turning that 'island paradise' into a nuclear test area and in the Condominium of the New Hebrides they indulge in more flag waving than their co-partners the British."[42] The following year, the paper noted that France's actions were resisted by the residents of the South Pacific, reporting that "the 85,000 inhabitants of the 125 scattered islands forming French Polynesia [were] apprehensive": "The effects of the towering, mushroom clouds are dreaded all over this South sea paradise covering an area the size of Europe."[43] Stressing this point worked to highlight the imposed nature of France's nuclear tests on the Pacific, implicating the French in outdated modes of imperial and colonial control. But France was not the only country Australians condemned for such behavior.

The danger of nuclear weapons was, for many student activists, intimately entangled with the perceived expression of US imperialism in Vietnam. At the Adelaide-based Flinders University, students writing for their union's newspaper—*Empire Times*—spent far less time examining the issue of French nuclear testing between 1966 and 1972 than they did vehemently and frequently condemning the Vietnam War. Nevertheless, the students' anti-imperial critiques of the United States' war efforts in Vietnam were often accompanied by antinuclear sentiment: "America, Go Fuck Yrself with Yr Atombomb," one headline read.[44] In another issue, a poem flanked by an image of a ballooning mushroom cloud captured one student's explanation of American imperialism offered to their imagined son, twenty years in the future, in which the poet lamented the dual inhumanity of the war in Vietnam and the development of nuclear technology.[45] Such contributions reflected the fear held by many members of the public—in Australia and elsewhere—that the United States government would revert to the use of nuclear weapons in Vietnam as it had in Japan two decades earlier. Students sought to remind their fellow citizens that, should nuclear weapons ever be used in aggression again, the consequences would impact all humankind.

As Australia entered the 1970s and a federal election loomed, the public condemnation of French nuclear testing became more pronounced. This was especially so in relation to the program's potential environmental consequences as widespread public concern over pollution, overpopulation, and resource exploitation promoted a global environmental consciousness in the late 1960s.[46] Environmental and antinuclear efforts blended in the

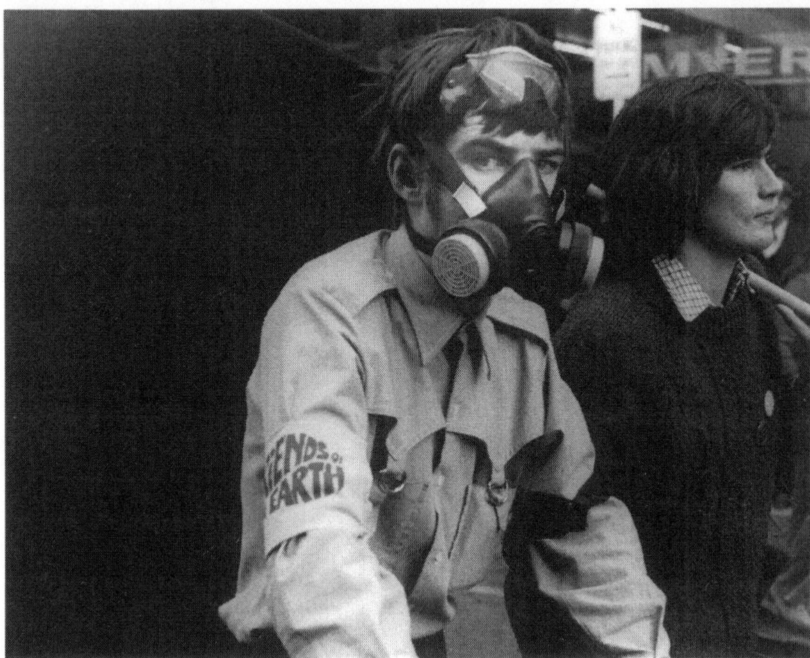

FIGURE 6. The invisibility of radioactivity ensured contamination was a particular concern of Australian environmentalists demonstrating against French nuclear testing in the Pacific in 1972. Photograph courtesy of Soc Hedditch and the National Library of Australia. NLA: PIC/6563/5.

early 1970s as both movements sought to expose the West's overconsumption of the world's exhaustible resources and overreliance on technology.[47] These overlapping concerns came under a generalized "green" politics, characterized by a fear of dual human and energy crises and increasingly obvious anthropogenic impacts on the environment across the world (fig. 6).[48] Many realized that these entangled—and markedly global—issues were not going to be solved by individuals, precipitating activists' pursuit of larger-scale action: "the picket, the blockade, the rally."[49]

Many of the antinuclear articles published in *On Dit* and *Empire Times* in the early 1970s linked French nuclear testing to environmental contamination, against which students were encouraged to demonstrate en masse. For example, in March 1973, the Committee Against Nuclear Testing (CANT) posted an advertisement in *On Dit*, the University of Adelaide's student newspaper, asking for donations to fund its "protest boat." Following in the footsteps of other protesters—mostly from New Zealand—CANT intended to sail a boat into France's testing zone near Mururoa, the ad explained, to "demonstrate to people in France and the rest of the world that many Australians want an end to the radioactive pollution of our planet by nuclear fallout."[50] In an arguably more alarmist tone, the Flinders Environmental Action Group implored readers of *Empire Times*: "KILL YOUR FAVOURITE FRENCHMAN SOON, BEFORE HE KILLS YOU, OR YOUR KIDS."[51] Many Australian environmentalists harbored particular concern over the contamination of Australia's scarce and vulnerable water sources, especially given the continent's propensity for drought.[52] By 1972, then, public denunciations of French imperialism in Australia focused on the tests' proximity to Australian shores.

Despite the threat of environmental contamination in Australia as a result of nuclear testing, the government refused to take any tangible steps toward condemning France's tests, angering large pockets of the public in the process. To counteract the government's perceived silence on the issue, their aggrieved constituents took action. In April 1973, various student newspapers circulated a letter addressed to the French president, Georges Pompidou, urging him to "stop this threat to the health and welfare of Australians and other peoples of the Pacific."[53] Readers were instructed to cut the letter out, affix a stamp to it, and put it in the mail, "in the name of future generations who cannot speak for themselves."[54] Students were also encouraged to attend antinuclear marches organized by recently formed environmental groups and to assist in funding CANT's aforementioned protest voyage. In perhaps the most extreme demonstration of opposition, Andrew Small—presumed to be a student at Flinders University—set fire to the roof of Adelaide's Renault showroom in the early hours of 1 August 1973.[55] In justifying his actions, Small told *Empire Times*: "France . . . in her typical arrogant fashion chooses to do her testing at the opposite corner of the globe where a few poor unfortunate Pacific islands plus insignificant countries such as New Zealand, Australia, and the South Americas will cop most of the radio-active fallout."[56] When Small was later charged with arson, his fellow students at *Empire Times* raised funds for his defense, arguing that his act reflected the spirit of radicalism inherent in student activism in this period.[57]

The focus on the environmental impacts of radioactive contamination was a central tenet of the burgeoning antinuclear movement across the world but was afforded little attention at a government level in Australia prior to the election of Labor Prime Minister Gough Whitlam in December 1972.[58] Potential impacts on fertility through the ingestion of irradiated produce was of particular concern. The historian Traci Brynne Voyles has identified similar concerns in the US movement, where "women's bodies provided a map of the health consequences of ionizing radiation, bringing nuclear consequences home in the most intimate ways: in kidneys, muscles, lungs, and ovaries."[59] The invisibility of radioactivity in the environment, including in food, compounded this perceived threat.

Accordingly, from the early 1960s on, Australian newspapers of various political persuasions reported on the potential impact of French nuclear testing on the Australian environment and—by association—its resources. "Nuclear Fallout Detected," "'Fall-Out on Australia' Warning," and "Sea Life 'May Be Threatened'" were all headlines in the *Canberra Times*.[60] The *Tribune* opted for more alarmist openings, including "Leukemia!" and "The Pacific in Danger."[61] Later headlines included "France Accused of Disregard for People" and "Radioactive Fish Swimming towards US."[62] The intangibility of radioactivity's effects in this period, coupled with its invisibility, raised significant concerns over its impact on Australians, both directly and as a result of the contamination of Australia's lands and waters.

Aboriginal Activism and the Condemnation of Nuclear Weapons

While public fears regarding France's potential contamination of Australia grew substantially, antinuclear protest ephemera rarely drew connections between this fear and the recently concluded British nuclear tests. Instead, most Australians projected their criticisms outward. Consequently, antinuclear discussions failed to grapple with the consequences of nuclear testing on Aboriginal peoples during the 1960s, despite the movement's development alongside a transformation in Aboriginal politics during the 1960s and 1970s.[63] Nevertheless, increased agitation from Aboriginal peoples for rights and recognition in this period ensured that, long term, Australia's implication in global nuclear injustices would not go unnoticed.

Aboriginal agitation in the 1960s increased both in support of and in response to several landmark events, which provide vital context for the discussion of nuclear colonialism for the remainder of the book. Initiating a wave of political agitation, a group of senior Yolŋu people from Arnhem Land in the Northern Territory created the Yirrkala bark petitions in 1963 to protest the Australian government's approval of bauxite mining on their Country. These petitions marked the first formal representation of Aboriginal peoples' connection to Country to be recognized by the Australian Parliament.[64] This public assertion of Yolŋu land rights was later followed by the 1966 Gurindji walk-off, during which approximately two hundred Aboriginal domestic workers, stockmen, and their families walked off Wave Hill station in the Northern Territory in response to the station's owners refusing to pay its Aboriginal workers' wages. This strike action kick-started a seven-year dispute that ended with the partial return of the Gurindji people's homelands by Gough Whitlam in formal acknowledgment of their dispossession.[65]

These (and other) public articulations of Aboriginal land rights created the political conditions necessary for Aboriginal activists to seek constitutional change through the 1967 Referendum. Prior to the success of this referendum, Aboriginal people were not recognized in the Australian Constitution as part of the population. They were not included in the Australian census, and individual states (rather than the Commonwealth government) were given the power to legislate on Aboriginal peoples' behalf. In its response to a groundswell of activism from Aboriginal people and their non-Indigenous allies, the 1967 Referendum asked citizens to vote on two constitutional amendments, first, to include Aboriginal people in the census and, second, to provide the federal government with the power to legislate on Aboriginal peoples' behalf.[66] The referendum succeeded in a landslide; 90.77 percent of voters agreed to the changes.

Those activists who had campaigned tirelessly for this constitutional change hoped that the positive outcome of the referendum would be the start of Aboriginal liberation in Australia, but it soon became clear that the country remained intimately bound to its colonial past. In the years following the referendum, many campaigners expressed significant disillusionment over the fact that constitutional recognition had appeared to change little in the everyday lives of Aboriginal people.[67] One such individual was Oodgeroo Noonuccal, a Noonuccal poet and activist who had been heavily involved in the referendum campaign.[68] Noonuccal was formerly a believer in the need for Aboriginal inclusion in the Australian nation, but by the end of the 1960s her politics had shifted toward a more radical articulation of Aboriginal liberation and the prioritization of a distinct Aboriginality. She argued in 1969 that the referendum had only worked to ease "the guilty conscience of white Australians."[69] In the same year, she published her "Black Commandments," which reflected the radical shift occurring in Aboriginal politics in this period: "Thou shalt gather thy scattered people together," "Thou shalt resist assimilation with all thy might," and "Thou shall think black and act black."[70] Disillusionment in the wake of the referendum, the rise in land rights claims, and an air of radicalism thus inspired a generation of Aboriginal activists who facilitated the emergence of a particular anticolonial pan-Aboriginal nationalism.[71]

As with Australia's non-Indigenous population, young Aboriginal activists felt that the 1960s was "an era of youth rebellion."[72] Gumbainggir activist and scholar Gary Foley asserts that this young generation of Aboriginal activists sought to act on this radicalism at a time when their "white counterparts were challenging the white political mainstream over issues to do with imperialism and neo-colonialism (Vietnam)."[73] With greater access to both secondary and tertiary education, and increased social and physical mobility, young Aboriginal activists became the conduits through which fresh ideas flooded into Aboriginal politics.[74] This included the emergence of the modern land rights movement, whereby small, previously localized land rights claims were subsumed into a national land rights agenda, supported by the politics and unity promoted by organizations such as the Federal Council for the Advancement of Aborigines and Torres Strait Islanders, or FCAATSI.[75]

As the emergence of Aboriginal youth activism occurred alongside that of non-Indigenous youth movements in Australia, the issue of Aboriginal rights—in particular, land rights—made its way into university newspapers and other media, though rather superficially. In 1968, the University of New South Wales's *Tharunka* supplied readers with its "Special Lift-Out Supplement on Aborigines," detailing the "depressing" state of Aboriginal land rights across the country.[76] Three years later, the University of Adelaide's *On Dit* highlighted the issue of racial discrimination against South Australia's Aboriginal populations specifically.[77] And while Flinders University's *Empire Times* was marginally more inclusive than *Tharunka* or *On Dit*, it too published on Aboriginal issues infrequently.

A shift began in the early 1970s when Aboriginal activism became particularly pronounced. As an example, in 1972 *Empire Times* published an exclusive penned by Foley titled "Boong Power," in which he discussed "what the Blacks living in Australia at the moment want."[78] Referencing the demands of the newly formed Aboriginal Tent Embassy outside of Australia's Parliament House in Canberra, he cited the Aboriginal community's desire for "the handing back of the land" belonging to Aboriginal peoples, as well as "some compensation for the land stolen since 1770."[79] In conjunction with funding from white Australians, Foley argued that the return of stolen lands would "provide black people with an alternative to the genocidal assimilation policies of the present government."[80] However, this engagement with Aboriginal politics did not mean that student activists, on the whole, made any connections between the plight of Australia's Aboriginal population and those subjected to nuclear testing in this period. Foley's piece "Boong Power" was printed directly above an article titled "French Litter," which condemned the French nuclear tests at length.[81] No links were drawn between the two. Perhaps most surprisingly, given the amount of outrage regarding French nuclear testing in the Pacific, no mention was made of Britain's nuclear tests in Australia within the pages of *On Dit* or *Empire Times* between 1966 and 1972.

Such absences reflect the persistence of the Australian public's ignorance toward its own country's role in perpetuating nuclear injustices against Aboriginal peoples. French and US nuclear imperialism remained front of mind for many student protesters and participants in the antinuclear, environmental, and moratorium movements during this period. And while the absence of Australia's nuclear history from these debates can be credited—at least in part—to the secrecy that continued to shroud

Britain's testing program, perpetuated by a long period of conservative leadership, such silences cannot be solely blamed on Menzies and his successors. As the rest of this book will uncover, numerous successive governments, Labor and Liberal, encouraged or benefited from controlling the narrative around Australia's (nuclear) past, present, and future. This included Whitlam, the charismatic Labor prime minister from 1972 to 1975.

Whitlam's Strategic Ambiguity

Gough Whitlam personified the radical change demanded by student activists across Australia's major cities in the 1960s. As deputy party leader of the ALP and leader of the opposition prior to his election in 1972, Whitlam publicly curated a "grand vision of a post-Menzies era," replete with emphases on Australia's geopolitical place in the Pacific, the formal end of the White Australia policy (which had limited non-British migration to Australia since 1901), recognition of the People's Republic of China, commitment to Aboriginal rights, the condemnation of French nuclear testing, and the ratification of the Nuclear Non-Proliferation Treaty.[82] With such policies at the forefront of his campaign, Whitlam swept into power in 1972 with the slogan "It's time," two words that captured the shifting mood of Australian politics.[83]

Although opposition to nuclear testing existed well before Whitlam's victory, the 1972 federal election presented an opportunity for those who condemned France's continuing program to have their hopes of its end realized. Whitlam's conservative forebear—John Gorton—signed the Nuclear Non-Proliferation Treaty in 1970, but he did so reluctantly.[84] The treaty's prohibition of horizontal proliferation—that is, of knowledge and technology *between* states—meant that Australia, by signing the treaty, was giving up any aspirations it might have to develop its own weapons.[85] Dragging its feet, Canberra was yet to ratify the treaty by 1972, but its ratification was included among Whitlam's many election promises. As such, Labor's vehement antinuclear stance presented the Australian public with a remedy to the Liberal-Country coalition's decades-long unwillingness to act meaningfully on the issue of disarmament.[86] According to Whitlam, his forebears' noncommittal approach had ensured that the French government would "no longer take Australia's protests seriously."[87] All Australia had done up to this point, Whitlam lamented, was to show "the world that it is not dinkum in its protests against French nuclear tests in the Pacific."[88] But exactly what Whitlam meant by a "dinkum" protest was up for interpretation.

Labor equivocated on its policy commitments prior to the 1972 election.[89] But this ambiguity meant that Australians could project their own hopes and expectations onto the party.[90] In light of burgeoning social progressiveness and radicalism within the Australian Left in particular, it was time for the country's leaders to accept that the world was changing and Australia needed to change too.[91] The election of progressive Labor/Labour governments in both Australia and New Zealand represented a public embrace of this shift in the South Pacific, one that required both major countries to commit to decolonization and détente, the easing of geopolitical tensions between states. This would necessitate a stronger stance on nuclear testing. In this area—as well as many others—the Whitlam government differed markedly from its forebears.[92] However, taking action against French nuclear testing did not necessarily require Whitlam to condemn nuclear testing or the nuclear order writ large. And, as with Menzies, condemning French nuclear testing in the Pacific did not necessitate Whitlam's reckoning with Australia's own role in nuclear colonialism.

It was clear from the day Whitlam was elected prime minister that he would have to move swiftly on French nuclear testing in the Pacific.[93] Scrawled on a letter dated 5 December 1972—the day he took office—marginalia in an unknown hand speculated, "The PM's first test in foreign affairs is likely to be the French matter."[94] Within a fortnight of the election, Don Dunstan, a close friend of Whitlam and the Labor premier of South Australia at the time, had advised the prime minister, "The time factor is now all-important if the next series of tests is to be stopped."[95] This was, in large part, due to immense public pressure built up by CANT, FOE, and a variety of other student, peace, and environmental organizations, as well as numerous trade unions. But this haste was equally prompted by France's intention to begin a new round of atmospheric tests in the Pacific, the nature of which had the potential to significantly increase the radioactivity detected in the region.[96]

Where Menzies had expressed regret over French testing due to its facilitation of France's emergence as a fourth nuclear power, Whitlam opposed France's contamination of the Pacific as a breach of Australian sovereignty, citing environmental concerns. Early in his prime ministership, Whitlam promised his constituents that he would take the issue of French nuclear testing to the International Court of Justice (ICJ).[97] The resumption of France's testing program in the Pacific was viewed as "itself a manifestation of French colonialism," which to Whitlam reflected a "clear abrogation of its responsibilities to its dominion territories."[98] Whitlam's view was cemented when Australian scientists predicted that French atmospheric tests in the Pacific would lead to a potential increase in Australian cancer deaths due to the tests' likely irradiation of the Australian environment. This particular revelation encouraged Whitlam's cabinet to argue that French testing posed an environmental risk within Australia's sovereign borders.[99]

Whether fallout from French tests legally constituted a breach of Australia's sovereignty was central to Whitlam's pursuit of a case in the ICJ.[100] Thus, on 3 January 1973, and ahead of France's next proposed series of Pacific nuclear tests the same year, the Australian government issued a strong statement to the French government. "In the opinion of the Australian Government," the statement read, "the conducting of such tests would not only be undesirable, but would be unlawful—particularly in so far as it involves modification of the physical conditions of and over Australian territory; pollution of the atmosphere and of the resources of the sea."[101] This statement established "clearly" that there was "a legal dispute between Australia and France."[102] Should the French refuse to refrain from further testing in the Pacific, Australian officials declared that they would be forced to pursue "appropriate international legal remedies."[103]

The Australian government's resistance to French nuclear testing rested largely on environmental concerns, exacerbated by radiation's cumulative effects. Whitlam himself articulated his government's opposition as relating to "the fact that these tests [could] harm countries in the track of the winds."[104] Australian Attorney General Lionel Murphy similarly admonished the French government's Pacific program, through which France had "exposed the people of Australia to the unnecessary danger of increased nuclear radiation."[105] Murphy cited "increased incidence of cancer and potential genetic defects as well as increased total genetic damage leading to a deterioration of physical and mental health" as grounds for pursuing legal action against the French.[106] "The Australian Government does not consider that the French Nuclear defence experiments should proceed at the expense of peoples in the Pacific basin," he stated, arguing that, under such circumstances, "we would be justified in seeking an international legal remedy to the threat posed to the welfare of the people of this country by continuation of the tests."[107]

French authorities resented the suggestion that France's nuclear program would endanger Australians and other inhabitants of the Pacific. In January 1973, Australian officials from the Department of Foreign Affairs met with a representative of the French Embassy, who expressed his view that Australia's stance against France's tests "had already had an unsettling effect on French business circles and amongst the French business community in Australia."[108] France's representative expressed hope that "the Government could give a lead in dampening down some of the ill-informed public criticism of the tests which . . . did not represent a significant health hazard."[109] In response, an Australian official told his French counterpart: "In my view it was a mistake to regard the tests from the rather narrow point of view of whether or not they represented a health hazard. . . . The long-term effects were unknown, and public opinion not only in Australia but throughout the world was becoming increasingly sensitive to any threats to the environment."[110] Australian government officials declared that while they could not take a definitive stance on the environmental risks of France's testing, they were required to take into account "a growing body of opinion that atmospheric testing was *morally* wrong."[111] Morality aside, Australia's case to the ICJ was a delicate geopolitical maneuver.

Leveling a case against the French in the ICJ fulfilled an election promise Whitlam had made—namely, to stop the tests—while attempting to maintain geopolitical ties with China.[112] Where Menzies had feared the emergence of China as a nuclear power due to the perceived implications of more communist-controlled nuclear weapons, the Whitlam government sought "the development of a mutually useful working relationship" in various fields with the emergent power.[113] The government held acute fears that a general case against France in the ICJ "could lead to a judgement logically applicable . . . to China."[114] This apprehension included arguments pertaining to fallout. Government representatives believed that accusations leveraging the hazards of fallout "could lead to the stimulation of domestic pressures in other countries—including in Australia—to take China itself to the Court or to step up political action against China in the UN and elsewhere."[115] This belief was especially so since while Australian scientists had determined that "the radiation dose from a French explosion in the atmosphere in the Pacific would be greater than that from an identical explosion in China," Chinese tests would still increase global fallout levels.[116]

Ultimately, Whitlam thought that Australia needed to refrain from "a broad attack on nuclear testing generally" in order to protect Sino-Australian relations.[117] Representatives concluded that the case to the ICJ must focus on "restraining French atmospheric testing in the Pacific on the grounds that the resultant spread of pollution around the *southern hemisphere*" was a "violation" of Australia's "national sovereignty."[118] Their focus on the Pacific was paramount, supported by evidence of "damage and hazard to life in the *Pacific* area, including the prospects of the damage or hazard being accumulative."[119] "If the Australian case before the ICJ is confined solely to the question of French atmospheric testing in the Pacific," government officials deduced, "the repercussions on Sino-Australian relations would be minimal."[120] As a result, the government pursued "a case based solely on France's using colonial territory for its testing," to which China was "unlikely to react."[121]

In addition to protecting the Sino-Australian relationship, the condemnation of French nuclear testing in the Pacific supported Whitlam's desire for Australians to be "the natural leaders" of the region.[122] Australia's central role in the case at the ICJ allowed the state to position itself as "the vanguard in the public campaign against France" in the Pacific.[123] It also allowed Australian officials to assuage their concerns that New Zealand's acute antinuclearism would jeopardize Australian security. In the 1970s, many New Zealanders supported regional calls for a nuclear-free zone in the South Pacific, but the implementation of such a zone had the potential to jeopardize the Australia, New Zealand, and United States Security Treaty (ANZUS) by restricting the movement of both nuclear-armed and nuclear-powered US Navy vessels through the region's waters.[124] Despite Whitlam's rather rocky relationship with the United States, ANZUS remained a foreign policy priority, and Australian officials determined that "given the stated policy of the Government to maintain ANZUS as a defensive alliance," it would "remain essential to ensure that no steps [be] taken such as to cause the United States to review its own attitudes towards the alliance."[125] By taking on a leading role in ICJ negotiations, then, Whitlam's government demonstrated Australia's commitment to being the South Pacific's major power, rather than merely a southern outpost of the British Empire, beholden to the whims of its neighbors.[126]

In 1973, Whitlam's government proceeded with a case against France in the ICJ. By December 1974 it was all but settled, as France declared that it had the technological means to take its tests underground.[127] As the Australian government's case had rested on the condemnation of atmospheric tests in alignment with the provisions of the 1963 Partial Test Ban Treaty, the court ruled on 20 December 1974: "France has undertaken the obligation to hold no further nuclear tests in the atmosphere in the South Pacific."[128] In light of that, the court determined, "the claim of Australia no longer has any objective."[129] The case was closed.

As Australia's case in the ICJ demonstrated, Whitlam's government was not against nuclear testing writ large. Nor was the case put forward in opposition to nuclear proliferation more generally.[130] Rather, the ICJ provided the Whitlam government with a platform on which to perform geopolitically. Nevertheless, Whitlam's approach to nuclear issues in Australia's immediate region responded to a marked shift in Australians' opinions on the necessity, morality, and potential consequences of nuclear energy more generally, and nuclear weapons specifically. The Australian public had begun to demand genuine action from its government representatives. Thus, as the twentieth century wore on, Australia's engagement with the region and the world, through the provision of uranium, for example, could not remain divorced from the very real human consequences of the nuclear order. And as Aboriginal political demands in the form of land rights became increasingly difficult for Australians and their state and federal governments to ignore, considerations of Aboriginal people's subjugation on Australian soil at the hands of the nuclear industry became more acute. Change was undoubtedly afoot.

Changing Tides

Between the 1950s and 1970s, Australia's relationship to the nuclear order, as represented by public and political opposition to French nuclear testing, shifted considerably. During this period, the prospect of foreign powers testing nuclear weapons in colonial territories within proximity to Australian shores became increasingly unacceptable. However, opposition—at a political level at least—remained geopolitically and environmentally motivated. This is clear in the marked avoidance of discussions relating to Britain's nuclear testing program in Australia under both conservative Prime Minister Robert Menzies and Labor Prime Minister Gough Whitlam. For Menzies, resisting French testing worked to provide a precedent for Australian resistance to the acquisition of nuclear weapons by communist states, namely, China, while for Whitlam, protecting Sino-Australian relations necessitated specific resistance against French tests on account of environmental risks, rather than broad-brush condemnation.

But as evidenced by the growth of antinuclear sentiment in this period, the (largely settler) public maintained a hostile attitude toward French nuclear testing. This challenged Australia's relationships with its great and powerful friends (Britain and the United States), as these were relationships many Australians began to recognize as being fundamentally underpinned by imperial interest and exploitation. Yet the antinuclear movement's outward projection of anti-imperial sentiment was also implicated in the perpetuation of a nuclear colonial silence about British testing in Australia. This silence would be only redressed as Aboriginal politics relating to land rights became increasingly influential in debates surrounding Australia's nuclear order in the final decades of the twentieth century. In fact, as chapter 4 will show, in a short period of time and due to a confluence of social and political issues, Aboriginal politics, the legacies of Australian colonialism, and the nuclear industry became inextricably entangled with one another. The global social upheaval of the period between 1966 and 1972 had facilitated this shift.

FOUR

Paving the "Yellowcake Road"

After thirteen years of planning and the construction of approximately A$750 million worth of infrastructure, South Australia's Olympic Dam mine finally began its operations in November 1988. Given the purported importance of the mine to the Australian economy, its official opening spared no expense. Over six hundred guests were treated to a lengthy ceremony at the mine site, replete with a live orchestral performance. The event was, according to the *Canberra Times*, a "who's who of business and politics."[1] But for the *Australian Financial Review*, the opening of Olympic Dam was not merely an opportunity for the mine's operators to show off to the upper echelons of Australian society. Rather, it reflected "a new agenda in the uranium debate," one that epitomized the seeming triumph of the uranium industry over the anti–uranium mining movement of the previous decade.[2]

Irrespective of the notable absence of protesters at Olympic Dam's opening ceremony, simmering beneath the spectacle of the event was the mine's unavoidably controversial history. To some, the mine represented a complete disregard for the rights and welfare of workers and Aboriginal communities due to the potential for its contamination of people and the environment, while to others, the capital accrued by Olympic Dam's uranium held the potential to guide Australia away from the perils of economic stagflation and toward a prosperous neoliberal future. At the center of the tensions between these viewpoints was Olympic Dam's—and other large-scale uranium mines'—contribution to the global nuclear fuel cycle. Unlike other forms of large-scale mining in Australia, the mining of uranium was linked to the highly politicized human and environmental consequences of both military and civilian nuclear energy, as well as its potential promise amid a global energy crisis.

Opened as a polymetallic mine brimming with precious metals such as copper, gold, and silver, Olympic Dam remains the largest-known single deposit of uranium in the world. To this day, it is one of Australia's biggest mines and is set to continue operating until 2036, with the potential for a fifty-year extension after that.[3] The deposit exploited at Olympic Dam was identified by Western Mining Corporation (WMC) for commercial use in 1975, and in 1979 British Petroleum (BP; formerly the British Petroleum Company) and WMC signed a joint venture agreement, enabling the two companies to begin preparations to mine the lode together.[4] Thus, 1979 signaled the official birth of Olympic Dam and earned BP and WMC the collective moniker "the Joint Venturers." Exploration for shafts began in the same year, and in 1982 the South Australian state government passed the Roxby Downs (Indenture Ratification) Act, which provided the legal framework for the mine's operations.

In the 1960s and 1970s, however, a confluence of social and political issues ensured that uranium mining could not go ahead without controversy in Australia. Not only was antinuclearism taking off across the world, but among the critics of Olympic Dam were those who supported the provision of Aboriginal land rights, debates over which questioned the unfettered access to land enjoyed by mining companies. In Australia, links were explicitly drawn between the nuclearity of uranium mining and its potential to negatively impact Aboriginal communities across the country. However, as the 1970s waned and the postwar economic boom came to an unceremonious end, economic stagflation set in and facilitated renewed engagement with the notion of settler Australia's *right* to resource development and the exploitation of minerals, especially radioactive ones. By the 1970s and 1980s, then, rhetoric relating to land rights and Aboriginal heritage protection was actively manipulated by proponents of uranium mining to erase, undermine, or override attempts by Aboriginal people to protect their lands in favor of mining interests.

The desire to prevent land rights claims to mineral-rich lands across South Australia undoubtedly influenced both the mining industry's and government officials' approach to Aboriginal demands at Olympic Dam. Proponents of uranium mining chipped away at the perceived integrity of Aboriginal claims in the Olympic Dam area by playing into public fears that Aboriginal land rights would impede settler Australians' rights to development, and thus any economic benefits that might come from mining and its related industries. This strategy undermined Aboriginal rights to both heritage protection and potential land claims under new South Australian legislation developed in the 1960s and exacerbated unfounded claims that Aboriginal people were intent on preventing development for the wider population. One tangible consequence of such attempts to undermine Aboriginal claims to mineral-rich lands was the destruction of a sacred site of particular significance to the Kokatha people: Canegrass Swamp.

The desecration of Canegrass Swamp is certainly not the only historical example of a mining company destroying Aboriginal artifacts or compromising sacred sites. However, the Canegrass Swamp incident—especially when placed in the broader narrative of this book—cannot be separated from Olympic Dam's nuclearity. The minerals WMC and BP extracted from Kokatha Country were destined for the nuclear energy programs of Australia's allies, and proponents of Australia's fledgling uranium industry were not willing to allow burgeoning land rights debates to impede those ties. The Joint Ventures' destruction of Aboriginal sacred sites at Olympic Dam is thus illustrative of Australia's long-held perceptions of settler superiority and right to (nuclear) development.

Uranium, Stagflation and Land Rights in 1970s Australia

Optimism regarding the possibilities of an Australian uranium industry existed alongside rampant antinuclear sentiment in the 1960s and 1970s. By the early 1970s in the United States and across Western Europe, this antinuclear sentiment had manifested in fierce campaigns against nuclear energy production. In Australia, nuclear energy was less of an issue, as the government had shelved extant plans for an Australian nuclear power capability in 1971 on account of its significant financial cost. In its place, environmentalists and others opposed the mining and exporting of uranium due to its contribution to perceived dual human and energy crises and its potential to lead to an environmental catastrophe of global proportions.[5] This opposition followed the discovery of huge uranium deposits in Australia (estimated to constitute at least 20 percent of the world's supply) and the fluctuation of global uranium prices in alignment with the growing popularity of nuclear power.[6] As other countries expanded their nuclear energy programs, Canberra recognized the significant economic and geopolitical opportunities presented by the potential provision of Australian uranium to the global market.

From the early 1970s on, the issue of what to do with Australian uranium plagued those in power.[7] Initially, Gough Whitlam's government imposed an embargo on uranium exports, as global oversupply had led to a significant drop in the global value of the mineral at the beginning of the decade. However, not long into Whitlam's prime ministership, and amid the 1973 oil crisis, foreign governments keen to purchase Australian uranium oxide challenged the logic of this embargo.[8] Various discussions between the British government, Whitlam, and his minister for minerals and energy, Rex Connor, demonstrate a marked disparity between Whitlam's and Connor's approach to uranium export. For Connor, it was necessary to prioritize the Australian industry, which—he believed—would involve developing an independent uranium enrichment program to facilitate Australia's exportation of enriched uranium at a much higher cost than non-enriched uranium oxide. For Whitlam, as global uranium prices climbed during the oil crisis, prioritizing Australia's interests involved considering the possibility of simply exporting Australian uranium oxide to foreign powers, such as Britain and Japan.[9]

In the process of attempting to thrash out a future for Australia's uranium industry, Whitlam called for an inquiry into the environmental impacts of exploiting several recently discovered uranium deposits in the Northern Territory's Alligator Rivers Region (map 3). The Ranger Uranium Environmental Inquiry—later known as the Fox Inquiry after its chair, Justice Russell Fox—sought to assess the environmental impacts of mining various uranium deposits in the territory, including those in the Ranger, Koongarra, and Jabiluka leases.[10] But before its results could be made public, Whitlam was (in)famously dismissed as prime minister by Australia's then-governor-general over a confluence of issues, including a significant budgetary crisis.[11] In the wake of growing anti-imperial sentiment in pockets of the Australian public, the sacking of the prime minister by Queen Elizabeth's representative in Australia was highly controversial and is popularly remembered as one of the most significant constitutional crises in the country's history.[12] Deepening the contentiousness of the

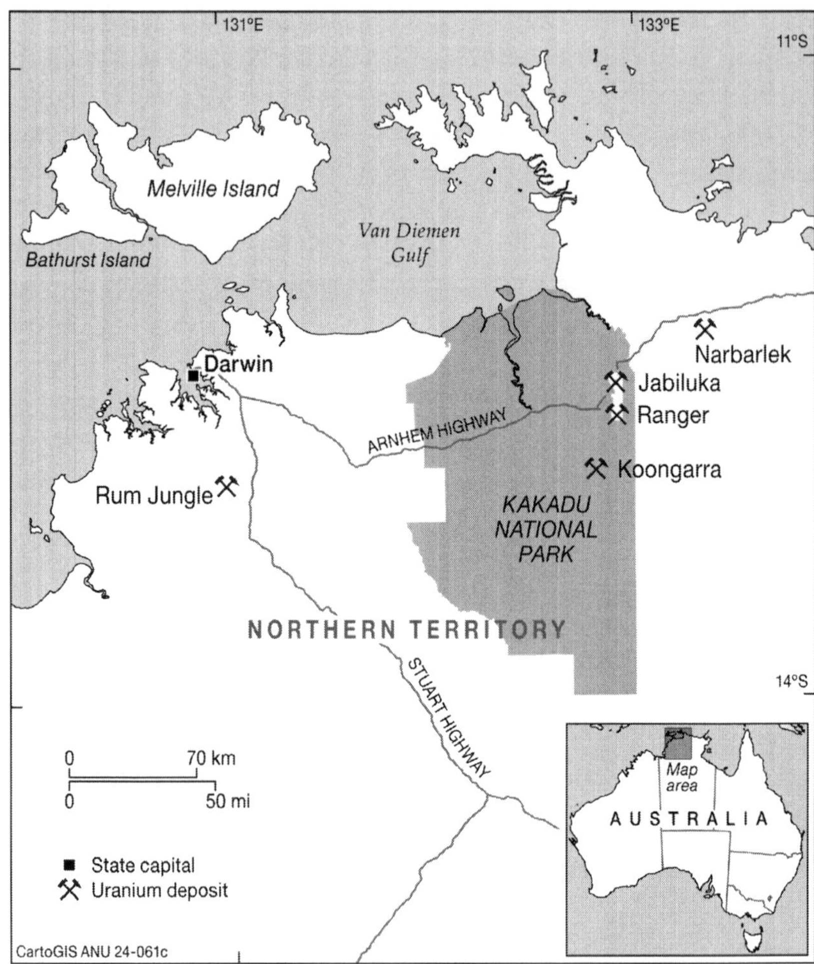

MAP 3. Several uranium deposits were earmarked for exploitation within the confines of the environmentally important Kakadu National Park, in the Alligator Rivers Region of the Northern Territory, during the 1970s. While not all of these deposits were exploited by settlers (thanks in part to large protest campaigns to prevent the expansion of Australia's uranium industry in the 1990s), Ranger was one of the biggest uranium mines in the world until 2021, when it ceased operations. Map provided by CartoGIS, Australian National University, Canberra.

situation, the governor-general immediately replaced Whitlam with a caretaker prime minister and the leader of the opposition, Malcolm Fraser, who would officially give the "green light" to uranium development.

Following Whitlam's unceremonious removal from power, the Fox Inquiry handed down its findings to Fraser, detailing the various risks and benefits posed by the pursuit of a large-scale uranium industry in Australia. Fox's extensive report considered—among other things—the economic benefits of uranium mining, the environmental risks of the industry, and the impact of the mine on the region's Aboriginal communities. While the mine was economically feasible, Fox made clear that any significant development in the region would need to take seriously the Northern Territory's seasonal rains, ecologically rich wetlands, and subterranean aquifers. Fox cited scientific evidence that suggested there was a very real possibility of the mine contaminating significant water bodies in the Alligator Rivers Region, the environmental consequences of which would undoubtedly outweigh any potential economic gains.[13] The contamination of Country—created by mine runoff, tailings, and the infrastructure and personnel required for operations—would have a disruptive impact on the region's Aboriginal peoples, whose rights had only recently been formally acknowledged in the Aboriginal Land Rights (Northern Territory) Act of 1976.

Aboriginal demands for land rights proliferated alongside growing concerns over persistent colonialism, environmental degradation, and the scourges of the nuclear industry. These demands emphasized the need for substantial legal reform that would acknowledge communities' entitlement to land.[14] The first reform of this nature—the Aboriginal Lands Trust Act—was rolled out by the South Australian government in 1966 under the initiative of the then-minister for Aboriginal affairs, Don Dunstan. This early piece of legislation established the Aboriginal Lands Trust, which took over the title and administration of all lands formerly designated Aboriginal reserves in South Australia. Previously, tracts of land had been designated as "reserve" lands and set aside for the sole use of Aboriginal people—including those within proximity to the Maralinga and Emu Field nuclear test sites—but these lands were not owned by communities, nor were they managed by the government for the betterment of these communities. In its creation of a trust designed to control lands on behalf of all South Australian Aboriginal peoples and with exclusively Aboriginal membership, the act effectively granted Aboriginal peoples the rights to their lands for the first time since Anglo-European invasion.[15] In response to the growing incursion of mining companies into Aboriginal lands in the 1960s and 1970s, the act was amended in 1973 to make it more difficult (but not impossible) for exploration, prospecting, or mining to take place on lands vested in the Trust.[16]

A decade later—in 1976—progress on inalienable land rights was made in the Northern Territory with the passage of the Aboriginal Land Rights (Northern Territory) Act. This act was devised on the recommendation of the Woodward Royal Commission, a federal government inquiry initiated by the Whitlam government in 1973 and undertaken by Justice Edward Woodward to determine the best way to recognize Aboriginal land rights in the Northern Territory. The ensuing act granted Aboriginal communities inalienable freehold title to approximately 32 percent of the territory, endowing title holders with rights to negotiate development on their lands.[17] This marked the first piece of Australian legislation to grant Aboriginal people direct control over their lands and coincided with exploration for what would later become the Ranger Uranium Mine. Under the act, former Aboriginal reserve lands became Aboriginal owned and could not be sold or acquired by state or federal governments. This legislation empowered Aboriginal communities to negotiate with companies seeking to explore or mine on their Country.

In the wake of this legislative change, Fox's investigations into uranium mining in the Northern Territory necessarily involved consultation with the region's Aboriginal communities. Overwhelmingly, Fox detailed, Aboriginal people expressed their opposition to *any* uranium mining in the region, citing concerns for their welfare and interests, not least in the land. Aboriginal witnesses to the inquiry made it abundantly clear that they would happily forgo any material benefits of mining (including potential royalties, cars, hunting licenses, and so on) "in exchange for an assurance that mining would not proceed."[18] Northern Land Council chairman and Alewa man Silas Roberts expressed Aboriginal peoples' concern: "We are losing a little bit, a little bit, all of the time." "We keep our ceremony, our culture, but we are always worried," he told the inquiry; "we are very worried that the results of this enquiry will open the doors to other companies who want to dig up uranium on our sacred lands."[19] "If you destroy our land, you destroy us," he stated plainly.[20] In an accompanying National Press Club address in November 1977, Roberts reiterated to politicians and media representatives present: "We insist we don't want uranium mining."[21] Consequently, Fox's final report acknowledged Aboriginal opposition to the venture and recommended that uranium mining should be pursued "with caution after due public discussion and debate."[22]

Fox was adamant that Australian governments should take seriously Aboriginal opposition, not least as the nation had reached a political "turning point." The 1973 Woodward Royal Commission had been a historic step toward the recognition of Aboriginal land rights. Nevertheless, Fox was aware of lingering resistance to land rights and openly admitted that many Australians would "regard [this] solicitude for the welfare of Aboriginal people as misplaced." In his report, Fox reiterated his belief that the shift in attitude toward land rights was "not . . . a matter of conscience, but of justice, based on a fuller and better understanding of Aboriginal people, their ways and their beliefs."[23] He concluded that uranium mining would compromise these ways and beliefs but that there could be "no compromise with the Aboriginal position." "Either it is treated as conclusive," he argued, "or it is set aside."[24] In a move conceived by many to be a shocking betrayal of Aboriginal peoples' newly won rights, Prime Minister Fraser set the inquiry's findings aside.

According to Fraser, this was an issue not of race, but of geopolitics. "If we just leave Australia's uranium in the ground," he argued, "Australia will not be able to act with any effect, with any force, in matters which are important to all of us and to our children."[25] Citing a strong sense of national responsibility, the prime minister argued that there was a need both to control uranium exports under "Australia's obligations as a good international citizen" and to supply uranium to a world that was "short of energy."[26] With regard to the impact on the Aboriginal communities of the Alligator Rivers Region, Fraser's minister for Aboriginal affairs publicly stated, "The Government's decision to allow mining of uranium in the Alligator Rivers Region will certainly have profound effect on the lives of the Aboriginal people" but that the opinions of the communities "should not be allowed to prevail."[27] Government representatives hoped that their decision to allow uranium mining to go ahead in the Northern Territory would not be viewed "in a racial light."[28]

To many, however, the decision to mine the Ranger uranium deposit seemed highly racialized. At a 1978 Special Unions Conference on uranium, Yiman and Bidjara scholar and activist Marcia Langton told the audience, "There can be no compensation for the destruction of our culture."[29] Warren Snowdon of the Northern Territory Trade and Labor Council expressed his opinion on the approval of the Ranger mine more colorfully, telling the conference, "We are participating in the genocide of a whole population."[30] And in the same year, famed public servant and champion of Aboriginal rights Herbert Cole (Nugget) Coombs expressed his opinion that the environmental assessment prepared for Ranger was "a travesty . . . exhibiting profound ignorance of Aboriginal people, a complete disregard for the recorded evidence of the effects of other large scale mining projects on Aboriginal communities and a contemptuous indifference to preferences of the Aboriginal people concerned."[31] A mixture of apprehension and outrage accompanied the Fraser government's announcement that uranium mining would proceed in Australia.

Although Whitlam and Connor had supported uranium export in one form or another prior to their government's loss of power, there was significant grassroots opposition to the uranium industry among Labor supporters and members of the labor movement in Australia. In response to growing (and rather vehement) anti–uranium mining sentiment across the country, from 1977 onward the Australian Labor Party (ALP) officially endorsed a uranium moratorium until various assurances could be made, not least in relation to worker safety.[32] Concerns over workers' handling and transportation of radioactive materials, the potential contribution of Australian uranium to nuclear proliferation, and the impacts uranium mining would have on the environment punctuated debates in the ALP's ranks. However, the party's newly minted moratorium was controversially challenged when the president of both the ALP and the Australian Council of Trade Unions (ACTU) at the time, Robert (Bob) Hawke, supported Fraser's decision to give the green light on uranium. And while Hawke's support of an Australian uranium industry was in line with the beginnings of a markedly neoliberal turn in the ALP during the 1970s and 1980s in response to economic downturn, it was nonetheless contentious.[33]

Hawke's seeming support of the soon-to-be Ranger mine facilitated a split in the ALP that reflected the broader tensions harbored within Australia about uranium mining. At the Labor conference of 1977, leaders of the South Australian and Victorian Labor parties publicly acknowledged the problems arising from Australia's provision of uranium to the global nuclear fuel cycle.[34] Citing threats to "Australian sovereignty, the environment, the economic welfare of our people, and the rights and well-being of Aboriginal people," not least on account of uranium's potential contribution to nuclear proliferation, they actively implored Hawke and the ALP to hold out on making any decisions relating to uranium mining until the ALP was "satisfied" that these problems had been solved.[35] Hawke ignored their request. At the 1982 Labor conference, the party agreed to allow uranium exports in situations where uranium mining "was incidental to the mining of other minerals."[36] Despite arguments over whether the uranium that would eventually be mined at Olympic Dam was truly "incidental" to the mine's operations—as many disputed the mine's profitability without it—this stance ensured that Ranger and Olympic Dam would be allowed to continue operating even if the ALP was to win at the next federal election.[37] Ultimately, this concession did away with the ALP's formal opposition to uranium.

Labor constituents were outraged by Hawke's support of the industry. One Labor voter wrote to him while in the pub with some mates, informing the ALP and ACTU president, "We, sitting here having a beer, think that you're being weak as piss on the uranium issue."[38] Another went to great lengths to mail Hawke photographs of the aftermath of Hiroshima and Nagasaki in an attempt to drive home the potential consequences of Australia contributing to the global nuclear fuel cycle (a reality that, in the United States two years later, would be starkly demonstrated by the Three Mile Island incident in Pennsylvania). And an "Outraged Territorian" declared that Hawke's "irresponsible outburst on uranium" was "as moral and logical as the proposition that Australia grow and export dope."[39] While many echoed such sentiments, opposition to uranium mining across the continent could not contend with arguments that the industry would prove an effective salve for Australia's economic woes.

Underpinning the promise of uranium mining's prosperity was settlers' perceived entitlement to national development, which stubborn stagflation had fueled anew. Stagflation, or the experience of higher inflation and unemployment alongside simultaneous lower growth in gross domestic product, had signaled the end of the postwar boom in several countries, including Australia and the United States.[40] For everyday Australians, this translated to diminished affluence, especially when compared with previous decades.[41] Anxiety about Australia's economic state spread rapidly. But in the shadows of recession, Australia's extensive mineral resources remained a source of great potential wealth.[42] By the late 1970s, a sense that mining was the life raft that would keep both state and federal economies afloat was growing across several of Australia's states, encouraged by increasingly popular neoliberal principles that permeated both government and industry.[43]

South Australians were particularly attuned to the economic potential of uranium mining. In the wake of the discovery of the Olympic Dam uranium deposit by WMC in 1975, many emphasized the need to exploit the lode in an effort to improve the state's economic position relative to those states with independent and prosperous industries, such as New South Wales and Victoria.[44] Capturing this sentiment during a visit to South Australia's Chamber of Commerce in 1979, Prime Minister Fraser's deputy and minister for national resources noted, "Unfortunately . . . the picture here in South Australia is not as bright as it is in other States."[45] Many South Australians had harbored hope since before Federation that mineral wealth would transform the state's economy, facilitating greater economic and political independence. Demonstrating the maintenance of this expectation into the 1970s, the minister assured the Chamber of Commerce, "The prospects for mining hold out . . . great hope for the economy and wellbeing of South Australia."[46] To *not* mine uranium at Olympic Dam would be "to sit back while the rest of the world surges ahead into the nuclear age," according to the minister.[47] The South Australian government agreed.

The state's conservative Liberal government led by David Tonkin heralded the recently discovered Olympic Dam uranium deposit as a "tonic" to many of South Australia's economic and developmental anguishes. In a letter to Prime Minister Fraser in 1979, Premier Tonkin noted that the minerals discovered at Olympic Dam were "of substantial National and State significance."[48] For Tonkin, the approval of the mine was a "great triumph" for both his government and his constituents.[49] Many of the latter appeared to agree. In a letter to the editor of *The Bulletin* in 1982, a "former resident" of South Australia wrote, "SA has never been a 'great' state," but the exploitation of uranium at Olympic Dam "enables SA to show this country that it is not the laughing stock and sinking ship most regard it to be."[50] The mine existed as a demonstration of how Tonkin's cabinet was "prepared to put the long-term interests of the State before any apparent short-term electoral advantage."[51] Prime Minister Fraser agreed, himself considering Australia's mining and export of uranium key to the country's role as a middle power, policing global nuclear proliferation and fueling the reactors of its allies through the supply of uranium.[52] It was exactly this justification that accompanied Canberra's green-lighting of uranium mining and export from the Northern Territory in 1977, with Ranger's official opening in 1980 paving the way for Olympic Dam.[53] Until Ranger closed in 2021, these two mines remained among the largest uranium mines in the world.[54]

By the 1980s, proponents of mining were encouraged by the promise that uranium's monetary and geopolitical value would catapult South Australia out of stagflation. At the same time, Aboriginal communities continued to agitate for land rights, pushing back against mining on their lands. Despite the promise with which many regarded the growing rights' agenda in this period, uranium's nuclearity—its contribution to the continually expanding global nuclear fuel cycle—took precedence over Aboriginal claims for recognition. In fact, vocal proponents of Olympic Dam ensured its success by actively undermining Aboriginal land claims in the name of economic prosperity, national development, and Australia's moral obligations as a responsible international citizen.

The Legitimate Right of All Citizens

Settlers have historically justified settler-colonial expansion in the name of "progress" as inevitable: a *right* of settlers.[55] Such notions remain relevant in analyzing uranium mining in 1980s Australia, as the industry's proponents considered the mining of uranium integral to Australia's economic growth and progress as a nation.[56] For many Australian neoliberal politicians and businesspeople during the 1980s, mineral development denoted moral progress, an appropriate use of the environment, and a modern manifestation of the late nineteenth- and early twentieth-century desire of settlers to civilize and domesticate the "unfamiliar."[57] Uranium's contribution to global nuclear development only elevated these perceived benefits. As such, proponents of the industry viewed its development as both a right and an expectation in the 1970s, perhaps none more so than conservative politician Roger Goldsworthy, the South Australian deputy premier and minister of mines and energy (1979–82), and his peers.

Goldsworthy was a keen advocate for uranium mining in South Australia both prior to and throughout his term as minister. In parliamentary debates during 1977, he questioned the incumbent South Australian premier, Don Dunstan, about the latter's resistance to mining the recently discovered Olympic Dam deposit, drawing into question the premier's concerns about safety and waste disposal. Goldsworthy argued that Britain's expansion of its nuclear power program following the 1957 disaster at its Windscale nuclear reactor site should dismiss any concerns Dunstan had about the industry.[58] Goldsworthy used Britain's expansion of its nuclear capability after the Windscale fire and its resulting contamination of the environment as ample evidence that scientific development could adequately deal with the issue of waste, imploring Dunstan not to ignore the "great potential" offered by Olympic Dam on account of what he considered frivolous fears of the uranium industry.[59]

As minister, Goldsworthy continuously advertised the benefits of an Australian uranium industry, arguing that the nation had a "moral obligation to supply energy to an energy-hungry world."[60] In fact, he argued that there was "no other option" for the future of the world's energy needs than nuclear energy, citing the increasing commitment of the United States, Canada, France, Sweden, Britain, and Japan to nuclear power.[61] He was by no means alone in this view, with one of his colleagues applauding the minister's commitment to uranium mining as "a return to sanity!" following years of antinuclear sentiment at a state level.[62] By 1981, however, new land rights legislation looked to threaten the prosperous nuclear future that Olympic Dam promised.

In 1981, South Australia's government assented to the Aṉangu Pitjantjatjara Yankunytjatjara Land Rights Act, granting the Pitjantjatjara Council rights to over 62,000 square miles (102,000 square kilometers) of Country in central South Australia. A landmark piece of legislation, this act shifted control of the lands in question from South Australia's Aboriginal Lands Trust directly to the Pitjantjatjara people.[63] This historic act responded to the Pitjantjatjara's desire for more than the communally designated land rights previously legislated in South Australia and the Northern Territory. It endowed the Pitjantjatjara people with autonomy over the use of their lands, including by prohibiting mining without express community permission.[64] This had profound implications for numerous communities in the vicinity of Roxby Downs station, where the Olympic Dam deposit had been identified by mining companies. The high-profile act precipitated similar land claims from the Pitjantjatjara's neighboring communities—such as the Kokatha—and the formation of Aboriginal organizations, including the Southern Land Council (SLC).[65] But as Aboriginal communities requested greater access to and control over their traditional lands in response to such legislative changes, the relationship between land rights and resource extraction grew increasingly complicated.

Much of Goldsworthy's most vehement opposition to Aboriginal land rights followed the South Australian government's passing of this land rights act. To Aṉangu, their granting of land rights had been formal recognition of their connection to land, *manta*, as "the land's inherent and perpetual custodians."[66] However, many settler Australians—not least conservative politicians and mining executives—considered such recognized rights "a fundamental threat to the political status quo," as well as state and private economic interests.[67] Goldsworthy appeared to share these sentiments; the Pitjantjatjara's lawyers described him as "disinterested and antagonistic" during negotiations for the act.[68] But he was not alone in his disdain. Many others resented the fact that while the act did not provide the Pitjantjatjara Council with veto rights over mining on Pitjantjatjara lands, it did shift some power back toward Traditional Owners.[69] Mining companies were now required to seek permission from the state government and the Pitjantjatjara Council before exploration could begin.[70]

In light of this development, Premier Tonkin had to consider with greater urgency what impact Aboriginal land rights claims might have on resource extraction within his state. Goldsworthy reminded his leader that "industries based on the extraction and processing of natural resources" were "key elements in the economic and social development of South Australia."[71] Goldsworthy implied that such priorities were at odds with granting Aboriginal people land rights. He argued that the government's "sensitivity to aboriginal questions" had the potential to impact mineral developments of national (and international) importance.[72] Even entertaining Aboriginal land claims "could prejudice exploration and development unless they are firmly rejected," Goldsworthy argued.[73] Reflecting the views of various proponents of mineral development in Australia at the time, he presented the granting of land rights as a direct impediment to uranium mining. The implication was that the two were mutually exclusive.

Goldsworthy argued that listening to Aboriginal voices would jeopardize the rights enjoyed by other South Australian citizens. A draft statement prepared in 1981 by staff members of his department expressed concern over Aboriginal land rights' impact on uranium mining, the benefits of which they viewed as "the legitimate right of all citizens of the State."[74] According to this logic, Aboriginal rights to land could not exist in conjunction with the rights of "other" South Australians. To reconcile this issue, Goldsworthy argued that, when making decisions relating to land rights, "the Government must . . . consider the legitimate expectations of all citizens of South Australia and their right to share in the benefits of development."[75] Hugh Morgan, the executive director of WMC starting in 1986, held similar prejudices.

Morgan was a proud proponent of the 1980s New Right, a group that existed as the antithesis to the global New Left. Where the New Left saw itself as the steward of progressive politics and counterculture, the New Right championed economic freedom and considerable social conservatism, especially when it came to Aboriginal affairs.[76] Representing a generation of mining moguls whose unfettered access to Aboriginal land was being challenged in the early 1980s by increased calls for land rights and articulations of Aboriginal politics, Morgan and his peers made it clear that the property rights of settlers should take precedence over the rights of Aboriginal communities when it came to uranium mining.[77] In 1984, he gave a reportedly "explosive" speech at the annual meeting of the Australian Mining Industry Council in which he challenged Aboriginal peoples' attempts to protect sacred sites within mining-rich areas. He argued, "[The Australian] public should reject Aboriginal claims to sacred sites in the same manner as it has refused to sanction other features of early Aboriginal life such as cannibalism, infanticide, and cruel initiation rights."[78]

Such opinions reflected the anti–land rights agenda pursued by pockets of Australia's mining industry in this period. This agenda was anchored in the long-held notion that settlers maintained a right to mining. Many Aboriginal peoples' maintenance that they held specific *Aboriginal* rights to land was challenging this position. To undermine the political potency of such claims, individuals like Morgan chose to interpret land rights legislation as inhibiting mining and exploration "for the benefit of *anyone*."[79] During the early 1980s, the political journalist David Barnett, an adviser to Fraser, likened land rights to South African apartheid in the conservative broadsheet *The Bulletin*, evoking ire from the Left. This comparison aimed to imply that land rights sought to elevate one group over others, based on race, while evoking the sense that the mining industry "wanted nothing more than equal treatment for everyone" so that "mining could continue to do its public-spirited work for the good of all."[80] Or as the director of Legal Services at the Central Land Council described it in the 1980s, Morgan and his peers "chose to depict land rights as creating Berlin-type walls built by black hands across the state," closing off lands from deserving settlers.[81]

Such arguments failed to account for the fact that legislation such as the 1981 Aṉangu Pitjantjatjara Yankunytjatjara Land Rights Act only prejudiced mining insofar as companies now had to consult Aboriginal communities ahead of commencing exploration. Despite the claims of mining proponents and their allies, this legislation did not give communities veto powers over mining. Moreover, many communities—including the Pitjantjatjara and the Kokatha—made it clear that they were in fact not opposed, in principle, to mining on their lands. Rather, they asked that companies hoping to explore Aboriginal lands for minerals seek permission and consult with communities in order to preserve Aboriginal cultural knowledge and heritage, protect sacred sites, and ensure that long-term benefits were negotiated for the communities in question. These requests both encapsulated Aboriginal peoples' willingness to allow development on their lands and acknowledged their long-held connection to Country.

For Aboriginal communities, it was (and remains) this long-held connection to Country that empowered them to make decisions on behalf of the land. This connection was acknowledged in the guiding principles of the SLC, a body formed in 1981 to address the issue of Aboriginal rights and resource extraction across South Australia. Constituted of representatives from several South Australian Aboriginal communities, the SLC created a forum within which the Kokatha could seek support from neighboring communities in their endeavor to have WMC and BP guarantee the protection of Aboriginal sacred sites at Olympic Dam. The Kokatha's campaign was inspired by the Pitjantjatjara's; the SLC provided them the space within which to learn from their neighbor's campaign.

During the SLC's inaugural meeting in October 1981, attendees agreed to a set of guiding principles for the council. Foremost among them was acknowledging the primacy of Aboriginal physical and spiritual connections to their land.[82] The SLC explained that this connection was "based on prior occupation and permanent spiritual attachment."[83] Pitjantjatjara representatives in the SLC reiterated to their Kokatha counterparts that maintaining and asserting this connection was paramount. Aboriginal power, they argued, came from their deep knowledge of their Country, including its flora, fauna, stories, and people. But as Aboriginal activists vocally laid claim to Country (fig. 7), proponents of mining told alternative stories of the land that centered on the pioneering spirit of the pastoralists and prospectors upon whose shoulders modern settler Australia stood.

Goldsworthy took particular umbrage at the assertion that Aboriginal people had a "primary interest" in Olympic Dam. So while the SLC did acknowledge that "miners and Europeans ha[d] a temporary and secondary interest based . . . on economic value," he insisted that pastoralists and miners maintained more significant connections to the Roxby Downs area by virtue of having made proper *use* of the land.[84] "It is simply not

FIGURE 7. Kokatha Country, and thus Kokatha culture, came under threat from uranium mining in the 1980s. Recognizing the power of Kokatha knowledge of, and connection to, Country, Kokatha boys Stanley Wingfield, Sydney Amos, Glen Wingfield, and Terry Strangeway hold an Aboriginal flag on their Country near Olympic Dam, circa 1983. Photograph courtesy of the Wingfield family.

true to say that aborigines are the only people with permanent spiritual attachment to the land," Goldsworthy argued in the South Australian Parliament in 1981. "Pastoral and . . . agricultural activity has taken place in many areas of the State . . . since before the middle of the last century." Underpinning the minister's response to the SLC's claims was his view that the use of land in a strictly European sense was key evidence that settlers were economically and spiritually invested in the area, perhaps even more so than Aboriginal people were. As such, Goldsworthy sought to enlighten Parliament on the "history of the Roxby Downs area," stating, "There is a limit to which this generation and future generations can be required to atone for the so-called sins of our forebearers."[85] At some point, he implied, it was necessary to consider the darker aspects of Australia's colonial past as having given way to an era of settler prosperity through which non-

Indigenous peoples had forged an unquestionably strong bond to the land, one that overrode previous Aboriginal connections.

For Goldsworthy, the true history of the region began in 1876, when the first pastoral lease was taken up by a South Australian settler at what would later become Roxby Downs. As far as Goldsworthy was concerned, the Joint Ventures' Roxby Downs had seen "almost 130 years" of occupation, ensuring that Europeans had "developed as much spiritual attachment to the land as ha[d] previous aboriginal occupants." "In view of this lengthy history of activity," he pointed out, "it is perhaps surprising that only recently has there been a move by aboriginals to assert claims to control of the area."[86] Goldsworthy then made the point that the Joint Venturers had been "undertaking exploration in those areas for some years," thus "a requirement that companies enter into consultations with the Kokatha" or other Aboriginal communities "would be onerous."[87] Aside from evading the deep history of Aboriginal occupation of Australia and the importance of the labor of Aboriginal people to Anglo-European settlement and prosperity, his reference to Aboriginal people as the "previous aboriginal occupants" worked to rhetorically sever Aboriginal peoples' connection to the region, effectively removing the "onerous" task of consultation on the part of the Joint Venturers.[88] Ultimately, Goldsworthy's claims that Aboriginal interests in and occupation of the land had appeared minimal until significant mineral deposits had been discovered overlooked the disruptive effects of settler colonialism on the Kokatha.

Goldsworthy's clear suspicion over the "recent" nature of Aboriginal claims in the area drew on public fears that land rights would facilitate Aboriginal people making claims to land almost anywhere and everywhere. Writing to the Kokatha's lawyer in March 1981, Goldsworthy acknowledged: "The Government notes the concerns of your client with regard to the protection of sacred sites [within Olympic Dam]."[89] By Goldsworthy's admission, he understood that the Kokatha did not appear to be claiming blanket land rights to the region, but rather were demanding the ability to protect individual sites. Yet drawing the distinction between these two desires hardly mattered to Goldsworthy. His letter continued, drawing the Kokatha's claims into direct suspicion: "The companies concerned have been undertaking their investigations with regard to, and in exploration in, that area over a considerable period of time." In comparison with these heavily invested mining corporations, Goldsworthy asserted, "the representations of your client are very recent."[90] Here Goldsworthy attempted to discount Kokatha claims on the basis that many years of exploration had taken place prior to Aboriginal claims to land or sacred site protection. But he also alluded to the Joint Venturers' significant investment of capital in the region.

Such rhetoric afforded no acknowledgment of the impact of colonization on Aboriginal communities in the region. Kokatha attempts to protect sacred sites were overlooked time and again by the Joint Venturers and politicians, dismissed under the guise that no obvious evidence of Aboriginal occupation had been uncovered during mineral exploration. This justification not only failed to account for colonization's "unpeopling" of such spaces but also elided the various structural mechanisms of White Australia that had forced Aboriginal peoples off their lands and into white settlements over the preceding decades, including the assimilation policies of the 1950s. So, while Aboriginal claims may have appeared to miners and others as recent, they were largely inconceivable before this period. The Kokatha's insistence that their sacred sites be protected from mining was the product of Aboriginal peoples' increasing empowerment and political mobilization, engendered by the political and social changes occurring across the nation.

Despite these changes, resentment of and cynicism toward land rights persisted among decision-makers. During negotiations between the Joint Venturers and the Kokatha Peoples Committee (KPC), the Department of Mines and Energy demonstrated opposition to protections afforded to Aboriginal peoples by various new pieces of legislation, including South Australia's 1979 Aboriginal Heritage Act. This act provided Aboriginal people with mechanisms to have sacred sites (or "Aboriginal heritage") identified and protected from destruction, in response to the increased incidence of mineral exploration across the state. One of the department's key concerns was that "the definition of 'aboriginal people'" and "the definition of 'item of Aboriginal Heritage'" were "too wide," thereby increasing the risk that any number of people could claim connection to the land and its heritage on the grounds that it constituted "Aboriginal heritage."[91]

Similarly, representatives within the department feared that the act would cause "considerable difficulty and delay to mining companies" at Olympic Dam by attempting to legislate how the excavation of Aboriginal sites was to occur across South Australia.[92] In response, and in an attempt to limit the powers of land rights and heritage legislation, the department made a strategic decision to agree to acknowledge sacred sites at the expense of greater protections.

The Department of Mines and Energy understood that protecting *some* sites significant to Aboriginal groups would assist in counteracting broader land claims. In May 1981, representatives from the department met with South Australia's director general of environmental planning to express several of the department's concerns about the Aboriginal Heritage Act. First, they questioned the fact that, under the act, the minister for mines and energy did not have to be consulted for an item of heritage to be protected under the law. This was despite such protection having the potential to impede mining interests. In response, all parties present agreed that a representative of the department would be appointed to the Aboriginal Heritage Committee, while the director general of environmental planning would be required to discuss any submitted sacred site protection proposals with the minister of mines and energy directly. It was also decided that the registration of any sites "should not be interpreted as recognition of a proprietary interest in the land on which they [were] situated." However, the director general inferred that it would be unwise to too tightly police the protection of sacred sites, as "a decision to refuse to recognise further land claims would be 'sweetened' by protection of sites" under the act.[93] So while the department wanted to make clear that the protection of sacred sites did not endow Aboriginal groups with land rights, it was forced to acknowledge that granting some protections to Aboriginal heritage could be useful for counteracting larger and more consequential claims.

Even though Goldsworthy and the Joint Venturers were reluctant to recognize Aboriginal claims concerning Olympic Dam, the mine was necessarily subjected to an anthropological survey as part of its Environmental Impact Statement (EIS). To complete this assessment, the Joint Venturers had to consult with relevant Aboriginal communities to identify any sites of significance. Once recorded by an anthropologist, these recognized sites would be protected by the EIS for the life of the mine. The completion of an EIS for mining and other development projects was made compulsory under the 1974 Environmental Protection (Impact of Proposals) Act (the EPIP Act), passed by the Whitlam government.[94] However, by the mid- to late 1980s, the limits of the EPIP Act and its environmental impact assessments were clear. State reluctance to comply with their provisions made them almost entirely ineffectual in their protection of the environment.[95] This was certainly the case with Olympic Dam. While the 1982 Roxby Downs (Indenture Ratification) Act required the Joint Venturers to complete a thorough assessment of the area from an environmental, archaeological, and anthropological perspective, these assessments would ultimately be made by individuals hired by the Joint Venturers.[96] The limitations were clear, not least as the EIS relied on mining Aboriginal knowledge of place.

Kokatha Claims for Country

Arid desert Country abounds around the Olympic Dam mine, fed by the life-giving waters of the Great Artesian Basin. The Great Artesian Basin houses approximately 65 million gigaliters of fresh underground water, spanning from the north of Queensland down through New South Wales, the Northern Territory, and South Australia. The springs, creeks, wetlands, rivers, and groundwater that characterize this basin provide permanent water to otherwise incredibly dry Country.[97] These waters feed plants, animals, and peoples, ensuring the red sands of South Australia's desert region are a highly vegetated and abundant environment, replete with rock holes, bilbies, emus, wedge-tailed eagles, kangaroos, sleepy lizards (or shingleback or bobtail lizards), thorny devils, mulga trees, bluebush, and saltbush. The plants, animals, and waters of this Country have sustained Kokatha for millennia. It therefore comes as little surprise that the establishment of a uranium mine on this Country raised significant questions about spiritual, cultural, and environmental preservation, not least due to the industry's potential to produce environmental contamination *and* its need to access a considerable water supply to maintain its operations.

For Kokatha, faced with the imposition of uranium mining, it was their knowledge of this Country that remained central to the community's power. A key tenet in the organizational ethos of the SLC—of which the Kokatha were a part from its inauguration in 1981—was thus recognizing and respecting the importance and secrecy of Aboriginal knowledge, especially when in negotiation with mining companies.[98] As much of this knowledge was "secret and sacred and only aboriginal people [we]re experts in its understanding," it provided communities with control over their sacred sites.[99] But at Olympic Dam, the Joint Venturers and politicians such as Goldsworthy were undermining and replacing this knowledge with their own. "Roxby Downs is big history for the Kokatha people," Kokatha representatives explained to those gathered at the SLC's inaugural meeting, and "[it] was secret and sacred to Aboriginal people before white man came along." But now, "Aboriginal history" had been "chucked aside by white man," and, as a result, Kokatha representatives were "afraid that many sacred sites may already have been destroyed at Roxby." Irrespective of their fears, Kokatha representatives in the SLC supported the council when it insisted, "The first rule in dealing with mining companies or the government is not to let them see a map of Aboriginal sacred places."[100] Unfortunately for the Kokatha, the environmental protections enabled by the EIS were contingent on Aboriginal people divulging their sacred knowledge to settlers.

Working with an anthropologist hired directly by the mining companies compromised the root of the Kokatha's negotiating power: their knowledge of the landscape and its sacred sites. In keeping with the SLC's principles, the Kokatha refused to work with anthropologists on the Joint Venturers' payroll, reiterating their need to protect Aboriginal knowledge. This refusal was a particularly important articulation of Aboriginal resistance, reflective of prevailing arguments among Indigenous groups at the time that communities had specific rights to land because of their close connection to and knowledge of Country. To maintain control of their stories—and thus sacred sites—the KPC instead asked the South Australian state government and the Joint Venturers for funds to employ their own anthropologist for recording the location of sites of archaeological and anthropological significance.

In mid-1981, Kokatha woman Joan Wingfield, secretary of the KPC, wrote to the company contracted to complete Olympic Dam's EIS—Kinhill

Engineering—to explain her community's position. The Kokatha were "not prepared to accept the prospect of an anthropologist gaining access to secret and sacred information on matters of aboriginal history," she stated, "when our people have no control over the use to which that information will be put."[101] In its response to Wingfield, Kinhill Engineering confirmed the KPC's fears, acknowledging that any knowledge of sacred sites divulged to anthropologists other than those affiliated with Kinhill would have no bearing on the environmental assessment of the mine. And even if the Kokatha did divulge the location and nature of sacred sites to Kinhill and its anthropologist, this information, the KPC was cautioned, did not need to be taken into account by the Joint Venturers.[102] Wingfield articulated in response that "this proposal ma[de] no provision for the special interests of the Kokatha people."[103] Rather, the information gathered by Kinhill would be used as necessary, assessed alongside submissions made by the public. A stalemate between Kinhill and the KPC ensued.

Goldsworthy used this impasse as an opportunity to cast further doubt over Kokatha claims, implying they were dubious, to say the least. He expressed this belief to his cabinet: "[If] the aboriginal people have refused to cooperate unless provided with their own anthropologist," that "must cast severe doubt upon the degree to which aboriginal people do retain knowledge of their traditions and laws." He continued, arguing that if the Kokatha held specialized knowledge of the Roxby Downs area, then they "would not require the assistance of white advisors in this matter, and would be too proud to accept it."[104] In making claims so painfully ignorant of the colonial nature of legislative processes relating to land rights, Goldsworthy dismissed the validity of Kokatha knowledge, not least by implying that the Kokatha knew little about the region. But Goldsworthy's attack also sought to dispel any hope the Kokatha might have for pursuing land rights over their lands.

The suspicion cast by Goldsworthy over the KPC's request for an anthropologist was accompanied by a vehement rejection of any inkling that the South Australian government would be willing to entertain land rights claims. In April 1981, the Kokatha's lawyer had written to Goldsworthy to advise him that the Kokatha's decision to hire their own anthropologist for the EIS may slow down the formal negotiation process.[105] Goldsworthy drafted three letters in reply. Two of these were never sent, but their tone is unmistakable.[106] In the first—boldly crossed through and accompanied by a stern note that it was "NOT TO BE SENT"—Goldsworthy wrote, "I wish to make it quite clear that claims to land at Roxby Downs or elsewhere in the region will not be recognised by the Government and would seek to dispel false expectations which might be nurtured now that could lead to disappointment . . . in the future."[107] In the second, he declared, "Claims for land rights at Roxby Downs . . . [do] not have the support of the State Government."[108] And the final letter included a diluted version of the two drafts, exaggerating the Kokatha's attempts to negotiate on their own terms in such a way as to suggest that they were attempting to deceive the government to secure land rights, and thus veto resource extraction.

Such suggestions contradicted the desire of the community, which was—first and foremost—to protect their sacred sites. In an exchange between Wingfield and Kinhill Engineering, the former powerfully reiterated that the Kokatha were not interested in preventing Olympic Dam from going ahead. Rather, they wished to have their sites protected, which Wingfield felt "obliged" to reiterate: "The fundamental concerns of the Kokatha Group is to have the sacred sites of our people preserved. In that regard, we are as anxious as you are to have an anthropological survey done as soon as possible, our concern is more immediate than one based solely on proposed new developments."[109] This was not news to the Department of Mines and Energy. In 1981, a South Australian Liberal senator made this exact point to Goldsworthy, imploring his colleague to take the claims of the Kokatha seriously given the increasingly tense relationship between resource extraction and Aboriginal affairs. The senator wrote to the minister, acknowledging "the need to develop the area concerned in the interests of the economic welfare of the State." However, he also articulated his fear that the Kokatha would be alienated in the process. "I am . . . aware of the history of previous Australian mining ventures and the way in which the aboriginal people have been accommodated," he wrote. He emphasized, "It was made clear to me that the Kokatha Committee is not against developments but would appreciate a continuing dialogue to ensure that the significant sacred areas are preserved."[110] Goldsworthy did not heed that warning.

Further complicating matters for the Kokatha, the state government amended the Aboriginal Heritage Act in 1981 to reduce its powers. To ensure that bids to protect sacred sites could not continually plague resource extraction, the Department of Mines and Energy proposed that Aboriginal sites and items, as defined by the Aboriginal Heritage Act, be restricted "to those identified and acknowledged by the Government to be significant at the time the EIS [wa]s completed."[111] This amendment created significant time pressure for the Kokatha by ensuring that only those sites identified prior to the completion of the mine's EIS were recognized as in need of protection. Predictably, the Kokatha were unable to secure the funding to hire their own anthropologist in time, and Olympic Dam's EIS was accepted incomplete.

When the Joint Venturers published their EIS in 1982, its section on Aboriginal heritage excluded considerations of anthropological significance. In place of its anthropological assessment, the report included a note that detailed the apparent difficulty the Joint Venturers had encountered while negotiating with the Kokatha. As an "agreement on an approach to anthropological research was still to be reached with the Kokatha," the report concluded that it had "not been possible to conduct anthropological surveys of the Study Area."[112] Despite the fact that the Kokatha had attempted to negotiate with the Joint Venturers and Kinhill on recognizing their specific interests in and knowledge of the Olympic Dam area, their claims could not be legally substantiated without the approval of a designated anthropologist. As with many contemporary negotiations between mining companies and Aboriginal communities, the onus had been placed on the community to muster (and then pay for) the resources necessary to negotiate within short timeframes.

However, in November 1982, South Australia's Labor Party defeated Goldsworthy and his fellow ministers at the polls and returned to power, renewing hope that progress on land rights would be achieved in the state. Many within John Bannon's Labor party had been fierce opponents of the Liberal party's approach to both uranium mining and Aboriginal issues between 1979 and 1982, with the new premier himself openly criticizing Olympic Dam's Joint Venturers for their "uncompromising and cynical attitude" toward Aboriginal people.[113] Prior to taking over the premiership,

Bannon had argued that the Liberal party could not—morally—commit South Australia to an unknown nuclear future by zealously approving Olympic Dam within months of an election and years ahead of the mine being ready to operate. Bannon was a strong proponent for honoring Labor's commitment to phasing out uranium mining, arguing that allowing Olympic Dam's unfettered operation through the passage of the 1982 Roxby Downs (Indenture Ratification) Act would "commit the people of this State to the nuclear fuel industry as of 1982, with no regard to the circumstances or the conditions that might prevail if and when the project d[id] go ahead." He continued, "It means that now in 1982, we give up our right to decide this vital question for the rest of this decade and beyond."[114] For many Labor politicians, Bannon among them, uranium mining at Olympic Dam promised to tie the broader Australian population into a nuclear future that many resisted and feared.

But with an election to win, Bannon conceded to the state's development goals, promising that Olympic Dam would go ahead if Labor won the 1982 South Australian election over the incumbent Liberal government. The project theoretically aligned with the ALP's federal policy on uranium mining in Australia, which permitted the mining of uranium alongside other minerals such as copper, silver, and gold.[115] Olympic Dam was abundant in all of these minerals. Thus, in taking power, Labor "acted in good faith in honouring the Indenture and all existing Government commitments to the [Olympic Dam] project," including the EIS, which Bannon acknowledged had significant shortcomings.[116] One of these shortcomings was its lack of an anthropological survey. The EIS neither recorded nor acknowledged any Kokatha sacred sites.

The Destruction of Canegrass Swamp

On the morning of 20 July 1983, dust kicked up behind an old four-wheel drive (4WD) as it traversed the sandy hills surrounding Roxby Downs. Driven by Kokatha Elder Ningel Reid, the beat-up 4WD handled badly; the brakes were sticky, and the going was slow.[117] The vehicle was accompanied by new 4WDs, vehicles that took the turns and bumps of the sandhills and claypans with ease. Tailing them was a bulldozer, headed for Canegrass

Swamp, a small seasonal wetland named for its tussocky cane grass, nestled within the Olympic Dam mine site, nearly 62 miles (100 kilometers) north of Woomera, west of Lake Torrens. Rocky outcrops dot the region, indicating where Aboriginal Dreaming sites—sites associated with creation—track the desert.

At Canegrass Swamp, several important places intersected. The anthropologist Rod Hagen confirmed in 1983 that the area was the home of the *kalta*, an ancient sleepy lizard who rests underground. Mining disturbs the *kalta*, evoking its wrath and upsetting Country. Sleepy lizards abound in the central deserts and are reflective of the health and abundance of Country for Kokatha and other communities. The evocation of the angered *kalta* is still mobilized today by anti–Olympic Dam protesters through campaigns such as Lizard's Revenge, organized by the late Arabunna Elder Kevin Buzzacott.[118]

Hagen also noted, along with other anthropologists, that the claypan was significant to the story of the Seven Sisters, a foundational narrative of "flight and pursuit, as the sisters flee the unwanted attentions of a sorcerer who pursues them." Reflected in the Pleiades constellation, the Seven Sisters forged the landscape as they fled their pursuer, manifesting in "a landscape that seethes and ripples with [the] sexual desire" and violence of the pursuer and the strength and resilience of the Sisters.[119] In July 1983, millennia after it was forged by this pursuit, the landscape was once again being traversed, this time by surveyors intent on constructing a road designed to service mining vehicles and heavy machinery for Olympic Dam.

As the day wore on, Reid and the Kokatha men who accompanied him—KPC chairman Max Thomas and Elder Willie Williams—expressed their concern about the reliability of their 4WD.[120] Still, the party pushed on, identifying various sites of significance and negotiating deviations in the proposed road as they went. Representatives of Roxby Management Services (RMS)—the body tasked with the construction of the mine—agreed to these shifts in course, drawing on Kokatha knowledge of the landscape to guide them. As the convoy ran out of daylight, the parties agreed that they would reconvene the following day. The Kokatha men camped 11 miles (19 kilometers) from Andamooka, but when they woke the following morning, their vehicle would not start. Futile efforts to start the engine resulted in two of the party hiking three hours to Andamooka for help. The men arrived at the rendezvous point several hours late. Upon arrival, their 4WD broke down entirely, shedding "metal and oil in great profusion," rendering it useless. With the lifeless 4WD before them, RMS representatives accepted that the Kokatha's delay was outside of their control.[121] Alas, in their absence, the show had to go on. The bulldozer proceeded without Kokatha guidance.

Hearing this news, the Kokatha men hastily asked to assess the damage. Proceeding along the route, the men explained to their lawyer that the bulldozer had destroyed a sacred site, disrupting several rocky outcrops that may have appeared insignificant to RMS workers but which, for the Kokatha, were representative of the *kalta* and Seven Sisters Dreamings.[122] John Showers, of RMS, admitted that he had permitted the continuation of bulldozing without the Kokatha, as "he had been unwilling to hold up work."[123] In its own report on the incident, RMS noted that "the aboriginal party expressed concern at the RMS decision to bulldoze the remaining short section without joint agreement."[124] Unfortunately, it was too late.

From this point onward, negotiations between RMS and the Kokatha broke down. Angry and frustrated letters flew back and forth. Several telegrams from neighboring Aboriginal communities and other interested parties requested that the state government halt the development of Olympic Dam until the protection of Aboriginal sacred sites could be guaranteed. Unfortunately for the Kokatha, South Australia's new minister for mines and energy emphasized that the destruction did not technically breach the Olympic Dam EIS, for "protection provided under the Roxby Downs Indenture to Aboriginal people with associations in the area had been limited because of the non-completion of site surveys by the specified date."[125] However, in an effort to try and alleviate this public relations disaster, Bannon and the Labor government did commit to having the area reassessed. Meanwhile, Kokatha people—including Elder Max Thomas, who had inspected RMS's destruction at Canegrass Swamp—protested at the mine site alongside environmentalists who had traveled from the nation's major cities (fig. 8).

In light of this incident, the government hired renowned anthropologist Ronald Berndt to compile a report on the significance of Canegrass Swamp and its sacred sites to the Kokatha. In agreement with earlier assessments

FIGURE 8. The destruction of Canegrass Swamp drew ire from neighboring Aboriginal communities and passionate anti-uranium activists, some of whom traveled to Kokatha Country to join Kokatha Elders Eileen Wani Wingfield (*center*) and Max Thomas (*center, leaning against a car*) in protest. Photograph courtesy of the Wingfield family.

by anthropologists, as well as the Kokatha's own claims, Berndt concluded: "The Kokatha people (and those affiliated with them) not only have a continuing, traditionally-phrased interest in the Olympic Dam mining area, but look upon that area as their land." He continued, "[This] constitute[s] a legitimate, traditionally based interest and justif[ies] their right to insist on the protection of sites which they designate."[126] In receiving Berndt's report, Premier Bannon's advisers noted that his conclusions had the potential to create further fears regarding purported "land grabs" by Aboriginal communities. Providing Bannon with notes on Berndt's report, an adviser wrote: "[The report] introduced the notion of land rights for Aboriginals who are not living traditionally. It should be recognised that the Project Area is not Aboriginal land in that sense. The result of favouring the KPC in this respect may be a proliferation of land claims by other groups, including over existing projects, and conceivably in areas not related to mining."[127] In other words, Berndt's conclusions supported the provision of inalienable land rights to areas subject to development.

Such a stalwart commitment to land rights made government officials uneasy. Consequently, while the Labor government committed to granting money for the completion of Berndt's study, it decided that it could not accept the anthropologist's recommendation of granting inalienable land rights to the Kokatha. Doing so, officials argued, "would establish significant precedents in the areas of land rights and compensation which would have a far reaching effect both on new and existing development." Land rights for the Kokatha, which would inevitably jeopardize Olympic Dam, had the potential to inspire further land rights claims from communities across the state and the country. Considering this possibility, the Bannon government agreed that it "should maintain some degree of detachment from the Berndt Report, not treating it as a brief . . . but rather as an input into the decision making process."[128] Olympic Dam would go ahead unimpeded.

Half a decade later, at the mine's grand opening in November 1988, Bannon stated that uranium mining "remain[ed] an emotional and divisive issue."[129] This was certainly the case for the KPC, whose secretary Joan Wingfield had spent several months in the lead-up to the mine's opening trekking across Europe "driven by a determination to focus world attention on the plight of her people." She was met with considerable sympathy in West Germany in particular, and "the Germans turned out in their hundreds for Ms Wingfield."[130] For Wingfield, who had just turned thirty when Olympic Dam opened, the mine represented the potential destruction of her Country and, with it, her people, her culture, and the livelihoods of future generations. For the Bannon government, the mine marked a new "chapter in the development of one of th[e] country's great adventures in mineral exploration."[131] With this characterization, and the acknowledgment that Olympic Dam remained "emotional and divisive," the South Australian premier encapsulated the clash inherent between development and Aboriginal rights at the mine. By demonstrating how, in this instance, uranium mining took precedence over meaningful engagement with Aboriginal land rights, the destruction of Canegrass Swamp is emblematic of broader processes of colonial imposition that wrestle land rights away from Indigenous communities for the benefit of the nuclear industry.

As Kokatha and others predicted, Olympic Dam has been implicated to date in a number of environmental calamities. First, the mine's entitlement to pump up to 42 million liters of water per day from the Great Artesian

Basin has raised significant questions over Aboriginal water rights in the region. Arabunna Elder Kevin Buzzacott was particularly vocal about this issue, advocating for both the cessation of pumping by the Broken Hill Proprietary Company (BHP) and payment to communities for the theft of their water.[132] More recently, the drying up of desert springs across South Australia has drawn greater attention to the mine's use of artesian water.[133] Second, the mine's tailings ponds, where mine refuse is mixed with water and stored, have plagued operations. Contaminants produced by the mine have poisoned innumerable animals that flock to these ponds thinking they are wetlands. Over the years, numerous investigations have been undertaken into the death of waterbirds, which, alighting on these toxic water bodies to drink, bathe, and feed, have died in the hundreds.[134] Government investigations have also drawn attention to the inadequacy of the mine's tailings system, which experts suspect have facilitated the contamination of the surrounding environment and its waters for decades.[135] Present alongside these calamities have been Aboriginal voices imploring the government and the companies responsible to treat Country with the respect and care it deserves.

A Great Adventure?

In the 1980s, nuclear issues contended with increased Aboriginal visibility on the subject of land rights. Previously, proponents of radium mining and nuclear testing had capitalized on structural and racial silences that ensured such activities could take place with little resistance. However, by the time Canegrass Swamp was destroyed, uranium mining's nuclearity was well-founded and Aboriginal land rights had come rapidly to the fore. The economic and geopolitical promises of an Australian uranium industry now contended with the unprecedented Aboriginal political mobilization of the 1970s and 1980s.

As a result, Olympic Dam was simultaneously subject to greater scrutiny from critics than were other large-scale mining projects *and* viewed as one of the "great adventures" of mineral exploration in Australia. For proponents of Australia's exportation of uranium, this adventure relied on companies' freedom to explore, mine, and acquire wealth, unhindered by Aboriginal claimants. And for many of the mine's critics, the venture risked ending up a reckless foray into the global nuclear industry, with the potential to further alienate Aboriginal communities and their rights. By mobilizing colonial rhetoric and manipulating emergent legislation, Goldsworthy and his colleagues were able to ensure the alienation of potential Aboriginal claimants, such that uranium mining would proceed unfettered. For their role in this process, successive South Australian Liberal and Labor governments, as well as proponents of mining, demonstrated their prioritization of (nuclear) development over Aboriginal assertions of their rights to protect their lands.

While the same might be said of other large-scale mining ventures in Australia—both in this period and since—the intergenerational and insidious nature of radioactive contamination, and uranium's potential to contribute to unthinkable human and environmental catastrophes, sets uranium mining apart. Even proponents of the industry lauded its uniqueness, citing Australia's moral obligations to extract and export uranium in order to fuel an energy-hungry world. This singularity was captured by Bannon in 1988 when he noted that uranium mining remained an "emotional and divisive issue" in South Australia.[136] After all, it was—and is—the nuclear aspect of this development that divided and provoked most vehemently, partnering hope for economic wealth with persistent colonial subjugation *and* the potential contamination of environments and those who enjoy them.

Public fears regarding the potential of contamination from nuclear processes were crystallized in the mid-1980s as several scientific studies undertaken at Emu Field and Maralinga shed light on the inadequacy of previous cleanup efforts. Prompted by these studies, politicians and the public called on Australia's prime minister to conduct a formal inquiry into the British nuclear tests in Australia, which led to the establishment of a Royal Commission. In large part due to the testimonies of Aboriginal witnesses before this commission, growing numbers of the Australian public began to draw clearer links between ongoing Aboriginal dispossession, displacement, and colonialism and Aboriginal peoples' experiences of Australia's nuclear past, present, and future.

FIVE

Unearthing the Hidden Histories of the Tests

Against the backdrop of burgeoning land rights, the imposition of new large-scale uranium mines, and growing concerns over contamination, Britain's nuclear tests in Australia came under greater scrutiny from an increasingly educated public. In June 1984, Tina Saunders wrote to the editor of the *Canberra Times* to call "as an Aboriginal of Australia . . . for a Royal Commission into this issue": "the Maralinga issue."[1] The impact of Britain's tests, she described, was a "blot on the conscience of humanity, a disgrace that has been with us, the Aboriginal people, for almost 30 years." She spoke of the long-lasting impact of the blasts: decades of "whispers around campfires," recollections of people dying, "hacking coughs," "running eyes," and "peeling skin." All the while, she said, "the perpetrators of this crime walked amongst us protected." At the time that Saunders put pen to paper, discussions of Maralinga Tjarutja's dispossession from their irradiated lands were circulating, eliciting questions as to whether the return of contaminated land was "the price" to "pay (as the original inhabitants of this land) for land rights."[2]

The contents of Saunders's letter reflected the transformative nature of land rights debates in Australia. The contamination of Country was no longer an acceptable consequence of technological and military superiority to Australians, not least Aboriginal peoples within Australia, whose voices were becoming difficult for the government to ignore. However, it was not a straightforward progression from the denial of Aboriginal voice to its embrace. Nor was it a case of the Australian government *choosing* to platform Aboriginal experiences of dispossession in acknowledgment of the persistent nature of colonialism. Rather, when Bob Hawke's Labor government gave in to public pressure and called the Royal Commission into British Nuclear Tests in Australia (1984–85), the inquiry's parameters were designed to actively shy away from discussions of Australia's colonial complicity. Instead, the commission applied a "hierarchy of tragedy" to its investigations, with irradiation firmly at the top.[3]

Royal Commissions—Australia's highest form of investigation into matters of interest to the Australian people—are designed to examine events, determine accountability, and make recommendations to the government on policy and legislative changes. The Royal Commission into British Nuclear Tests in Australia aimed to investigate the safety standards of Britain's nuclear tests in the 1950s (chapter 2). But, in many ways, it became an opportunity for those in power to challenge the Anglophilic predilections of Robert Menzies's government and put distance between the contemporary Australian government and people and the consequences of the tests. The Royal Commission ultimately placed blame for the tests' worst impacts on the British government and its "Anglophilic" allies, including Prime Minister Menzies and Australia's scientific representatives. However, Aboriginal testimonies to the commission demonstrated that Aboriginal dispossession was one of the tests' key human costs and that there was no denying the Australian government had been fundamentally complicit in this process. These revelations expanded Australians' consideration of nuclear colonialism's impacts. So, while the commission was not designed to consider the broader effects of colonization on the peoples of desert South Australia, the stories Aboriginal people told the Royal Commission revealed the multifaceted effects of nuclear colonialism as experienced in the central deserts over a period of more than thirty years.

As a result of its engagement with Aboriginal nuclear survivors throughout its hearings, the Royal Commission was ultimately unable to ignore the issue of displacement. Aboriginal dispossession and displacement were thus revealed as particularly devastating consequences of the tests, despite the commission's initial intent to focus on irradiation effects only. According to the historian Heather Goodall, who worked on the Royal Commission, this focus on irradiation indicated settler Australians' reluctance to accept forms of catastrophe—such as colonialism—"for which we, as much as the British generals, could be held responsible."[4] The emphasis Aboriginal survivors of the tests placed on dispossession and displacement, as well as Australia's active role in such processes, assisted in fueling Aboriginal mobilization against nuclear issues over the preceding and succeeding decades and continue to underpin contemporary engagement with Australia's nuclear past.

Initiating an Inquiry

A lot occurred in the three decades between Britain's first inland nuclear test, which had ripped through the central deserts on 15 October 1953, and the initiation of the Royal Commission into British Nuclear Tests in 1984.[5] Throughout that time, many Aboriginal communities remained barred from their lands, housed in missions, and suffering the consequences of systemic colonialism, mourning their separation from Country. Politicians and members of the public who voiced their concerns regarding contamination were consistently reassured of the test sites' safety. Cleanups had tried—and largely failed—to remove contaminants from the region, while the public's attention often turned to French nuclear testing in the Pacific, an issue of great consequence to Australia's environment. By the early 1980s, it was clear that Britain's conduct during its testing program had far-reaching consequences for Australians, and many endeavored to draw attention to its impact.

It is in this context that calls for a national inquiry into the tests began, culminating in the Royal Commission into British Nuclear Tests. Kick-starting discussions in 1977, the leader of the Labor Party, then in opposition, demanded that a judicial inquiry be held into inconsistent statements made by various Australian ministers about the safety of Britain's testing program on Australian soil.[6] Following this demand, a large amount of abandoned plutonium was discovered at the Taranaki testing site, one of Maralinga's more heavily contaminated sites used for testing Britain's weapons during Operation Antler in 1957. In the wake of this discovery, South Australian Premier Don Dunstan implored Prime Minister Malcolm Fraser to conduct an inquiry into the disposal of nuclear waste at Maralinga, the process of which had clearly been inadequate.[7] Fraser successfully negotiated the removal of the plutonium by the British government, but he did not initiate a formal inquiry. In fact, no inquiry was held under his leadership. But calls continued, gaining momentum. The demands of politicians were soon accompanied by those of the public, who were becoming increasingly aware of the (nuclear) atrocities inflicted on Aboriginal communities across the central deserts.

In 1983, Yankunytjatjara man Yami Lester lodged a writ with the South Australian Supreme Court to claim damages as a result of negligence during the tests.[8] As a young boy, Lester had lived in the central deserts with his family and had experienced what survivors refer to as the "black mist," a roiling, oily black cloud that engulfed communities camped at Wallatinna following one of Britain's nuclear tests. As described in the opening pages of this book, Lester went blind in the years after this cloud rolled through his Country. He maintained until his death that it had been his exposure to radioactive contamination that had blinded him.[9]

Lester's writ coincided with surges in the peace and antinuclear movements that encouraged protesters to march in support of nuclear disarmament across Australia and the wider world. Where previously Australian members of the New Left had paid attention to the nuclear tests underway in the Pacific, in March 1983 protesters wielded picket signs that referenced Britain's tests in the deserts.[10] Only a month later, an investigative journalist at the British newspaper *The Observer* reported that "Aborigines were blinded, burnt, and 'perhaps died in appreciable numbers' following British nuclear tests in Australia."[11] And in July 1983, the University of New South Wales's student newspaper *Tharunka* reported that "10 representatives of the Aboriginal people" were in Vanuatu "at a conference for a Denuclearised and Decolonised Pacific" to publicize the use of Aboriginal land for "nuclear testing . . . dumping of waste" and uranium mining.[12] This conference was hosted by the Nuclear Free and Independent Pacific movement, which had been established nearly a decade earlier, in 1975, and would become an increasingly influential source of antinuclear activism in the Pacific region.[13] By the early 1980s, Australia's nuclear past was being drawn into a broader history of global nuclear atrocities, a conversation that was occurring alongside burgeoning calls for land rights.

It was in light of such developments that, in early 1984, John Bannon's government declared its intention to return the Maralinga lands to their Traditional Owners through the Maralinga Tjarutja Land Rights Act.[14] The region in which the nuclear tests had taken place belonged predominantly to the Southern Pitjantjatjara and Yankunytjatjara people. At the time the act was handed down, the community's lawyer explained that

"'Tjarutja' means 'down from.'" Thus, referring to the community represented by the 1984 Maralinga Tjarutja Land Rights Act as Maralinga Tjarutja reflected their experiences of being "the people brought down from Maralinga."[15] By recognizing the community as such, this act acknowledged Maralinga Tjarutja dispossession and made provisions for their return to Country.

However, the lands at Maralinga had not been adequately decontaminated for human habitation. As the historian Tim Rowse evocatively put it: "There were no political costs in giving Aṉangu title to radioactive dirt."[16] As a result, the "return" of these unceded lands remained largely symbolic due to the risk of residual contamination to community members. Understandably, Maralinga Tjarutja possessed a strong desire to return to their Country as soon as possible.[17] But the community also remained genuinely concerned about residual contamination on that Country.[18] Cleaning up Maralinga Tjarutja lands to a level fit for habitation would require significant resources and money, neither of which Maralinga Tjarutja possessed. And to complicate matters further, the initiation of a formal inquiry, such as a Royal Commission, would considerably delay the process of cleaning up the lands.[19]

Echoing the concerns of Maralinga Tjarutja, general and widespread public and political anxiety over the health effects experienced by those exposed to the tests resulted in several scientific studies into the residual contamination at Maralinga and Emu Field. These studies drew into significant doubt the safety of the purportedly rehabilitated sites. The most consequential study was undertaken by the Expert Committee on the Review of Data on Atmospheric Fallout Arising from British Nuclear Tests in Australia. Formed in May 1984 after the discovery of widespread nuclear contaminants across the Maralinga range, this study catalyzed greater discussion of the tests and their long-term impacts.[20] Sydney-based physician and professor Charles Kerr, president of the Expert Committee, handed down its report in June 1984, concluding that there was need for a national inquiry into the tests due to fears that the sites' contamination was far more severe and widespread than previously thought.[21] This recommendation received support from those who had been imploring the government to look more closely at the conduct of the tests. One such individual was John Bannon, South Australia's Labor premier.

Bannon had appealed to the Hawke federal government for a national inquiry into Aboriginal health effects before the formation of the Expert Committee. Bannon wrote to the prime minister in March 1984 announcing his initiation of a South Australian–specific study into the effects of weapons testing on the state's Aboriginal population. The premier's aim was "to determine whether or not Aboriginal people ha[d] suffered radiation illness."[22] By April—and much to the federal government's embarrassment—the premier had informed the British government of an even larger-scale inquiry he planned to undertake.[23] Writing to British Prime Minister Margaret Thatcher, Bannon requested that "the British Government release all relevant material relating to the Maralinga tests."[24] When Kerr handed down the report of the Expert Committee (also known as the Kerr Report) in June, he recommended that the Australian government follow Bannon's lead, "subsuming" his inquiry and conducting a "major investigation into the effects and consequences of British nuclear tests on Aboriginal people."[25] Following the tabling of the Kerr Report, and amid conversations among politicians, the federal minister for resources and energy, Peter Walsh, and his colleagues began debating options for the inquiry.[26]

As rumors of a possible public inquiry into the nuclear tests trickled out of the halls of Parliament, pressure mounted on the government to account for damages incurred by Aboriginal communities in particular. Importantly, these requests were not limited to past damages, or even just to health effects, and insisted that less tangible impacts be considered. The Aboriginal Land Rights Movement Incorporated, writing on behalf of the community displaced to Yalata, contended that the inquiry needed to account for "the possible problems Aboriginal people may face today and in the future as a result of the tests."[27] Such problems included dispossession and dislocation, as well as the negative effects of communities having lived in and around missions, indefinitely barred from Country and exposed to alcohol through a beer canteen opened at Yalata in 1969 and other proximate licensed venues. John Liddle and Trevor Cutter from the Central Australian Aboriginal Congress implored Walsh and Hawke to consider those "people [who] died as a direct result of . . . dislocation."[28] These requests were echoed by the federal minister for education and youth affairs, Susan Ryan, who wrote to Walsh in June 1984 suggesting that the "consequences of forceable relocation of Aboriginal people away from the testing sites" be a focus of the inquiry. She noted that the effects of such dislocation "could be more widespread, and less immediate" than direct exposure to radiation.[29]

Suggestions that any inquiry should include dispossession as a consequence of the nuclear tests were swiftly and clearly dismissed. Walsh wrote to Ryan, as well as several others who had highlighted the need to account for effects beyond irradiation, arguing that such a "proposed extension of the terms of reference to include the effects of dislocation . . . would introduce much broader issues than the intended focus of the Inquiry."[30] Instead, the preference within the government was for a public inquiry that would extend well beyond Aboriginal communities. This would ensure that the concerns of Aboriginal communities and their spokespeople and allies could be addressed by the commission's investigations, but would be sufficiently limited to avoid questions of Australia's colonial complicity.

When Hawke wrote to Bannon in July 1984 with the news that he would soon call for the establishment of a Royal Commission into the British nuclear test, the announcement did not receive the praise the prime minister might have expected. Bannon in his response had "no doubt that a Royal Commission into these tests [wa]s justified," but he was concerned that it fell short of expectations.[31] The chairman of the Pitjantjatjara Council had expressed the same concern as Bannon only weeks prior, writing to the prime minister with his view that it was time the federal government took the conclusions of the Kerr Report seriously.[32] A Royal Commission, Premier Bannon highlighted, was only "part of the package of measures" he and others had "sought from the Commonwealth."[33] Bannon expressed disappointment that the health effects experienced by Aboriginal people would not be the sole focus of the inquiry. Nor would the impacts of colonialism.

The government had been careful not to open up the inquiry to questions of colonialism for fear of opening a floodgate. Walsh's opinion on the matter was that including questions of dislocation during the nuclear testing in the inquiry's investigations would lead to discussions of "the dislocation of traditional aboriginal life since the settlement of Australia by white men began."[34] This was not something that Canberra wanted to emphasize during the inquiry, as it risked connecting Australia directly to the negative impacts Aboriginal people experienced during the testing program. It would also draw attention to the structural inequalities created by colonialism that persisted even under the Hawke government.

The topic of *who* was complicit in Australian colonialism was especially sensitive in the mid-1980s, as the bicentenary of Anglo-European invasion loomed in 1988. In this context, the Royal Commission appeared to respond to a contemporary Australian mood, punctuated by a growing anti-British nationalism. This was a mood, *The Times* (London) noted, "that look[ed] at the British-dominated past, in the run-in to the country's bicentennial, with a deep distaste."[35] But Hawke's vision for the celebration of the bicentenary also echoed his approach to the issue of the nuclear testing: Australians could acknowledge the "grim and harsh reality of the origins of modern Australia," but the history of the first two hundred years of Australia should not be reduced to "collective and irredeemable guilt."[36] Across the Australian political spectrum, this sentiment reflected a general fear of the consequences of admitting fault for the dispossession and dislocation of Aboriginal people.

In particular, the federal government held concerns about the impact such admissions could have on land rights claims. In discussing the need for an inquiry, the Hawke cabinet acknowledged: "Maralinga is just one of the many instances of past dispossession and dispersal—indeed taken to its extreme," but "the whole continent is involved."[37] This encouraged his cabinet to speculate that including such discussions in the inquiry could be risky, as any "formal recognition of past dispossession and dispersal (or 'loss of use and enjoyment of land')" as a result of the tests would "set a precedent for a multitude of similar demands." Making the government's stance on the matter abundantly clear, the cabinet concluded that "the facts of the matter," as they saw them, were that "the Maralinga lands were not formally recognised as Aboriginal land at the time of the tests" and that "the provision of compensation for dispossession would therefore set a precedent for other claims from Aboriginals in respect of lost traditional land."[38] Moreover, the cabinet believed that the nation's obligations to Maralinga Tjarutja had already been fulfilled by South Australia's granting of formal title to their lands through the 1984 Maralinga Tjarutja Land Rights Act. The federal government viewed any further concessions—such as compensation for dispossession or the contamination of Country—as a "danger," capable of opening "a Pandora's box in Aboriginal Affairs."[39]

Nestled together in this Pandora's box were Labor's divisive and controversial policies on both nuclear issues and land rights in the early 1980s. In the years of the Royal Commission, both nuclear and land rights debates were wrought with emotion, dividing both the Australian Labor Party (ALP) and its supporters.[40] Yet both debates were largely avoided during the Royal Commission.Their absence is noteworthy for several reasons. First, the extent to which constituents resented Hawke's 1977 turn toward uranium mining should not be underestimated. It is conceivable that the government established the Royal Commission to alleviate some of the public pressure placed on Labor in the wake of Hawke's abandonment of the party's uranium moratorium in the late 1970s. By committing itself to investigating the British nuclear tests, the ALP could demonstrate that it took nuclear issues seriously, despite continuing to support the development of both the Ranger and Olympic Dam uranium deposits under its newly minted "three-mines policy." This policy, adopted by the ALP in 1984, restricted uranium mining to a maximum of three mines across the country, protecting uranium exports while failing to acknowledge and legally recognize Aboriginal land rights over such resource-rich regions.[41] This policy prompted a fracture in the ALP, one that birthed the Nuclear Disarmament Party.[42]

In addition to Labor's complicated relationship with uranium mining, the Hawke government struggled with issues of national land rights following its election in 1983. Running up to the election, Hawke had promised "national, uniform land rights legislation" if his party was successful at the polls.[43] Yet, once in power, the Western Australian Labor premier refused to comply with such reform and made a successful push to protect mining in his state. The Western Australian government's vehement opposition to land rights, in support of and backed by outspoken bodies and companies such as the Western Australian Chamber of Mines and Energy, Australian Mining Industry Council, and Western Mining Corporation, put an end to Labor's national land rights promise.[44] As prominent Aboriginal activist Kevin Cook articulated: "Once again Aboriginal people are left with only scraps."[45] In light of such failures, the federal Labor government sought to avoid discussions of land rights during the Royal Commission, conceptualizing such conversations as well beyond the scope of the inquiry.

After much speculation and debate about the form that the inquiry should take, on 5 July 1984 Walsh officially announced that his government was initiating a Royal Commission, the highest level of inquiry available to it. Detailing the scope of the commission, the press release heralded: "Following consideration . . . the Government will be recommending to the Governor-General-in-Council the establishment of a Royal Commission to inquire into the British nuclear tests in Australia between 1952 and 1963."[46] The announcement detailed the commission's intent to investigate the "measures that were taken for protection against the harmful effects of exposure to ionising radiation . . . on any persons but with particular reference to Australian service personnel and civilian employees . . . Royal Australian Navy personnel . . . Royal Australian Air Force personnel . . . Aboriginals and other civilians."[47] The parameters that bound the Royal Commission determined a scope that would cover issues from the nature of the firing conditions to the disposal of materials. Importantly, the human impacts of the tests on Aboriginal people and others were only to be considered in relation to evidence that suggested "exposure to ionising radiation" or direct irradiation. For the commissioners, therefore, their focus would be on whether people were irradiated, excluding the broader suite of colonial catastrophes entangled with the tests. The dispossession and dislocation of communities would not be under scrutiny.[48]

Despite these arguably limited parameters, what the commissioners ultimately explored deviated from what the inquiry had set out to investigate. Largely, this was on account of the visceral images conjured up by the Royal Commission's evidence, both in the form of archival material and oral testimony. In fact, the commission's condemnation of the British and their "Anglophilic" allies in pursuit of an Australian nationalism could not avoid—and was in large part predicated on—narratives that highlighted Aboriginal exclusion both from the consideration of politicians and from their lands, at the times of the tests and in the decades since.

The Royal Commission Proceeds

The McClelland Commission, as the Royal Commission became known, has been popularly historicized as a one-man show due to its enigmatic commissioner and namesake, Justice James (Diamond Jim) McClelland.[49] But this inquiry was far from such. With proceedings undertaken in both Australia and Britain, and evidence collated through interviews and the gathering of documents, the Royal Commission's conclusions were indebted to a large team of commissioners, lawyers, scholars, and witnesses both on Australian soil and overseas. In Australia, the commission received submissions in the hundreds, and witnesses appeared before McClelland and his fellow commissioners, Jill Fitch and Worimi man William Jonas, in Sydney, Melbourne, Perth, Adelaide, Brisbane, Karratha, and desert South Australia. In England, the commissioners were received warmly by the press, as well as by witnesses who had managed to reap little from their own government in the way of compensation or information. The commission spent over a month in London, hearing the testimonies of British veterans and scientists who represented the United Kingdom during the testing program, while also attempting to wrangle classified documents from the tight fists of the British establishment. It was in London that McClelland became a "hero" figure for Australians looking to sever ties with Britain and its colonial legacies. But, through its nationalistic high theater, the commission drew greater attention to the ways that Aboriginal people were treated during the tests, not least in connection to the displacement many experienced.

Viewed retrospectively, the Royal Commission was a narrative-building exercise that supported the notion that the British were responsible for neglectfully subjecting their former colonies to unspeakable nuclear injustices.[50] Integral to the construction of this particular narrative was McClelland himself. A notable Labor man, "Diamond Jim" was described as an "embittered, colourful relic of the Whitlam Government" by one member of the conservative opposition.[51] Known for his dislike of the British—as well as for his flamboyance—McClelland's personal politics ensured that nationalism was central to the commission's inquiries. Capturing that, one Australian journalist likened the commission process to "a long, long cricket Test match between Australia and England": "We not only consistently outplayed the Poms, thanks to the Bradmanesque Diamond Jim McClelland, but also caught them cheating, bowling underarm, etc, again and again and made them look unspeakably shifty."[52] In juxtaposition to Britain's "shiftiness," McClelland and the Labor Party appeared "as the chief custodians of an independent Australian nationalism."[53] Meanwhile, Labor's predecessors, namely, Menzies's respective governments, were cast as "'anglophile' conservatives" or "local agents for British Imperial, rather than Australian national, interests."[54] This characterization was not lost on the British. *The Times* (London) reported that McClelland's conduct in Britain had "made him something of a folk hero in Australia," echoing the growing social consciousness and anti-British nature of pockets of the Australian population in the 1980s.[55] This is reflected in the popular characterization of McClelland as a Labor "hero" for his role in "sticking it" to a "perfidious Britain."[56]

McClelland's punishment of the British on behalf of an increasingly nationalistic and independent Australia has been recalled fondly by historians due to the flair with which it was executed.[57] Described as a "colorful raconteur with a sparkling wit," McClelland mobilized his proclivity for drama and "devastatingly sharp tongue" during the commission toward the goal of humiliating the "mother country."[58] This was aptly captured in the satirical Australian magazine *Matilda*. In its November 1985 issue, McClelland said of the British establishment: "Their attitude was that we'd find it too cold and if it was too hard to get what we wanted, we'd pack up and go home." McClelland's self-declared attitude was, "Fuck you bastards, we'll get what we want out of you."[59] His bluntness conjured glee within those who enjoyed watching the judge "tip buckets" on Britain and Australia's "sycophantic Anglophiles."[60]

However, McClelland's attempts to punish Britain failed to account for the intricacies in the Britain-Australia relationship during the 1950s, a relationship fostered by both liberal and conservative politicians. Casting the tests as a one-dimensional tale of imperial lust triumphing over a subservient dominion demonstrates a strategic ignorance toward the nuances of Britain and Australia's shifting relationship. The public condemnation of characters such as Menzies in pursuit of a "new," and decidedly anti-

British, Australian nationalism overlooked the broader facilitation of the testing program. Not only had Menzies's Labor predecessors in John Curtin and Ben Chifley paved the way for an Australian nuclear posture, but entrenched paternalistic policies toward Aboriginal communities facilitated their displacement. These aspects of the history were markedly absent from the commission's questioning of conservative politicians and scientists during the proceedings. Instead, and marking "the arrival of a post-imperial Australia," the commission became an important opportunity for Australia to symbolically sever ties with Britain.[61] In fact, the Royal Commission, according to an expert who worked on gathering evidence for the proceedings, "allowed the government to indicate . . . that the act of testing bombs in Australia was a British decision, supported by those with Anglophile tendencies with general (but predictable) colonial attitudes to those Aborigines who might be inconvenienced."[62] Those narratives that centered the negligence of the British and their Anglophilic allies in Australia had the effect of highlighting the exclusion faced by Aboriginal people during this historic episode, both literally from Country and figuratively from the consideration of experts and policymakers.

One way the commission shirked the idea of broader Australian complicity was its emphasis on the ignorance of those deemed part of the Anglophilic "old" order in Australia. These were individuals who, according to the commissioners, had failed to protect Aboriginal people. This charge was most vehemently laid against Menzies; the first dozen of the commissioners' conclusions referred to Menzies's blind support of the British and his active culpability in relation to the tests' worst outcomes, notably the irradiation of Aboriginal people.[63] The commissioners' condemnation of Menzies was discussed freely in the media, with even British journalists likening the commission to a posthumous trial of Menzies's character, referring to it as "a regicide." Menzies was put on "trial as a British quisling," *The Times* (London) reported.[64] Central to the trial of Menzies's character—and that of some of his contemporaries—was the assertion that he held Aboriginal life in contempt and consequently failed to protect communities.

This accusation was also leveled at the nuclear physicist Ernest Titterton, whose credentials as an Australian scientific representative at the tests were questioned for numerous reasons, including his British heritage, his involvement in the United States' first nuclear test at Alamogordo, and his vociferous support of all things nuclear.[65] Raised and educated in Britain, Titterton played an integral role in the Manhattan Project, facilitating the development of the United States' first nuclear weapon through his expertise in telemetry. Following the Second World War, Titterton returned to Britain, before being appointed the foundation head of physics at the Australian National University in 1951. By 1952, just months after Titterton's move to Canberra, Menzies asked him to represent the Australian scientific community during Britain's nuclear tests. Throughout the commission's proceedings, Titterton was repeatedly asked to answer for his nationality, accused of treachery by McClelland as a result of his Britishness. For McClelland and his fellow commissioners, Titterton's nationality and his unwavering dedication to the development of nuclear technologies (including weapons) cast a dubious light on his character, ensuring he fit the bill of a traitorous spy. The commissioners concluded that Titterton "played a political as well as a safety role in the testing program," with the physicist demonstrating that he was "prepared to conceal information from the Australian Government and his fellow Committee members if he believed to do so would suit the interests of the United Kingdom."[66] He was accused of being tasked by Britain with concealing information and, as a consequence, betraying Australia's people throughout the testing program. Integral to this interpretation was the commission's understanding that Menzies had charged Titterton with the job of protecting Aboriginal people, which he had evidently failed to do.

According to Titterton, in 1952 he received a summons from Menzies to meet him at Parliament House. Titterton hopped on his bike and rode the short distance from the Australian National University to the prime minister's office. There Menzies asked Titterton to be an Australian representative at the tests. Recalling this episode, Titterton told the commission that Menzies had professed: "In view of your experience, which is unique in Australia, of three nuclear weapons tests around the world, I would be glad if you would be prepared to go to the Monte Bellos to lend whatever help you can to Dr Penney's team . . . and at the same time to—well, essentially stick your oar in to make as certain as it is humanly possible . . . that there will be no adverse effects on the Australian people, flora and fauna, and in particular the aborigines."[67] Titterton reiterated, "From the first five minutes I was involved a major concern of the Australian Prime Minister was aborigines."[68] This comment became a key point of conflict between Titterton and the commission, as it provided the commissioners with what they understood as a clear indication of exactly *who* was to blame for the adverse impacts Aboriginal communities experienced, while Titterton asserted that various others bore responsibility.

During the extensive questioning of Titterton, the commissioners suggested that blame for harm to Aboriginal people should be placed on the physicist. In particular, the commissioners' questions returned frequently to the conversation Titterton had with Menzies in his office in 1952. "Did you understand that the prime minister, in saying those things to you, was casting on you some special responsibility with respect to the aboriginals?" the commissioners asked.[69] Titterton adamantly contested that, no, that was not how he or Menzies interpreted the brief. On another occasion, McClelland failed to conceal his contempt for both the physicist and the former prime minister, asking the physicist, "But Sir Ernest, do not I recall you saying that . . . one of the things that was impressed on you very early and very earnestly by the great constitutional lawyer, Sir Robert Menzies, was his concern for the aborigines?"[70] Bristling at the slight, Titterton responded yes, "that is right."[71] However, it did not naturally follow that Menzies's brief had conferred responsibility on Titterton. In fact, Titterton recalled, it was his Australian colleague and defense scientist William Butement's job to ensure the protection of Aboriginal people. By the 1980s, Butement's health had deteriorated substantially, and his interrogation by the commission was comparably brief. The commissioners made little attempt to pin Aboriginal harm on the ailing scientist. In contrast, Titterton's persecution fed seamlessly into the nationalistic politics of the commissioners and reinforced the narrative that Menzies was a hopeless Anglophile. Moreover, Titterton's clear ignorance of Aboriginal communities and their ways of life reiterated their exclusion from consideration both at the time of the tests and in the years thereafter.

During the Royal Commission, Titterton made numerous remarkably ignorant comments that assisted in both condemning his character and exposing the perceived contempt of Aboriginal life that he and others held.

When asked why he did not investigate the Monte Bello tests' potential impact on Aboriginal communities along the coast of Western Australia, Titterton retorted, "My university['s vice-chancellor], who wished to have me doing my job in Canberra, was not at all keen for me to do totally unnecessary work." "I think he would have taken a great deal of umbrage had I suggested that I should become an anthropologist and start investigating the people living on the north-west corner of Australia," he continued.[72] On another occasion he implied that Aboriginal people should not have been within the testing zone if they did not want to be affected. When pressed on this view, Titterton doubled down, suggesting that Aboriginal people should not have voted for the Menzies government if they disagreed with the tests, explaining that "democracy is a system where people elect the government to make decisions on their behalf."[73] Titterton was subsequently reminded that "Aborigines did not vote in those days," to which he responded that he did "not know about that."[74] Clearly, Titterton's consideration of Aboriginal people's claims throughout the Royal Commission worked to delegitimize and often belittle their accounts. And while the blame for harm inflicted on the Aboriginal population lies with the Australian and British governments writ large, Titterton became the face of the Menzies government's apparent neglect of Aboriginal Australians and blind support of its great and powerful friends.[75]

Such attempts to place blame for the injustices Aboriginal people experienced during the nuclear tests reflected a significant shift in the way that the Australian government and its constituents considered Aboriginal rights. Where, in the 1950s, the safety of Aboriginal communities was a mere footnote among the serious concerns of the Australian government, by the 1980s there was an inability to overlook the injustice of the tests given the shifts in social consciousness facilitated by local Aboriginal groups such as the Pitjantjatjara Council, land rights debates, and the emergence of various social movements. These shifts were highlighted by the United Kingdom's submission to the Royal Commission, which expressed Whitehall's opinion that the commission could only be useful if the tests were "not judged on the strength of 30 years' hindsight."[76] Nor, Britain argued, should the tests be considered independently of the "awareness that Australia's own attitude to the likely future use of the test sites and to the needs of its Aboriginal peoples ha[d] changed radically since the time of the tests."[77] Despite these pleas, in their 1985 report on the commission, McClelland and his colleagues concluded that "attempts to ensure Aboriginal safety" during the tests demonstrated the "ignorance, incompetence and cynicism on the part of those responsible for that safety."[78] Titterton was most vehemently implicated in this narrative, followed closely by Menzies. Continuing on, the commissioners argued: "The inescapable conclusion is that if Aborigines were not injured or killed as a result of the explosions, this was a matter of luck."[79]

But it was not just the effects of the physical explosions that McClelland, Fitch, and Jonas referenced in their conclusions. They also highlighted the "detrimental effects" of Aboriginal people being "kept away" from their lands, which the commissioners described as "important places."[80] They identified, too, the impact of their interactions with "intruders," evoking the sense of invasion many Aboriginal people would have felt as a result of the influx of scientists and military personnel to the region. The commissioners emphasized this point in their conclusions, irrespective of the Hawke government's attempts to avoid questions of Australia's colonial complicity during the proceedings.

Peter Walsh, the minister for resources and energy, had made it clear in 1983 that the issue of Aboriginal displacement was well outside the scope of the Royal Commission. There were seemingly too many potentially negative consequences of opening up the inquiry to issues of dispossession, including exposing the wrongs committed by settlers "since the settlement of Australia by white men began."[81] The Royal Commission nevertheless highlighted the visceral experience of displacement as a key manifestation of nuclear colonialism in Australia. Politicians and the public no longer understood the effects of the nuclear tests solely in relation to radiation. The tests were now implicated in the efforts of the state to remove Aboriginal people from their Country in pursuit of nuclear development.

Dislocation and Dispossession

In 1984, the lawyers Geoff Eames and Andrew Collett, anthropologists Maggie Brady and Kingsley Palmer, and historian Heather Goodall were all employed by various bodies and councils to work on the Royal Commission. While the commissioners were largely conducting their investigations in the comfort of courtrooms across Australia's major cities, Eames, Collett, Brady, Palmer, and Goodall joined a group of dedicated individuals whose roles took them to central South Australia. Collectively, they focused on determining what had happened to Aboriginal people as a result of the tests. In support of this mission, Brady and Palmer were tasked with interviewing as many people as they could from the Maralinga lands.[82] Goodall, based north of the testing sites at Ernabella, worked through the archived interview transcripts of Aboriginal people from Wallatinna and Ernabella.[83] And the Aboriginal legal counsel, consisting of Collett and Eames, built a legal case around this evidence to "represent all Aboriginal interests."[84] Those with whom Brady, Palmer, Eames, Collett, and Goodall spoke told harrowing stories of loss, physically, spiritually, and culturally; many recalled the confusion caused by the lack of information provided to them by authorities, while others alluded to the intergenerational trauma inflicted on their peoples by the dispossession at the heart of the tests.

The testimonies Aboriginal people provided to the Royal Commission highlighted a plethora of colonial impositions linked to the nuclear testing and its legacies. Their content was undoubtedly influenced by the developments in Aboriginal politics taking place across the twentieth century. The accounts of Aboriginal nuclear survivors placed their experiences during the tests (and since) into a broader political context, with pointed references to Aboriginal subjugation on missions, their lack of access to Country, the desires of communities to have their "homelands" returned, and the primacy of Aboriginal knowledge of Country. Importantly, these accounts were not isolated to the Royal Commission's proceedings. The stories told by Aboriginal witnesses garnered significant media interest and manifested in tangible cleanup efforts. Their revelatory power remains pertinent to contemporary understandings of the tests' greatest impacts.

In response to Aboriginal requests for meaningful inclusion in the Royal Commission, McClelland and his fellow commissioners undertook hearings in proximity to communities.[85] On 20 April 1985, McClelland commenced an open-air court in the central deserts at Marla Bore.[86] He was flanked by Fitch and Jonas, the latter of whom has since been described as a "powerful advocate for the rights" of Indigenous peoples, not least for his role as the principal of the Australian Institute of Aboriginal and Torres Strait Islander Studies.[87] Jonas's presence is thus notable. "Ladies and gentlemen," McClelland addressed the first informal hearing, held in the shelter of a garage, "I declare open the central Australian sittings of the royal commission."[88] "Nobody needs to stand up," he assured the seated attendees; "the proceedings will be completely informal."[89] Conducting the hearing as such was aimed at making "it possible for the Aboriginal people to give their evidence in circumstances which maximise[d] the convenience for themselves."[90] But it also marked an acknowledgment of the importance of the lands subjected to nuclear testing to those communities who had been displaced from them.

Eames, the Aboriginal communities' legal counsel, began the proceedings by acknowledging that those in attendance were seated on Aboriginal land. Such acknowledgment, he posited, existed as "an indication . . . that things may have changed since October 1953 in terms of the consideration, power and relevance accorded to Aboriginal people."[91] It was with such sentiments front of mind that the Royal Commission heard a week's worth of Aboriginal testimony across four remote South Australian locations: Marla Bore, Wallatinna, Maralinga (fig. 9), and Ceduna. At Marla Bore and Wallatinna, witnesses spoke of the "black mist" that rolled through the desert in 1953, making people sick, while at Maralinga, those who were "missed" or "moved" by authorities were encouraged to give evidence.[92]

Of particular interest to the Royal Commission was the question of the "black mist."[93] This event was recalled by Aboriginal people at Wallatinna, Mintabie, and Marla Bore. Aboriginal witnesses, including Lallie Lennon, who was noodling for opal near Mintabie (detailed in chapter 2), described a low, dark cloud roiling above the desert's surface, engulfing them.[94] Afterward, witnesses told the commission, many fell sick with ailments such as vomiting, diarrhea, sore eyes, and eventual blindness. The "black mist" was described in these accounts as "sticky," "dark," "nasty," and "quiet," "like a smog."[95] Yankunytjatjara man Yami Lester explained that "the old people were frightened," fearful of what they understood as *mamu*, or a malevolent spirit.[96] Following his exposure to the black mist, Lester's eyes became sore, and he slowly went blind. In their investigations, the commissioners

FIGURE 9. Holding informal desert hearings of the Royal Commission was considered imperative if those communities most impacted by Britain's nuclear weapons tests were to have their experiences understood and accounted for. This particular hearing, held at Oak Valley ("Maralinga Camp") in 1985, featured Justice James McClelland (*seated on a chair in the center*), fellow commissioners William Jonas (*left*) and Jill Fitch (*right*) the anthropologist Maggie Brady (*center left*), and Aboriginal witnesses Alice Cox, Rene Sandimar, Dulcie Watson, and Mabel Queama (*right of McClelland*). Photograph courtesy of Kingsley Palmer and Maggie Brady.

were unable to accurately quantify the amount of contaminated material that would have been carried by the cloud witnesses described. However, the consistency of the accounts from Wallatinna and other locations in the line of the "black mist" pointed to a meteorological phenomenon, the commission concluded, that had occurred because of the testing, tracking across Wallatinna, Marla Bore, and Mintabie with the winds.

Conversely, the severe ailments experienced by Aboriginal people from Ernabella—north of Emu Field, quite a distance from Wallatinna, and outside the path of the winds—present a different story. Extensive interviews with the people of Ernabella link their experiences of illness during the testing period to several outbreaks of measles that had swept through missions and communities in the central deserts in both 1948 and 1957, devastating Aboriginal peoples and decimating their population.[97] The communities at Ernabella Mission were hit particularly severely; it was a catastrophe for the mission's residents. Goodall's work with the Ernabella community during the commission revealed that the traumatic memories from these outbreaks had become, by the 1980s, entangled with those of the nuclear tests happening concurrently. As Goodall notes, this was a period of "intensifying colonisation for these desert landowners."[98] The conflation of the impacts of nuclear testing and the devastation of measles in the interviews of Ernabella people point to an attempt by the community to reconcile experiences for which they had little contextual information or understanding, experiences that were world altering and devastating. Yet the commission's need to focus on the nuclear tests, and to differentiate between contamination and colonialism, ensured it failed to actively expose "the full effect of invasion and colonisation, which included *both* disease and nuclear weapons."[99] Nor did this differentiation account for the true devastation wrought by disease and displacement, colonial tragedies many were intent on ranking below irradiation during the Royal Commission. This was exacerbated by the preoccupation with nuclear weapons' effects as *the* most conceivably catastrophic impact of the Cold War period on the central deserts' Aboriginal populations.

It is worth noting that there remains little evidence to concretely link both veterans' and Aboriginal peoples' experiences of ill health to radiation exposure during the British nuclear tests in Australia. Despite that, many survivors—Indigenous and non-Indigenous—remain stalwart in their commitment to exposing the tests' health implications. In 2006, a study into the health and mortality rates of Australian military personnel working on the tests concluded that while cancer deaths among participants were 18 percent higher than in the average population, there was no evidence that this directly correlated to their exposure to radiation.[100] Many of these deaths were speculated to be due to veterans' exposure to other substances throughout their careers in the military, including asbestos, proximity to which precipitated increased cases of mesothelioma among test veterans. Medical professionals were less willing to link many of the rare cancers and other illnesses that veterans and their family members experienced in the wake of the tests to radiation exposure, regardless of many veterans' experiences working in contaminated areas with inadequate protective clothing and ineffective monitoring systems in place.

In the case of Aboriginal survivors, the ability to assess health impacts has proved even more difficult. Due to the exclusion of Aboriginal people from the Australian census until 1967, there is almost no historical data with which scientists can compare health and mortality rates in order to assess potential radiation effects.[101] Historic state discrimination against Aboriginal peoples has ensured that even less evidence exists to determine whether or not the health of individuals and broader communities was negatively affected by irradiation. Regardless, Aboriginal people described harrowing scenes to the commission, detailing the fear, uncertainty, and illnesses they had experienced as a result of the tests.

The story of Edie Milpuddie and her family was one that particularly shocked commissioners and has been retold in media publications and popular histories as emblematic of the flaws in authorities' monitoring of Aboriginal peoples in the region.[102] Having traveled from Ernabella in the north down toward Ooldea (described in chapter 2), the family was discovered by military personnel within proximity of the crater created by Marcoo. Following their discovery, each family member was forced by range personnel to scrub themselves with soap under a shower located in a service caravan not far from the crater.[103] Their subsequent trip to Yalata in a military jeep was the family's first experience riding in a car; Edie suffered serious motion sickness and recalled vomiting throughout the drive.[104] Upon their arrival at the mission, military personnel shot their dingoes under instruction from government officials who feared they were contaminated.[105] Unsurprisingly, the family struggled to reconcile the events that had led them so far south to Yalata.

All of these events were recalled by Edie and others as highly traumatic. Witnesses to the commission detailed the ailing mental health of Edie's husband, Tjanyindi, in the years thereafter, while Edie's son, Henry, was diagnosed with tuberculosis at age twenty-four. Several more children born to Edie suffered short and painful lives. And while some of the details of this story were known prior to the Royal Commission, what was revealed during the proceedings was Edie's experience of stillbirth following this incident. Edie told the commissioners that she had been pregnant when discovered near the Marcoo crater. Shortly after arriving at Yalata, she gave birth "out bush," burying her stillborn child in secret.[106] Edie and other women attributed the death of her stillborn baby to "the poison" from the bombs.

In addition to explicit references to radiation exposure, as in the case of the Milpuddies, the testimonies provided by Aṉangu affected across the central deserts highlighted grievances that included the effects of various colonial processes connected to, and facilitated by, the nuclear tests. This was especially important for communities such as the Southern Pitjantjatjara and Maralinga Tjarutja, as their experience of the testing program was largely defined by their displacement from Country to the Lutheran missions at Koonibba and later Yalata. It was at the Yalata Mission that many were exposed to colonialism as they had never experienced it before, with the community struggling with poor living conditions and access to addictive substances such as alcohol. As a young anthropologist, Brady had become familiar with the Yalata community through her research into both substance abuse and juvenile crime and detention.[107] She was later hired by lawyers Eames and Collett due to her familiarity with the people living there, telling the communist newspaper the *Tribune* in 1986 that Yalata had been an "unhappy place" since the testing program began.[108] Brady referred to the "social problems" stemming from the colonial impositions present at Yalata: "alcoholism, petrol-sniffing among the kids, a high rate of juvenile crime."[109] All of these issues "could have been ameliorated" if the community "had access to their country," Brady argued.[110]

The lack of access to Country due to both displacement and persistent contamination was unsurprisingly a topic of interest among those testifying to the Royal Commission. Pitjantjatjara and Antakirinja woman Tjunmutja Watson, interviewed at Marla Bore, described her childhood experience of having been "round up" by the missionaries at Ooldea and put into the mission school.[111] Despite her displacement from Country, Watson was able to show the commissioners on a map provided during the hearings where her family would hunt. "This is Maralinga now," she said; "it used to be—Aboriginal name is *Muyan*," a rich hunting ground pitted with rock holes.[112] Watson, like others displaced from the central deserts, later lived at Yalata Mission.[113] She lasted only three years there on account of people "drinking and fighting."[114] She told the commissioners that her sisters, Alice Cox and Rene Sandimar, lived at Lake Dey-Dey, part of their family's old hunting ground, but that "they were upset" as a result of radiation on Country.[115] It "should be cleaned up," she stated, so that "our people over there" can use "that place."[116] This would facilitate many people being able to move from Yalata back to their traditional lands.

The experience of being barred from Country and kept within proximity of the Yalata Mission was viscerally represented in the testimonies of both men and women at the mission. In preparing McClelland for the testimonies of two groups from Yalata residing at Maralinga Camp at Lake Dey-Dey, Eames informed the commissioner that their stories would focus on "what they described [as] the country being blocked to them by the army, which meant that they could not go back in to use the country."[117] Tommy Queama, assisted by an interpreter, told the commission that after the closure of Ooldea and the commencement of nuclear testing, his people were prevented from hunting on their own lands: "Whitefella sent us away," he told them. [118] Most were moved to Yalata Mission, but many attempted to return north, to "spinifex country," where authorities "stopped them and turned them back."[119] As Alice Cox recalled, "I saw Mr MacDougall and he said to go back."[120] "Did he tell you why?" Eames questioned. "Because of a bomb," she responded.[121] When asked whether people were concerned about being blocked from Country, Hughie Windlass responded, "Course they were worried about it. People used to be to and fro, you know."[122]

Beyond highlighting the restriction put on Aboriginal mobility by the tests, and perpetuated over the proceeding decades, those interviewed in relation to Yalata wished to discuss the particular and enduring "importance of the country" and their "concern about harm that might have been done to" it.[123] Interviewing Alice Cox, Gracie Peters, Rene Sandimar, Dulcie Watson, Mabel Queama, Edie Milpuddie, and Elizabeth Illie as a group, the women's interpreter described their disdain for the dusty, gray sand of Yalata.[124] This was Country with which the women were unfamiliar. Afterall, it was not *their* Country. In stark contrast, the women described their own Country's sand as being a rich red. Eames asked the women whether the red sand indicated "good country," to which they answered with a resounding yes. In a similar vein, Eames asked about the "Maralinga Camp" established at Oak Valley in lieu of the lands' return to community: "Is that a good camp? Is that a better camp than Yalata was?"[125] "Yes, it is a good place," Sandimar responded; "there was too much noise at Yalata," plus "Oak Valley—it has got the real sand-hill red sand."[126] This was, the women reiterated, their Country, marked by "dreaming tracks" and from which they had been displaced.[127]

A group of men McClelland and Eames interviewed, consisting of Joe Smart, Hughie Windlass, Kumana Cook, Jack Baker, Jackie Cox, Kumana Queama, Mervyn Day, and Tommy Queama, expressed similar sentiments. Their recollections, like those of the women, suggest the primacy of Aboriginal relationships to the land. When Eames asked why the men were concerned for Country, Windlass told the lawyer: "That is where they are born and reared and that is their home all the time."[128] "They were not related to that country down south and they wanted to go back," an interpreter relayed on behalf of Baker, "back to the country to which they were related."[129] The physical exclusion of Aboriginal communities from Country was of particular focus in these interviews, drawing into view the importance of reconnecting communities to their land, a conversation assisted by the development of land rights.

As the inclusion of contemporaneous discussions of dispossession and the desire to return to Country demonstrate, the testimonies provided to the commission had notable political motivations. Windlass, on behalf of several men living at Maralinga Camp (later referred to as Oak Valley), noted to Eames and the commissioners the importance of reclaiming the Country from which he had been displaced. The establishment of outstations across Maralinga Tjarutja land in this period reflected a desire, as the lands' displaced inhabitants described, to return to "where they are born . . . their particular land they know well."[130] Witnesses reiterated this by referring to the 1981 South Australian legislation that granted land rights to the Pitjantjatjara and Yankunytjatjara communities immediately north of Maralinga. "So you want to have homelands . . . the same way the Pitjantjatjara got homelands?" Eames asked Windlass.[131] "Same way," he responded. "That is the future now we are looking at. Fix up their homelands."[132] Fundamental to "fixing" Aboriginal lands was a comprehensive cleanup, a point witnesses reiterated during these hearings.

While various attempts had previously been made to clean up after the tests, considerable contamination remained at the sites. The earliest attempts by the British authorities to clean up the sites were Operation Clean-Up and Operation Hercules in 1963 and 1964, respectively. These were supposedly "decontamination" programs that focused solely on the removal of large hazards to facilitate the continued use of the sites for military operations.[133] Following the cessation of Britain's minor nuclear tests in the mid-1960s—a series of experiments that spread significant amounts of contaminated material across the deserts—British authorities conducted Operation Brumby, a more comprehensive attempt to remove contamination and debris from the sites. Undertaken in 1967, Operation Brumby largely focused on tilling contaminated soil and using fresh soil to cover the former testing sites' most contaminated areas. Authorities also dug large pits and filled them with highly radioactive debris in an attempt to centralize residual waste.[134] However, Australian authorities later deemed Operation Brumby to have been wholly inadequate, as the British government's so-called cleanup efforts had failed to alleviate the risks of residual contaminants in the soil. Thirty years later, fallout products such as cobalt-60, strontium-90, caesium-137, and europium-152 and 155, as well as considerable amounts of plutonium, were still identifiable across the region in alarming quantities.[135] Low levels of plutonium were found by Australian scientists as far away as Maralinga Camp in 1987, several years after it had been resettled by those testifying at the commission.[136]

Many who had resettled at Maralinga Camp spoke to the commission about the need to adequately clean up and rehabilitate their lands. As Windlass noted, "The damage has been done; the land has been spoiled" and the "poison" should "be taken away."[137] Mervyn Day seconded Windlass's comments, referencing the fencing off of the most contaminated sections of Maralinga. "The fence does not stop" the poison, he stated; "if the wind takes it the fence does not stop that being carried."[138] As such, "the ones who put it there should take it away."[139] Windlass's assertions were later confirmed by scientists, who recorded with concern the lax containment of radioactive soil behind a chain-link fence.[140] Easily spread by wind and other environmental conditions, this soil presented a risk to Aboriginal people living on the land. And "though it might have poison on it now," witnesses told the commission, it "is still Aboriginal land."[141]

The establishment of Maralinga Camp and the tone of the testimonies given to the Royal Commission reflected many individuals' desire to resettle their "homelands" after decades of displacement.[142] Undoubtedly influenced by debates on land rights, this desire was also characterized by the growing momentum of the "homelands movement." According to a 1987 Standing Committee on Aboriginal Affairs report titled "Return to Country," the homelands movement was "very much an Aboriginal initiated movement," considered "one of the most significant developments in Aboriginal affairs" over the previous decade.[143] It was a movement that reflected a "concerted attempt" by Aboriginal peoples to "leave government settlements, reserves, missions and non-Aboriginal townships . . . to re-occupy their traditional country."[144] Several of the outstations conceived during the homelands movement responded to poor labor conditions and damage inflicted on sacred sites across Central Australia by mining companies during the 1970s.[145] Moreover, the homelands movement was facilitated by two major shifts in Aboriginal politics: the abandonment of assimilation policies in pursuit of self-determination and greater engagement with land rights, with the legislation surrounding it further inspiring Aboriginal returns to Country.[146]

Linking the testimonies given at the Royal Commission and the burgeoning homelands movement, the Standing Committee's report directly cited the nuclear tests. It referred to the "effects of the removal of people from" the lands used for "atomic testing in the 1950s at Maralinga" as one reason for the proliferating movement in the central and western desert regions.[147] Quoting from evidence given to the committee, the report noted that both "the land and the social conditions at Yalata were foreign and the people have never been comfortable in that environment[,] leading to serious incidences of violence and alcohol abuse."[148] This statement echoes many of the sentiments expressed in testimonies at the Royal Commission, not least that for many people displaced by the tests Yalata was not "home" due largely to a lack of familiarity with and affinity for the environment. The testimonies of those displaced from their Country by the Maralinga and Emu Field tests mobilized the political language of self-determination and recompense that had been building over the previous decades, and which had begun to enter into public discourse.

These testimonies exist in stark contrast to settler narratives that sought to sever Aboriginal connections to Country. They also differ markedly from the paternalistic considerations of Aboriginal peoples' contribution to the Australian nation that dominated in the 1950s. The testimonies provided to the Royal Commission reflect the entanglement between Australia's nuclear order and colonialism, the adequate acknowledgment of which was impossible under the Royal Commission's parameters but was meaningfully captured in Aboriginal testimonies during its proceedings.

Exposing Nuclear Colonialism

When Prime Minister Bob Hawke called for a Royal Commission into the British nuclear tests in Australia in 1984, Aboriginal survivors of the tests were low on the government's priority list. They represented, once again, a "problem" that threatened to render unstable an emergent and independent Australian nationalism leading up to the nation's bicentenary. Their very existence, and the nuclear tests more generally, pointed to Australia's involvement in, perpetuation of, and persistent inability to grapple with the insidious forms of colonialism on which the state was built. Yet less than a decade later, dispossession was front of mind when discussing the British nuclear tests owing to the strength of Aboriginal testimony.

Despite the Royal Commission's focus on "the harmful effects of exposure to ionising radiation," ample evidence existed to indicate that myriad harms were imposed on Aboriginal people during and following the tests.[149] However, because the commission created a hierarchy of tragedy, with irradiation firmly at the top, the inquiry itself commented very little on the broader, decidedly colonial, impacts of the tests, including dispossession and displacement. The only conclusion in the commission's final report with regard to impositions of this nature referred to the "detrimental effects" of Aboriginal people being "kept away" from their lands while exposed to "intruders."[150]

Rather than grapple with the intricate and multifaceted colonial legacies of the tests, the commission blamed individuals such as Menzies and

Titterton for the neglect and mistreatment Aboriginal people experienced. These individuals, McClelland suggested, represented the Anglophilia woven into the fabric of the program. It was Australia's Anglophilic allies in cahoots with the British, McClelland strongly implied, who had facilitated the mistreatment of Aboriginal people. However one-dimensional this narrative framing was, it pointed to Aboriginal survivors of the tests as in need of greater consideration in its history. It was, after all, the complete disregard for and potential irradiation of Aboriginal people within the testing zone that represented the most shameful aspect of Britain's program. Yet as evidenced by Aboriginal testimonies at the commission's proceedings, nuclear colonialism seeped into their lives in less tangible but markedly more destructive ways than radiation alone.

While the entangled nature of nuclear colonialism would not be represented in the commission's findings, it exists within its testimonies. These were testimonies that detailed Aboriginal peoples' and their Country's exposure to contamination and reflected several of the key developments in Aboriginal politics that had taken place in the preceding decades, not least in relation to land rights and Aboriginal reclamation of and return to Country. As Aboriginal survivors described the fear, confusion, and health impacts facilitated by the tests, both on account of radiation exposure *and* their dispossession, the wider Australian public began to be able to draw tangible links between broader colonial processes and the nuclear tests. This shift created space for discussions of compensation as well as the cleanup and return of the Maralinga lands. Thus, irrespective of the Royal Commission's parameters, the evidence collected by the Aboriginal legal counsel and presented to the commission pointed to dispossession and dislocation as clear consequences of nuclear colonialism in Australia. These were consequences able to be remedied only through meaningful engagement with affected communities and greater acknowledgment of the influence and legitimacy of Aboriginal politics, knowledge, and connection to Country.

SIX

Finding a Seat at the Table

In October 1991, a delegation of Maralinga Tjarutja spokesmen visited London. It had been six years since the McClelland Royal Commission had recommended—among other things—that the British and Australian governments compensate Maralinga Tjarutja for the contamination of their Country.[1] Despite this recommendation, negotiations had proved slow. And so the men—Archie Barton, Barka Bryant, and Hughie Windlass—decided to take their request for compensation directly to Whitehall. They were accompanied by their legal counsel, Andrew Collett, who had been by their side since the beginning of the commission's investigations seven years earlier. Cameras flashed as Australian media correspondents captured the moment the delegation walked through Westminster on the way to confront the British government directly.

The delegation met with several politicians in London that October to discuss options for compensating Maralinga Tjarutja. This trip had been purposefully planned to coincide with the BBC's airing of *Secrets in the Sand*, a documentary that sought to expose the treatment of British servicemen alongside Maralinga Tjarutja.[2] The media was abuzz with dissatisfaction over how the British had handled their nuclear mess in the Australian deserts. When the delegation first met junior defense minister Lord Cranborne, the Elders presented him with woomeras, spear-throwing devices whose namesake had been crudely appropriated for the Woomera long-range missile testing facility near Maralinga in the central deserts.[3] Lord Cranborne reportedly asked the men where the spears to accompany the woomeras were. Barton responded, "You clean our land up and pay us some damages, then we'll give you the spears."[4]

Described by Collett as an invaluable "publicity ploy," the Maralinga delegation's first trip to London was the perfect opportunity for the men "to put pressure on the British government to cough up some money."[5] The trip also demonstrated that several historic shifts had occurred in the years following the Royal Commission, shifts not yet explored by histories of the nuclear tests. By the late 1980s, and as evidenced by their trip to London, Maralinga Tjarutja were central to negotiations about cleaning up contaminated sites at Maralinga and Emu Field. These negotiations, in many ways, were guided by Aboriginal use of and connection to Country. But the community had become notably more mobile, connecting with international audiences and Pacific nuclear survivors of the United States' weapons tests through a series of international trips.

The international mobilization of Maralinga Tjarutja was a product of broader trends in Indigenous politics during the 1980s, both abroad and in Australia. From the late 1970s on, there was greater engagement with the plight of Indigenous peoples the world over. In this context, Aboriginal activists were increasingly connecting with communities subject to similar forms of colonization and subjugation. And, in the specific case of Maralinga Tjarutja, this increased mobilization coincided with the proliferation of information about the British nuclear tests. Maralinga Tjarutja's efforts to connect beyond the local and the national represented a new era in the history of opposition to nuclear colonialism in Australia, characterized by the increased political clout of nuclear survivors. The Australian government and its constituents could no longer ignore the voices of Aboriginal nuclear survivors, especially when placed in conversation with international communities with comparable experiences of colonization.

Consolidating a Seat at the Table

In January 1986, just over a month after the publication of the Royal Commission's conclusions and recommendations, Bob Hawke's cabinet ministers met to consider which of the commission's findings they thought should be discussed in an upcoming meeting with delegates from the British government. The cabinet agreed that "the Royal Commission had raised expectations in Australia and was the subject of continuing public, media and State Government interest."[6] Hawke's government was under pressure to give genuine consideration to the commission's recommendations, the most pressing of which centered on the question of environmental cleanup and compensation and, importantly, who would pay for it. The Royal Commission, while flawed, had added fuel to discussions

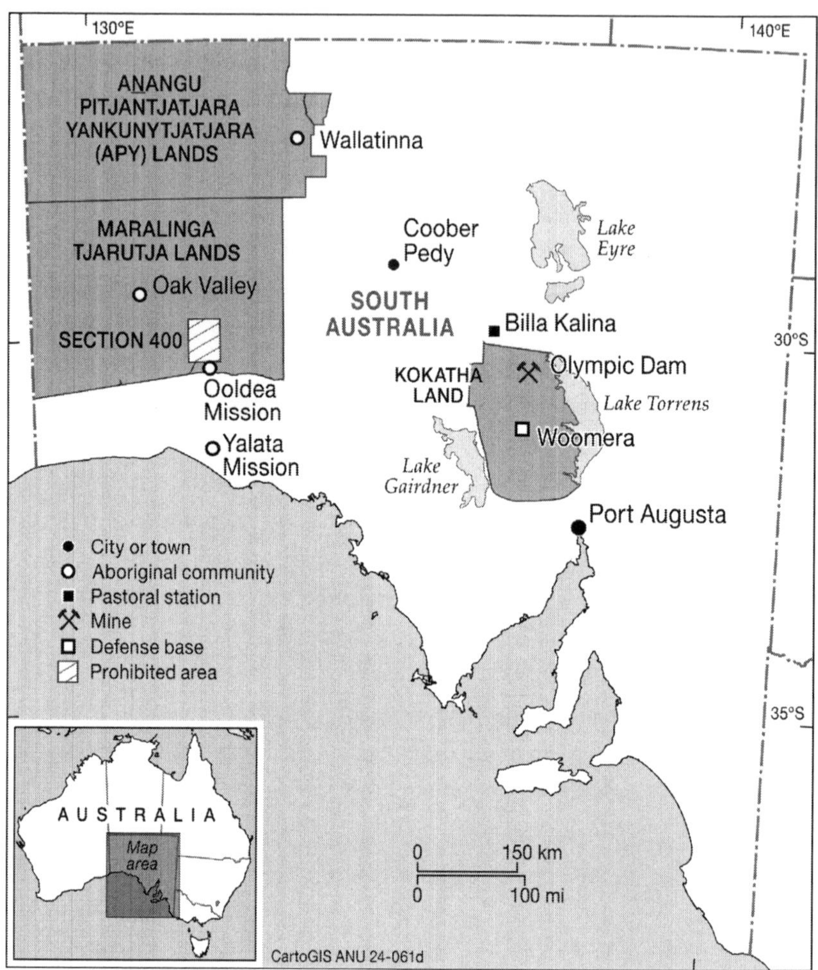

MAP 4. By the late 1980s, those lands used for nuclear weapons testing had been formally handed back to their Traditional Owners. Despite this hand-back, sections of this Country (Section 400 in particular) remained contaminated and thus uninhabitable. Map provided by CartoGIS Services, Australian National University, Canberra.

surrounding the restriction of Aboriginal peoples from their lands (map 4). It had also sparked conversations about compensation for damage to, and loss of enjoyment from, said lands.

When Australian representatives suggested that the British were responsible for paying for a comprehensive cleanup of the Maralinga Prohibited Area, the British accused them of "moving the goal posts."[7] By virtue of what Her Majesty's Government perceived as a change in heart in Australia regarding the treatment of Aboriginal people, the British delegates expressed distrust and resentment toward the Royal Commission's recommendations. When a UK delegation visited Canberra in January 1986, it reiterated that Whitehall was unconvinced the lands really needed to be cleaned up, regardless of the clear presence of dangerous contaminants across Maralinga Tjarutja lands.

Despite the difficulty of measuring plutonium contamination in the 1980s, Australian studies undertaken throughout the decade confidently identified significant plutonium occurrence across the lands subjected to Britain's nuclear testing program. Studies undertaken in 1984, 1985, and 1986 identified notable levels of plutonium contamination at both Maralinga and Emu Field in samples of submillimeter particles, soil, and heat-fused sand, or "glazing."[8] The presence of plutonium was especially high in the vicinities of Britain's so-called minor tests, as several of these experiments were designed to determine the spread of plutonium caused by potential accidents involving nuclear weapons, including fire or accidental detonation. In some cases, plutonium contaminants traveled more than 60 miles (100 kilometers) downwind.[9] As a result of the spread of contaminants across the region, and Maralinga Tjarutja's desire to regain access to and use of their lands, scientists were anxious to determine the risks posed by airborne contamination to humans, not least as a result of dust storms and other environmental conditions specific to the arid central desert region. Australian Radiation Laboratory scientists determined that while the airborne concentrations of plutonium and other contaminants were low at the Maralinga site, "dust levels in places inhabited by Aboriginal people living a semi-traditional lifestyle [were] much higher."[10] These levels posed a significant risk to human life.

Faced with these results and Canberra's ensuing demand for a comprehensive cleanup of the former testing sites, British authorities insisted that between 1967 and 1968 Operation Brumby had purportedly "reduce[d] residual radioactivity to a minimum."[11] Any further liability Her Majesty's Government had for the sites had been relinquished in 1979, when approximately 44 pounds (20 kilograms) of plutonium discovered in the site was removed by British authorities at the request of Prime Minister Malcolm Fraser. As far as the British government was concerned, the "Australian government confirmed in writing that this had been carried out to their complete satisfaction and that there was no obligation on the UK government to complete any further decontamination."[12] With this in mind, the British delegation questioned the necessity of an extensive, costly, and environmentally destructive cleanup that would facilitate the "uninterrupted habitation" of the area by its Traditional Owners.[13] Avoiding Aboriginal use of the area appeared to be Britain's preferred approach, but this approach was no longer acceptable to many Australians, as Aboriginal people's perspectives and relationship to Country were gaining a new level of prominence and legitimacy.

Following tense negotiations, both parties agreed that further research needed to be done to determine exactly how much contamination remained in the range. Until further investigation was undertaken, the Hawke government decided to refrain from insisting that the British government pay for a cleanup. Senator Gareth Evans, Australian minister for resources and energy at the time, stated in a press release: "Satisfactory progress was made not only in identifying the matters on which the Australian and UK Governments have, at this stage, differing views, but—more importantly—on establishing procedures and processes which may ultimately enable those differences to be resolved."[14] The first of these processes was the establishment of the Technical Assessment Group (TAG) to undertake extensive studies into the contamination of the former range, beginning over a decade of scientific investigation, negotiation, and jostling for compensation. Central to the question of whether compensation was due, and, if so, how much, was first determining whether the lands really were still contaminated. Despite the British delegation's agreement to "undertake work to assist TAG," it made clear to Senator Evans: "The sharing of studies in no way affected the UK view that we had no legal obligation to contribute to the cost of further clean-up."[15]

During the Royal Commission, previous cleanup efforts and scientific studies were drawn into considerable doubt. Not only were large amounts of contaminated soil (and even plutonium) left behind, but no consideration of Aboriginal people's unencumbered use of the land into the future had been taken into account during said cleanup efforts. In order to facilitate Maralinga Tjarutja's safe return to Country, more in-depth scientific and anthropological assessments were needed to determine the risks posed by the community's traditional use of their lands. The establishment and completion of the TAG studies involved the Maralinga Tjarutja Council and community from the very beginning, demonstrating the extent to which these studies afforded validity to Aboriginal voices and land use. Moreover, the dissemination of information facilitated by the commission and then the TAG studies mandated Maralinga Tjarutja's continued engagement with both the Australian and British governments.

In February 1986, Hawke's government formed the TAG with the aim of addressing the technical conclusions of the Royal Commission.[16] Consisting of British, Australian, and American experts, the TAG was tasked with scientifically assessing the former testing sites to determine the level of contamination left by Britain's experiments, the greatest risk in terms of contamination uptake for Aboriginal land users, and the best cleanup options.[17] A significant aspect of the studies was thus observing Aboriginal use of and interaction with the land to determine the various scenarios within which individuals might encounter contaminants. Two anthropologists with existing relationships to Maralinga Tjarutja undertook this element of the study: Maggie Brady and Kingsley Palmer. Previously employed in the Royal Commission, Brady and Palmer were under contract with the Maralinga Tjarutja Council during the studies, marking a shift toward incorporating Aboriginal knowledge, evidence, and concerns in assessing the tests' residual dangers.[18]

The anthropological aspects of the TAG studies sought to create a model of "semi-traditional Aboriginal lifestyle" for determining the extent of contamination risk.[19] This largely involved measuring the amount of contamination exposure created by all aspects of Maralinga Tjarutja's life on Country. Community members and TAG experts were required to wear devices that both caught dust and monitored radiation as Brady and Palmer observed the Traditional Owners going about their usual activities in the desert (fig. 10). The data collected necessarily referred to kilograms of "bush foods" gathered and consumed and summaries of "factors influencing ingestion, inhalation and absorption."[20] Palmer and Brady observed with concern the ingestion of large quantities of dust by Maralinga Tjarutja through cooking processes (food "cooked in the ashes"); traditional medicinal practices ("the application of ashes" to burns and wounds); the absence of sanitation or health facilities; childhood games (wheeling toys along dusty roads and "throwing handfuls of dust"); weather patterns ("small but powerful willy-willies [that] spin regularly through camp"); and driving vehicles (from tires).[21] These observations highlighted the nuances of Aboriginal land use that had been negligently and comprehensively overlooked when initial safety precautions for the tests had been determined by both British and Australian authorities over three decades earlier.

Throughout the studies, Maralinga Tjarutja continued to conduct "business" in order to sustain their culture. "There's all this scientific stuff going on," Brady recalled; "meanwhile the Aṉangu are trying to keep their cultural life alive."[22] "One minute they're initiating boys, the next they're driving down to Adelaide for a research meeting with their lawyers and us," she explained.[23] These recollections point to a growing appreciation of Aboriginal use of land as legitimate. "It's the first time . . . people have gone into this subject of Aboriginal lifestyle and precisely how they live in so much detail," the journalist and author Robert Milliken acknowledged in relation to Brady and Palmer's work.[24] In the 1950s, the nuclear tests had taken place at Maralinga and Emu Field by virtue of government authorities being unwilling to recognize the legitimacy of Aboriginal connection to and use of Country. Even in the early 1980s, Kokatha claims to Canegrass Swamp at Olympic Dam had been ignored both by government officials and by proponents of mining in place of seemingly more legitimate land use. So by taking seriously Aboriginal land use, the TAG studies were radical: "for the first time" a scientific study considered it "important

FIGURE 10. Centering Maralinga Tjarutja knowledge was integral for the TAG studies' findings. The anthropologist Maggie Brady (*pictured center*) described the process of working in 1985 with Maralinga Tjarutja—including Rene Sandimar (*left*) and Mabel Queama (*right*)—as a significant exchange of information. Photograph courtesy of Kingsley Palmer and Maggie Brady.

to understand how Aboriginal people live and utilise this countryside."[25] This attention to Aboriginal land use had the additional effect of educating Maralinga Tjarutja on the nature of radioactive contamination and its potential consequences, and on how to negotiate with the government.

The BBC's 1991 documentary *Secrets in the Sand* used footage taken during the TAG studies to put a human face on the scientific descriptions and concerns voiced by TAG researchers.[26] In one scene, Brady explains to Alice Cox, a Maralinga Traditional Owner, why they are both wearing monitoring devices around their necks while digging for witchetty grubs. Cox walks barefoot across the red sand to an acacia bush, where she digs at its base using a stick. As she pulls a furled piece of bark out of the sand, the viewer catches a glimpse of a large monitor worn around her waist. Accompanying this image is panning video footage of a young child seated in the dirt with a puppy, face caked with mucus and dust. In most situations, the image of a dirt-covered child would appear completely innocuous, perhaps even evocative of childhood folly, but at Maralinga such footage exists as evidence of the child's potential exposure to radioactive contaminants. In another scene, Maralinga Tjarutja Council chair Archie Barton walks down a laboratory corridor, looking uncertain. He is then shown a machine that detects plutonium in the human body. The narrator explains to the viewer that Maralinga Tjarutja were offered the opportunity to be individually tested for plutonium.[27] The community declined. The community's choice to reject subjection to this test reflects the deep-seated distrust among Maralinga Tjarutja in the years after the Royal Commission, created by decades of misinformation and denial regarding their experiences. It was during the TAG studies that Maralinga Tjarutja began to grapple with the severity of the situation thrust on them. "In terms of their consciousness of the damage that had been done," Brady recalled, "those TAG studies were really when it . . . began to sink in."[28]

By 1988, two years into the TAG studies, it was clear that Maralinga Tjarutja had developed the "lingo" to communicate their demands to government officials.[29] Both learning a specific language of compensation and honing their negotiating skills, Brady argues, reflected an increasing awareness among the community not only of what had happened to their lands but also of their entitlement to payment for damages done.[30] Importantly, 1988 was also the bicentenary year and thus an occasion for the Hawke government to reinforce its desire to champion unity among the Australian population.[31] However, it also created an air of recompense, "an atmosphere of reconciliation . . . [and] compensation," according to Brady.[32] It was around this time that discussions of reparation were being taken up by Maralinga Tjarutja with Australian government representatives. Brady recalls writing in her diary at this time: "This is the first time Jack [a member of the community] has mentioned compensation."[33] As the notion of payment for damages incurred was importantly becoming entwined with Aboriginal responsibilities for and custodianship of the land, in the context of the widespread contamination of Aboriginal land, calls for compensation were fitting. This included a comprehensive cleanup of the lands in question.

Scientific analyses of the data collected during the TAG studies highlighted that there was a very real risk Maralinga Tjarutja would be exposed to unsafe levels of radioactivity on their lands if remediation did not occur. Radioecological analyses of the various flora and fauna traditionally eaten by Maralinga Tjarutja, the dusts and sands of their campsites, and the rock holes from which the community drew seasonal water demonstrated that Maralinga Tjarutja would likely exceed a "safe" level of exposure if they were to permanently resettle certain parts of the former testing sites. Moreover, there remained a risk that individuals could ingest abnormally "hot" particles while drinking, cooking, or wearing dusty clothing on Country. Several samples of kangaroo meat returned unusually high traces of radioactivity, and high levels of soil measured in water tanks and on clothing prompted experts to encourage the Australian government to consider the remediation of contaminated lands.[34] When the TAG's final report was handed down, nine options were presented to the government, ranging both in cost—mostly in the tens to hundreds of millions of Australian dollars—and in approach.[35] The options put to the government included fencing the most contaminated areas of the former testing sites, reburying previously buried contaminants and debris, diluting contaminated surface soils with clean soil, and ensuring the ongoing surveillance of the sites' "hottest" areas. These remediation options, however, would have varying impacts on the short-, medium-, and long-term use of this land by Maralinga Tjarutja.

TAG experts were highly sensitive to the need to rehabilitate the Maralinga lands such that they could be resettled permanently by their Traditional Owners. As detailed in the TAG's final report, "The scale of the rehabilitation measures to control radiation dose is predominantly determined by Aboriginal life style." A substantial amount of the estimated cost of the cleanup was thus directly attributed to "those options relating to the release of land for unrestricted entry and use."[36] In other words, the most expensive options put forward by the TAG were those that accounted for unrestricted use of the land by Aboriginal groups. This is significant, not least because the options presented were in stark opposition to requests from the British government to consider the *necessity* for Aboriginal communities to have unimpeded access to the former test sites. Unimpeded access was a given.

However, as the Australian government hoped the British would pay for the cleanup, Hawke's cabinet was forced to consider how the British government would react to the TAG studies' conclusions. In reference to options that attempted to ensure the lands were entirely and freely usable by Aboriginal communities, the cabinet acknowledged that "the UK w[ould] regard" such options as "excessive."[37] This was due to Britain's inability to "consider itself liable for rehabilitation measures specifically intended to allow Aboriginal occupation of contaminated areas."[38] In particular, the cabinet referenced the proliferation of land rights rhetoric in Australia, noting that the United Kingdom would consider "the relatively recent growth of the Aboriginal land rights movement as something which could not have been envisaged during earlier clean-ups at test sites [and] for which it has no responsibility."[39] Despite acknowledging the difficulties that the Australian government looked to face from the British, the cabinet concluded that—irrespective of which cleanup option was selected—"a substantial contribution [will] be sought from the UK Government."[40] Moreover, the Australian government recognized the importance of involving Maralinga Tjarutja directly in consultations.

As the British dragged their feet, the Hawke government and Maralinga Tjarutja representatives came to a consensus in early 1991 on their preferred cleanup option. Taking their time to seriously consider every option, the Maralinga Tjarutja Council concluded by the following year that option 6(c) was the most practical and achievable. This option had an estimated cost of A$90 million and involved the tilling of contaminated soil, fencing around highly contaminated areas, and permanent patrolling of the range.[41] In a press release given in March 1991, council spokesperson Archie Barton acknowledged that while the community recognized that it was "technically feasible to clean up this land by removing the top soil and replacing vegetation"—as outlined in the most extensive cleanup option—such activity risked solving "one environmental disaster by creating . . . another."[42] This conclusion followed investigations that Barton and Andrew Collett conducted into whether the revegetation of areas where contaminated soil would need to be removed and reburied was possible. The advice the men received from an eminent South Australian botanist was that revegetation was certainly possible. However, when Collett inquired how long successful revegetation would take, he was advised that it would take approximately one hundred years. The community was unwilling to wait that long for the restoration of their Country.

The thorough, though still partial, cleanup presented in option 6(c) would largely avoid the creation of new environmental issues through the complete removal of soils and vegetation, while allowing Maralinga Tjarutja access to most of their lands within a few years.[43] Section 400, the most contaminated part of the former Maralinga Prohibited Area, would remain permanently fenced off, albeit with material that would allow local fauna to pass through. Maralinga Tjarutja had expressed concern over the potential for native animals, such as kangaroos, to become entrapped by traditional fencing options in the highly contaminated Section 400. The community therefore agreed to have the government fence it off with posts and a series of warning signs in exchange for compensation for their indefinite loss of access to that particular stretch of Country. With the addition of compensation, option 6(c) was estimated to cost upward of A$100 million.

Although Maralinga Tjarutja and the Australian government had agreed on a single option for cleanup, the latter was not willing to bear the entire cost. While the cabinet supported the pursuit of option 6(c), it maintained: "What can be achieved in terms of rehabilitation of the sites will depend on negotiations with the UK Government."[44] "The MT [Maralinga Tjarutja] should appreciate that no substantive rehabilitation work will proceed without a significant UK contribution," the government upheld.[45] With such a substantial bill sitting before it, the British government dug in its heels, and negotiations drew on for several more years.

Despite Britain's refusal to pay up, the TAG studies and their aftermath demonstrated a new era in the Australian government's approach to issues stemming from the nuclear tests. By the late 1980s, there was no room for the government to act on Maralinga outside of consultation with its Traditional Owners. Where, in the 1950s, Aboriginal peoples' traditional uses of land were little accounted for, let alone acknowledged as legitimate, forty years of reckoning with the legacies of nuclear colonialism in Australia and six years of negotiation with the Australian government during and after the Royal Commission had given Maralinga Tjarutja a "seat at the table."[46] The commission, its recommendations, and the ensuing TAG studies undoubtedly contributed to the process of legitimizing in the minds of settler Australians the knowledge and experiences of Aboriginal nuclear survivors. Not only had the TAG studies placed Aboriginal traditional land uses at the center of scientific considerations (an almost entirely novel idea), but concerns about what exactly should be done with contaminated sites had to account for such uses. In search of answers about the best way forward in terms of both environmental remediation and community compensation, representatives of Maralinga Tjarutja began to look beyond the local and the national. Utilizing the webs, networks, and circuits forged by nuclear colonialism, several Maralinga Tjarutja sought out the experiences of other nuclear survivors in an effort to grapple with their uncertain futures.[47]

Creating Connections

Seeking compensation was no easy feat for Maralinga Tjarutja. In pursuit of recompense, the community sought solidarity with groups who had also experienced forms of nuclear colonialism and who had successfully negotiated financial reparations. Such interactions promised both precedents for compensating victims of the global nuclear order and lessons on how best to approach the subject of compensation. Moreover, forging relationships with others who had sought to hold their oppressors to account provided Australians affected by nuclear testing with models for surviving, thriving, and fighting under the forces of nuclear colonialism. Finally, it created tangible links between Australia and the atrocities of the global nuclear order, forcing the Australian government to account for its role in Britain's testing program.

While antinuclear movements have existed as long as nuclear weapons have, the politics of the 1980s drew the public's attention to the highly racialized nature of global nuclear imposition. Connections forged among nuclear survivors across the globe starkly exposed the relationship between colonialism, militarism, and the nuclear, as those affected were predominantly Indigenous. The shared experience of Indigenous nuclear survivors involved dispossession, subjugation, and silencing by nuclear processes, though the experiences of survivors varied across the globe, as nuclear colonialism manifested in myriad ways.[48] Irrespective of the inherent experiential differences of nuclear survivors, bringing their voices together worked to empower those previously left in the dark about the nuclear past.

The active and increased discussion of the rights of Indigenous peoples in international forums such as the United Nations created the opportunity for nuclear survivors to draw attention to their plight.[49] In particular, the notion of the "Fourth World" proliferated globally in this period, highlighting those marginalized within so-called First World countries and excluded from mainstream society. The links between nuclear weapons testing and colonial imposition were made explicit by Indigenous activists across the Pacific in the mid- to late 1970s as antinuclear sentiment grew in the region alongside various independence movements in Fiji, Papua New Guinea, the Solomon Islands, Kiribati, and Vanuatu, among other nations.[50] The confluence of antinuclearism and a growing hunger for independence among Pacific nations fostered a strong Nuclear Free and Independent Pacific movement, the meetings of which were frequented by Aboriginal representatives from Australia.

Of particular note is the involvement of Aboriginal spokespeople in the creation of the 1978 Pohnpei Charter, a document designed to "establish the Rights of Indigenous Peoples." This radical declaration existed as the culmination of discussions among attendees of the second Nuclear-Free Pacific Conference, held in 1978 on Pohnpei, in Micronesia (now the Federated States of Micronesia). The charter was a promise numerous communities across the Pacific made to protect the world's oceans and peoples from nuclear testing. Described by the late Pacific scholar Tracey Banivanua Mar as "the first of its kind in the brave new decolonising world," this meeting provided a forum in which nuclear-affected Indigenous communities could publicly expose nuclear testing for what they believed it to be: a form of colonialism.[51] Nuclear testing, the charter asserted, had forced many Indigenous communities into a "position of subjugation in their own lands."[52]

Both the meeting and the charter responded directly to nuclear testing across the Pacific, asserting "'the rights of indigenous peoples' against 'the degrading influences of Imperialism and Colonialism.'"[53] In highlighting the creation of a "Fourth World" by nuclear colonialism and other impositions, the charter fundamentally challenged the accepted "saltwater thesis" of decolonization, which inferred that "the only colonized peoples entitled to sovereign self-determination were those living in territories 'geographically separate' from their rulers."[54] Better transport, increased information exchange, and the support of international forums, such as the United Nations, assisted in forging transnational Indigenous networks and allowed messages—such as those encapsulated in the charter—to be broadcast globally.[55] This represented a shift in international attention—at least in part—to Indigenous communities living and remaining subjugated within established states, such as Australia.

Maralinga Tjarutja were increasingly aware of the potential connections to be made with other nuclear survivors through such activist networks. Accordingly, in 1987 Archie Barton, Maralinga Tjarutja spokesperson, and Graham Knill, a representative from the South Australian Department of Aboriginal Affairs, wrote a proposal to the federal government for an overseas study program to visit nuclear survivors in the Pacific and the United States. The proposal sought A$30,000 of funding to send Barton and Knill on a trip to determine the "sociological aspects of resettlement on lands affected by nuclear weapons testing," with reference to "political implications," "health, social [and] cultural aspects of resettlement," and "compensation issues."[56] The men proposed liaising with "two indigenous groups whose homelands ha[d] been contaminated by nuclear wastes" as well as with the Japanese *hibakusha*, the survivors of the United States' attacks on Hiroshima and Nagasaki.[57] The proposal specified that the trip would complement the TAG studies by occurring alongside them, while also assisting in informing Maralinga Tjarutja decision-making regarding the best cleanup option for their Country. The written proposal stated that the trip would give the "Australian and State Governments . . . a unique opportunity to atone for the insensitive approach of the past."[58] Sending Knill and Barton to speak with the Marshallese, the Navajo, and the *hibakusha* would, they suggested, help to redress wrongs committed and facilitated by the Australian government during the testing program.

The primary goal of this proposed trip was to ascertain how other nuclear survivors had accounted for their displacement and dealt with the rehabilitation of their lands. Knill envisioned that the trip would assist the community, among other consultative groups, in making "more critical judgements on the clean-up options of the Maralinga lands."[59] This was due to the importance of international experiences in seeking compensation and negotiating the rehabilitation of nuclear sites.[60] The South Australian Department of Aboriginal Affairs, in pursuing this trip, recognized that key to Maralinga Tjarutja's plight was their involvement in international conversations.[61] The trip had the express goal of elevating the demands of Maralinga Tjarutja from a state or federal issue to one of international importance by engaging in dialogue with other survivors of nuclear colonialism in Japan, the Marshall Islands, and the United States.[62] Connecting Maralinga Tjarutja with and to the worlds' most well-recognized nuclear-affected communities would put increased pressure on the British and Australian governments to pay appropriate compensation to the community.

Where the TAG studies focused on anthropological issues—primarily in relation to traditional land use—Knill and Barton's proposed trip sought sociological information. They hoped to gain insight into how other communities had dealt with the breakdown of their own traditions and cultures as a result of nuclear processes. In reference to this knowledge-gathering exercise, the proposal outlined some of the sociological consequences of nuclear testing witnessed elsewhere in the world, including the "breakdown in traditional authority and culture" of nuclear-affected communities, citing alcohol abuse and dependence as one such manifestation of this "breakdown."[63] Considering the extent to which such issues plagued Yalata, the trip was arguably "consistent with the welfare and needs of the Aboriginal people most affected and disadvantaged by the British Nuclear Test Programme," not just due to the contamination of land, but also in relation to the cultural and social issues stemming from separation from Country.[64] These were issues shared with other Indigenous groups similarly subjected to nuclear testing.

While the South Australian state government was on board, the federal government was less enthusiastic about the trip. On 15 April 1987, Gareth Evans received a minute in his capacity as minister of resources and energy to warn him of this impending study proposal. "Mr G Knill . . . is seeking funds for a study that will concentrate on an assessment of comparative sociological factors on settlement on lands affected by nuclear contamination," the minute read.[65] In reference to the requested funds, Evans annotated the document: "Am sure State Govt will be delighted to provide."[66] Then, when advised to give a "non-committal response" to the request, Evans noted he would be "inclined to be slightly more pointed."[67] When the South Australian minister of Aboriginal affairs, Greg Crafter, sent Evans his support of the proposal, Evans noted: "[The] US Indian exercise *may* have a bit more justification than the Bikini one" and "*certainly* more than the Japanese one (which seems a real try on)."[68] The federal government questioned whether Maralinga Tjarutja would benefit from forging connections with other communities of nuclear survivors. The assistant secretary of the Test Site Management and Investigations branch in charge of Maralinga agreed with Evans, noting, "The whole South Australian proposal was a bit of a try on and . . . we would see little value for money coming out of the study."[69] However, he conceded that it was important for the government to maintain positive consultation with Maralinga Tjarutja. This justified at least partial Commonwealth support.

In the end, the government agreed to commit two-thirds of the funds sought if Barton and Knill adequately refocused the study.[70] While Evans preferred that the men simply travel to the United States, as he saw the parallels between the situation of Maralinga Tjarutja and Navajo most clearly, his opinion did not prevail. Knill wrote to the Department of Resources and Energy in September 1987, noting, "The program has been substantially modified."[71] Taking on a less ambitious form, the revised proposal suggested "to undertake a study of the Bikini Islanders in relation to the resettlement of the Maralinga Lands by the traditional Aboriginal owners."[72] The new terms of reference detailed the necessity to "examine the cultural, social, political, economic and legal effects on the Bikini people after 30 years of scatteration and resettlement."[73] The government's reservations did not go unspoken, but representatives decided that it was "important to provide some measure of support" as a result of Maralinga Tjarutja's "important role" in the ongoing TAG studies.[74] In addition, Barton's role as a community leader and spokesperson was recognized by federal officials as "particularly important."[75]

Despite the extensive paper trail left by this proposal, there is far less documentation of the actual trip Knill and Barton undertook. However, there is some scattered evidence that Barton visited Kili Island, where many of the displaced Marshallese were residing.[76] Barton and Knill's initial intention had been to spend up to a week on Bikini Atoll, but following their meeting with its mayor, Tomaki Juda, it became clear that this visit would prove fruitless given no one resided on the atoll due to its severe contamination.[77] Luckily, those hosting Bartin and Knill had already devised a plan for their visit: "[a] few days in Majuro, including a visit to nearby Ejit, and a week in Kili."[78] No trip to Bikini had been planned by the hosts, as there were "no regular flights" and there were "no people to talk to there."[79] As representatives of the federal government considered a visit to Bikini central to the trip's aims, Australian officials negotiated a charter flight to the atoll so that Knill and Barton could spend at least one day there. After further stops in Honolulu, San Francisco, Washington, DC, and New York for meetings with scientists, officials, and lawyers, Knill and Barton returned home.[80] The trip lasted just three weeks.

A lack of Australian press coverage of Knill and Barton's trip has left historians in the dark about the minutiae of their travels. Seemingly few records of the trip remain in Australian government archives. But what is known is that the trip led to the Marshallese visiting Australia in turn. Clearly of greater interest to the Australian press was this reciprocal trip undertaken in June 1988 by six Marshallese, their lawyer, and a liaison officer to Maralinga. The extensive press coverage of this subsequent trip demonstrated the power of shared experience for mobilizing survivors of nuclear colonialism and their narratives. It also highlighted the differences inherent in these experiences, differences that allude to the nuanced nature of nuclear colonialism.

Two Worlds Collide

Reciprocity was central to the connections made by Barton and Knill in the Marshall Islands. Irrespective of these communities' differences, the trip had facilitated an exchange of experiences, ideas, knowledge, and culture between those removed from Bikini and Maralinga Tjarutja. Honoring this reciprocity, approximately two months after his return from the Pacific, Barton rang the Australian Department of Primary Industries and Energy to request that a delegation of Maralinga Tjarutja and Marshallese be permitted to stay at the government-owned and operated Maralinga Village.[81] A month later, on 20 June 1988, a packed six-seater plane touched down at Maralinga. Inside was the delegation of Marshallese, whose landing was received by approximately fifty Maralinga Tjarutja.[82] Aboard the three planes that accompanied them were the press and a documentary crew sent to film the formal meeting of the two communities.[83] A *Sydney Morning Herald* reporter captured the moment that Bikini Atoll mayor Tomaki Juda "sat in the red dust of the Australian desert . . . and told the Aborigines how his people were rebuilding their lives after the atom bomb."[84] This was a meeting that would not be forgotten in a hurry.

Both Maralinga Tjarutja and the Marshallese had specific reasons to engage with each other through this trip. For Maralinga Tjarutja, the Marshallese offered a lesson in how to negotiate successfully with offending governments, providing guidance for their pursuit of compensation from both Australia and Britain. For the Marshallese, they hoped the media exposure that the trip garnered would put further pressure on the US Congress to honor the payments it had promised to those displaced from Bikini Atoll under the Nuclear Claims Tribunal established in 1983. For both communities, the trip placed their respective experiences into an international framework. But for this trip to be of any consequence, the media was of paramount importance.

Much of the media coverage relating to the Marshallese's trip to Maralinga referenced the shared experiences of the two communities. Adelaide's *The Advertiser* reported that, at the invitation of Maralinga Tjarutja, the Marshallese had come to Australia to "discuss matters of concern arising from the common experience of Bikinian and Maralinga peoples in having both had their homelands taken from them for nuclear testing."[85] An issue of *Land Rights News* trumpeted the headline "Two Peoples Share an Atomic Legacy." Within, the article referred to the "common experience of nuclear weapons testing." Reinforcing the narrative of a shared experience, *Land Rights News* quoted Barton as having said that through discussions with the Marshallese, "[Maralinga Tjarutja] learnt that we were not the only ones who suffered the tragedy of relocation and all the other consequences of nuclear tests on their homelands." Their shared experience created an "immediate bond" as a result of their being "black people who had been treated in the same way."[86]

At the center of this shared experience was the issue of dispossession. Where the *hibakusha* had suffered the horrific effects of radiation as a result of being victims of an act of war, the Marshallese and Maralinga Tjarutja shared a mutual—and indefinite—dispossession from traditional lands. This was highlighted in the press. At a media conference following the visit to Maralinga, a member of the Marshallese delegation said that the key issue witnessed at Maralinga was not the testing's impact on physical health, as many would expect, but "something very common to my own people," the delegate explained, "and that's the way we feel about our land." "We're being kept away from something that is very treasured by us," the delegate continued. "This fact alone creates many problems."[87] An article in the national broadsheet *The Australian* drew additional attention to the centrality of environment and place to both communities. The paper reported that the enjoyment of their lands was being integrally compromised by lingering contamination, so much so that the Marshallese expressed apprehensions "about possible radiation risks" during their visit.[88]

A key topic of discussion between the communities was the struggle of rehabilitating contaminated Country while maintaining its natural and spiritual integrity. For Marshallese displaced from Bikini Atoll ahead of the United States' nuclear testing program, the atoll was (and remains) home, a bountiful environment replete with resources and cultural significance. Pikinni—the atoll's Marshallese name—pays homage to the island's towering coconut palms (*pikin* is Marshallese for "flat land," and *ni* is a general term for all varieties of coconut trees and fruit). Coconut palms provided innumerable cultural and material benefits to the island's inhabitants, integral for environmental protection from the sun, wind, and erosion and an important source of food, fuel, sap, syrup, sweetener, and fiber. But various radiological surveys undertaken by US scientists in the early 1980s determined that the most significant pathway for humans to be exposed to radiation on Bikini Atoll would be through the food chain, impacting any potential permanent resettlement of the island.[89] In the

1990s, the International Atomic Energy Agency confirmed these findings, determining that the resettlement of the atoll and the community's return to subsistence on locally grown foods would be impossible due to the risk of radiation.[90] The only possible path forward would be for experts to remove the atoll's topsoil and replace it periodically with potassium fertilizer, a process that would "cause serious environmental harm to the island and have social consequences," according to the agency's experts.[91]

Similarly, the health of Maralinga Tjarutja's Country was of paramount importance to the community. The desire of Maralinga Tjarutja to maintain use of their lands for hunting, camping, and ceremony, if not permanent habitation, drove much of their activism and guided their discussions with the Marshallese. However, as on Bikini Atoll, Matthew Warren of *The Australian* reported, "the only sure way of removing all radioactive material" from contaminated lands was to remove "the top 16cm of soil and all plant life."[92] This process would fundamentally alter the existing environment, the revegetation of which would take longer than a human lifetime.

The question on many lips was thus that of compensation for the loss of land suffered by these communities: Would Maralinga Tjarutja get the money they sought for environmental and cultural damages that might never be able to be remediated? The media had a lot to say in this regard, quoting Barton extensively. "A spokesman for the Maralinga-Tjarutja people, Archie Barton, said they were seeking $7 million compensation from the Australian Government," one report detailed, adding for its readers that "this money would be used to help the Maralinga people resettle."[93] It was this pursuit of compensation, several newspapers suggested, that had inspired the connection with those from Bikini Atoll. "They are further advanced in their efforts through negotiation and through the courts to obtain compensation from the US Government," Barton was quoted as having said. "They have much they can share with us."[94] Subsequently, *The Advertiser* titled an article "N-Test Aborigines to Study Tactics" in reference to Maralinga Tjarutja's bid to learn how to lobby from the Marshallese.[95] The *Sydney Morning Herald* referred to the exchange as enabling Maralinga Tjarutja to "study the legal tactics used by Bikini Islanders against the United States during compensation claims."[96] Whether such coverage was designed to reflect compensation in a positive or negative light is up for contention. What it did do, however, was draw the public's attention to the similarities in the experiences of and connections between Indigenous nuclear survivors across the globe.

Yet as much as these communities found similarity and solidarity in their experiences of nuclear colonial imposition and dispossession, their lived environments differed considerably. Following the return of the Marshallese delegation to Kili Island, a representative of the Department of Primary Industries and Energy briefed her colleagues on the days spent at Maralinga. While she acknowledged that the filmed conversation between the two groups had gone "very well," once the cameras had stopped rolling the situation shifted. It became clear to government officials that the Marshallese were "apprehensive about possible radiation risks" at Maralinga. But beyond this, they were "intimidated by the remoteness of the place."[97] The Marshallese expressed "unease" at the "physical environment" of Maralinga and were shocked by the living conditions of its people.[98] Representatives of the Australian government expressed bitterness over the impression Maralinga Tjarutja left on the Marshallese. A handwritten annotation of the brief reads: "I think O'Shea [Maralinga Tjarutja's lawyer] has used up all of his credits during this fiasco." "MT should really get its act together before we agree to any further use by them of facilities at Maralinga," it continued.[99]

Bikini liaison officer Jack Niedenthal later reflected on the apparent "culture shock" that the Marshallese had felt at Maralinga.[100] In his recollections of the meeting, his language invoked the differences between the two groups' homelands, referring to Maralinga Tjarutja Country as "desolate" and "dry" and the Aboriginal population as "dust-coated" and "nomadic." Niedenthal described the trees dotting the landscape as "scraggly," the remoteness of the village making "it just a bit too rustic" for the visitors from Bikini. These descriptions inadvertently evoked the water-flanked islands of Kili, Bikini, and Rongelap, all of which are pitted with tall and dense palm and coconut trees, their turquoise oceans brimming with fish. In contrast to the irradiated coral at Bikini, the seemingly desolate nature of the vast central deserts shocked the visitors: "The Bikinians had the same looks on their faces that I did, i.e., this is really, really different,"

Niedenthal recalled.[101] Difference, as much as similarity, punctuated this exchange and served as a reminder to the public that the dispossession of Indigenous peoples for nuclear testing had occurred all over the world.

These exchanges denoted a new era of mobility among Maralinga Tjarutja facilitated by the internationalization of Indigenous activism and the information provided by the TAG studies. The aim of this mobility was to share, educate, and agitate. Arguably, the merging of these communities' narratives in media discourse put greater pressure on both Canberra and Whitehall to honor their commitments to compensating survivors. With the stories of Maralinga Tjarutja existing alongside the Marshallese, Australia's nuclear past had burst out of the national frame. As the anthropologist Maggie Brady put it, "It had leapt out . . . beyond Australian borders."[102] The result, she noted, was that "the government couldn't contain it anymore."[103] This was made most evident in 1991 when Maralinga Tjarutja decided to take their claims to the heart of the empire.

London Calling

By October 1991, the British government had made little progress on compensating survivors, and no commitment appeared forthcoming. Discontented with this situation, Archie Barton and fellow Maralinga Tjarutja representatives, Barka Bryant and Hughie Windlass, jetted across the world to put direct pressure on the British. This trip was "history-making," as the original delegation was the first to travel directly to the former metropole to discuss Maralinga with the British government.[104] The 1991 trip to London was intended to "embarrass the British Government" and draw attention to the inadequacy of the British response to Maralinga and Emu Field.[105] Integral to this process was putting a "human face on the issue."[106] While it had been "easy to ignore a problem which [was] 12,000 miles away," the *Canberra Times* noted, the Maralinga delegates were living examples of Britain's ill-use of Australian lands and peoples.[107] Their presence in London was designed to make it impossible to reduce the issue of Maralinga's cleanup to "scientific facts and debate over . . . costs."[108]

Whitehall both recognized and feared the trip's indication that the Maralinga issue was once again gaining momentum.[109] Maralinga Tjarutja's presence in London drew attention to what the British considered "the thorniest problem" in their "bilateral relations with Australia."[110] With the timing of the delegation's visit intended to coincide with the airing of the BBC's *Secrets in the Sand*, the British government expressed concern that the documentary was "likely to be highly critical of HMG [Her Majesty's Government]" and that the presence of Maralinga Tjarutja in London would only fuel this criticism. To mitigate increased scrutiny from the public, while also maintaining the British government's noncommittal stance in relation to compensation, British officials decided: "It would not be appropriate nor sensible to do more than hear what they have to say," except to "repeat HMG's position on legal liability for clean up and compensation" and "make it plain that . . . the proper way to deal with this matter is between governments."[111] In the face of criticism, Whitehall was determined to stick to its accepted line of argument: that all British liability for any cleanup at Maralinga had already been met.

Members of the British cabinet agreed initially that the best course of action was to maintain that Maralinga was a domestic issue for Canberra to solve. In sentiments similar to those expressed by British officials during the tests (discussed in chapter 2), several authorities insisted that the testing sites were within Australian sovereign territory and were therefore an Australian issue. This view was supported by agreements signed alongside the Australian government in both 1968 and 1979 that reportedly absolved Britain of legal liability for its former test sites. This legal argument ensured that Whitehall could maintain that "any question of compensation is not a matter for HMG."[112] Even so, doubts within the British government were beginning to grow about the legalistic and moralistic argument that Britain was absolved of all past, present, and future obligations at its former nuclear testing sites.

As in the 1950s, some British members of Parliament questioned whether Her Majesty's Government really did have grounds to dismiss Australia's requests. One government official, for instance, noted: "The UK's legal position is not cut and dried" and "although the UK has some good grounds for arguing that the 1968 Memorandum released the UK from liability . . . there would be some risk in assuming that the UK is in the clear."[113] Furthermore, the Maralinga issue had the potential to sour geopolitical relations between Britain and Australia, not least due to the shift in Australian attitudes toward the British Empire. "The overwhelming majority of Australians will feel that it was British tests that caused the problem," the British high commissioner to Australia wrote to his colleagues in the Ministry for Defence. "Australia of 1990 . . . for the most part regards the then Menzies Government as having been subservient to HMG and the relationship at that time as being close to colonial in nature." "Thus," the letter concluded, "whatever the legal arguments, Britain's moral responsibility is clear."[114] But the majority were unwilling to concede to the Australians just yet.

Representatives of the British government were instead instructed to welcome the delegation to London, but they were to reiterate that Britain held no legal responsibility to assist Maralinga Tjarutja.[115] According to British accounts, the delegation's lawyer, Collett, was warned ahead of the meeting that Whitehall did not intend to budge on its position. He reportedly countered by warning the British high commissioner that he was "sharpening . . . [his] jemmy to prise open the door." In conversations since, Collett has maintained that he has no recollection of this exchange, though the commissioner reports responding that "as a solicitor he should know what happens to housebreakers."[116] The meeting was cordial, though it achieved very little in terms of securing any British commitment to compensation. Despite that, Collett told the *Canberra Times* in the days after the meeting that the delegation had been greeted with respect and sympathy by British politicians.[117]

At the meeting, the delegation was able to discuss with British representatives the effect of the tests on Aboriginal peoples and their way of life. Those present were informed of the cultural significance of the Maralinga area, such that the "denial of access or of right to transit the area for hunting . . . was a severe loss." While some British officials cast doubt on the traditional nature of Aboriginal use of these lands (some citing the community's use of vehicles for hunting, for example), the meeting closed "with mutually amicable expressions of interest."[118] Collett later reflected that "these government representatives would never have expected to have sat around a conference table with traditional Aborigines . . . [to] discuss such complex issues." They were "clearly moved," he maintained.[119] Nevertheless, the British continued to stall in negotiations. Within a year, a second trip was proposed.

By 1992, Maralinga Tjarutja were mounting pressure on the Australian government to respond to their requests for compensation. This pressure was fueled by a growing fear that negotiations over cleanup and compensation would not be resolved before the next Australian federal election, to be held in 1993. Should a change in government occur at that election, the payment of A$7 million for infrastructure at Maralinga Tjarutja's camp at Oak Valley would be in jeopardy.[120] Barton and Collett expressed concern that "the [current] Government's decision to pay these funds might not be honoured by an incoming Government."[121] This would have significant impacts on Maralinga Tjarutja's ability to permanently reside at Oak Valley, due to the funds' contribution to critical infrastructure such as housing and water tanks at the remote desert settlement. But an even greater concern for Barton and Collett was the compensation worth A$43 million sought from the United Kingdom. In light of that, Maralinga Tjarutja decided to send a second delegation to London. Canberra held clear reservations about this plan, expressing the opinion that the "very positive atmosphere" created by the first meeting could be jeopardized by "any subsequent visit [which] might be seen by the British as weakening [its] position."[122] But, the Australian government ultimately concluded, it was up to the community to decide.

With the decision left in the hands of Maralinga Tjarutja, in September 1992 a second delegation traveled to London to continue pressing for compensation amid British filibustering.[123] The delegation held out hope that another international trip would create some "interest in why, after nearly 12 months, the British Government ha[d] not responded to Australia's representations."[124] *The Advertiser* quoted Barton as stating that Whitehall's inaction was "causing the Maralinga people great physical and mental strain as they [could] not fully re-settle their lands or properly plan for their future."[125] This time, Barton and Bryant were accompanied by Elder Mervyn Day in place of Windlass, and the trip included several more stops.[126] Of particular importance was the delegation's decision to attend the World Uranium Hearing in Salzburg, Austria.[127]

This meeting, organized by German antinuclear journalist Claus Biegert, brought together representatives from nearly thirty countries and twenty-five Indigenous communities to share their experiences of the destructive nature of nuclear technologies. It was designed to expose the promises of nuclear development as "a delusion" by demonstrating through human testimony the social, cultural, environmental, and spiritual impacts of both military and civilian nuclear energy production.[128] At the hearing on 16 September 1992, Barton spoke about the injustice his community felt at the contamination of their land by the British. Introducing Bryant and Day, he explained that these men, while not well-versed in English, had been sent to Salzburg and London to represent their community.[129] He powerfully explained that for decades Maralinga Tjarutja had been kept in the dark by government officials about Britain's nuclear tests, forced to remain ignorant about what had happened on their lands until the 1980s. Even then, he explained, "the Royal Commission was unable to determine the risks posed to the Maralinga Aboriginal people by the remaining radioactive contamination, since all risk estimates made by the British government assume[d] a western lifestyle."[130] Such assumptions included the wearing of protective clothing and footwear, as well as infrequent or impermanent habitation of contaminated lands.

It was only during the TAG studies of the late 1980s, Barton explained, that Maralinga Tjarutja had begun to understand the impacts of radioactive contamination on their Country. His Country remained uninhabitable on a permanent basis due to the irradiation of native flora and fauna, the presence of considerable radioactivity in loose desert sands, and the possibility of the community's exposure to radiation through traditional food gathering practices. "Unless this environmental disaster is cleaned up," Barton continued, "my people are sentenced to life amongst the pollution for the next quarter of a million years. We are determined that this will not happen."[131] This speech caught the ears of many in the global community, gaining Maralinga Tjarutja international support. However, as the trip's next stop in London unfolded, it was clear that the delegates were most determined to have their pleas heard by the British government.

As they had a year earlier, the spokesmen arrived in London bearing gifts for British officials. *The Advertiser* described a gleeful Lord Cranborne telling the delegates: "I hear you were going to bring me more presents." It can be safely assumed that he expected spears to accompany his previously gifted woomeras. Unable to see any obvious present in the room, Lord Cranborne reportedly mused that he "didn't think they [had] been brought in yet."[132] Barton spoke up, ensuring the junior minister that the gift was, in fact, at his feet, having been briefly confiscated by security upon the delegation's arrival at Whitehall and subsequently returned to the men during the meeting. Heaving a large bag onto the table between themselves and the officials, the men explained that they had brought them some sand from Taranaki, Maralinga's most contaminated site.

Those in the room physically recoiled; some gasped. Unbeknownst to them, the sand's radiation level was so low that the delegation's adviser had certified prior to the trip that the best way to dispose of the sand "was to throw it in a rubbish bin."[133] Despite its low levels of radioactivity, this bag of sand, inconspicuously carried into the room and placed at the feet of the minister, was representative of the actions of the British nearly forty years ago. The stunt was a clever demonstration of the senselessness of British claims that there was no need to clean up their contaminated lands. The delegation reminded the minister of what they had told him a year earlier: "You clean our land up and pay us some damages, then we'll give you the spears."[134]

As the Maralinga Tjarutja representatives hoped to pressure the British government by creating a spectacle in London, not least by "embarrassing" the British, media exposure was once again of paramount importance to the delegates. Collett later recalled that during both trips the press followed the delegation everywhere, "falling over themselves to get footage," as the trip constituted "the biggest story for Australian correspondents in London for quite a while."[135] During both trips, pictures of Barton, Bryant, Windlass, and Day graced the pages of British and Australian newspapers, and footage of them walking down Whitehall or seated in Westminster would later feature in documentaries about the community's fight for compensation.[136] With the attention of both local and international news outlets focused on the delegates, their stunt with the sand was the perfect ploy for exposing Whitehall's inaction.[137] In the aftermath, the press reported that the British decided they were "keen to clean the slate," perhaps "anticipating more potent gifts."[138] Following the trip, the defense minister committed to compensating Maralinga Tjarutja within a matter of months.

The following decade was punctuated by the numerous results of Maralinga Tjarutja's lobbying. By early 1993, the British government had agreed to assist in funding the desired cleanup. Consequently, the Australian government established the Maralinga Rehabilitation Technical Advisory Committee (MRTAC) to oversee the rehabilitation of the Maralinga lands. In the same year, the Australian government also accepted and paid in full all claims for compensation put forward by Collett on behalf of individual Aboriginal people and the Wallatinna community for personal injuries arising from the tests. Two years later, in 1995, Maralinga Tjarutja received a further A$13.5 million in compensation to be held in trust by the community's council. And, between 1995 and 2000, the MRTAC removed and disposed of contaminated soil, debris, and vegetation from the region's most contaminated sites; retrieved residual uranium fragments from the environment; identified and exhumed buried waste from inadequate, unmarked, and previously unknown storages; treated and reburied waste; and established a boundary fence to demarcate areas that remained unsafe for full-time occupancy.[139]

By 2000, all but Section 400 (just shy of 1,000 square miles) was considered safe for human habitation.[140] Maralinga Tjarutja's efforts in demanding the return and rehabilitation of their Country culminated in 2009 when the South Australian government officially handed back Section 400 and Maralinga Village to the community.[141] This marked the return of the final section of Maralinga Tjarutja Country to its Traditional Owners.

Land, Livelihoods, and Legitimacy

The trips that Maralinga Tjarutja delegates took between 1988 and 1992 stand in stark contrast to the decades that the Australian government kept the community in the dark, their experiences sidelined by historic attempts to obfuscate Aboriginal voices. Rather, these trips provided the community with an unparalleled opportunity to have their voices heard, which forced both the British and Australian governments to commit to an adequate cleanup, one negotiated by the Traditional Owners. But this cleanup process was also indebted to the TAG studies (1986–90), without which there would be far less knowledge about the residual contamination at Maralinga.

While they were initiated as a result of the Royal Commission's recommendations, the TAG studies took on a life of their own. Most consequentially, they centered Aboriginal land use in their investigations. As a result, Aboriginal connection to and use of Country was vital to the process of determining the impact of nuclear testing on the desert landscape, and Aboriginal knowledge and traditional land use was recognized by the team of experts as legitimate. The thoroughness of these studies provided Australian politicians, scientists, and anthropologists with deeper knowledge of the far-reaching impacts of nuclear testing on human populations and their lived environments, fostering greater regard for how the testing program had affected both Aboriginal peoples' livelihoods and their use of Country.

Increasing their impact, these studies coincided with the internationalization of Indigenous politics in the 1980s. Attempts to forge networks and connections between the community and others who had survived nuclear colonial impositions gained traction. Indicative of this increased connection were the various efforts Barton and others made to foster conversations with nuclear survivors from around the world. And while the experiences of Maralinga Tjarutja and other survivors, including the Marshallese, did not always neatly align, the act of bringing their voices together to share their common experience of dispossession and colonial imposition added pressure to both the British and Australian governments to acknowledge the damage incurred by Maralinga Tjarutja, both in the 1950s and in the years since.

Exploring the increasing political mobility of Maralinga Tjarutja between 1986 and 1992 demonstrates the extent to which adequate knowledge empowered communities to advocate for themselves. But it also highlights how attitudes toward this community—and nuclear issues—had shifted in the decades following the tests. With the transnational political mobilization of Maralinga Tjarutja emerged a shifting awareness of the global impacts of nuclear colonialism. In large part due to nuclear survivors' utilization of transnational activist networks, various governments (not least the Australian and British governments) were forced to acknowledge the existence of survivors *and* their possession of legitimate grievances against their mistreatment and the destruction of their lands. From this point onward, their voices and stories could not be unheard.

SEVEN

Irati Wanti

In a lavish ceremony held in San Francisco in April 2003, Yankunytjatjara and Antakirinja woman Eileen Kampakuta Brown AM and Kokatha woman Eileen Wani Wingfield were jointly awarded the internationally prestigious Goldman Environmental Prize on behalf of the Kupa Piti Kungka Tjuta, the Coober Pedy Senior Women (known as the Kungka Tjuta, meaning "many women").[1] Prize founders Richard and Rhoda Goldman awarded the women this globally recognized accolade for their collective role in spearheading a campaign against a nuclear waste repository proposed for remote South Australia. The Kungka Tjuta had tirelessly campaigned against the establishment of the waste dump on their Country since the late 1990s, fueled by their responsibility for the land, desire to protect future generations, and lifelong experiences of nuclear colonialism.

Speaking of Mrs. Wingfield's relationship to the nuclear at the Goldman Environmental Prize award ceremony, her daughter Rebecca Bear Wingfield drew the audience's attention to three key dates.[2] "The first one is 15 October 1953," she explained, "the date of the first atmospheric [nuclear] explosion at a place called Emu Junction. My mother was a young mother to my oldest sister . . . and they didn't know about the bomb. Nobody knew." "The second occasion . . . is about twenty years ago," she continued, "when they were planning to establish a uranium mine at Western Mining's Roxby Olympic Dam site, not far from where we live." Referencing Mrs. Wingfield's involvement in protesting against the Olympic Dam uranium mine and for the protection of Kokatha sacred sites in 1983, she noted: "My mother camped out bush with all the children and my late uncle. They spoke publicly about their concerns about the establishment of the uranium mine. They protested." And, to a room of hollering audience members, she said: "My mother . . . she laid down in front of the bulldozers. And still they didn't want to listen." Finally, she directed the speech to Mrs. Wingfield's most recent fight, in 1998, recalling, "We found out about a waste dump being planned for the Billa Kalina region of South

Australia." Mrs. Wingfield chose to fight again. "She's been doing this for nearly fifty years," her daughter told the audience.[3]

Kokatha woman Eileen Wani Wingfield (née Allen) was born on Ingomar station in 1935.[4] When she was young, her family was camped at Mabel Creek in remote South Australia during the British nuclear tests; her mother later developed aggressive breast cancer and passed away before she could be treated.[5] But Mrs. Wingfield's life story is as equally intertwined with the history of uranium mining as it is with nuclear testing: the Kokatha's traditional Country encompasses the Olympic Dam uranium mine. It was the pain and suffering of her people and Country as a result of the tests that inspired Mrs. Wingfield to fight to protect Canegrass Swamp from uranium mining in 1983 (chapter 4). As this book has explored, Australia's journey down the "yellowcake road" had taken many twists and turns by the mid-1990s, but as the story of the Kungka Tjuta suggests, it was set to take more.[6]

While most discussions of nuclear colonialism focus on radioactive mineral extraction and nuclear weapons testing and their aftermaths, less tangible (but still linked) forms of nuclear violence, such as waste disposal and storage, have also "given Australia a history to ponder."[7] In 1998, conservative Prime Minister John Howard announced the establishment of a national radioactive waste repository in a remote region of South Australia, Billa Kalina, approximately 60 miles (95 kilometers) northwest of Olympic Dam and 80 miles (130 kilometers) southeast of the remote opal-mining town of Coober Pedy. The repository was his government's solution to increasing public anxieties over the proximity of nuclear contaminants to Sydney's suburban population. Aboriginal representatives from the Kokatha, Pitjantjatjara, Yankunytjatjara, Antakirinja, and Arabunna communities implored the government to consider how the contamination of their Country—including of traditional food sources—would make life harder for those attempting to live on and maintain connection to the land. "It was time to put a stop to things and make people realise that . . . [radiation] has made a big impact on Aboriginal people and they don't want that happening again," family members of the Kungka Tjuta recall.[8]

This chapter focuses on the government's proposed repository, and the Kungka Tjuta's response to it, to examine the clash between urban and desert anxieties inherent in contemporary nuclear colonialism. It demonstrates that, by the 1990s, urban Australia had become increasingly resistant to the presence of nuclear contaminants within its spaces, requiring their removal. What ensued was a struggle between the necessary discussion of radioactivity's relative danger and the perceived expendability of desert landscapes for its disposal. Importantly, this chapter highlights how Aboriginal responses to more contemporary nuclear processes are steeped in the broader history of nuclear colonialism in Australia. This, I argue, impelled—and continues to impel—resistance against, and negotiation with, those attempting to impose unknown nuclear futures on Indigenous communities.

This chapter is therefore not just a story of urban populations once again attempting to facilitate the pollution of desert spaces, but also a story of triumph for those resisting nuclear colonialism and a celebration of Aboriginal women's specific cultural knowledge. As such, the Kungka Tjuta's struggle against nuclear imposition on their Country is a necessary addition to the broader history of women's global antinuclear campaigning.[9] And it serves as a reminder that Australia's nuclear past extends well beyond the British nuclear tests, while embodying similar legacies. One such legacy is the disproportionately toxic burden borne by Indigenous peoples the world over.

Through their campaign Irati Wanti—meaning "the poison, leave it"—the Kungka Tjuta demonstrated that Aboriginal people are not mere victims of nuclear processes. Rather, the Kungka Tjuta's approach to resisting the nuclear order highlights the pressing need to have greater consideration for our lived environments, to better understand the intergenerational impacts of nuclear colonialism on peoples and landscapes, and to hold decision-makers to account.

"No Time to Waste"

While Britain's nuclear tests had been in Australian headlines and discussed heatedly for decades by the mid-1990s, the issue of nuclear waste disposal was largely overlooked by the public for most of the twentieth century. Australia's lack of nuclear power may in part be the reason. Canberra toyed with the idea of nuclear power in the late 1960s under Prime Minister John Gorton, with prominent chemical engineer Philip Baxter and telemetry expert Ernest Titterton advocating relentlessly for an Australian nuclear power capability.[10] Though a site for the first reactor for this power network was found, and tenders were opened for an appropriate reactor design in 1969, by 1971 the Treasury had deemed the venture too expensive, and plans for a nuclear power network across New South Wales were shelved.[11] Subsequent attempts by proponents of nuclear power to get the industry off the ground have also failed. Without nuclear power, Australia's waste has historically consisted of low- and intermediate-level by-products of nuclear medicine, research, and the country's sole nuclear reactor, the High Flux Australian Reactor (HIFAR).[12]

The Australian Atomic Energy Commission (AAEC) built HIFAR in the bush to the southwest of Sydney, near the northern edge of the Royal National Park, in the late 1950s. Britain exchanged the technology and components for the reactor in light of Australia's provision of nuclear proving grounds and uranium to the empire.[13] It went critical in 1958 and was used by the AAEC (which became the Australian Nuclear Science and Technology Organisation [ANSTO] in 1987) for research and the production of radioisotopes for medicine and industry, until it was decommissioned in 2007.[14] HIFAR was built near Sydney at the Lucas Heights facility, and the proximity of the reactor and its stored nuclear waste to Sydney's outer suburbs appeared to go largely unchallenged for much of this period.[15] But as Sydney expanded, and suburbia began to actively rub up against the reactor, murmurs of opposition began to emerge.[16] In a 1986 plan devised to cope with potential accidents at the facility, Lucas Heights' one-mile "buffer zone" erred remarkably close to the nearby suburbs of Engadine and Heathcote.[17] In light of the reactor's proximity to suburban Sydney, many residents preferred the idea of nuclear waste in someone else's backyard, and as fears that urban populations might be exposed to potentially hazardous radioactive waste became more acute, the government sought alternative spaces to store it.[18]

Historically, the storage of nuclear waste has come up against public discontent and suspicion all over the world.[19] Public fears over the ability to adequately secure waste from entering the surrounding biosphere have been bolstered by the fact that radioactive waste disposal is deeply rooted in and closely associated with the fear and devastation wrought by nuclear weapons and their contamination.[20] This situation was (and is) no different in Australia, regardless of the seemingly "moral" argument for Australia storing its own *and* others' nuclear waste, as it is an extractor and exporter of uranium (and thus an active contributor to global nuclear waste production). In making this case, the 1997 Australian Senate Select Committee on Uranium Mining and Milling argued that it was "morally indefensible" for Australians to assume that the government had no obligation to consider how Australian uranium's waste products were disposed of given Australia's contribution to global uranium exports from the Ranger and Olympic Dam mines.[21] Yet discontent and fear over nuclear waste disposal during the 1990s exposed Australia as a "Janus-faced nuclear power," willing to export uranium but reluctant to site nuclear waste on its own soil.[22] Unlike that of other South Pacific nations, including New Zealand, Australia's relationship to nuclear processes has been in a constant state of flux: sometimes contradictory, and often highly political. This was certainly the case for radioactive waste disposal, an issue that reared its head vehemently in the 1990s.

The need for Australia to establish a national disposal facility for its nuclear waste was brought into stark relief in the 1990s following an incident involving mishandled contaminated soil. ANSTO triggered contestations in 1991 when it accepted a request from the Commonwealth Scientific and Industrial Research Organisation to take and store contaminated soil from its experimental plant at Fishermans Bend, on the Yarra River in Port Melbourne. Set up for radioactive laboratory experiments between 1941 and 1965, the facilities at Fishermans Bend closed in 1989, and nearly ten thousand drums of radioactive waste were stored temporarily at Lucas Heights by ANSTO.[23] Before long, Sydney's Sutherland Shire, where Lucas Heights is located, expressed significant concern over the storage of nuclear waste in the outer suburbs of Sydney, taking the issue to the New South Wales Land and Environment Court.[24]

As a result of this dispute between state and federal authorities, Australia's Commonwealth government was ordered by one of its state courts to remove the waste from Lucas Heights. The government thus made plans for the soil to be transported for temporary storage to the Woomera airfield, owned and operated by the Department of Defence. Having once contributed to Australia's nuclear past by servicing the Maralinga and Emu Field testing sites, Woomera once again became embroiled in Australia's nuclear politics when a truck carrying drums of contaminated soil from Lucas Heights to the defense facility was stopped by an inspector for a routine check outside Port Augusta. The inspector found that one of the drums had been leaking contaminated material throughout its journey.[25] Later referring to the incident in Parliament, the minister for science and technology insisted that "the incident posed no threat to the health and safety of workers or the public."[26] Despite this reassurance, news traveled fast, and South Australian residents, both within and outside of Port Augusta, expressed their concern at the lax way Australia's nuclear waste appeared to be managed, transported, and stored.

On 9 March 1995, in response to these events, the Australian Senate formed the Select Committee on the Dangers of Radioactive Waste.[27] And while the committee determined that much of Australia's low-level waste was of little concern, its report—"No Time to Waste"—recognized the importance of heeding warnings presented by public anxiety over the issue. "Public anxiety about radioactive waste is real and should not be ignored," the committee's report detailed.[28] "This anxiety," the report acknowledged, "arises from the special features of radiation," including "the genuine uncertainties about some of its long term effects; the imponderable element in valuing uncertain, unlikely or far-off risks; the strong emotional content of some of the issues raised (such as radiation as a possible cause of cancer or congenital abnormalities); or the lack of information or lack of trust of authorities in charge of radiation safety."[29] In its investigation of this last point, the committee witnessed a significant disconnect between the way ANSTO stored waste on behalf of the Australian government (constituting 90 percent of Australia's nuclear waste in 1995) and the approaches taken by various actors contributing privately to nuclear waste (the other 10 percent).[30] The lack of a cohesive approach to Australia's storage and disposal of nuclear waste, not to mention the confused and inarticulate nature of such codes, was cause for concern.[31]

The committee's key recommendation was the establishment of a national waste repository. Such a facility would provide both the Australian government and individual institutions, such as universities, hospitals, and industry, with a centralized location to deposit their nuclear waste. This would address several of the public's key concerns, namely, that waste was stored in populous areas and that its monitoring by the government was not adequate. Furthermore, the recommended repository would be not a disposal site, where nuclear material would be buried, but rather a storage site, where the government could house nuclear waste until technology had evolved enough to usefully repurpose it. However, *national* waste repository or not, a facility of this kind would have to be housed within a state or territory whose constituents would likely reject its existence. Irrespective of the reservations of several senators, the Howard government was committed to the recommendation, and by June 1998, after an in-depth investigation into various sites across Australia, it had chosen its final location: Billa Kalina, South Australia.

Billa Kalina is a 42,000-square-mile (67,000-square-kilometer) region of arid Country to the northwest of Olympic Dam.[32] Named after an operational sheep and cattle property in the same location, the proposed repository site was in a region in the southwestern reaches of the Great Artesian Basin, its low scrub and abundant flora and fauna fed by significant underground water reserves and mound springs.[33] However, experts and government officials considered this location the ideal waste storage site for the same reasons the land immediately to its west had been used for nuclear weapons tests: its remote location and geological stability.[34] But those living within the region had long associations with Australia's nuclear past and did not take lightly to the suggestion that Billa Kalina would house the nation's radioactive waste repository. In their opposition to the dump, residents highlighted the injustice of considering desert regions as ideal for getting rid of waste because of their apparently "uninhabited" nature.[35] Such arguments reflected a persistent tension between urban and desert spaces over this issue, drawing attention to the disproportionate (and radioactive) burden borne by South Australians in particular.

MP Lyn Breuer, taking on the fight of her constituents (both Indigenous and non-Indigenous), addressed the South Australian House of Assembly in June 1998, arguing against the establishment of a national waste repository in her electorate. This was an electorate, she reminded her colleagues, that incorporated the Maralinga lands. "The Labor Party fought long and hard for the clean up of the Maralinga lands," she stated. For the three years prior, the newly minted Maralinga Rehabilitation Technical Advisory Committee had been overseeing the slow and painstaking rehabilitation of the former test sites in accordance with agreements reached by scientific experts, Traditional Owners, and the Australian government (see chapters 5 and 6). "It took many years, a lot of money, a lot of hard work, lobbying, etc. to get those lands cleaned up," Breuer reminded her colleagues; "[yet] now, we have the very strong possibility that some waste will be dumped back into the Billa Kalina area."[36] A mere three years into efforts to clean up the testing sites, the government was once again considering the region as the ideal site for Australia's nuclear waste.

The prevailing notion that Billa Kalina's remoteness made it the perfect nuclear waste disposal site angered those communities who called it home. While "Billa Kalina . . . is hundreds of miles from many places," Breuer noted, "it is there somewhere."[37] Expressing a similar sentiment, Yankunytjatjara woman Karina Lester reflected on what government officials were saying about these sites: "'[They're] nowhere,' 'out of sight, out of mind,' so they don't have to deal with it, because it is in the 'Outback.'" They do this, she said, "without any real understanding about what their actions are imposing on Aboriginal people across the globe, not only in Australia."[38] Billa Kalina was, in fact, a region of great importance to Aṉangu, many of whom had memories of the nuclear tests. "They remember what it was like," Breuer told her parliamentary colleagues. "They remember the clouds coming over; and they were frightened. And the results are still there today. Those people are still suffering effects from this, and they are very concerned about the possibility of waste in their area."[39] Those with memories of Totem I's "black mist" included members of the Kupa Piti Kungka Tjuta, the Coober Pedy Senior Women's group. When they heard the news that Howard's government intended to dispose of nuclear waste at Billa Kalina, they implored the government to "take it back to Sydney." They had had "enough of the poison."[40]

Irati Wanti (The Poison, Leave It)

The Kupa Piti Kungka Tjuta was formed in the late 1980s by three Yankunytjatjara and Antakirinja Elders of the South Australian central deserts: Ivy

Makinti Stewart, Eileen Unkari Crombie, and Emily Munyungka Austin. These women rallied together to tackle community issues surrounding the loss of traditional culture in the Coober Pedy region.[41] They expressed concern that "the young people didn't have the Women's culture," starting the Kungka Tjuta in pursuit of "a better world for their grandchildren," not least through the pursuit of cultural continuity.[42] "We are the women who are fighting to keep the culture going," they emphatically maintained; "we've been teaching the younger women and the women that were taken away, teaching the people that lost the culture" as a result of ongoing colonial imposition and intergenerational trauma.[43] In support of these aims, in the mid-1990s Mrs. Crombie asked Michele Madigan (a Sister of Saint Joseph, living in Coober Pedy at the time) to assist the women with the administration associated with maintaining the Kungka Tjuta as an officially registered organization. And by 1998, the Kungka Tjuta's numbers had swelled to around a dozen.

The mobilization of women against nuclear impositions all over the world has been the subject of much discussion among scholars. The women who took up camp outside Britain's Royal Air Force base Greenham Common in Berkshire in the 1980s, for example, have been analyzed at great length.[44] The experiences of mothers having to face their children's futures in a world plagued by potentially imminent nuclear catastrophe have also preoccupied many whose research explores the role of women peace protesters in influencing nuclear security discourse.[45] Accompanying such work are feminist critiques of the nuclear weapons regime as a patriarchal structure.[46] Yet Indigenous women have a unique stake in the nuclear order, not least due to its inherently colonial nature.[47]

In the case of the Kungka Tjuta, they were, first and foremost, custodians of specific women's knowledge. Gender dynamics differ across Aboriginal nations, but for many communities women hold specific cultural knowledge that allows them to nurture Country. "Women hold the genealogical knowledge" essential to protecting Country (as well as for making claims to Country), according to the late historian Peggy Brock.[48] This is knowledge that is endowed and entrusted to them by the ancestors and which is their responsibility to pass on to younger generations. However, Anglo-European assumptions about gender have historically silenced

Aboriginal women's contribution to land claims and politics, irrespective of their importance as custodians of knowledge and culture.[49]

As the historian Heather Goodall articulates it, "women's rights in land are substantial"; "holding" or "caring for" Country has many implications for women, centered on learning, performing, and thus teaching "the ceremonies belonging to the Dreaming for that land." Through holding, caring for, and teaching about Country they "protect the land, its species and people from damage and unauthorised use."[50] This is not to imply that men do not have comparable or even similar connections to and responsibilities for Country, but women, through their role as nurturers and educators within the community, have historically expressed a unique stake in protecting Country from nuclear imposition.[51] Reflecting this, Mrs. Wingfield's daughter recalls that it was her mother who taught her how to collect food in the desert, how to make bush medicines, and how to catch and care for the land's creatures.[52]

Fulfilling their obligations to caring for Country, the Kungka Tjuta placed great emphasis on "their role as nurturers of people, land and relationships."[53] Their "major responsibilities" were in the "'growing up' of people and land," maintaining "harmonious relations between people and culture" through "the *Tjukur*—the important stories of the land," "the *Inma*-song and dance of the culture, all part of the land as well," "the bush tucker," language, and family.[54] According to the Kungka Tjuta, "all this is law" and is relied on for the preservation and protection of their Country, not least from extractive or polluting industries like mining or waste disposal. The Kungka Tjuta understood the protection of Country as providing them with guidance and nourishment—physically, spiritually, and emotionally—while also fulfilling their responsibility as Aboriginal women. But the announcement of a national waste repository threatened to impose on all of these responsibilities, as nuclear testing had decades earlier.

With all this in mind, it comes as little surprise that the Kungka Tjuta would strongly oppose the disposal of radioactive waste on their Country. Commenting on the nuclear industry's legacy, several of the Kungka Tjuta reflected on the "black mist" that rolled over Wallatinna in the 1950s.[55] "Years ago, we know a lot of bad things went on after the Bomb that went off up here," members of the Kungka Tjuta explained to the *Coober Pedy Times* in 1999. They remembered seeing "people living off the land . . . and then dying after the bomb went off."[56] Others had memories of Native Patrol Officer Walter MacDougall encouraging their people to move out of areas considered too close to the testing sites.[57] When the Kungka Tjuta heard about the government's decision to dump nuclear waste at Billa Kalina in 1998, Sister Madigan recalls, Mrs. Crombie stood up and declared, "We cannot have this!"[58] They were vehement: "We've had enough of this poison, enough sickness, from the bomb."[59]

The Kungka Tjuta's campaign amplified women's experiences (and associated fears) of radiation exposure as a result of the tests and radiation's disproportionate impact on female physiology and fertility.[60] The role of Aboriginal women in gathering bush foods, making and administering bush medicines, and passing down cultural knowledge about Country exposed the Kungka Tjuta and other women in the central deserts to increased levels of radioactivity. "They couldn't even give their babies breast milk," Janice Wingfield maintains, for fear of contamination from the bomb.[61] Even today, the suffering of women is readily recalled by those whose family members were exposed to the tests; many struggle to reconcile the unexplained birth defects and health issues continuing to plague communities across the central deserts.[62] Given the Kungka Tjuta's commitment to nurturing future generations, "We knew we had to fight it," Mrs. Crombie asserted at the time; "straight out we said *wanti*—leave it . . . we were frightened properly."[63] The Kungka Tjuta's memories of the nuclear tests formed the basis for what would become a tireless campaign to resist the establishment of the national waste repository, a campaign rooted in the desert landscape and articulated through the experiences and knowledge of these women.[64]

The Kungka Tjuta officially began the Irati Wanti campaign with a refusal.[65] In April 1998, just a month after the Kungka Tjuta had been made aware of the repository proposal, the Department of Industry, Science and Resources sent the director of its Radioactive Waste Management Section to Coober Pedy to begin the government's consultation with potentially affected communities. The director was armed with an instructional video, which aimed to encourage those within and around Coober Pedy to get behind the proposal. The Kungka Tjuta refused to partake in the viewing. Mrs. Crombie insisted, "We're not going to be watching your film, we're going to talk, and we're going to show them." The Kungka Tjuta requested a private meeting with the director and spoke "for two hours . . . strongly about their Tjukur—Dreaming and their responsibilities for the country." After each woman spoke, the officials had to wait to hear the English translation of the women's speeches, given in Yankunytjatjara or Antakirinja. Sister Madigan recalls the director's shock when "the ladies told them straight out, 'we're not going to watch the film, we want to talk to you—you're the boss.'"[66] When the government representatives left Coober Pedy after this meeting, the Kungka Tjuta put pen to paper, kick-starting Irati Wanti's national campaign.

With the help of Madigan, the Kungka Tjuta drafted a statement for circulation across Australia. Within it, they summarized their key concerns, drawing attention to the ways desert regions and their Aboriginal populations were forced to bear the burdens of the nuclear order.[67] As critics of the original proposal had also worried, the Kungka Tjuta did not want Australia's nuclear waste to become "out of sight, out of mind."[68] Billa Kalina was out of the sight of those creating the waste but was very much at the center of the worlds of communities such as those represented by the Kungka Tjuta. They reiterated in the statement that while many Australians commonly assumed the desert was desolate and lifeless, it sustained them and their culture. "Never mind our country is the desert," they wrote, "that's where we belong. And we love where we belong." "Listen to us! The desert lands are not as dry as you think!" they continued. "Nothing can live without water. . . . We know the poison from the radioactive dump will go down under the ground and leak into the water."[69] This water provided sustenance to the plants and animals of the desert ecosystem considered fundamental to the Kungka Tjuta's physical and spiritual nourishment. And, perhaps most importantly, they identified themselves by name, asserting, "We are the people born on *manta*, born on the earth . . . we know the Country. We know what we're talking about."[70]

Throughout the Irati Wanti campaign, the Kungka Tjuta performed their commitment to Country through various Inma, ceremonial performances of dance and song that assert their knowledge of the land.

Inma are accompanied with song to tell and teach of the Tjurkurpa, "Dreaming," "a performed oral library of knowledge."[71] Articulating this, the Kungka Tjuta described the dancing of various Inma as "the proof of how we know what the Tjukur says, what the Dreaming says." In particular, the Dreaming emphasized the importance of leaving uranium in the ground, as the Kunga Tjuta articulated: "Aboriginal people were always obedient to that law, they don't touch the poison."[72] Thus, at every opportunity during their campaign, the women performed Inma for their audiences, reiterating the importance of their message: *irati wanti*, "the poison, leave it." This tradition was handed down to younger women and became an integral articulation of the Kungka Tjuta's resistance to threats to Country. And radioactivity was a threat that the women were markedly familiar with.

A<u>n</u>angu had maintained for generations that uranium should be left in the ground. "Irati needs to be kept safely where it is in the ground," Yankunytjatjara woman Karina Lester has said; "but then Western culture has worked out that you can make certain things with it."[73] "Old A<u>n</u>angu people taught us to not disturb the *manta* because this mineral non-Aboriginal people call uranium was too powerful to deal with, too dangerous," Mrs. Wingfield's daughter Rebecca Bear Wingfield has explained. "It killed people who did the wrong things," she continued.[74] Elders used to say to "just leave that thing under the *manta*, no good, poison, leave it," another of Mrs. Wingfield's daughters, Janice Wingfield, recalls.[75] This was *manta* that, for over a century, had been reduced to empty desert in the Western psyche: land whose utility was limited to its role as a nuclear testing site, a source of uranium, and now, a nuclear waste dump. But desert landscapes are full of life, physically, spiritually, and culturally. The Kungka Tjuta made it their mission to inject this message into urban spaces, pushing back against the tendency of settlers to silence Aboriginal voices as if they have "no language for the land."[76]

In alignment with their cultural responsibilities, care for Country was inherent to Irati Wanti, guided by the Kungka Tjuta's connections to the environment and everything within it. Family members of the Kungka Tjuta tell of the women teaching them "how to track animals, lizards, and identify their footprints," pointing out, they say, "what we can and what we can't eat out in the bush," while sharing other knowledge.[77] The Kungka Tjuta taught their relatives to "always care for the animals, always care for the Country," as well as how to use plants and animals to make bush medicines.[78] "This was the land they lived on, the land they depended on for their bush food," Mrs. Wingfield's niece, Kokatha woman Lynette Allen, noted.[79] But contamination from the proposed repository threatened this land, seeping into the soil, air, food, and water, existing for generations. "All our natural beauty is all going to go one day . . . no animals, no trees, no nothing," Janice Wingfield stated; "that's just the way of the greed" inherent to colonialism. In the face of colonial impositions, it was important for the Kungka Tjuta to "stand tall, stand strong."[80]

In 2003, Mrs. Wingfield implored Australia's settler populations residing in urban areas to rethink their use of the land. "If the whitefella stands still, not blowing things up, not mining the earth, the land will stay as it is," she said.[81] In addition to imploring settlers to slow down their exploitation of the land, the Kungka Tjuta encouraged them to listen to Aboriginal people: "We tell them there's something there before they dig it out," Mrs. Crombie stated. "Old people know. They know before whitefella came for it. They told them don't touch it. Aboriginal people know it's poison." "Listen to old people . . . you got to listen. Take it in," Mrs. Crombie begged, "don't just hear the words and go."[82]

One way the women sought to make settlers listen was through their engagement with urban-based environmentalists. From its very inception in Australia, Friends of the Earth (FOE) had been heavily involved in community action against nuclear issues. From picketing uranium mines to riding bikes in large numbers across the country, FOE aimed to create spectacles that were hard to ignore. In 1990, FOE went on its first Nuclear Exposure Tour, traveling to South Australia's nuclear hot spots. Aimed at "letting people witness and experience the nuclear industry at first hand," these tours facilitated white environmentalists' engagement with Aboriginal communities affected by the nuclear order, encouraging them "to see and walk on the country affected, hear what Aboriginal people had to say, . . . support traditional owners in their opposition to the nuclear industry" and then "return to their colleges, work places and communities with the story of their experience."[83] These tours are still held today. One consequence of an early Nuclear Exposure Tour was the creation of a collective that, in 1997, organized the Roxstop Action and Music Festival in protest of Olympic Dam. Over three hundred people attended.

With antinuclearism once again spreading across Australia in the wake of both a proposed expansion of the Ranger mine and France's recommencement of nuclear testing in the Pacific, the Kungka Tjuta recognized the benefits of engaging urban-based environmentalist groups in their cause. In the months after Roxstop, the Kungka Tjuta wrote to its organizers in search of solidarity. "Dear Greenies," their letter read, "we are just dropping you a few lines to let you know we want help. We are trying hard about this rubbish, the radioactive dump. . . . We've been talking to the Government, but they've taken no notice. . . . We want help! We want you to come up here to Coober Pedy and have a meeting with the Aborigine people, and any whitefellas from here who want to come."[84] This letter drew on the support that FOE networks had demonstrated toward Aboriginal communities in their struggle against environmental concerns in Australia, endearing themselves to groups such as the Kungka Tjuta. In Melbourne, FOE established the Indigenous Solidarity Group and aimed to foreground Indigenous issues. In November 1998, the group held a gathering in Maribyrnong, Victoria, called "Global Survival and Indigenous Rights." According to FOE Melbourne, "Of special interest was the attendance of almost 20 Kupa Piti Kungka Tjuta women from Coober Pedy who were building momentum to stop the nuclear waste dump on their lands."[85] Those at the event recalled that just being in the presence of the Kungka Tjuta was incredibly moving; several attendees (all women) would later move to Coober Pedy to assist with Irati Wanti.[86] According to *The Age*, the Kungka Tjuta used their attendance at this FOE event as another opportunity to voice their discontent at the proposed waste repository.[87] Their attendance cemented their relationship with FOE.

By 1999, Irati Wanti had taken more concrete shape. Inspired by the Kungka Tjuta's attendance at FOE's "Global Survival and Indigenous Rights" conference, a group of women from FOE Melbourne threw their support behind Irati Wanti. In assisting the cause, these Melbourne-based environmentalists utilized their standard methods of protest to further the reach of the Kungka Tjuta's stories, diversifying the campaign's tools.

By fundraising, conducting phone calls, rallying other environmentalists, and generally supporting the Kungka Tjuta's efforts, they "provided vital friendships as well as logistical support." The Kungka Tjuta's book *Talking Straight Out* acknowledges that "initially, the campaign relied heavily on the resources" of these women and their urban connections, and that "over time, [they] . . . came to play a crucial role in building the national profile and support base of Irati Wanti."[88]

In addition to assistance from urban environmental groups, the Kungka Tjuta enjoyed local support in Coober Pedy. The groundswell of anti-dump activity in this remote town included forming committees, organizing petitions, countering misinformation, networking with anti-dump groups, and protesting at the annual Opal Festivals.[89] At the April 1999 Coober Pedy Easter Street Parade, the Kungka Tjuta joined other locals protesting the waste dump, entering their Toyota Troop Carrier as a float. Emblazoned with banners and accompanied by the Kungka Tjuta performing various Inma on foot, their convoy was awarded the parade's "Best Walking Float." According to Sister Madigan, it was important for the Kungka Tjuta to have local support from settlers, not only to bolster the women and provide encouragement but also to reinforce the Kungka Tjuta's message and to see them "in the terms they wish[ed] to be seen."[90]

The involvement of white environmentalists reinforced and strengthened Irati Wanti, but there were also subtle tensions within the relationship between them and Indigenous activists.[91] While the relationship between the Melbourne environmentalists who moved to Coober Pedy and the Kungka Tjuta was undoubtedly productive, the anthropologist Eve Vincent, who counted herself among the "Melbourne Greenies" (as the Kungka Tjuta affectionally called them), has discussed at length the "unstable dynamics" that are always at work in such relationships, not least since "non-Indigenous desires for contact with Aboriginal people, idealisation of cultural otherness, and postcolonial guilt combine to shape, constrain and sometimes wreck these relations."[92] In the case of Irati Wanti, tensions were relatively veiled, overwritten by the success of the campaign. But they were nonetheless present.

Subtle pressures highlighted the slight differentiation between the goals of the Kungka Tjuta and the goals of urban-based environmentalists.[93] Australian activists turned academics have highlighted the tendency for environmentalists to claim the views and identities of those Aboriginal groups with whom they work closely, consequently viewing Aboriginal people holding opposing views as somehow illegitimate, irrespective of how that conflict is managed within or between communities.[94] As Melbourne Greenie Clare Brown articulated it, "There's not a right and a wrong way to be Aboriginal, or to be more Aboriginal or less Aboriginal, you know. But greenies seemed to be saying, 'This is the real, proper way to be Aboriginal, and these [other Aboriginal] people . . . have sold out.'"[95] The solidarity claimed by white environmentalists often served to "obscure, possibly unwittingly, a much more conflicted reality," that environmentalists are, in fact, "in support of *particular* Aboriginal people, on the condition that they share their political goals."[96] Such a point is, in itself, contentious, and opinions on the matter vary greatly. Regardless, in the case of Irati Wanti, the goals of those environmentalists who joined them in Coober Pedy appeared decidedly antinuclear, while those of the Kungka Tjuta are better understood as tied intimately to the safeguarding of cultural knowledge, which relied on their care for Country. This commitment was articulated through specific expressions of resistance, distinct from, but complementary to, those deployed by environmentalists, such as through the performing of Inma. By the end of Irati Wanti in 2004, the Kungka Tjuta had performed various Inma in front of desert and urban audiences, on and off Country, in despair and in celebration.

In September 1999, in a strange twist of fate, Hollywood star Val Kilmer of *Top Gun* and *Batman* fame heard about the Kungka Tjuta while filming in Australia. Sister Madigan tells of returning with the Kungka Tjuta to Coober Pedy after a big trip campaigning and being approached by someone who said, "Val Kilmer would like to meet the ladies." Not knowing who Kilmer was, Madigan suggested that the women would be too tired, but she asked Mrs. Wingfield about speaking with him anyway. Overhearing the conversation, one of Mrs. Wingfield's daughters screamed with excitement: "You've got to speak with him! He used to be Batman!" When Madigan later said to Kilmer, "I heard you were Batman," he modestly responded, "I was one of them."[97]

FIGURE 11. Val Kilmer's star power was met with unbridled excitement by members of the Kupa Piti Kungka Tjuta when he asked to meet with the women in November 1999 while he was filming in the desert. Captured in this image alongside Kilmer are Rebecca Bear Wingfield, Lucy Wilton, Eileen Wani Wingfield, Eileen Unkari Crombie, Sally Cullinan, and Emily Munyungka Austin (*left to right*). Not adequately captured here is the bright orange hue of Kilmer's matching tracksuit. Photograph courtesy of the Wingfield family.

The *Sunday Mail* reported that while shooting *Red Planet* in the South Australian central deserts, the Hollywood "actor took time out . . . to meet local Aboriginal leaders at a dusty Coober Pedy campsite to learn about their culture." Kilmer met with them to talk "about the land on which he . . . [was] making the film." Newspapers quoted members of the Kungka Tjuta as saying that "he wanted to know from the old people": "He spent about an hour sitting under the stars, listening to the Dreaming stories told by the women and their families."[98] He returned several nights later "for a ceremonial dancing of the Seven Sisters Dreaming."[99] With over five hundred people reportedly in attendance for Kilmer's return visit to the Kungka Tjuta, the women shared "their concerns over a proposed radioactive waste dump in the region, as well as indigenous Americans' experiences with the uranium industry" (fig. 11).[100] Rebecca Bear Wingfield later told the media that the meeting was "really powerful," characterized by a "lot of spiritual togetherness."[101] Several of the women who were there still laugh at the memories of the Kungka Tjuta charming—and being charmed by—the film star. Others recall with amused annoyance that they had not been there to meet him. Nevertheless, this undeniable contrast between Kilmer's Hollywood "star quality" and the desert raised the Kungka Tjuta's profile in urban spaces significantly.[102]

This publicity came when the Howard government was attempting to reassure the public that a national waste repository was necessary, a claim resisted by many. Despite the overall lack of local support for the facility, Canberra forged ahead, forced to address the question of Aboriginal heritage surrounding the six identified proposal sites. According to a Commonwealth document published in 1999, the government "wished to minimize the risk of damage to Aboriginal objects, remains, sites of spiritual, archaeological, anthropological or historical significance" caused by the waste repository.[103] Despite this apparent olive branch, the proposal treated Aboriginal objections to the repository as hollow, uninformed, and unnecessary, failing to acknowledge the importance of whole environments to contemporary Aboriginal peoples. A federal senator reiterated this sentiment in a letter to Sister Madigan: "There is no factual basis for the concern by Kupa Piti Kungka Tjuta that its members would be endangered by a repository in the central-north region." "The repository," he continued, "will not contribute to a higher level of background radiation than would otherwise be encountered in the region."[104] The response of the government demonstrated starkly that it would not seriously consider the concerns of the Kungka Tjuta because of what it regarded as their apparent lack of rationality. Nor, it seemed, could the government recognize the historical circumstances that left so many concerned about the proposal.

Rounding out the millennium, in November 1999 the Australian Conservation Foundation (ACF) hosted a large public meeting at Adelaide Town Hall to discuss the future of the national waste repository. To get to the meeting, the Kungka Tjuta bundled into a van and drove over 500 miles (approximately 850 kilometers) from Coober Pedy to Adelaide. However, outside of Port Augusta, the van carrying the women hit a bullock. Miraculously, no one was hurt, but the Kungka Tjuta decided they could not continue on their journey. They chose instead to stay the night in Port Augusta before turning around and heading home. Yet, Madigan recalled, "when they woke up in the morning, they all decided they wanted to go."[105] So, after a visit to the doctor, the Kungka Tjuta got back on the road to finish the trip.

Arriving in Adelaide, the Kungka Tjuta were met by the largest crowd they had faced thus far in their campaign. The meeting was attended by a reported one thousand to fifteen hundred people.[106] Headlining the meeting was the frontman of the popular Australian rock band Midnight Oil and former ACF president Peter Garrett, South Australia's shadow environment minister John Hill, and other government representatives.[107] Accompanying them was Rebecca Bear Wingfield, speaking to the audience about the Kungka Tjuta's cultural obligations, and Punch Gibson, Mrs. Crombie's uncle and the spokesperson for the Kungka Tjuta on this specific occasion.[108] Following speeches, senior Kungkas Mrs. Eileen Brown and Mrs. Lucy Wilton performed an Inma in black outfits painted with white and yellow dots to reflect the *irati*, the poison.[109] Spontaneously, the most senior Kungka, Mrs. Ivy Stewart, began to sing to the enraptured audience: "I left it [*irati*—poison] in the ground, you leave it in the ground."[110] The meeting was met with extensive media coverage and launched Irati Wanti into the new millennium with great momentum.

In 2000, the Sydney Olympics provided an international stage on which the Kungka Tjuta could present Irati Wanti. Arabunna Elder Kevin Buzzacott planned to use the event to highlight his community's opposition to Olympic Dam's use of water from the Great Artesian Basin, organizing a walk from Lake Eyre in central South Australia to Sydney, a journey of over 1,000 miles (1,650 kilometers). It would take him three months.[111] The Kungka Tjuta performed an Inma as Buzzacott and his supporters set off on their journey. From the outset, Buzzacott acknowledged the Kungka Tjuta's support, writing later that their presence made it "a very special day" because his "mob" was there.[112] Like the Kungka Tjuta's Irati Wanti campaign, the importance of land was central to Buzzacott's activism, as the Elder wrote: "We are walking our land in the company of the Old People and the old spirits of the ancient land. We are walking from Lake Eyre to Sydney, to arrive before the Olympic Games, carrying the real flame with us, the sacred firestick with our big message of peace to the world."[113] The Kungka Tjuta would later meet the walkers in Sydney. By virtue of being hosted in the same city as the Lucas Heights Nuclear Reactor, the global spectacle that was the Olympic Games presented the Kungka Tjuta with the ultimate platform for voicing their opposition to the proposed national waste repository. It was a chance for the Kungka Tjuta to finally—and quite literally—take the issue of nuclear waste back to Sydney.

In traveling to Sydney, the Kungka Tjuta had taken their fight right to the root of the problem. Sister Madigan recalls that the Kungka Tjuta were apprehensive about the trip, as they worried about what they would face in Sydney knowing that the Australian government would want to save face with the eyes of the world on the harbor city. They went anyway. "They were brave women, anything could have happened," Madigan recalls. While there, they watched the rehearsal of the Olympics opening ceremony, and some accompanied Buzzacott on a boat tour of Sydney's harbor, during which he conducted a traditional smoking ceremony over the water, performed to ensure safe passage for visitors to Country.[114] They also organized a visit to Lucas Heights, where the Kungka Tjuta met with members of the Sutherland Shire Council, with whom they discussed the women's fears over the national repository and highlighted the disproportionate burden borne by Aboriginal communities as a result of Australia's nuclear industry. In addition to meeting government officials and members of ANSTO, the Kungka Tjuta extended an invitation to "all the whitefellas": "Come and sit with us by the fire [at Buzzacott's camp in Victoria Park] and listen and learn the Aboriginal way." "By listening to us talking for our country," Mrs. Emily Austin said, "you're helping to save our land, our Australia."[115]

The trip garnered both national and international media coverage. The national Aboriginal newspaper the *Koori Mail* documented the women's Sydney trip in a second-page feature, reiterating the importance of the Kungka Tjuta's relationship to the land. "The message from the desert women is quite simple," a reporter explained, "and goes a little way in highlighting the extremely close affinity between Aboriginal people and the land."[116] The newspaper quoted the Kungka Tjuta at length, reinforcing their key messages: "There has to be no more Maralinga, no more radiation . . . we want clean land!" In an interesting role reversal, the report noted that the women suggested that "the proposed waste be sent to a place such as Sydney."[117]

Over the next few years, the Kungka Tjuta's profile continued to grow. In March 2000, Lucy Brown, an environmentalist from Melbourne, moved to Coober Pedy to support the Kungka Tjuta full-time. Her establishment of a permanent office for Irati Wanti ensured the campaign had a tangible and visible headquarters. Five more Melbourne women relocated to Coober Pedy throughout the campaign, facilitating its proliferation. In the years between 2000 and 2003, the Kungka Tjuta continued to write to politicians, and, as they reminded people time and time again, they traveled everywhere: "We went to Melbourne, we went to Adelaide, we went to Canberra, we went to Sydney . . . we even had a car crash and just kept going!"[118] These were travels that took significant bravery and stamina from these women, many of whom were elderly.

Nevertheless, the Kungka Tjuta refused to be bound by borders. The women strove to highlight their solidarity with other nuclear-affected communities, such as the Japanese *hibakusha*. They held festivals and performances. They even had a website launched and merchandise created: "They had tentacles everywhere."[119] All the while, the Kungka Tjuta maintained their original message: "We had enough [of the poison] at Maralinga and Emu Junction. . . . This time we say 'NO.'" "You fellas got to listen to us," they implored. This was not just a fight the women took on for themselves, it was for "everybody."[120] Karina Lester, Eileen Kampakuta Brown's granddaughter and a frequent interpreter for the Kungka Tjuta, noted that the women "were concerned with fulfilling their cultural obligation as law women to pass on that knowledge to their children, but they were also very concerned about the wider community."[121]

The Greenie Nobel Prize

The Kungka Tjuta's ability to highlight the importance of Aboriginal knowledge to all Australians has afforded them much praise since the late 1990s and directly contributed to the success of Irati Wanti. A significant recognition of their efforts came from the United States when, in 2003, Eileen Wani Wingfield and Eileen Kampakuta Brown received the Goldman Environmental Prize on behalf of all the Kungka Tjuta. Nicknamed the "Greenie Nobel Prize," and endowed by philanthropists Richard and Rhoda Goldman, the prize aims to "demonstrate the international nature of environmental problems, draw public attention to global issues of critical importance, reward ordinary individuals for outstanding grassroots environmental achievements, and inspire others to emulate the examples set by the Prize recipients."[122] Awardees also receive a generous cash prize. For the Kungka Tjuta, their selection as recipients of this accolade was unparalleled recognition of their campaign to care for Country. It also represented the reality that it had taken significant international recognition of the Kungka Tjuta's fight before they could be widely celebrated within Australia.[123]

In April 2003, Mrs. Wingfield made her first international trip when she jetted to San Francisco to receive the Goldman Prize. Accompanied by her daughter Rebecca Bear Wingfield, Mrs. Wingfield was presented with a whirlwind itinerary by Goldman Prize staff. Her time in the United States was split between San Francisco and Washington, DC, and included speech coaching and media orientations, press interviews and photography sessions, meetings with the World Bank, the World Wildlife Fund, National Geographic, and FOE, as well as a luncheon with the prize's donor Richard Goldman and dinner with Ethel Kennedy, widow of Robert F. Kennedy.[124] The trip also included the award ceremony, during which Mrs. Wingfield formally accepted the Goldman Prize. Speaking on Mrs. Wingfield's behalf, her daughter told the audience that it had been a very emotional journey to that stage in San Francisco. Nevertheless, she said, "my mother kept going."[125]

It was not just Mrs. Wingfield's daughter who honored the tenacity of the Kungka Tjuta in the face of hardship. The prize citation acknowledged the Kungka Tjuta's intimate experiences of nuclear imposition, justifying Mrs. Wingfield's and Mrs. Brown's receipt of the award. The citation acknowledged that their Country had been subjected to "half a century of government sanctioned nuclear contamination" from both "weapons tests and [the] exploitation of one of the world's largest uranium mines."[126] But, it was also their desire to highlight Aboriginal knowledge of and connections to the environment that made them worthy recipients. The citation reiterated that the women would "continue to fight for a healthy environment and pass on vital cultural and environmental lessons learned from their grandmothers."[127] These lessons were passed down from Mrs. Wingfield and Mrs. Brown to other women in their lives.[128]

The women's efforts against the waste dump—and their recognition by the Goldmans—elicited support from other Indigenous groups across the world. Haunani Apoliona, chairperson of the Board of Trustees of the Office of Hawaiian Affairs, wrote personally to Mrs. Wingfield, welcoming her to the United States: "To you *kapuna* (elders) of the aboriginal people of Australia, on behalf of the indigenous native Hawaiian people, I bid you welcome." "Our Hawaiian elders," Apoliona went on, "have cautioned us to *mālama 'āina* (care for the land) to ensure the survival of our people. Therefore, we support your efforts to protect your homeland from practices which poison your land and its people."[129]

Similar sentiments were expressed by the National Congress of American Indians. "Your demonstrated leadership in the campaign to block construction of a nuclear waste dump in your South Australian desert homeland is to be commended and we congratulate you on receiving this distinguished award," wrote Tex G. Hall, president of the congress, to Mrs. Wingfield and Mrs. Brown. "It is our honor," he continued, "to have two distinguished and respected aboriginal elders represent indigenous people worldwide and be recognized on our homelands."[130] Hall's letter was accompanied by an invitation to a reception hosted by the congress and designed to informally welcome the women to the United States. Reflecting the shared experiences of Indigenous peoples the world over, Mrs. Wingfield's family still recalls her particular connection to Native American groups, citing the sadness she felt: "Them poor people are just like us, being treated wrongfully on our own Country, own dirt, own *manta* . . . no recognition, no nothing."[131] Many of the dream catchers she collected in her lifetime hang in the house of her daughter to this day.

Following her receipt of the Goldman Prize, Mrs. Wingfield returned to Port Augusta, where the local newspaper, the *Transcontinental*, ran a modest piece congratulating her and Mrs. Brown, alongside the other members of the Kungka Tjuta. "Aboriginal Elder Awarded World Environmental Prize," the headline ran. And despite acknowledging that the award, "dubbed the Nobel prize for the environment," is "the largest award in the world for grassroots environmentalists" and that these women belonged "to an elite group, with only four other Australians previously winning the prize," the *Transcontinental*'s coverage was scant.[132]

Politicians from across South Australia made up for that, congratulating the women in Parliament and in person. On 23 April 2003, Labor politician Gail Elizabeth Gago noted in Parliament that the "internationally prestigious" Goldman Environmental Prize had been "awarded to two South Australian Aboriginal women."[133] The South Australian minister for Aboriginal affairs and reconciliation explained to his parliamentary colleagues that Mrs. Wingfield and Mrs. Brown were "two elderly Aboriginal women" who had "elder status within their community" and had "worked hard for the recognition" afforded by the Goldman Prize. "The prize is recognised as the Nobel prize for the environment," he stated, "which makes it even more important for two relatively obscure, unknown and almost hidden Aboriginal women within this state." It is important to acknowledge that, to their communities and supporters across the country, these were not "relatively obscure, unknown and almost hidden Aboriginal women."[134] The impact of the Kungka Tjuta was profound, and it continues to be.

In 2004, the Howard government made the decision to ax its plan to dump nuclear waste at Billa Kalina. This decision was reached owing largely to the South Australian government's decision to take the Commonwealth to the Federal Court over attempts to extinguish state legislation to make way for the repository.[135] And while the justification for abandoning the repository was complex, many South Australian politicians nonetheless acknowledged the Kungka Tjuta's relentless fight against the dump in their responses to Howard's decision. The Kungka Tjuta's mobilization of Aboriginal ways of knowing and being was celebrated. South Australia's Labor premier personally addressed the Kungka Tjuta in his announcement that the proposal had been scrapped, describing them as having "continued to share their personal stories of the impact from the atomic tests in Maralinga on their people and continued their opposition to the radioactive waste dump through a dignified campaign, based not on science or law but on their personal experience and connection with the land."[136]

"Be Strong like Us"

The Howard government's proposal to dump the nation's radioactive waste at Billa Kalina sought to combat anxieties about the contamination of urban spaces. At its core, the proposal reflected settler attitudes toward the disposability of desert ecosystems and the peoples who inhabit them, a tool of nuclear colonialism since its beginning. As with the case for nuclear testing, the proposal reiterated the notion that, where urban spaces remain indispensable, remote regions are comparably expendable. As such, the proposal echoed decades of nuclear history both in Australia and abroad, where nuclear processes were actively imposed on and thus were—and continue to be—disproportionately borne by marginalized communities. More often than not, these communities are Indigenous.

This historical episode elucidates key characteristics of nuclear colonialism, not least the struggle between urban and desert landscapes, and the tensions between settler and Indigenous attitudes toward lands and waters. The clear juxtaposition between the Kungka Tjuta's approach to protecting the desert by emphasizing care and preservation and that of the government in seeking seemingly uninhabitable landscapes for waste is reflective of these stark historical differences. Yet, in the face of a proposal that aimed to make Australia's nuclear waste someone else's problem, Irati Wanti sought to center the knowledge of Aboriginal women, highlighting the importance and indispensability of desert landscapes to peoples who, generation after generation and in countries all around the world, have borne the burden of the global nuclear order.

Through their tireless efforts, the Kungka Tjuta demonstrated that desert spaces are not mere dumping grounds for the waste of urban populations. Nor are they proving grounds for working through urban anxieties about the potentially hazardous nature of radioactivity. Rather, they are inhabited landscapes steeped in cultural, spiritual, and physical importance, worthy of recognition as something other than "out of sight, out of mind." The Kungka Tjuta worked assiduously to highlight the inherent connection between Aboriginal peoples, the lands, waters, plants, and animals that make up Country *and* the persistent environmental impacts of nuclear processes. The Kungka Tjuta's efforts thus reflect their place in a broader history of global Indigenous politics, shaped by decades of nuclear imposition and Indigenous resistance that (while still developing) demonstrated the legitimacy of Aboriginal knowledge of and connection to Country.

The lessons endowed by Irati Wanti deployed decidedly Indigenous articulations of resistance against ongoing nuclear imposition, guided by the Kungka Tjuta's role as cultural women with a duty to their communities and by their exposure to the intergenerational impacts of nuclear colonialism in South Australia. Their knowledge continues to guide Aboriginal antinuclear resistance across Australia, inspiring individuals and communities "to stand up and talk."[137] These women implored their contemporaries, and future generations, "Be strong like us." "Don't be scared of the government," they told anyone who would listen; "we weren't scared and we are elderly ladies!"[138]

CONCLUSION

Fallout

In 2017, Yankunytjatjara woman Karina Lester implored the international community to consider the impact of the nuclear order on Indigenous peoples globally. When she spoke to the United Nations General Assembly as a member of civil society, she was there to represent Yankunytjatjara people, on whom nuclear colonialism has been a long-term imposition. She noted that her trip to the UN had become "a personal journey," a journey to share a story, she said, "that was so close to myself and my family as well." "We were doing it for our people, for our families, who would have been completely overwhelmed by going through these experiences." But she also spoke on behalf of Indigenous nuclear survivors worldwide, reflecting that her presence in New York was an "amazing opportunity" to demonstrate that nuclear colonialism is "not just a local issue, it's not just a black issue, it's not just a state issue, or an Australian issue." It is "a global issue," she said, and "what happened in our backyard, happened in other people's backyards."[1]

In speaking with me as I researched this book, Lester reflected on her own understandings of, and relationship to, nuclear colonialism. First, she poignantly described how the environmental responsibility placed on contemporary Aboriginal peoples—fundamental to inherited cultural obligations—is integrally undermined by nuclear processes. She implored people more generally to think of the Kungka Tjuta and recognize that when Aboriginal peoples' responsibilities to Country are "undermined by bigger and more powerful industries and companies that are there to reap and pillage and take away in the name of economics," it "is certainly colonialism."[2] But she also articulated the relationship at the core of nuclear colonialism in reference to its deeper, less contemporary implications. She likened it to pastoralism, evoking the ways that, as she described, pastoralists "came in, didn't even speak to Aṉangu, didn't engage with Aṉangu Tjuta, used our land and our country, put all [their] stock there, over grazed [their] cattle, [and] destroyed our sites and places," cementing their places in Australia's history as "great legend[s]."[3] Nuclear colonialism, Lester articulated, is part of a much bigger structure, one particularly insidious cog in the colonial machinery of contemporary Australia.[4]

Colonialism has fundamentally shaped Australia's nuclear past, present, and future. From the early twentieth century onward, the nuclear ambitions of Australia and its closest allies were fueled by settler-colonial visions of the island continent and its utility. But as the twentieth century wore on, challenges to settler-colonial structures and policies by Aboriginal peoples and others forced the nation to face its involvement in and enactment of nuclear colonial injustices. Nuclear colonialism should thus be understood as a complex and malleable phenomenon, defined by the overlapping influences of historically contingent imperial and settler-colonial ambitions, Aboriginal mobilization, and humans' differentiated relationship to the environment. Placed in an Australian context, these intersections reveal a great deal about the parallel—and often interconnected—historical development of both settler and Aboriginal politics on state, national, and international levels. Where in the early twentieth century Aboriginal peoples were actively rendered invisible by the state in pursuit of nuclear development—irradiated, dispossessed, and silenced—by the century's end they were active citizens of the nation, agitating for recognition and advocating for Country.

Nuclear colonial injustices both assisted in engendering this shift and were exposed by it. The development of Aboriginal politics described throughout this book would likely have occurred in some form or another without the enactment of nuclear colonialism on Australia's lands and peoples. However, the insidiousness of the nuclear industry's role in contaminating and degrading Country and dispossessing Aboriginal peoples undoubtedly influenced land rights debates and contributed to ballooning antinuclear sentiment across the nation. In turn, the environmental and human injustices facilitated by nuclear development in Australia encouraged specific Aboriginal mobilization against the industry, exposing and challenging the settler-colonial ambitions that have historically propped up development in Australia.

From the beginning of the twentieth century, settlers' visions of the land as theirs for the taking dictated individuals' relationships to the emergent nuclear industry. Early manifestations of nuclear colonialism in Australia were defined by the same settler-colonial ambitions as other forms of exploration, pursued in the name of scientific discovery and development. As geology formalized the appraisal of nature for its economic value, radium prospecting in countries such as Australia, the United States, and Canada relied on the knowledge and labor of Indigenous peoples to identify minerals and other natural resources in areas considered ripe for development. Such was the case on Australia's inland frontier, its "red" or "dead" heart. Radioactive minerals, and later nuclear testing, assisted in colonizing lands whose aridity had precluded it from traditional colonial settlement.

However, as the explosive potential of radium and uranium became more apparent, Canberra's desire to obtain a national supply of radioactive minerals grew, supplemented by British imperial ambitions. The convergence of British nuclear imperialism and Australian settler colonialism transformed nuclear colonialism in Australia, shifting the phenomenon from one that encouraged individual ambition for radioactive riches to one defined by the perceived exceptionalism of nuclear weapons. This purported exceptionalism presented an alternative source of importance and power for previously "great" but slowly shrinking empires, encouraged the centralization of control over radioactive minerals, and offered modernization and purpose to a region settlers had largely dismissed as useless.

Rather than creating something entirely "new" or "exceptional," then, nuclear colonialism effectively co-opted existing colonial practices and mechanisms. Nuclear weapons testing did not *replace* settler colonialism in the central deserts but relied on it to succeed. Britain's obtainment of a so-called Commonwealth nuclear posture in the 1950s, and Australia's direct involvement in the process, required both states to justify nuclear development on occupied lands. Against the backdrop of settlers' prevailing beliefs about the uninhabitability and hostility of Australia's inland reaches, such justification was not hard to find. For Australian authorities, the dispossession of desert communities would enable the modernization of these arid lands, while bolstering Australia's geopolitical standing and scientific development. For the British, the empire's nuclear ambitions relied on the unpeopling of the central deserts, though this process was purportedly not theirs to oversee. Rather, it was a process enabled by the settler-colonial mechanisms and policies of Australian authorities, many of which had existed for decades prior to the tests and prevailed long after their conclusion.

By this token, nuclear exceptionalism justified dispossession that was already underway. So, while the insidiousness of radioactive contamination can be considered exceptional, the conduct of both Britain and Australia in pursuit of their nuclear ambitions during the mid-twentieth century was anything but. Their ambitions reflected long-held preoccupations with imperial prestige, territorial control, and geopolitical influence, enacted through tried-and-tested mechanisms of settler-colonial command and the subjugation of Indigenous peoples. The perceived exceptionalism of nuclear technology may have *justified* the usurpation of Aboriginal lands, but the physical act of dispossession was enabled through extant forms of colonial control—through missions, stations, and superstitions—themselves embedded in Australia's political and social fabric. This duality reveals the influence of British nuclear imperialism on Australian nuclear colonialism *and* the centrality of dispossession to both.

Dispossession has been fundamental to the pursuit of nuclear development in Australia's central deserts and inland region over the past century. The declaration of uranium as a Crown possession in 1946 assumed territorial ownership over any radioactive minerals on Aboriginal-occupied land. The management of Aboriginal people around Maralinga and Emu Field in the late 1940s and 1950s drew on the influences of missions, stations, and superstitions to move peoples from and then indefinitely prevent them from returning to Country. And this persistent perception of settler Australians' "right" to development paved the way for two of the world's largest uranium mines. Reckoning with Australia's nuclear past thus requires an acknowledgment of the industry's embeddedness in the broader colonial project of the Australian state, at the center of which is dispossession.

But histories of nuclear colonialism are not all about imposition. The history of nuclear colonialism in Australia is also a history of political evolution. In the decades following Britain's nuclear tests in Australia, both anti- and pro-nuclear sentiments intersected with broader political developments among settler and Aboriginal populations. As reflected around the world, the period 1966–72 was one of great social change as progressives and youth culture pushed back against Australian conservatism and demanded greater engagement with international issues relating to peace, imperialism, and Indigenous self-determination. International social movements catalyzed an important development in how nuclear weapons possession and testing were viewed publicly and politically in Australia. Calls to emancipate France's colonial subjects in Algeria and across the Pacific, and to protect Australia's environment from radioactivity, accompanied growing anti-imperialism. And while there was little to no engagement with Maralinga and Emu Field during these discussions, developments in Aboriginal politics, including engagement with an anticolonial pan-Aboriginal activism and greater interest in land rights, ensured that Australia's own nuclear processes could not go on unquestioned, especially in relation to their colonial dimensions.

Charting the interplay between the development of Aboriginal politics and Australia's nuclear past is pivotal in understanding both nuclear colonialism and resistance to it. At Olympic Dam, local, national, and international interest in uranium mining actively came up against advances in land rights and Aboriginal heritage protection. Legislative developments in South Australia, such as the A<u>n</u>angu Pitjantjatjara Yankunytjatjara Land Rights Act of 1981, precipitated greater engagement with land rights debates and Aboriginal interests in the lands encompassed by the state, while also leading to greater anxiety among proponents of mining that their rights to development would be impeded. Ebbing prosperity, brought by the end of the postwar boom, increased settler optimism for nuclear development. However, greater political mobility among Aboriginal groups and antinuclear sentiment in the broader Australian public challenged this optimism, revealing the potential costs of Australia's pursuit of a nuclear industry. Faced with the prospect that mining companies might have to concede to Aboriginal communities, proponents of mining reasserted both settlers' rights to and connections with mineral-rich lands.

By the 1980s, Aboriginal communities were actively challenging settlers' interests in nuclear processes. This was especially important for Maralinga Tjarutja, whose lands had been formally returned in 1984 without being adequately decontaminated. The potential danger posed by environmental contamination, alongside a greater sense among politicians and the public that information about the nuclear tests thirty years earlier needed to be released, precipitated the calling of the Royal Commission into British Nuclear Tests in Australia (1984–85). The parameters that guided the commission sought to actively avoid the colonial consequences of the nuclear tests on Aboriginal peoples, instead focusing solely on irradiation. Delving into the less tangible consequences of the nuclear order's colonial dimensions, such as dispossession, displacement, and exposure to poor conditions on missions or at stations, was not considered an option by the Hawke Labor government. Instead, the commission created a stage on which Hawke and his contemporaries could divorce Australia from the "mother country," placing blame for the nuclear testing and its ongoing consequences on the British government and its Anglophilic allies, the Menzies government.

Nevertheless, Aboriginal testimonies during the Royal Commission's proceedings demonstrated that the tests had deeply colonial consequences. Supported by growing land rights and homelands movements, individuals from across numerous communities gave voice to the layers of colonialism overlapping at the heart of Britain's postwar nuclear program. Not only had people been irradiated, but they had also been displaced from Country, indefinitely dispossessed due to contamination, manipulated into not returning to their ancestral lands by authorities, and exposed to addictive substances, abuse, and violence at missions. The active acknowledgment of these testimonies by both the commissioners and the media during the 1980s led to greater public discussion of and engagement with the colonial consequences of nuclear processes writ large. Australia's nuclear past also bore witness to the emergence of a decidedly Aboriginal antinuclear movement, one that did not necessarily mobilize in the same ways as the social movements of the 1960s and 1970s, but which brought together Aboriginal voices on both nuclear issues and discussions of colonialism.

The active involvement of nuclear survivors in formalizing compensation agreements following the Royal Commission reflects the growing demand of Indigenous peoples all over the world to be taken seriously as experts in their use of and connection to Country. Dispossession, destruction, and contamination had not severed communities' connections to their land. This was made evident by the internationalization of Indigenous issues in the late 1980s to 1990s, during which Maralinga Tjarutja were able to place their experiences in direct comparison with those of other nuclear survivors. Finding solidarity with others who had been displaced by nuclear impositions, including the Marshallese removed from Bikini Atoll, enabled Maralinga Tjarutja and other communities to share and reconcile their experiences of indefinite dispossession from traditional lands. It was under these circumstances that the experiences of Australia's nuclear survivors could be placed into transnational discussions of monetary compensation for the impositions of nuclear colonialism experienced by Indigenous peoples over the previous four decades.

These impositions came to a head in the late 1990s when Canberra proposed establishing a national radioactive waste repository near Coober Pedy. The Irati Wanti campaign was thus the culmination of nearly a century of Aboriginal political engagement with and challenge to Australia's nuclear order. This campaign encapsulated the ways in which the relationship between nuclear processes and colonialism had shifted across the twentieth century, from their pursuit being perceived as the right of the settler to being defined in relation to their imposition on Aboriginal responsibilities to Country, responsibilities laid bare by key developments in Aboriginal politics. The Kungka Tjuta's relentless campaigning exposed the centrality of Indigenous refusal to the understanding of nuclear colonialism. Aboriginal peoples (as well as their non-Indigenous allies) have consistently challenged colonial practices and narratives, exposing the deeply colonial nature of Australia's nuclear past by evading authorities in the testing area, lobbying for the protection of sacred sites, jostling for their return to Country, and refusing to be silenced. The efforts of Indigenous people globally have ensured that nuclear colonialism's impacts and impositions cannot be overlooked or underestimated.

A history of nuclear colonialism in Australia offers much more than merely charting the impact of nuclear processes on Aboriginal peoples. It demonstrates the persistence and contemporary relevance of colonial structures, narratives, and ambitions. It highlights the insufficient periodization afforded by considering nuclear colonialism an exceptional product of the post-1945 "nuclear age." And perhaps most importantly, such a history serves as a reminder that nuclear colonialism has not been and is not merely enacted upon peoples, but has been and continues to be challenged, resisted, and forced to adapt.

There is no doubt that the relationship between nuclear processes and colonialism in Australia has changed since the settler "discovery" of radioactive minerals. But it is set to continue shifting. Since 2017, furious debates over the establishment of a national waste repository in South Australia have raged as renewed attempts to dispose of the nation's nuclear waste have been challenged by Aboriginal and non-Indigenous communities alike. Meanwhile, the Treaty on the Prohibition of Nuclear Weapons has rendered these weapons of mass destruction illegal. And yet former opponents of nuclear power in Australia have begun to flirt with the idea of developing nuclear energy to ensure Australia meets its carbon emission targets under the terms of the Paris Agreement.

As elsewhere in the world, a nuclear renaissance is afoot in Australia. The continent's abundance of uranium is considered by politicians and members of the public as an enticing solution to the world's fossil-fueled woes, not least as uranium is frequently touted by conservative politicians and the media as the apparent solution to climate change. Mentions of "clean" nuclear energy punctuate pressing discussions of the very real consequences of our warming planet. And as a result, experts, politicians, and laypeople argue over the viability of pursuing nuclear energy into the future; they debate the pros and cons, list the positive and negative environmental impacts, and attempt to crunch the numbers. But regardless of whether Australia embarks on a nuclear-powered future, the nation and its people are plagued by the residues of its nuclear past. From the soil, machinery, and debris that remain contaminated and fenced off at Maralinga to the large tailing ponds that flank Olympic Dam, Australia's nuclear past has an unavoidable present and future.

NOTES

Introduction Fission and Fusion

1. For clarity in the first instance, I have included Karina Lester's Aboriginal nation *after* her name. For the remainder of this book, the specific Aboriginal nation of individuals—where known—will come before their names.

2. Further to the "Note to the Reader" at the beginning of this book, I want to acknowledge here that when I refer to the "central desert region" or "central deserts" I am referring to the varied arid regions at the center of the Australian continent, encompassing varied ecological and cultural geographies extending across South Australia and into the Northern Territory and Western Australia. This region comprises various arid ecosystems—some stony, some replete with low vegetation, and some with rolling sands—that can be collectively understood as "deserts," given the region's inclusion of the Great Victoria Desert (which covers the majority of this region), Pedirka Desert, Simpson Desert, and Strzelecki Desert, among other arid environments. The "central deserts" or "central desert region," as this area is referred to throughout this book, are known and valued by different groups of Aboriginal people who hold knowledge of their lands and waters, understand complex religious and philosophical narratives about them, and know themselves to belong to these arid places. My use of these terms is not to be confused with the capitalized Central Australia or Central Desert, which are geographically discrete areas in the Northern Territory.

3. "Karina Lester Addresses the Second Meeting of States Parties to the TPNW," 2023, video via YouTube.

4. "Nuclear Test Survivor Sue Coleman-Haseldine," 2017, video via YouTube.

5. Karen Percy, "Indigenous Anti-Nuclear Activist Tells of Her Personal Work with Nobel Prize–Winning ICAN," *ABC News* (Sydney), 7 October 2017.

6. Treaty on the Prohibition of Nuclear Weapons, United Nations, New York, 7 July 2017, 1–2, https://documents-dds-ny.un.org/doc/UNDOC/GEN/N17/209/73/PDF/N1720973.pdf; emphasis in the original.

7. "Nuclear Test Survivor Sue Coleman-Haseldine."

8. Urwin, "The Radioactive Dr Mawson," 33.

9. Reynolds, *Australia's Bid for the Atomic Bomb*, 63; Broinowski, *Fact or Fission?*, 44.

10. For more on Britain's inland and offshore nuclear tests in Australia, see Tynan, *Atomic Thunder*; Tynan, *The Secrets of Emu Field.*

11. Reynolds, *Australia's Bid for the Atomic Bomb*; Walker, *Maralinga*, 1; Parkinson, *Maralinga: Australia's Nuclear Waste Cover-Up*, 3; Broinowski, *Fact or Fission?*, 51–74; Lowe, *Long Half-Life*, 3.

12. Lowe, *Long Half-Life*, 2–3.

13. Broinowski, *Fact or Fission?*, 127–58, 241–54; Lee, *The Second Rush*, 276–81.

14. Urwin, "'The Old Colonial Power Can Stand Proxy.'"

15. Broinowski, *Fact or Fission?*, 277–90.

16. Note that for some of these listed scholars, the process of nuclear colonialism is ongoing and is not tied to historical nuclear weapons tests: Endres, *Nuclear Decolonization*, 37–45; Endres, "From Wasteland to Waste Site"; Runyan, "Disposable Waste, Lands and Bodies." See also Hogan, *What Is Colonialism?*

17. Bullard, *Environment and Morality*; Bullard, "Dismantling Environmental Racism"; Bullard, *Confronting Environmental Racism*; Malin, *The Price of Nuclear Power*; Voyles, *Wastelanding*; Bullard et al., "Toxic Wastes and Race at Twenty"; Endres, "From Wasteland to Waste Site"; McGurty, "From NIMBY to Civil Rights."

18. Maddock, *Nuclear Apartheid*; Jacobs, "Nuclear Conquistadors."

19. Bullard, *Environment and Morality*; Bullard, "Dismantling Environmental Racism"; Bullard, *Confronting Environmental Racism*; Malin, *The Price of Nuclear Power*; Voyles, *Wastelanding*; Bullard et al., "Toxic Wastes and Race at Twenty"; Endres, "From Wasteland to Waste Site"; McGurty, "From NIMBY to Civil Rights"; Johnston, *Half-Lives and Half-Truths*; Endres, "The Rhetoric of Nuclear Colonialism."

20. Malin, *The Price of Nuclear Power*; Voyles, *Wastelanding*; Endres, "From Wasteland to Waste Site."

21. Voyles, *The Settler Sea*; Voyles, *Wastelanding*; Gómez, *Nuclear Nuevo México*; Leddy, *Serpent River Resurgence*. For other works, less focused on nuclear contaminants and interested in other forms of waste, see Müller, *The Toxic Ship*; Hecht, *Residual Governance*.

22. Horowitz et al., "Indigenous Peoples' Relationships to Large-Scale Mining"; Fan, "Nuclear Waste Facilities on Tribal Land"; Johnston, *Half-Lives and Half-Truths*; Pellow, *Resisting Global Toxics*.

23. Hill, "Britain, West Africa and 'The New Nuclear Imperialism'"; Gerster, "Anzac, New Mexico"; Jacobsen, *The Nuclear Era*; Keown, "Waves of Destruction"; Shiga, "The Nuclear Sensorium"; Maurer and Hogue, "Introduction: Transnational Nuclear Imperialisms."

24. Maurer and Hogue, "Introduction: Transnational Nuclear Imperialisms," 27; Hecht, *Entangled Geographies*, 4–5.

25. Hecht, "Globalization Meets Frankenstein?," 3.

26. Hecht, "Globalization Meets Frankenstein?," 3; Hecht, "Rupture-Talk in the Nuclear Age."

27. Moreton-Robinson, *The White Possessive*, xi.

28. Moreton-Robinson, *The White Possessive*, xi–xii.

29. Echo-Hawk, "Colonialism and Law in the Post-Colonial Era," 160.

30. Relatedly, scholars argue that "it is often indigenous people whose sovereignty is most profoundly challenged by the colonial and post-colonial processes of state formation," to which resource extraction has been fundamental. See Howitt, Connell, and Hirsch, "Resources, Nations and Indigenous Peoples," 1.

31. Malin, *The Price of Nuclear Power*, 2–50; Johnston, *Half-Lives and Half-Truths*, 2–6; Fan, "Nuclear Waste Facilities on Tribal Land"; Tatz et al., *Aborigines and Uranium*.

32. Hecht, *Being Nuclear*; Voyles, *Wastelanding*; Gómez, *Nuclear Nuevo México*; Leddy, *Serpent River Resurgence*.

33. Kuletz, *The Tainted Desert*, 13; Voyles, *Wastelanding*. For a discussion of how rhetorical constructions of nuclear spaces have played out in nondesert environments, such as in the Pacific, see Kahn, *Tahiti beyond the Postcard*.

34. For more on settlers' hopes for the modern utility of the central deserts in the 1950s, see chapter 2. "Woomera," *The Advertiser* (Adelaide), 7 July 1947, 2.

35. Endres, "From Wasteland to Waste Site," 926; Voyles, *Wastelanding*, 7–11.

36. Edwards, "Nuclear Colonialism and the Social Construction of Landscape," 112.

37. Bongiorno, *Dreamers and Schemers*, 186.

38. The acknowledgment of Indigenous resistance to nuclear colonial imposition is part of a growing global scholarly trend of account for Indigenous resistance and refusal more generally. See Endres, *Nuclear Decolonization*; Leddy, *Serpent River Resurgence*; Runyan, "Indigenous Women's Resistances"; Allman, "Nuclear Imperialism and the Pan-African Struggle"; Simpson, "Indigenous Resurgence and Co-resistance."

39. The use of Adnyamathanha to describe the communities of the northern Flinders Ranges during the early twentieth century risks appearing anachronistic, as this region was then the land of several Aboriginal groups, including the Kuyani, Wailpi, Yadliaura, Pilatapa, and Pangkala. However, these nations are contemporarily grouped under the Adnyamathanha and are historically difficult to differentiate, and thus Adnyamathanha is the most accurate way to refer to these grouped nations today. See Brock, *Yura and Udnyu*, 5–8.

One Radioactive Riches

1. "Health in Radium, the World's Wonder Mineral, Its Enormous Value," *North West Post* (Tasmania), 5 March 1909, 4.

2. "Concerning Radium: An Interview with Mr. Mawson," *The Register* (Adelaide), 5 May 1906, 7.

3. Kaye, "The Romance of Radium," 56.

4. "Concerning Radium: An Interview with Mr. Mawson," 7.

5. "The Price of Radium," *Evening News* (Sydney), 23 January 1904, 4.

6. Malin, *The Price of Nuclear Power*, 32–58.

7. Radioactivity captured the imaginations of many countries globally. See Badash, "Radium, Radioactivity and the Popularity of Scientific Discovery"; Badash, *Radioactivity in America*; Priestley, *Mad on Radium*, 1–34.

8. "Is It Radium? Interesting Mineral Discovery," *The Register*, 4 May 1906, 5.

9. Articles with the headline "Is It Radium?" appeared in *The Register*, 9 May 1906, 4; *Evening Journal* (Adelaide), 10 May 1906, 2; *The Observer* (Adelaide), 12 May 1906, 36; *Glen Innes Examiner and General Advertiser* (New South Wales), 22 May 1906, 4; and *Clarence and Richmond Examiner* (Grafton, New South Wales), 2 June 1906, 8.

10. McLean, *Why Australia Prospered*, 63–79.

11. To this day, Australia is a leading exporter of gold, approximately 60 percent of which comes from Western Australia.

12. Commissioner of Crown Lands and Immigration, "South Australia: A Brief Account of Its Progress and Resources" (E. Spiller Government Printer, 1882), 6.

13. Lionel C. E. Gee, chief registrar of mines, *A General Synopsis of the Mining Laws of the State* (R. E. E. Rogers, Government Printer, 1918), GRS/111328/1, State Records of South Australia (SRSA), Adelaide.

14. "Bulletin Issued by the Directors of Australian Radium Corporation on the Radium Bearing Ores of Australia" (Harston, Patridge & Co. Pty. Ltd., date unknown), GRS/11322/00002/1/0009, SRSA.

15. Gee, *A General Synopsis of the Mining Laws of the State*, GRS/111328/1, SRSA.

16. For a discussion of the difficulties of engaging in pastoralism in the central deserts and other arid lands in Australia, see Palmer, *Unmaking Angas Downs*.

17. Griffiths, *Hunters and Collectors*, 186–87; Hirst, *Sense and Nonsense in Australian History*, 174–96.

18. Griffiths, *Hunters and Collectors*, 178–79; Hains, "Mawson of the Antarctic, Flynn of the Inland," 154.

19. Examples of such expeditions include the Elder Scientific Exploring Expedition (1891–92), the Horn Scientific Expedition (1894), and the Calvert Scientific Exploration Expedition (1896–97).

20. Jones, *Ochre and Rust*, 94.

21. Bsumek, *The Foundations of Glen Canyon Dam*, 57.

22. Griffiths, *Hunters and Collectors*, 178.

23. Gordon and Ryan, *Handbook of South Australia*, 299, 309.

24. Gordon and Ryan, *Handbook of South Australia*, 309.

25. For examples, see FitzSimons, *Mawson and the Ice Men of the Heroic Age*; Riffenburgh, *Racing with Death*. Scholarship that has sought to address Mawson and his legacy with more nuance includes Hains, *The Ice and the Inland*; Griffiths, "A Polar Drama."

26. Thomas, *Expedition into Empire*, 11.

27. Sendziuk and Foster, *A History of South Australia*, 100; Thomas, *Expedition into Empire*, 11.

28. Griffiths, *Hunters and Collectors*, 178.

29. Griffiths, *Hunters and Collectors*, 178; Hains, *The Ice and the Inland*.

30. Explorations of Mawson's contributions to geology within Australia do exist and have largely been written by geologists and others interested in mining. For examples, see Pring and Brugger, "Mawson and the Radium and Uranium Mineralisation at Mount Painter"; Jago and Pharaoh, "Pre-Antarctic Mawson in South Australia"; Stillwell, "Uraninite from Rum Jungle and Fergusson River, Northern Territory."

31. Mawson, "The Geology of the New Hebrides," 402; Jago and Pharoah, "Douglas Mawson's First Major Geological Expedition," 97–105.

32. F. J. Jacka, "Mawson, Sir Douglas" (1882–1958)," in *Australian Dictionary of Biography* (National Centre of Biography, Australian National University, 2006), https://adb.anu.edu.au/biography/mawson-sir-douglas-7531.

33. Mawson and Laby, "Preliminary Observations on Radio-Activity."

34. "Concerning Radium: An Interview with Mr. Mawson," 7.

35. Weidenbach, *Rock Star*, 29; Sprigg, *Arkaroola–Mount Painter*, 41.

36. "Radium Cancer Cure," *Evening News*, 21 August 1909, 11.

37. "A Radium Institute," *Sydney Morning Herald*, 8 March 1909, 6.

38. "A Radium Institute," 6.

39. Lawrence, *Radium: How and When to Use*, 49–74.

40. "What Is Radium? Latest Marvel of Science," *Express and Telegraph* (Adelaide), 2 May 1903, 4.

41. "Radium Manure," *The Observer*, 12 September 1914, 13.

42. "Radium Spray," *The Mail* (Adelaide), 31 May 1913, 9.

43. For more on the dial painters in the United States, see Moore, *The Radium Girls*.

44. "Radium's Power," *Northern Argus* (Rockhampton, Queensland), 30 March 1906, 6.

45. Caufield, *Multiple Exposures*, 80–81.

46. "Radium," *Ballarat Star* (Victoria), 19 October 1904, 1.

47. "Radium," *Ballarat Star*, 17 June 1904, 3.

48. "Price of Radium," *Cairns Post* (Queensland), 4 September 1909, 2; "The Price of Radium," *Evening News*, 23 January 1904, 4.

49. "Professor Bragg's Opinion," *Express and Telegraph*, 4 May 1906, 1.

50. "Radio-Active Carnotite," *The Week* (Brisbane), 11 May 1906, 15.

51. Letter from Douglas Mawson, 23 September 1906, Mawson Correspondence re. Radioactivity (1906), Mawson Collection, MI316, South Australian Museum (SAM), Adelaide.

52. Shumway, "A History of Uranium Mining on the Colorado Plateau," 6.

53. Letter from Mawson, 23 September 1906, Mawson Collection, MI316, SAM.

54. Sprigg, *Arkaroola–Mount Painter*, 12.

55. As I noted in the introduction, the Aboriginal communities of the Flinders Ranges historically included the Kuyani, Wailpi, Yadliaura, Pilatapa and Pangkala, among others. Adnyamathanha will be used in this book to reference these various nations on occasion, though at times it will be more appropriate to refer to groups simply as Aboriginal peoples. See Brock, *Yura and Udnyu*, 5–8.

56. Roberts et al., "Ochre, Flint and Violence," 329.

57. Jones, *Ochre and Rust*, 361.

58. Ellwood and Wegner, "Shared History Forgotten."

59. Ellwood, "Aboriginal Prospectors and Miners in Tropical Queensland."

60. Here I have referred to George as an Aboriginal man, rather than use his nation ahead of his name. This is due to the silence of the archive on exactly what nation George belonged to. As noted elsewhere, today he would be considered Adnyamathanha, but his specific nation is unknown.

61. Documents relating to the Radium Extraction Company, Reports—Mount Painter Uranium Project, GRS/11322/00002/1/0005, SRSA.

62. Mount Painter 1910, 1924, Mawson Collection, 30DM.3a, SAM.

63. Mount Painter 1910, 1924, Mawson Collection, 30DM.3a, SAM.

64. Mount Painter 1910, 1924, Mawson Collection, 30DM.3a, SAM.

65. Marsh and Green, "First Nations Rights and Colonising Practices by the Nuclear Industry."

66. Mawson and Hossfeld, "Relics of Aboriginal Occupation in the Olary District." Mawson's observations included "fine examples of native art," "remains of native camp fires," "pebble mounds," and "rock shelters embellished by native artists"; the drawings, Mawson noted, "are very primitive."

67. Letter from Douglas Mawson to Delta Metals Co. Ltd., February 1910, Delta Metal Co. (Letters), Mawson Collection, MI247, SAM.

68. "Radium," *The Register*, 25 November 1910, 6.

69. Mudd, "The Legacy of Early Uranium Efforts in Australia," 179.

70. Copies of Radium Extraction Co. Correspondence, GRS/11322/2/1/3, SRSA.

71. Copies of Radium Extraction Co. Correspondence, GRS/11322/2/1/3, SRSA; Notes and copies of letters sent by W. B. Greenwood concerning the Mount Painter Uranium Field, December 1910–July 1911, Greenwood Family Papers, PRG 274, State Library of South Australia (SLSA), Adelaide.

72. Copies of Radium Extraction Co. Correspondence, GRS/11322/2/1/3, SRSA.

73. Interview with Gordon (Smiler) Greenwood, ca. 1964, OH 389, SLSA.

74. Letter from William Greenwood to the Secretary, 23 May 1911, Copies of Radium Extraction Co. Correspondence, GRS/11322/2/1/3, SRSA.

75. Letter from William Greenwood to the Secretary, 7 July 1911, Copies of Radium Extraction Co. Correspondence, GRS/11322/2/1/3, SRSA.

76. "The Pastoral Industry—No. VIII, From Erudina to Mount Serle," *Adelaide Observer*, 21 August 1987, 2.

77. Corporal Alfred Burtt, Mount Serle, 8 June 1858, GRG52/12, file 585/1858, SRSA; Corporal Alfred Burtt, Mount Serle, 3 July 1858, GRG52/12, file 662/1858, SRSA; Corporal Alfred Burtt, Mount Serle, 30 September 1858, GRG52/12, file 893/1858, SRSA.

78. Burtt, Mount Serle, 8 June 1858, GRG52/12, file 585/1858, SRSA.

79. Brock, *Yura and Udnyu*, 11–30; Brock, *Outback Ghettos*, 121–37.

80. Brock, *Yura and Udnyu*, 12; Foster, Hosking, and Nettelbeck, *Fatal Collisions*, 94–114.

81. Brock, *Yura and Udnyu*, 13.

82. Brock, *Yura and Udnyu*, 14; Foster, "Rations, Coexistence, and the Colonisation of Aboriginal Labour."

83. Brock, *Yura and Udnyu*, 35.

84. Brock, *Yura and Udnyu*, 3–4.

85. Letter from the Protector of Aborigines to the Aborigines Office, Adelaide, 3 November 1902, GRG18/1/16, file 506/1902, SRSA.

86. Khatun, *Australianama*, 4.

87. Parkes, "Traces of the Cameleers," 88.

88. Vaarzon-Morel, "Camels and the Transformation of Indigenous Economic Landscapes."

89. Bongiorno, *Dreamers and Schemers*, 117; Khatun, *Australianama*, 99–100.

90. Cameleers were more ethnically diverse than the term "Afghan cameleers" reflects; however, it is the most historically specific term for this group in the late nineteenth century and into the twentieth century. Khatun, *Australianama*, 108.

91. Brock, *Yura and Udnyu*, 29.

92. Vaarzon-Morel, "Camels and the Transformation of Indigenous Economic Landscapes," 80.

93. Letter from William Greenwood to the Secretary, 7 July 1911, GRS/11322/2/1/3, SRSA.

94. Letter from William Greenwood to the Secretary, 4 June 1911, Copies of Radium Extraction Co. Correspondence, GRS/11322/2/1/3, SRSA.

95. Report by L. Keith Ward, 14 December 1912, Radium Mineral

Investigations—Correspondence and Related Papers, 1905–1954, Mawson Collection, 34DM, file 1, SAM.

96. Radium Extraction Company of Adelaide Ltd., June 1913, GRS/11322/2/1/5, SRSA.

97. Mudd, "The Legacy of Early Uranium Efforts in Australia," 169, 174.

98. Tame and Robotham, *Maralinga*, 13–41.

99. A. C. Broughton, "Precis Report on the Mount Painter Radium and Rare Earth's Deposit," 12 November 1923, in Radio Mineral Investigations—Correspondence and Related Papers, Mawson Collection, 34DM, file 4, SAM.

100. Letter from United States Department of Commerce to A. C. Broughton, 1926, Radio Mineral Investigations—Correspondence and Related Papers, Mawson Collection, 34DM, file 4, SAM.

101. Letter from Mount Painter Radium Company to A. C. Broughton, 1926, Radio Mineral Investigations—Correspondence and Related Papers, Mawson Collection, 34DM, file 4, SAM.

102. Radio Mineral Investigations—Correspondence and Related Papers, Mawson Collection, 34DM, file 1, SAM.

103. Evidence of A. Bowler, Australian Radium Corporation, 27 February 1929, Committee of Civil Research—Radium Sub-committee, Development of Australian Resources, MH 270, the National Archives (TNA), London.

104. Letter from Joseph Kenworthy, Member of Parliament (MP), to Neville Chamberlain, Ministry for Health, 16 February 1929, Committee of Civil Research—Radium Sub-committee, Development of Australian Resources, MH 270, TNA.

105. Oliphant's note on Australian metal supplies, Washington, DC, 15 September 1953, Uranium Australia, AB 1 83, TNA.

106. Mudd, "The Legacy of Early Uranium Efforts in Australia," 190–91.

107. Atomic Energy (Control of Materials) Act, 1946 (Commonwealth).

108. Mudd, "The Legacy of Early Uranium Efforts in Australia," 191.

109. Letter from Douglas Mawson to Smiler Greenwood, 21 February 1944, PRG 274, SLSA.

110. Letter from Mawson to Smiler Greenwood, 5 July 1944, PRG 274, SLSA.

111. Letter from Mawson to Smiler Greenwood, 5 July 1944, PRG 274, SLSA; Letter from Mawson to Mrs Greenwood, 25 July 1944, PRG 274, SLSA.

112. Letter from Mawson to Smiler Greenwood, 2 August 1944, PRG 274, SLSA.

113. Letter from Commonwealth Department of Supply and Shipping to G. A. Greenwood, 17 August 1944, PRG 274, SLSA.

114. Mawson, "The Nature and Occurrence of Uraniferous Mineral Deposits in South Australia," 334.

115. Letter from Charles Findlay Davidson, Geological Survey and Museum, to

Richard Sydney Sayers, British Ministry for Supply, 28 February 1945, Uranium Australia, AB 1 667, TNA.

116. For more on some of these scientists, see Hay, "Philip Baxter"; Holden, "'On the Oliphant Deign, Now to Sound the Blast'"; Keeble, "Frankenstein's Machine"; Urwin, "The British Empire's Dr Strangelove?"

117. Letter from Douglas Mawson to Samuel Benson Dickinson, Director of Mines, South Australia, 26 September 1956, Mawson Mineral Resources Correspondence, 1935–58, Mawson Collection, 40DM, SAM.

118. Letter from Mawson to Dickinson, 26 September 1956, Mawson Collection, 40DM, SAM.

119. Weidenbach, *Rock Star*; Sprigg, *A Geologist Strikes Out.*

Two Fields of Thunder

1. See Tynan, *Atomic Thunder*; Walker, *Maralinga.*

2. See Tynan, *Atomic Thunder*, 3; Tynan, *The Secrets of Emu Field*, 10.

3. Peel and Twomey, *A History of Australia*, 124–28.

4. Peel and Twomey, *A History of Australia*, 173.

5. Peel and Twomey, *A History of Australia*, 173.

6. Several historians have identified this tendency to consider Curtin as "turning" toward the United States, away from Britain. See Halvorson, *Commonwealth Responsibility and Cold War Solidarity*, 2; Reynolds, *Australia's Bid for the Atomic Bomb*, 25.

7. John Curtin, "Report on Improvements in the Machinery for Empire Co-operation," October 1944, Commonwealth Defence Co-operation (Policy), CAB 21/1799, the National Archives (TNA), London. See also Curran, "'An Organic Part of the Whole Structure,'" 52.

8. Moreton, *Fire across the Desert*, 3; Southall, *Woomera*, 7–10, 30–34.

9. Moreton, *Fire across the Desert*, 8.

10. Moreton, *Fire across the Desert*, 8.

11. "Informal Commonwealth Conference on Defence Science, Report by Australian Delegation," 18 July 1946, Informal Commonwealth Conference on Defence Science—Report, A1196 12/501/295, National Archives of Australia (NAA), Canberra.

12. "Informal Commonwealth Conference on Defence Science: Co-operation on Defence Research within the British Commonwealth," Note by the United Kingdom Delegation, 2 May 1946, A1196 12/501/298, NAA; "Commonwealth Collaboration on Defence Science," 10 December 1946, Informal Commonwealth Conference on Defence Science—Report, A1196 12/501/295, NAA.

13. Henry Tizard quoted in Reynolds, "Rethinking the Joint Project," 857.

14. "Informal Commonwealth Conference on Defence Science, Minutes," 3 June 1946, A1196 12/501/295, NAA.

15. "Dominion Contribution to Commonwealth Defence, Draft Memorandum by the Chiefs of Staff," 15 April 1946, Commonwealth Defence Co-operation (Policy), CAB 21/1799, TNA.

16. "Informal Commonwealth Conference on Defence Science: Item 4(a). Location of facilities for full scale development and testing of guided and propelled missiles and projectiles for all services; Draft Minutes of a Sub-committee Meeting, London," 4 June 1946, Informal Commonwealth Conference on Defence Science—Notes on Items of Agenda, A1196 12/501/298, NAA.

17. "Informal Commonwealth Conference on Defence Science," London, 4 June 1946, A1196 12/501/298, NAA.

18. Moreton, *Fire across the Desert*, 11.

19. Commonwealth of Australia, "Long Range Weapons Project—Statements by the Minister for Defence (The Hon John Dedman, MP) on 22nd November 1946 and 10th March 1947," Royal Commission into British Nuclear Tests in Australia—Aboriginal Collation, A6455 RC 819, Part 1, NAA; "Woomera," *The Advertiser*, 7 July 1947, 2.

20. "Woomera," 2.

21. "Woomera," 2.

22. Smith, *Peopling the Cleland Hills*, 1.

23. Arnold, *A Very Special Relationship*, 19.

24. Hogan, *Into the Loneliness*, 85. See also Paisley, "No Back Streets in the Bush."

25. Southall, *Woomera*, 1–2.

26. Endres, "From Wasteland to Waste Site"; Edwards, "Nuclear Colonialism and the Social Construction of Landscape"; Voyles, *Wastelanding*.

27. Voyles, *Wastelanding*, 9.

28. "With One Tree and Some Paradoxes—Woomera Now Oasis in the Desert," *Daily Telegraph* (Sydney), 6 November 1949, 17; "Woomera an Eden," *Sun News-Pictorial* (Melbourne), 10 August 1949, 3; "Wonder of Woomera, Desert Transformed," *Western Herald* (New South Wales), 18 November 1949, 8.

29. "Woomera Australia's Newest, Most Hush Hush Township," *The Advertiser*, 4 July 1949, 2.

30. Commonwealth of Australia, "Long Range Weapons Project—Statements by the Minister for Defence," A6455 RC 819, Part 1, NAA.

31. Foster, "True Lies," 70–76; Foster, "'An Ethnographical Laboratory'"; Foster, "'His Majesty's Most Gracious and Benevolent Intentions'"; Raftery, *Not Part of the Public*, 178.

32. Commonwealth of Australia, "Long Range Weapons Project—Statements by the Minister for Defence," A6455 RC 819, Part 1, NAA.

33. C. McCutcheon, "Letter to the Editor: Threat to Aborigines," *The Argus* (Melbourne), 19 February 1947, 6.

34. F. H. Wilson, "Letter to the Editor: Aborigines and Rocket Tests," *The Advertiser*, 14 August 1946, 10.

35. "Report by Australian Committee on Guided Projectiles and Its Meetings on 31 January and 1 February 1947," Aboriginal Collation, A6455 RC 819, Part 1, NAA.

36. "Australian Committee on Guided Projectiles," A6455 RC 819, Part 1, NAA.

37. Gray, "Aborigines, Elkin and the Guided Projectiles Project."

38. "Australian Committee on Guided Projectiles," A6455 RC 819, Part 1, NAA.

39. "Aborigines and Rockets," *Smith's Weekly* (Sydney), 12 October 1946, 31.

40. "Aborigines and Rockets," 31.

41. "Protest over Rockets," *News* (Adelaide), 15 May 1947, 1.

42. Charles Duguid quoted in Moreton, *Fire across the Desert*, 71.

43. "Australian Committee on Guided Projectiles," A6455 RC 819, Part 1, NAA.

44. Kerin, "'Doctor Do-Good'?," 59–98. See also Kerin, *Doctor Do-Good.*

45. Duguid, *The Aborigines of Australia*, 18. For more on detribalization, see McGregor, *Indifferent Inclusion*; Kerin, "'Doctor Do-Good'?"; Kerin, *Doctor Do-Good.*

46. Duguid, *The Aborigines of Australia*, 18.

47. "Australian Committee on Guided Projectiles," A6455 RC 819, Part 1, NAA; Rowse, *Indigenous and Other Australians since 1901*, 214.

48. "Australian Committee on Guided Projectiles," A6455 RC 819, Part 1, NAA. See also Thomson, "The Aborigines and the Rocket Range."

49. "Australian Committee on Guided Projectiles," A6455 RC 819, Part 1, NAA. In refuting the claim, Thomson argued: "The official [documents reflected] a serious misrepresentation of the facts and of my own warning as to the inevitable outcome of the policy now proposed by the Government." Thomson, "The Aborigines and the Rocket Range," 3.

50. Kerin, "'Doctor Do-Good'?," 61.

51. Raftery, *Not Part of the Public*, 178.

52. McGregor, *Indifferent Inclusion*, 97; Rowse, *Contesting Assimilation*, 3.

53. "Australian Committee on Guided Projectiles," A6455 RC 819, Part 1, NAA.

54. McGregor, *Indifferent Inclusion*, 31.

55. Kerin, "'Doctor Do-Good'?," 63; "Australian Committee on Guided Projectiles," A6455 RC 819, Part 1, NAA.

56. Arnold, *A Very Special Relationship*, 6.

57. Arnold, *A Very Special Relationship*, 6.

58. Letter from F. W. Marten, British Embassy Washington, DC, to Sir Roger Makins, Foreign Office, London, 20 October 1950, Testing of United Kingdom Atomic Weapon, CAB 126/325, TNA.

59. Draft telegram from Secretary of State to High Commissioner, Canberra, 15 September 1950, Testing of United Kingdom Atomic Weapon, CAB 126/325, TNA; letter from J. M. C. James, Commonwealth Relations Office, to Brigadier C. R. Price, Ministry of Defence, 21 September 1950, Testing of United Kingdom Atomic Weapon, CAB 126/325, TNA.

60. Letter from Marten to Makins, 20 October 1950, CAB 126/325, TNA; telegram from the United Kingdom High Commissioner, Canberra, 20 September 1950, Testing of United Kingdom Atomic Weapon, CAB 126/325, TNA.

61. Telegram from Cabinet Office, London, to B.J.S.M., Washington, DC, 5 September 1951, Testing of United Kingdom Atomic Weapon, CAB 126/325, TNA.

62. Tynan, *The Secret of Emu Field.*

63. Walker, *Maralinga*, 77; Tame and Robotham, *Maralinga*, 107.

64. Goodall, "Colonialism and Catastrophe."

65. Maggie Brady has written about the influence of rations, missions, and superstitions. See Brady, "The Politics of Space and Mobility."

66. McLisky, Russell, and Boucher, "Managing Mission Life," 121–23.

67. Yalata and Oak Valley Communities and Mattingley, *Maralinga*, 5.

68. Brockwell et al., "The History and Archaeology of Ooldea Soak and Mission."

69. Yalata and Oak Valley Communities and Mattingley, *Maralinga*, 12. It should be noted that Maralinga Tjarutja were originally part of the Southern Pitjantjatjara but in the 1980s adopted the name Maralinga Tjarutja in reference to their historic experiences of the nuclear tests (the name means "the community down from Maralinga"). So while using the term Maralinga Tjarutja in reference to the 1950s is an anachronism, referring to Alice Cox as a Maralinga Tjarutja woman here is an acknowledgment of the community's contemporary desire to be recognized as such.

70. Yalata and Oak Valley Communities and Mattingley, *Maralinga*, 12.

71. Yalata and Oak Valley Communities and Mattingley, *Maralinga*, 14.

72. Transcript of Proceedings 11 April–2 May 1985, Royal Commission into British Nuclear Tests in Australia, A6448 13, NAA, 7209.

73. Yalata and Oak Valley Communities and Mattingley, *Maralinga*, 21.

74. Yalata and Oak Valley Communities and Mattingley, *Maralinga*, 21.

75. Transcript of Proceedings 11 April–2 May 1985, A6448 13, NAA, 7194.

76. Transcript of Proceedings 11 April–2 May 1985, A6448 13, NAA, 7197.

77. Letter from Walter MacDougall to Secretary, Aborigines Protection Board, 4 February 1954, Aboriginal Collation, A6455 RC 819, Part 2, NAA.

78. MacDougall to Aborigines Protection Board, 4 February 1954, A6455 RC819, Part 2, NAA.

79. MacDougall to Aborigines Protection Board, 4 February 1954, A6455 RC819, Part 2, NAA.

80. MacDougall to Aborigines Protection Board, 4 February 1954, A6455 RC819, Part 2, NAA.

81. MacDougall to Aborigines Protection Board, 4 February 1954, A6455 RC819, Part 2, NAA.

82. Letter from Walter MacDougall to Superintendent of the Range, 10 December 1953, Aboriginal Collation, A6455 RC 819, Part 2, NAA.

83. MacDougall to Aborigines Protection Board, 4 February 1954, A6455 RC 819, Part 2, NAA.

84. Maggie Brady, interview with the author, January 2021.

85. Minutes from Walter MacDougall to Superintendent of the Range, "Re. Detailed Survey of the Jangkuntjara Tribe—Their Traditional Tribal and Ceremonial Grounds," April 1953, Aboriginal Collation, A6455 RC 819, Part 1, NAA.

86. Letter from C. S. Morrison, Security Officer, X200 Project, to Leo Carter, Chief Security Officer, Department of Supply, "Re. Briefing Station Personnel," 25 August 1953, Aboriginal Collation, A6455 RC 819, Part 2, NAA.

87. Foster, "Rations, Coexistence, and the Colonisation of Aboriginal Labour."

88. Letter from Walter MacDougall to Superintendent of the Range, 7 December 1954, Aboriginal Collation, A6455 RC 819, Part 2, NAA.

89. Submission of the Secretary, Aborigines Protection Board, Adelaide, November 1954, Aboriginal Collation, A6455 RC 819, Part 2, NAA.

90. Letter from Assistant District Officer, Eastern Goldfields, "Re. Influx of Natives—Cundeelee Mission," 24 July 1953, Aboriginal Collation, A6455 RC 819, Part 2, NAA.

91. Minutes from MacDougall to Superintendent of the Range, "Re. Detailed Survey of the Jangkuntjara Tribe," A6455 RC 819, Part 1, NAA.

92. Goodall, "Colonialism and Catastrophe," 70.

93. Walter MacDougall, "Report by Native Patrol Officer on Patrol Carried out from 9 May–22 July 1955," Aboriginal Collation, A6455 RC 819, Part 1, NAA.

94. Transcript of Proceedings 11 April–2 May 1985, A6448 13, NAA, 7145.

95. Transcript of Proceedings 11 April–2 May 1985, A6448 13, NAA, 7166.

96. Transcript of Proceedings 11 April–2 May 1985, A6448 13, NAA, 7147.

97. Transcript of Proceedings 11 April–2 May 1985, A6448 13, NAA, 7148.

98. Transcript of Proceedings 11 April–2 May 1985, A6448 13, NAA, 7149.

99. Transcript of Proceedings 11 April–2 May 1985, A6448 13, NAA, 7150.

100. Transcript of Proceedings 11 April–2 May 1985, A6448 13, NAA, 7151.

101. Transcript of Proceedings 11 April–2 May 1985, A6448 13, NAA, 7155.

102. Goodall, "Colonialism and Catastrophe," 57.

103. Letter from Walter MacDougall to the Commissioner of Native Affairs, Aborigines Department, 14 October 1955, Aboriginal Collation, A6455 RC 819, Part 3, NAA.

104. Report by Walter MacDougall to Department of Supply, 16 January 1956, A6456 R022/008, NAA.

105. Correspondence from William Butement, 16 March 1956, A6455 RC523, NAA.

106. Press extract, 14 January 1957, Report of Suffering by Australian Aborigines at Woomera, DO 35/10903, TNA.

107. Report of Suffering by Australian Aborigines at Woomera, DO 35/10903, TNA.

108. Telegram re. "Aborigines at Maralinga," 31 January 1957, DO 35/10903, TNA; emphasis in the original.

109. Telegram re. "Aborigines," 28 January 1957, DO 35/10903, TNA.

110. Report of Suffering by Australian Aborigines at Woomera, DO 35/10903, TNA.

111. Press statement by Howard Beale, "Conditions of Aborigines in Western Australia," 18 January 1957, DO 35/10903, TNA.

112. Transcript of Proceedings 11 April–2 May 1985, A6448 13, NAA, 7275.

113. Transcript of Proceedings 11 April–2 May 1985, A6448 13, NAA, 7274.

114. Transcript of Proceedings 11 April–2 May 1985, A6448 13, NAA, 7090.

Three Australia in the "Nuclear Playground"

1. George T. Eggleston, "Unspoiled Paradise," reprinted in *Goulburn Evening Post* (New South Wales), 23 November 1953, 7.

2. Firth, *Nuclear Playground,* ix.

3. "H-Bomb in Paradise," *Papua New Guinea Post-Courier* (Port Moresby), 20 June 1972, 5; "World's Dirtiest Nuclear Tests to 'Dust' Australia," *Tribune* (Sydney), 18 September 1963, 8.

4. Alexis-Martin, "The Nuclear Imperialism–Necropolitics Nexus," 153. See also Hill, "Britain, West Africa and 'The New Nuclear Imperialism,'" 276.

5. Hecht, "2012: An Elemental Force," 24; Hecht, "The Power of Nuclear Things," 3; Hecht, "Nuclear Ontologies," 321.

6. Hecht, "2012: An Elemental Force," 23.

7. Krell, "Genealogies of Technology and Prehistory in France," 158; Curran, "Australia at Empire's End."

8. Hecht, *The Radiance of France,* 2.

9. Robert Frank quoted in Hecht, *The Radiance of France,* 1–2.

10. Hecht, *The Radiance of France,* 2, 142; Jacobs, "Nuclear Conquistadors," 169–71.

11. Hecht, *The Radiance of France*, 2; Biswas, *Nuclear Desire*, 111.

12. "Atomic Warfare: Statement by the Minister for External Affairs, the Rt. Hon. R. G. Casey, 31 March 1954," *Current Notes on International Affairs*, Department of External Affairs, March 1954, 197.

13. Inward cablegram from Australian Mission to United Nations, New York, to Department of External Affairs, 4 November 1959, A1946 186/2/26, National Archives of Australia (NAA), Canberra.

14. Outward cablegram from Department of External Affairs to Australian Mission to United Nations, New York, 28 October, 1959, A1946 186/2/26, NAA.

15. Reynolds and Lee, *Australia and the Nuclear Non-Proliferation Treaty*, lii.

16. Peel and Twomey, *A History of Australia*, 220–21.

17. "Joint Intelligence Committee Report, January 1960," A1946 186/2/26, NAA. See also outward cablegram from Department of External Affairs to Australian Embassy, Paris, 6 September 1963, A1946 186/2/26, NAA.

18. Inward savingram from Australian Embassy, Paris, to Department of External Affairs, 20 November 1959, A1946 186/2/26, NAA.

19. Inward savingram from Australian Embassy, Paris, to Department of External Affairs, 20 November 1959, A1946 186/2/26, NAA.

20. Hill, "Britain, West Africa and 'The New Nuclear Imperialism,'" 278–79.

21. Internal cablegram from Australian Mission to the United Nations, New York, to Department of External Affairs, 13 November 1959, A1946 186/2/26, NAA.

22. Outward cablegram from Department of External Affairs to Australian Mission to United Nations, New York, 28 October, 1959, A1946 186/2/26, NAA.

23. While it never came to fruition, there is evidence to suggest that France considered testing on the Kerguelen Islands in the Southern Ocean. See French Nuclear Tests in the Kerguelen Islands, A1945 186/4/26, NAA.

24. Inward cablegram from Australian Embassy, Paris, to Department of External Affairs, 10 April 1963, A1946 186/2/26, NAA.

25. Inward cablegram from Australian Embassy, Paris, to Department of External Affairs, 10 April 1963, A1946 186/2/26, NAA.

26. Broinowski, *Fact or Fission?*, 86.

27. "Ban the French Tests," *Tharunka* (New South Wales), 31 July 1964, 4; Piccini, *Transnational Protest*, 6; Harvey, "How Far Left?," 118.

28. US Central Intelligence Agency report, "Restless Youth," September 1968, no. 0613/68, National Security File, Files of Walt Rostow, box 13, Lyndon B. Johnson Library, Austin, TX. Quoted and cited in Klimke, *The Other Alliance*, 1.

29. Harvey, "Nuclear Migrants, Radical Protest," 80.

30. Zelko, *Make It a Green Peace!*, 145.

31. Australian historian Michelle Arrow argues for 1966 as the year in which Australia's "seventies" began. See Arrow, *The Seventies*, 18.

32. Horne, *Time of Hope*, 7.

33. Irving, "Anti-Conscription Protest, Liberal Individualism and the Limits of National Myths," 189.

34. Christiansen and Scarlett, *The Third World in the Global 1960s*, 1.

35. "Another Day of Violence in Algeria," *Canberra Times*, 6 January 1962, 6; "Workers Crush Algeria Revolt," *Tribune*, 3 February 1960, 10.

36. "New Warnings on Fallout Follow Anger at French Test," *Tribune*, 11 January 1961, 9.

37. "French A-Bomb Anger," *Tribune*, 4 January 1961, 8.

38. "New Stage in African Liberation Struggle," *Tribune*, 3 May 1961, 6.

39. "French H-Peril to Aust.," *Tribune*, 25 January 1961, 4.

40. "The Pacific in Danger," *Tribune*, 11 May 1966, 7.

41. Notably, the union movement was particularly influential. See Waterside Workers' Federation of Australia, Federal Office Deposit 5, Peace—Nuclear Tests—France: vol. 1, correspondence, N114/995; vol. 2, correspondence and WWF and ACTU circulars, N114/996; vol. 3, correspondence; ACTU decisions, circulars, and minutes of Federal Unions meeting 10 May 1973; and WWF circulars and resolutions WWF All Ports Conference, Tahiti, New Caledonia, Chile, National Trade Unions Congress, N114/997, Noel Butlin Archive Centre (NBAC), Australian National University, Canberra.

42. A. J. Fitzgerald, "Tidying Up the Colonial Backyard," *Canberra Times*, 8 June 1965, 2.

43. "France N-Tests Likely in Few Days," *Canberra Times*, 29 June 1966, 4.

44. "America, Go Fuck Yrself with Yr Atombomb," *Empire Times* (Adelaide) 1, no. 10 (24 July 1969): 10.

45. I.C., "To My Future Son: Twenty Years (or More) from Now, an Explanation," *Empire Times* 4, no. 5 (c. 1972).

46. Hutton and Connors, *Australian Environment Movement*, 125–26.

47. Doyle, *Green Power*, 133.

48. Robin, *Defending the Little Desert*, 135.

49. Hutton and Connors, *Australian Environment Movement*, 126.

50. "A Boat against the Bomb," *On Dit* (Adelaide), March 1973, 15.

51. "French Litter," *Empire Times* 4, no. 7 (c. 1972).

52. "French Litter."

53. "Why Not Drop George a Line?," *On Dit*, 19 April 1973, 9.

54. "Why Not Drop George a Line?," 9.

55. "Small, French- and Labour-Test," *Empire Times*, issue unknown (1973).

56. "Small, French- and Labour-Test."

57. "Small, French- and Labour-Test."

58. Urwin, "'Better Active Today than Radioactive Tomorrow.'"

59. Voyles, "Anatomic Bombs," 669–70.

60. "Nuclear Fallout Detected," *Canberra Times*, 16 November 1966, 10; "'Fall-Out on Australia' Warning," *Canberra Times*, 28 May 1966, 3; "Nuclear Test: Sea Life 'May Be Threatened,'" *Canberra Times*, 3 June 1966, 12.

61. "Leukemia!," *Tribune*, 8 January 1964, 2; "The Pacific in Danger," *Tribune*, 11 May 1966, 7.

62. "France Accused of Disregard for People," *Canberra Times*, 10 May 1973, 8; "Radioactive Fish Swimming towards US," *Papua New Guinea Post-Courier*, 5 October 1977, 6.

63. Maynard, *Fight for Liberty and Freedom*, 2–3.

64. De Costa, *A Higher Authority*, 109–10; Walker, "Yirrkala Bark Petitions," 33–34; Wright, *N̲äku Dhäruk: The Bark Petitions*.

65. Ward, *A Handful of Sand*; Hokari, "From Wattle Creek to Wattie Creek"; Hokari, *Gurindji Journey*.

66. Attwood and Markus, *The 1967 Referendum*, 11–12.

67. McGregor, "Another Nation," 352; Banivanua Mar, *Decolonisation and the Pacific*, 187–89.

68. Oodgeroo Noonuccal, known as Kath Walker earlier in her life, was a prolific activist. Student newspapers from across the country referenced her activism and used it to encourage students to support Aboriginal peoples' activism. For example, see "Demonstration for Aborigines," *Tharunka*, 17 July 1964, 9.

69. Kath Walker (Oodgeroo Noonuccal), "Black-White Coalition Can Work," *Origin* 1, no. 4 (1969): 6, RS 21/21, Australian Institute of Aboriginal and Torres Strait Islander Studies (AIATSIS) Collection, Canberra.

70. Oodgeroo Noonuccal quoted in McGregor, "Another Nation," 348.

71. McGregor, "Another Nation," 343–44.

72. McGregor, "Another Nation," 348.

73. Foley, *Australian Indigenous Resistance*, 8.

74. McGregor, "Another Nation," 349.

75. McGregor, "Another Nation," 354; Rowse, *Indigenous and Other Australians since 1901*, 338–39.

76. *Tharunka*, 2 July 1968, 7–16.

77. See Bob Ellis, "Racism in South Australia," *On Dit*, 6 September 1971, 9; "Racism—the Debate Continues," *On Dit*, 22 October 1971, 15–17.

78. Gary Foley, "Boong Power," *Empire Times* 4, no. 5 (1972).

79. Foley, "Boong Power."

80. Foley, "Boong Power."

81. "French Litter," *Empire Times* 4, no. 5 (1972).

82. While the White Australia policy was officially dismantled by the Whitlam government through the introduction of the Racial Discrimination Act in 1975, it

had been slowly eroded over previous years as greater numbers of non-British migrants entered Australia following World War II. See Jordan, "'Not on Your Life.'"

83. National Archives of Australia, "Gough Whitlam: Before Office," accessed 25 July 2023, https://www.naa.gov.au/explore-collection/australias-prime-ministers/gough-whitlam/before-office#deputy-party-leader; Bongiorno, *Dreamers and Schemers*, 263.

84. Reynolds and Lee, *Australia and the Nuclear Non-Proliferation Treaty*, xvii.

85. Reynolds, "'To the Brink of Manufacture,'" 269–70.

86. Chen, "Shifting Interests."

87. "French Nuclear Tests," statement by E. G. Whitlam, Queen's Counsel (QC), MP, Canberra, 13 June 1972, Personal Papers of Prime Minister E. G. Whitlam—French Nuclear Tests, set 1, box 16, M170, 72/80, NAA.

88. "French Nuclear Tests," statement by Whitlam, 13 June 1972, M170, 72/80, NAA.

89. Doig, "New Nationalism in Australia and New Zealand," 560.

90. Doig, "New Nationalism in Australia and New Zealand," 560.

91. Doig, "New Nationalism in Australia and New Zealand," 560.

92. For a broader discussion of the many aspects of Whitlam's policy changes in this period, see Bramston, *The Whitlam Legacy*.

93. Chen, "Shifting Interests," 198–99.

94. Handwritten note, letter from D. P. O'Connell, Chichele Professor of Public International Law, Oxford, to Attorney General of South Australia, 5 December 1972, International Court of Justice—Advisory Opinions, French Nuclear Tests, Australia vs. France, A1838 1558/1/44, Part 2, NAA.

95. Letter from Don Dunstan, Premier of South Australia, to Gough Whitlam, Prime Minister, 19 December 1972, International Court of Justice—Advisory Opinions, French Nuclear Tests, Australia vs. France, A1838 1558/1/44, Part 2, NAA.

96. For more context on the concerns harbored in Australia over contamination and French nuclear tests in the Pacific, see Henningham, "Whitlam and Australia's Relations with France"; Whitlam, *The Whitlam Government*, 603–4.

97. Hocking, *Gough Whitlam*, 78.

98. Hocking, *Gough Whitlam*, 78.

99. Hocking, *Gough Whitlam*, 78.

100. Letter from O'Connell to Attorney General of South Australia, 5 December 1972, A1838 1558/1/44, Part 2, NAA.

101. Letter from the Australian Government to the Australian Embassy in Paris, 3 January 1973, A1838 1558/1/44, Part 2, NAA.

102. Follow-up telegram from Australian Government to Australian Embassy, Paris, 3 January 1973, A1838 1558/1/44, Part 2, NAA.

103. Letter from the Australian Government to the Australian Embassy in Paris, 3 January 1973, A1838 1558/1/44, Part 2, NAA.

104. Cablegram to Australian Embassies, from Minister of Foreign Affairs, January 1973 (specific date unknown), A1838 1558/1/44, Part 2, NAA.

105. Attorney General's Department, Statement by Attorney General of Australia, Senator Lionel Murphy, QC, French Nuclear Tests, 10 January 1973, A1838 1558/1/44, Part 2, NAA.

106. Statement by Murphy, 10 January 1973, A1838 1558/1/44, Part 2, NAA.

107. Statement by Murphy, 10 January 1973, A1838 1558/1/44, Part 2, NAA.

108. Record of conversation with M. Jean Morawiecki, Charge d'Affaires, French Embassy, French Nuclear Tests, 9 January 1973, Department of Foreign Affairs, A1838 1558/1/44, Part 2, NAA.

109. Record of conversation with Morawiecki, 9 January 1973, A1838 1558/1/44, Part 2, NAA.

110. Record of conversation with Morawiecki, 9 January 1973, A1838 1558/1/44, Part 2, NAA.

111. Emphasis added; record of conversation with Morawiecki, 9 January 1973, A1838 1558/1/44, Part 2, NAA.

112. Broinowski, *Fact or Fission?*, 106.

113. "The Implications for Sino-Australian Relations of an Australian Application to the ICJ on Nuclear Testing," 3 January 1973, International Court of Justice—Advisory Opinions, French Nuclear Tests, Australia vs. France, A1838 1558/1/44, Part 2, NAA.

114. "French Testing, the ICJ and China, M. J. Cook," 16 January 1963, A1838 1558/1/44, Part 2, NAA.

115. "French Testing, the ICJ and China, M. J. Cook," A1838 1558/1/44, Part 2, NAA.

116. "Radio-Active Fallout," from P. J. Flood, Assistant Secretary, Foreign Affairs, to A. H. Loomes, 11 January 1973, A1838 1558/1/44, Part 2, NAA.

117. "French Testing, the ICJ and China, M. J. Cook," A1838 1558/1/44, Part 2, NAA.

118. Emphasis added; "The Implications for Sino-Australian Relations of an Australian Application to the ICJ," A1838 1558/1/44, Part 2, NAA.

119. Emphasis added; "French Testing, the ICJ and China, M. J. Cook," A1838 1558/1/44, Part 2, NAA.

120. "The Implications for Sino-Australian Relations of an Australian Application to the ICJ," A1838 1558/1/44, Part 2, NAA.

121. "French Testing, the ICJ and China, M. J. Cook," A1838 1558/1/44, Part 2, NAA.

122. Chen, "Shifting Interests," 205; Gough Whitlam, "Election Speech

Delivered in Blacktown, NSW, November 13th 1972," Museum of Australian Democracy, accessed 21 July 2023, https://electionspeeches.moadoph.gov.au/speeches/1972-gough-whitlam.

123. Chen, "Shifting Interests," 200.

124. Broinowski, *Fact or Fission?*, 111.

125. "Draft Intelligence Report, Talks with Australian Prime Minister," 9 January 1973, A1838 1558/1/44, Part 2, NAA.

126. Chen, "Shifting Interests," 200, 211; Bongiorno and Cupit, "Australia before Whitlam," 18.

127. Henningham, "Whitlam and Australia's Relations with France."

128. Whitlam, *The Whitlam Government*, 613.

129. Whitlam, *The Whitlam Government*, 613.

130. Reynolds, "The Yellow Cake Road," 512.

Four Paving the "Yellowcake Road"

1. "Giant SA Mine Opening," *Canberra Times*, 6 November 1988, 2.

2. Peter O'Connor, "After Tumult and Shouting Dies, Olympic Dam Opens," *Australian Financial Review* (Sydney), 7 November 1988.

3. Mining Technology, "Olympic Dam Copper-Uranium Mine, Adelaide, Australia," 14 November 2012, https://www.mining-technology.com/projects/olympic-dam/.

4. Today Olympic Dam is administered by the Broken Hill Proprietary Company (BHP), as a result of WMC purchasing BP's 49 percent of holdings in the 1990s. BHP Billiton later purchased WMC in 2005. BHP Billiton rebranded as BHP in 2017. See Lee, *The Second Rush*, 323–26.

5. Urwin, "'Better Active Today Than Radioactive Tomorrow.'"

6. Clarke, Frühling, and O'Neil, *Australia's Nuclear Policy*, 49.

7. For more on uranium mining in this period, see Broinowski, *Fact or Fission?*; Lowe, *Long Half-Life*.

8. Cooperation with Australia on Uranium Enrichment, 1974, FCO 96/252, the National Archives (TNA), London.

9. Cooperation with Australia on Uranium Enrichment, 1974, FCO 96/252, TNA.

10. Department of Climate Change, Energy, the Environment and Water (DCCEEW), "Ranger Uranium Environmental Inquiry Final Report 1977," https://www.dcceew.gov.au/science-research/supervising-scientist/publications/ranger-uranium-environmental-inquiry-report-final.

11. Lim, *Australia's Constitution after Whitlam*, 36–90.

12. It should be acknowledged that the controversy of Whitlam's dismissal persists and has been subject to considerable debate, not only in relation to the role

of the monarch in Australia's democracy but also due to the secrecy that shrouded the governor-general's decision-making, until recent lobbying by historians and others facilitated the declassification of the correspondence between the governor-general and the Queen (colloquially referred to as the Palace Letters). See Hocking, *The Palace Letters.*

13. R. W. Fox, G. G. Kelleher, and C. B. Kerr, "Ranger Uranium Environmental Inquiry, Second Report" (Australian Government Publishing Service, 1977), 55.

14. Norman, *What Do We Want?*, xi, 4–5; Maddock, *Your Land Is Our Land*, 3.

15. Vincent, *"Against Native Title,"* 93; Rowse, *Rethinking Social Justice*, 73–79; Woollacott, *Don Dunstan*, 107.

16. Woollacott, *Don Dunstan*, 107.

17. Rowse, *Indigenous and Other Australians since 1901*, 296.

18. DCCEEW, "Ranger Uranium Environmental Inquiry Final Report 1977," 269.

19. Gundjehmi Aboriginal Corporation, "'We Are Not Talking about Mining': The History of Duress and the Jabiluka Project," July 1977, 2, https://tinyurl.com/49nsnzhz.

20. "Student Disarmament Group News," *Woroni* (Canberra), 1 April 1984, 18.

21. Gundjehmi Aboriginal Corporation, "'We Are Not Talking about Mining,'" 2.

22. Lee, *The Second Rush*, 277.

23. DCCEEW, "Ranger Uranium Environmental Inquiry Final Report 1977," 323.

24. DCCEEW, "Ranger Uranium Environmental Inquiry Final Report 1977," 9.

25. Malcolm Fraser, "Report to the Nation, 28 August 1977," Department of the Prime Minister and Cabinet, https://pmtranscripts.pmc.gov.au/release/transcript-4479.

26. Fraser, "Report to the Nation, 28 August 1977."

27. "Uranium—Australia's Decision, Statement by the Hon. Ian Viner, Minister for Aboriginal Affairs & Minister Assisting the Treasurer, Commonwealth of Australia," 25 August 1977, Uranium—Australian Council of Trade Unions (ACTU), Series RH10, box 35, folder 346, Robert Hawke Prime Ministerial Library (RHPML), University of Adelaide, Adelaide; Fox, Kelleher, and Kerr, "Ranger Uranium Environmental Inquiry, Second Report," 9.

28. "Uranium—Australia's Decision, Your Questions Answered, 25 August 1977," Uranium—ACTU—Meeting with Federal Ministers, March 29, Series RH10, box 35, folder 346, RHMPL.

29. "Lecture by Clifford B. Donn," undated, Uranium—Hawke, Series RH10, box 34, file 341, RHPML.

30. "Lecture by Clifford B. Donn," Series RH10, box 34, file 341, RHPML

31. Letter from H. C. (Nugget) Coombs to R. Groom, Minister for Environment, Housing and Community Development, 9 February 1978, Uranium—Current Northern Territory Papers, Series RH10, box 34, file 342, RHPML.

32. Parliament of Australia, "Chronology of ALP Uranium Policy 1950–1994," accessed 15 November 2023, https://parlinfo.aph.gov.au/parlInfo/search/display/display.w3p;query=Id:%22library/prspub/8FW10%22.

33. Humphrys, *How Labour Built Neoliberalism*, 1–18.

34. "Motion on Uranium Moved by D. Dunstan and C. Holding," Uranium Correspondence—19 March 1976–19 July 1977, Series RH10, box 33, file 335, RHPML.

35. "Motion on Uranium Moved by D. Dunstan and C. Holding," Series RH10, box 33, file 335, RHPML.

36. Lavelle, "'Conflicts of Loyalty,'" 184.

37. Lavelle, "'Conflicts of Loyalty,'" 184.

38. Letter from John Gray to Bob Hawke, 8 July 1977, Uranium Correspondence—19 March 1976–19 July 1977, Series RH10, box 33, file 335, RHPML.

39. Letter from Edna Williams to Bob Hawke, 29 September 1977, ALP Correspondence 1977, October- December, Series RH9, box 13, file 100, RHPML; telegram from "Outraged Territorian," Darwin, to Bob Hawke, 14 July 1977, Uranium Correspondence—19 March 1976–19 July 1977, Series RH10, box 33, file 335, RHPML.

40. McLean, *Why Australia Prospered*, 210.

41. McLean, *Why Australia Prospered*, 210. See also Lee, *The Second Rush*, 253–55.

42. McLean, *Why Australia Prospered*, 215–16.

43. Sendziuk and Foster, *A History of South Australia*, 193.

44. Sendziuk and Foster, *A History of South Australia*, 193–95.

45. Luncheon address by Acting Prime Minister and Minister for Trade and Resources, Rt. Hon. J. D. Anthony, MP, Chamber of Commerce, Adelaide, 1979, Roxby Downs—Western Mining Corporation—Uranium Venture, A1209 1979/990, Part 1, National Archives of Australia (NAA), Canberra.

46. Luncheon address by Anthony, Chamber of Commerce, Adelaide, 1979, A1209 1979/990, Part 1, NAA.

47. Luncheon address by Anthony, Chamber of Commerce, Adelaide, 1979, A1209 1979/990, Part 1, NAA.; Reynolds, "Australia's Quest to Enrich Uranium"; Reynolds, "The Yellow Cake Road."

48. Letter from Premier David Tonkin to Prime Minister Malcolm Fraser, 2 October 1979, Personal Papers of Prime Minister Malcolm Fraser, Hon. David Tonkin (Premier, South Australia), M1268, 188, NAA.

49. "Proposed Addition to Fraser's Speech, 1981," Personal Papers of Prime Malcolm Minister Fraser, Hon. David Tonkin, M1268, 188, NAA.

50. Steven Reynolds, "SA Never Great," *The Bulletin* (Sydney), 13 July 1982.

51. "Proposed Addition to Fraser's Speech, 1981," M1268, 188, NAA.

52. Fraser and Simons, *Malcolm Fraser: The Political Memoirs*, 564–65; Malcolm

Fraser, "Uranium—Australia's Decision, Statement by the Prime Minister," Commonwealth of Australia, 1977, https://pmtranscripts.pmc.gov.au/sites/default/files/original/00006007.pdf; Reynolds, "The Yellow Cake Road."

53. Fraser, "Uranium—Australia's Decision."

54. The only other uranium mine to open in Australia since this period has been the Beverley Mine in South Australia. Established on Adnyamathanha Country in the Flinders Ranges, it is a substantially smaller mine but has nevertheless drawn criticism from communities in the region.

55. See Moreton-Robinson, *The White Possessive.*

56. Trigger, "Mining, Landscape and the Culture of Development," 163.

57. Trigger, "Mining, Landscape and the Culture of Development." See also McEachern, "Mining Meaning from the Rhetoric of Nature"; Scambary, *My Country, Mine Country*, 1–30.

58. The Windscale accident occurred at a nuclear reactor site in Cumbria, United Kingdom. In October 1957, an error occurred during routine use of the reactor, causing a large fire that burned for several days and which resulted in the release of significant radioactivity into the atmosphere and surrounding environment. The Windscale disaster remains the United Kingdom's largest nuclear accident to date. See Wakeford, "Kyshtym and Windscale."

59. Commonwealth Hansard, Governor-General's Speech, Address-in-Reply, Senate, 28 February 1978.

60. *Backs to the Blast, an Australian Nuclear Story* (1981), National Film and Sound Archive, Canberra, https://aso.gov.au/titles/documentaries/backs-blast/clip1/.

61. *Backs to the Blast, an Australian Nuclear Story.*

62. Johns, *A Mirage in the Desert?*, 16.

63. Mazel, "Returning *Parna Wiru*," 167–68.

64. Department of Planning, Lands and Heritage, "A Brief History of the Aboriginal Heritage Act 1972" (Government of Western Australia, 2016), 1.

65. Bradshaw and Collett, "Aboriginal Land Rights in South Australia."

66. Toyne and Vachon, *Growing Up the Country*, 5.

67. Toyne and Vachon, *Growing Up the Country*, 53.

68. Toyne and Vachon, *Growing Up the Country*, 78.

69. I acknowledge that the moniker "Traditional Owners" does, in some ways, contravene Aboriginal peoples' views on Country, not as something anyone can possess (a highly Western notion), but as part of them, their history, and their culture. However, it is the accepted legal term to refer to Aboriginal land holders in Australia. That is how it is used throughout this book.

70. Jacobs, "Politics and the Cultural Landscape," 250; Bradshaw and Collett, "Aboriginal Land Rights in South Australia."

71. "Draft Discussion for Cabinet re. Aboriginal Sacred Sites and Areas of Significance in Areas Subject to Mining and Petroleum Exploration or Production Licences," 30 March 1981, Western Mining Corporation Olympic Dam Project Indenture Policy—Aboriginal Heritage, GRS/5505/14/16, State Records of South Australia (SRSA), Adelaide.

72. "Draft Discussion for Cabinet," 30 March 1981, GRS/5505/14/16, SRSA.

73. "Draft Discussion for Cabinet," 30 March 1981, GRS/5505/14/16, SRSA.

74. "Draft Discussion for the Minister of Mines and Energy," 3 September 1981, GRS/5505/14/16, SRSA.

75. "Draft Discussion for the Minister of Mines and Energy," 3 September 1981, GRS/5505/14/16, SRSA.

76. Compton, "The Function of 'Traditional Culture' in Australian Political Discourse," 80–81.

77. Bongiorno, *The Eighties*, 72.

78. Bongiorno, *The Eighties*, 72; Neale and Vincent, "Mining, Indigeneity, Alterity," 418–19.

79. Emphasis added; "Australian Mining Industry Council," Papers of Sister Michele Madigan, PRG 1686/4, file 2, State Library of South Australia (SLSA), Adelaide.

80. Bongiorno, *The Eighties*, 73.

81. Donald, "Aboriginal Land Council Attitudes to Mining Negotiations," 509.

82. "Minutes of Southern Land Rights Meeting," 4 October 1981, GRS/5505/14/16, SRSA.

83. "Statement to Be Made to Cabinet regarding Mining and Aboriginal Sacred Sites," 27 October 1981, GRS/5505/14/16, SRSA.

84. "Minutes of Southern Land Rights Meeting," 4 October 1981, GRS/5505/14/16, SRSA.

85. "Statement to Be Made to Cabinet," 27 October 1981, GRS/5505/14/16, SRSA.

86. "Statement to Be Made to Cabinet," 27 October 1981, GRS/5505/14/16, SRSA.

87. "Draft Discussion for Cabinet," 30 March 1981, GRS/5505/14/16, SRSA.

88. "Statement to Be Made to Cabinet," 27 October 1981, GRS/5505/14/16, SRSA.

89. Letter from Roger Goldsworthy, Minister for Mines and Energy, to C. J. Charles, 27 March 1981, Western Mining Corporation Olympic Dam Project Indenture Policy—Aboriginal Heritage, GRS/5505/14/16, SRSA.

90. Letter from Goldsworthy to Charles, 27 March 1981, GRS/5505/14/16, SRSA.

91. "Notes on the Aboriginal Heritage Act 1979 for the Minister of Mines and Energy," 27 May 1981, GRS/5505/14/16, SRSA.

92. "Notes on the Aboriginal Heritage Act 1979," 27 May 1981, GRS/5505/14/16, SRSA.

93. "Notes on the Aboriginal Heritage Act 1979," 27 May 1981, GRS/5505/14/16, SRSA.

94. Senate Environment, Communications, Information Technology and the Arts Committees, "Report on Commonwealth Environment Powers" (Senate Standing Committees on Environment and Communications, Parliament of Australia, 1999).

95. Formby, "The Australian Government's Experience with Environmental Impact Assessment."

96. Roxby Downs (Indenture Ratification) Act, 1982 (South Australia), 117.

97. Department of Climate Change, Energy, the Environment and Water, "Great Artesian Basin," accessed 13 June 2024, https://www.dcceew.gov.au/water/policy/national/great-artesian-basin.

98. "Minutes of Southern Land Rights Meeting," 4 October 1981, GRS/5505/14/16, SRSA.

99. "Statement to Be Made to Cabinet," 27 October 1981, GRS/5505/14/16, SRSA.

100. "Minutes of Southern Land Rights Meeting," 4 October 1981, GRS/5505/14/16, SRSA.

101. Letter from Joan Wingfield to Bryan Jenkins, 1 July 1981, GRS/5505/14/16, SRSA.

102. Letter from Bryan Jenkins to Joan Wingfield, 8 July 1981, GRS/5505/14/16, SRSA.

103. Letter from Joan Wingfield to Bryan Jenkins, 26 August 1981, GRS/5505/14/16, SRSA.

104. "Statement to Be Made to Cabinet," 27 October 1981, GRS/5505/14/16, SRSA.

105. Letter from C. J. Charles to Roger Goldsworthy, 28 April 1981, Western Mining Corporation Olympic Dam Project Indenture Policy—Aboriginal Heritage, GRS/5505/14/16, SRSA.

106. All draft letters also held in GRS/5505/14/16, SRSA.

107. Draft letter from Roger Goldsworthy to C. J. Charles, undated, GRS/5505/14/16, SRSA.

108. Draft letter from Roger Goldsworthy to C. J. Charles, undated, GRS/5505/14/16, SRSA.

109. Letter from Wingfield to Jenkins, 26 August 1981, GRS/5505/14/16, SRSA.

110. Letter from Donald Jessop, Senator for South Australia, to Roger Goldsworthy, Minister for Mines and Energy, 10 August 1981, GRS/5505/14/16, SRSA.

111. "Note to Minister of Mines and Energy on Amendment of the Aboriginal Heritage Act," 1 December 1981, GRS/5505/14/16, SRSA.

112. "The Olympic Dam Project: A Short Summary of the Environmental Impact Statement," October 1982, NLpf 333.8510994238, National Library of Australia (NLA), Canberra.

113. "Notes for the Premier on Roxby Downs, Berndt Report, Prepared by Sue Briton-Jones, Cabinet Office," 18 November 1983, Roxby Downs/Olympic

Dam—Berndt Report and Aboriginal Issues, 1983, BANN/033/Roxby Downs/04, Bannon Collection, Flinders University Special Collections (FUSC), Adelaide.

114. "A Case for Honouring Labor's Platform to Phase Out Uranium Mining and Export," 31 October 1983, Roxby Downs/Olympic Dam—Federal Government, BANN/033/Roxby Downs/05, FUSC.

115. Letter from Ron Payne, Minister of Mines and Energy, to J. James, Town Clerk, Fitzroy, 21 October 1983, Roxby Downs, General Correspondence and Legislation, GRS966/3/2, file 2/1982 TC 1, SRSA.

116. "Notes for the Premier on Roxby Downs, Berndt Report," BANN/033/Roxby Downs/04, FUSC.

117. Ningel Reid was referred to as "Richard" throughout documents. He was accompanied by KPC chairman and Kokatha Elder Max Thomas, Aranda-Kokatha Elder Willie Williams, and Christopher Charles, the KPC's lawyer.

118. R. M. Berndt, "Report on the Olympic Dam Mining Project in Relation to Aboriginal Interests," 4 November 1983, Roxby Downs/Olympic Dam—Berndt Report and Aboriginal Issues, BANN/033/Roxby Downs/04, FUSC.

119. Mahood, "The Seething Landscape," 32.

120. "Report to Ron Payne and Don Hopgood on Damage to Sacred Sites on the Pipeline Corridor from Olympic Dam to Borefield 'A,' Prepared by C. J. Charles, KPC Solicitor," 21 July 1983, Roxby Downs—Canegrass Swamp, Aboriginal Studies, vol. 2, GRS966/3/2, file 2/1982, vol. 2, SRSA.

121. "Report to Ron Payne and Don Hopgood," GRS966/3/2, file 2/1982, vol. 2, SRSA.

122. Note that specific descriptions of the sacred site in question are not available, and while various assumptions can be drawn about the nature of the site from available evidence, out of respect for Kokatha knowledge of this place, I have chosen not to describe it or speculate on its nature.

123. "Report to Ron Payne and Don Hopgood," GRS966/3/2, file 2/1982, vol. 2, SRSA.

124. "Report from Deputy Director-General, Department of Environment and Planning, to Minister for Environment and Planning re. Construction of Water Haulage Road from Borefield 'A' to Olympic Dam," (likely) August 1983, Roxby Downs, Minister of Mines and Energy, GRS/966/3/2, file 2/1982 TC 3, SRSA.

125. Letter from Ron Payne, Minister for Mines and Energy, to R. W. Davies, 26 August 1983, GRS/966/3/2, file 2/1982 TC 3, SRSA.

126. Berndt, "Report on the Olympic Dam Mining Project in Relation to Aboriginal Interests," BANN/033/Roxby Downs/04, FUSC.

127. "Some Notes for Consideration in Relation to the Berndt Report," November 1983, Roxby Downs/Olympic Dam—Berndt Report and Aboriginal Issues, 1983, BANN/033/Roxby Downs/04, FUSC.

128. "Some Notes for Consideration in Relation to the Berndt Report," BANN/033/Roxby Downs/04, FUSC.

129. Speech by Premier John Bannon at Olympic Dam Opening, 5 November 1988, "Opening Olympic Dam Operations, Roxby Downs," BANN/SP/1288, FUSC.

130. David Langsam, "Hard Slog for Envoy of Maralinga Blacks," *Sydney Morning Herald*, 25 June 1988, 11.

131. Speech by Bannon at Olympic Dam Opening, BANN/SP/1288, FUSC.

132. Watson, "Walking the Land for Our Ancient Rights: Interview with Kevin Buzzacott."

133. Senate Select Committee, "Report on Senate Select Committee on Uranium Mining and Milling" (Australian Parliament, 1997).

134. "SA Probes Bird Deaths at Olympic Dam Mine," *ABC News*, 10 January 2005, https://www.abc.net.au/news/2005-01-10/sa-probes-bird-deaths-at-olympic-dam-mine/616332.

135. Senate Select Committee, "Report on Senate Select Committee on Uranium Mining and Milling."

136. Speech by Bannon at Olympic Dam Opening, BANN/SP/1288, FUSC.

Five Unearthing the Hidden Histories of the Tests

1. Tina Saunders, "The Disgrace of Maralinga," *Canberra Times*, 6 June 1984, 20.

2. Saunders, "The Disgrace of Maralinga," 20.

3. Goodall, "Colonialism and Catastrophe," 55–57.

4. Goodall, "Colonialism and Catastrophe," 73.

5. Maggie Brady, interview with the author, January 2021. See also Transcript of Proceedings 11 April–2 May 1985, Royal Commission into British Nuclear Tests in Australia, A6448 13, National Archives of Australia (NAA), Canberra, 7252–61.

6. "Uren Seeks Inquiry on Bomb-Test Statements," *Canberra Times*, 11 August 1977, 7.

7. "Call for Inquiry into Maralinga," *Canberra Times*, 12 October 1978, 1.

8. "Atomic Tests Negligence Writ Lodged," *Canberra Times*, 4 February 1983, 8.

9. Experts still debate whether Yami Lester was blinded by fallout or as a result of contracting measles as a child. Lester himself does not recall having measles, and his family attributes his sight loss to the "black mist." See Rosamund Burton, "Rose and Karina Lester: How Illness Has Driven Our Anti-Nuclear Campaign Work," *Sydney Morning Herald*, 24 June 2017, https://www.smh.com.au/lifestyle/rose-and-karina-lester-how-illness-has-driven-our-antinuclear-campaign-work-20170619-gwuoem.html; Vincent, "Knowing the Country," 158.

10. Martin Peers, "Peace Movement Surges Forward as Big Rallies Planned," *Tribune*, 16 March 1983, 9.

11. The Australian *Tribune* wrote about *The Observer's* report at length. See "Maralinga Tests Contaminated Blacks—New Report," *Tribune*, 6 April 1983, 3.

12. Vicki Cowden, "Aboriginal Australia and the World Peace Movement," *Tharunka*, 25 July 1983, 9.

13. Banivanua Mar, *Decolonisation and the Pacific*, 1–3; Smith, *The Nuclear Free and Independent Pacific Movement*, 22–27.

14. For more information on the 1984 Maralinga Tjarutja Land Rights Act, see Hiskey, *Maralinga*.

15. O'Shea, "The Future Foreshadowed," 213; Mazel, "Returning *Parna Wiru*," 173.

16. Rowse, *Indigenous and Other Australians since 1901*, 298.

17. O'Shea, "The Future Foreshadowed," 212.

18. O'Shea, "The Future Foreshadowed," 212.

19. Bradshaw and Collett, "Aboriginal Land Rights in South Australia"; Mazel, "Returning *Parna Wiru*," 180.

20. "Cabinet Decision 3243—Atomic Testing at Maralinga, Possible Inquiry—Without Submission," A13979, 3243, NAA.

21. Expert Committee on the Review of Data on Atmospheric Fallout Arising from British Nuclear Tests in Australia, "Report of the Expert Committee on the Review of Data on Atmospheric Fallout Arising from British Nuclear Tests in Australia, 31 May 1984" (Commonwealth Government of Australia, 1984), 42.

22. Letter from John Bannon, Premier of South Australia, to Bob Hawke, Prime Minister of Australia, 8 March 1984, BANN/PR/071.3, Bannon Collection, Flinders University Special Collections (FUSC), Adelaide.

23. Letter from John Bannon, Premier of South Australia, to Margaret Thatcher, Prime Minister of the United Kingdom, 30 April 1984, BANN/065/MEU06, FUSC.

24. Letter from Bannon to Thatcher, 30 April 1984, BANN/065/MEU06, FUSC.

25. Expert Committee, "Report," 43.

26. Minute to the Minister regarding Reponses to Recommendations to the Kerr Committee, 1984, Royal Commission into British Nuclear Tests in Australia—Representation by R. A. Macaulay, A13064 DPIE86/002049, NAA.

27. Letter from Paul White, Aboriginal Land Rights Movement Incorporated, on behalf of the Yalata community, to Peter Walsh, Minister for Resources and Energy, 13 June 1984, UK Atomic Test Program, Calls for Public Inquiry, May–June 1984, A13064 DPIE84/001501, NAA.

28. Telex from John Liddle and Trevor Cutter, Central Australian Aboriginal Congress, to Bob Hawke, Clyde Holding, Neal Blewett, Gareth Evans, Susan Ryan, and Peter Walsh, 2 July 1984, UK Atomic Test, SA Aboriginal Health Inquiry, A13064 DPIE84/001697, NAA.

29. Letter from Susan Ryan, Minister for Education and Youth Affairs, to Peter

Walsh, Minister for Resources and Energy, 29 June 1984, A13064 DPIE84/001697, NAA.

30. Letter from Peter Walsh to Susan Ryan, 1 August 1984, A13064 DPIE84/001697, NAA.

31. Letter from John Bannon to Bob Hawke, July 1984, A13064 DPIE84/001697, NAA.

32. Cablegram from Canberra to London with letters between Bob Hawke and Donald Frazer, 19 June 1984, A13064 DPIE 84/001501, NAA.

33. Letter from Bannon to Hawke, July 1984, A13064 DPIE84/001697, NAA.

34. Draft telex reply to John Liddle and Trevor Cutter, prepared by parliamentary staff on behalf of Peter Walsh, Minister for Resources and Energy, 9 July 1984, A13064 DPIE84/001697, NAA.

35. Phillip Whitehead, "How the Bomb Broke Up the Family," *The Times* (London), 20 November 1985, 14.

36. Jane Robinson, "Two Faces of Aborigines in 1988," *Canberra Times*, 26 January 1988, 10.

37. Cabinet Submission on McClelland Royal Commission—Recommendation No. 7 Compensation for Dispossession, 1987, Royal Commission into British Nuclear Tests in Australia—Aboriginals Section, A3730, 1984/5108, Part 2, NAA.

38. Cabinet Submission on McClelland Royal Commission, A3730, 1984/5108, Part 2, NAA.

39. Cabinet Submission on McClelland Royal Commission, A3730, 1984/5108, Part 2, NAA.

40. See Woollacott, *Don Dunstan*, 214–35; Bongiorno, *The Eighties*, 85–118; Lavelle, "'Conflicts of Loyalty'"; Libby, *Hawke's Law*.

41. Knox, *Boom*, 290.

42. Strauss, "What Did We Want?"; Fisher, *Half-Life*.

43. Coral Dow and John Gardiner-Garden, "The Hawke Government 1983–1991," in "Overview of Indigenous Affairs: Part 1: 1901–1991" (Parliament of the Commonwealth of Australia, 2010), 20–27; Cook and Goodall, *Making Change Happen*, 175–76.

44. Bongiorno, *The Eighties*, 72–75.

45. Cook and Goodall, *Making Change Happen*, 255.

46. Peter Walsh's press release announcing the Royal Commission, 5 July 1984, A13064 DPIE84/001697, NAA.

47. Royal Commission Letters Patent (terms of reference) quoted in James McClelland, Jill Fitch, and William J. A. Jonas, "The Report of the Royal Commission into British Nuclear Tests in Australia: Conclusions and Recommendations" (Australian Government Publishing Service, 1985), 3–6.

48. Goodall, "Colonialism and Catastrophe," 57.

49. For an example of such scholarship, see Walker, *Maralinga*.

50. See Urwin, "'The Old Colonial Power Can Stand Proxy.'"

51. Alexander Downer, "McClelland Has Lost Credibility," *Sydney Morning Herald*, 19 December 1985, 12.

52. Ian Warden, "The Mess at Maralinga? Serves Us Right!," *Canberra Times*, 8 December 1985, 2.

53. Michel, "Villains, Victims and Heroes," 225.

54. Michel, "Villains, Victims and Heroes," 225.

55. Whitehead, "How the Bomb Broke Up the Family," 14.

56. Bongiorno, *The Eighties*, 117.

57. Some might describe McClelland as a "larrikin," an Australian colloquialism used to describe a mischievous person who is good-natured but might disregard social or political conventions. See Walker, *Maralinga*, 206–7.

58. Walker, *Maralinga*, 206–7.

59. Mungo MacCallum, "Diamond Jim . . . a Larger-Than-Life Legend," *Matilda*, November 1985, 37.

60. Walsh, *Confessions of a Failed Finance Minister*, 96; Bongiorno, *The Eighties*, 117.

61. Bongiorno, *The Eighties*, 118.

62. Palmer, "Dealing with the Legacy of the Past," 202.

63. McClelland, Fitch, and Jonas, "Conclusions and Recommendations," 1–32.

64. Whitehead, "How the Bomb Broke Up the Family," 14.

65. Urwin, "The British Empire's Dr Strangelove?"

66. McClelland, Fitch, and Jonas, "Conclusions and Recommendations," 11.

67. Transcript of Proceedings 5 May–30 May 1985, plus pp. 7541–8159, Royal Commission into British Nuclear Tests in Australia, A6448, 14, NAA, 7619.

68. Transcript of Proceedings 5 May–30 May 1985, A6448, 14, NAA, 7619.

69. Transcript of Proceedings 5 May–30 May 1985, A6448, 14, NAA, 7820.

70. Transcript of Proceedings 5 May–30 May 1985, A6448, 14, NAA, 7761.

71. Transcript of Proceedings 5 May–30 May 1985, A6448, 14, NAA, 7764.

72. Transcript of Proceedings 5 May–30 May 1985, A6448, 14, NAA, 7627.

73. Transcript of Proceedings 5 May–30 May 1985, A6448, 14, NAA, 7754.

74. Transcript of Proceedings 5 May–30 May 1985, A6448, 14, NAA, 7754.

75. Gara, "Ooldea, the Spinifex People and the Bomb."

76. "Final Submission of the Government of the United Kingdom," Royal Commission into British Nuclear Tests in Australia, September 1985, A6455 RC865, NAA.

77. "Final Submission of the Government of the United Kingdom," A6455 RC865, NAA.

78. McClelland, Fitch, and Jonas, "Conclusions and Recommendations," 20.

79. McClelland, Fitch, and Jonas, "Conclusions and Recommendations," 20.

80. McClelland, Fitch, and Jonas, "Conclusions and Recommendations," 20.

81. Draft telex reply to Liddle and Cutter, prepared by parliamentary staff on behalf of Walsh, 9 July 1984, A13064 DPIE84/001697, NAA.

82. Brady, interview.

83. Heather Goodall, interview with the author, April 2021.

84. Andrew Collett, interview with the author, June 2020.

85. Goodall, "Colonialism and Catastrophe."

86. Transcript of Proceedings 11 April–2 May 1985, A6448 13, NAA, 7080.

87. Australian Institute of Aboriginal and Torres Strait Islander Studies, "Vale Dr William Jonas AM," 3 June 2019, https://aiatsis.gov.au/whats-new/news/vale-dr-william-jonas-am.

88. Transcript of Proceedings 11 April–2 May 1985, A6448 13, NAA, 7081.

89. Transcript of Proceedings 11 April–2 May 1985, A6448 13, NAA, 7081.

90. Transcript of Proceedings 11 April–2 May 1985, A6448 13, NAA, 7083.

91. Transcript of Proceedings 11 April–2 May 1985, A6448 13, NAA, 7083.

92. Transcript of Proceedings 11 April–2 May 1985, A6448 13, NAA, 7089.

93. For a more in-depth investigation of the "black mist," see Tynan, *The Secrets of Emu Field*, 117–41.

94. Transcript of Proceedings 11 April–2 May 1985, A6448 13, NAA, 7148–51.

95. Transcript of Proceedings 11 April–2 May 1985, A6448 13, NAA, 7102, 7103, 7109, 7118.

96. Transcript of Proceedings 11 April–2 May 1985, A6448 13, NAA, 7119.

97. Goodall, "Colonialism and Catastrophe," 60, 63.

98. Goodall, "Colonialism and Catastrophe," 57.

99. Goodall, "Colonialism and Catastrophe," 60.

100. Michael Carter, Francis (Rob) Robotham, Keith Wise, Geoffrey Williams, and Philip Crouch, *Australian Participants in British Nuclear Tests in Australia*, vol. 1, *Dosimetry* (Commonwealth of Australia, Department of Veterans' Affairs, 2006), v–vi.

101. Geoff Eames, the Aboriginal legal counsel for the Royal Commission, made a very similar point to Justice McClelland during the proceedings. Transcript of Proceedings 11 April–2 May 1985, A6448 13, NAA, 7087.

102. See "Maralinga Royal Commission Hearings, Aboriginal Family 'Camped near A-Bomb Site,'" *Canberra Times*, 26 April 1985, 7; Tynan, *Atomic Thunder*, 191–94; Walker, *Maralinga*, 148–54.

103. Transcript of Proceedings 11 April–2 May 1985, A6448 13, NAA, 7280.

104. Transcript of Proceedings 11 April–2 May 1985, A6448 13, NAA, 7279–82.

105. Transcript of Proceedings 11 April–2 May 1985, A6448 13, NAA, 7283.

106. Transcript of Proceedings 11 April–2 May 1985, A6448 13, NAA, 7091.

107. Brady, interview.

108. Jo Stafford, "Aborigines and Maralinga—Pawns in a Deadly Game," *Tribune*, 19 March 1986, 12.

109. Stafford, "Aborigines and Maralinga," 12.

110. Stafford, "Aborigines and Maralinga," 12.

111. Transcript of Proceedings 11 April–2 May 1985, A6448 13, NAA, 7209.

112. Transcript of Proceedings 11 April–2 May 1985, A6448 13, NAA, 7210.

113. Transcript of Proceedings 11 April–2 May 1985, A6448 13, NAA, 7213–15.

114. Transcript of Proceedings 11 April–2 May 1985, A6448 13, NAA, 7214.

115. Transcript of Proceedings 11 April–2 May 1985, A6448 13, NAA, 7214–15.

116. Transcript of Proceedings 11 April–2 May 1985, A6448 13, NAA, 7215.

117. Transcript of Proceedings 11 April–2 May 1985, A6448 13, NAA, 7235.

118. Transcript of Proceedings 11 April–2 May 1985, A6448 13, NAA, 7237.

119. Transcript of Proceedings 11 April–2 May 1985, A6448 13, NAA, 7239.

120. Transcript of Proceedings 11 April–2 May 1985, A6448 13, NAA, 7270.

121. Transcript of Proceedings 11 April–2 May 1985, A6448 13, NAA, 7270.

122. Transcript of Proceedings 11 April–2 May 1985, A6448 13, NAA, 7241.

123. Transcript of Proceedings 11 April–2 May 1985, A6448 13, NAA, 7235.

124. Transcript of Proceedings 11 April–2 May 1985, A6448 13, NAA, 7284–90.

125. Transcript of Proceedings 11 April–2 May 1985, A6448 13, NAA, 7284.

126. Transcript of Proceedings 11 April–2 May 1985, A6448 13, NAA, 7284.

127. Transcript of Proceedings 11 April–2 May 1985, A6448 13, NAA, 7285.

128. Transcript of Proceedings 11 April–2 May 1985, A6448 13, NAA, 7242.

129. Transcript of Proceedings 11 April–2 May 1985, A6448 13, NAA, 7245.

130. Transcript of Proceedings 11 April–2 May 1985, A6448 13, NAA, 7246.

131. Transcript of Proceedings 11 April–2 May 1985, A6448 13, NAA, 7246.

132. Transcript of Proceedings 11 April–2 May 1985, A6448 13, NAA, 7246–47.

133. Department of Education, Science and Training (DEST), "Rehabilitation of Former Nuclear Test Sites at Emu and Maralinga (Australia) 2003; Report by the Maralinga Rehabilitation Technical Advisory Committee" (Commonwealth of Australia, 2002), 12.

134. DEST, "Rehabilitation of Former Nuclear Test Sites," 14.

135. DEST, "Rehabilitation of Former Nuclear Test Sites," 15.

136. DEST, "Rehabilitation of Former Nuclear Test Sites," 16.

137. Transcript of Proceedings 11 April–2 May 1985, A6448 13, NAA, 7248.

138. Transcript of Proceedings 11 April–2 May 1985, A6448 13, NAA, 7248.

139. Transcript of Proceedings 11 April–2 May 1985, A6448 13, NAA, 7248.

140. DEST, "Rehabilitation of Former Nuclear Test Sites," 12–30.

141. Transcript of Proceedings 11 April–2 May 1985, A6448 13, NAA, 7249.

142. Standing Committee on Aboriginal Affairs (SCAA), "Return to Country:

The Aboriginal Homelands Movement in Australia" (Australian Government Publishing Service, 1987), 1.

143. SCAA, "Return to Country," 1.

144. SCAA, "Return to Country," 7–8.

145. Myers and Peterson, "Outstations as Aboriginal Life Projects," 7–8.

146. SCAA, "Return to Country," 16; Myers and Peterson, "Outstations as Aboriginal Life Projects," 9–10, 17.

147. SCAA, "Return to Country," 10.

148. SCAA, "Return to Country," 10.

149. Letters Patent (terms of reference) quoted in McClelland, Fitch, and Jonas, "Conclusions and Recommendations," 3–6; Goodall, interview.

150. McClelland, Fitch, and Jonas, "Conclusions and Recommendations," 20.

Six Finding a Seat at the Table

1. As explained briefly in chapter 5, "Maralinga Tjarutja" means "the people brought down from Maralinga." When discussing the community that constitutes Maralinga Tjarutja, it is convention to refer to them as such, rather than as *the* Maralinga Tjarutja. See O'Shea, "The Future Foreshadowed," 213; Mazel, "Returning *Parna Wiru*," 173; Maralinga Tjarutja Land Rights Act, 1984 (South Australia).

2. Andrew Collett, interview with the author, June 2020.

3. "Hot Gift," *The Advertiser*, 17 October 1991, 27, in Maggie Brady Personal Papers.

4. "Hot Gift," 27.

5. Collett, interview.

6. "Agreed Summary Record of Discussions between British and Australian Officials, Canberra 9 and 10 January 1986," Royal Commission into British Nuclear Tests in Australia—Aboriginals Section, A3730 1984/5108, Part 2, National Archives of Australia (NAA), Canberra.

7. "Agreed Summary Record of Discussions between British and Australian Officials," A3730 1984/5108, Part 2, NAA.

8. Peter N. Johnston, Peter A. Burns, Malcolm B. Cooper, and Geoffrey A. Williams, "Isotopic Ratios of Actinides Used in British Nuclear Trials at Maralinga and Emu" (Australian Radiation Laboratory, Department of Community Services and Health, 1988), 1–8.

9. Johnston, Williams, et al., "Plutonium Resuspension," 117–19.

10. Johnston, Williams, et al., "Plutonium Resuspension," 129.

11. Brief to British Government, 28 October 1991, "Maralinga: Meeting with the Aboriginal Delegation, Wednesday 30 October 1991," DEFE 13/2584, the National Archives (TNA), London.

12. Brief to British Government, 28 October 1991, DEFE 13/2584, TNA.

13. "Agreed Summary Record of Discussions between British and Australian Officials," A3730 1984/5108, Part 2, NAA.

14. Press statement by Gareth Evans, Minister for Resources and Energy, 23 January 1986, A13064 DPIE87 1327, NAA.

15. Letter from Arthur Gore, Earl of Arran, Ministry of Defence, to Lord Brabason of Tara, Foreign and Commonwealth Office, 5 July 1990, DEFE 13/2584, TNA.

16. Technical Assessment Group (TAG), "Rehabilitation of Former Nuclear Test Sites in Australia: Report by the Technical Assessment Group" (Department of Primary Industries and Energy and Australian Government Publishing Service, 1990), v.

17. TAG, "Rehabilitation of Former Nuclear Test Sites," v.

18. Minute, Department of Resources and Energy, 15 February 1988, A13064 DPIE87 1327, NAA.

19. Minute, Department of Resources and Energy, 15 February 1988, A13064 DPIE87 1327, NAA.

20. TAG, "Rehabilitation of Former Nuclear Test Sites," 64–65.

21. TAG, "Rehabilitation of Former Nuclear Test Sites," 61–66.

22. Maggie Brady, interview with the author, January 2021.

23. Brady, interview.

24. Robert Milliken, Maggie Brady, and Kingsley Palmer, interview with Wendy Wicks, 26 June 1987, A13064 DPIE87 1327, NAA.

25. Milliken, Brady, and Palmer, interview, A13064 DPIE87 1327, NAA.

26. *Secrets in the Sand* (British Broadcasting Corporation, 1991).

27. *Secrets in the Sand.*

28. Brady, interview.

29. Brady, interview.

30. Brady, interview.

31. See Bongiorno, *The Eighties*, 241–47; Jane Robinson, "Two Faces of Aborigines in 1988," *Canberra Times*, 26 January 1988, 10.

32. Brady, interview.

33. Brady, interview.

34. M. S. Giles, J. R. Twining, A. R. Williams, R. A. Jeffree, and R. U. Domel, "Final Report to the Technical Assessment Group for the Maralinga Rehabilitation Project, Study No. 2 (Radioecology), April 1990" (Australian Government Publishing Service, 1990), 1–18.

35. TAG, "Rehabilitation of Former Nuclear Test Sites," 272–23.

36. TAG, "Rehabilitation of Former Nuclear Test Sites," 10.

37. Cabinet Submission 7479—Rehabilitation of Former British Nuclear Test

Sites, Technical Assessment Group (TAG) Report, Decision 14548, 15 October 1990, A14039, 7479, NAA.

38. Cabinet Submission 7479, A14039, 7479, NAA.

39. Cabinet Submission 7479, A14039, 7479, NAA.

40. Cabinet Submission 7479, A14039, 7479, NAA.

41. Cabinet Submission 7479, A14039, 7479, NAA.

42. Maralinga Tjarutja press release, 7 March 1991, Maralinga Rehabilitation—Discussions with Maralinga Tjarutja, A13064 DPIE91/2302, NAA.

43. Cabinet Submission 7479, A14039, 7479, NAA.

44. Cabinet Submission 7479, A14039, 7479, NAA.

45. "Minutes: Meeting with Maralinga Tjarutja," Department of Primary Industries and Energy, 1 November 1990, Maralinga Rehabilitation—Discussions with Maralinga Tjarutja, A13064 DPIE91/2302, NAA.

46. Collett, interview.

47. This idea of webs and circuits comes from influential work on the notion as it relates to imperialism. See Lester, "Imperial Circuits and Networks."

48. Banivanua Mar, *Decolonisation and the Pacific*, 1–3; Smith, *The Nuclear Free and Independent Pacific Movement*, 22–27.

49. Cook and Goodall, *Making Change Happen*, 315.

50. Alcalay, "The Ethnography of Destabilization," 244.

51. Banivanua Mar, *Decolonisation and the Pacific*, 2.

52. Quoted in Banivanua Mar, *Decolonisation and the Pacific*, 2.

53. Banivanua Mar, *Decolonisation and the Pacific*, 2.

54. Johnson, "Indigenizing Self-Determination at the United Nations," 211.

55. Kirchhof, "Spanning the Globe," 256.

56. "Proposal for Overseas Study Program 1987, Sociological Aspects of Resettlement on Lands Affected by Nuclear Weapons Testing," Visit from Australia by Mr Archie Barton and Mr Graham Knill, A13064 DPIE88/151, NAA.

57. "Proposal for Overseas Study Program 1987," A13064 DPIE88/151, NAA.

58. "Proposal for Overseas Study Program 1987," A13064 DPIE88/151, NAA.

59. "Proposal for Overseas Study Program 1987," A13064 DPIE88/151, NAA.

60. "Proposal for Overseas Study Program 1987," A13064 DPIE88/151, NAA.

61. "Proposal for Overseas Study Program 1987," A13064 DPIE88/151, NAA.

62. "Proposal for Overseas Study Program 1987," A13064 DPIE88/151, NAA.

63. "Proposal for Overseas Study Program 1987," A13064 DPIE88/151, NAA.

64. "Proposal for Overseas Study Program 1987," A13064 DPIE88/151, NAA.

65. W. G. McGregor, Minute, Department of Resources and Energy, 15 April 1987, annotated by Gareth Evans, A13064 DPIE88/151, NAA.

66. McGregor, Minute, annotated by Evans, A13064 DPIE88/151, NAA.

67. McGregor, Minute, annotated by Evans, A13064 DPIE88/151, NAA.

68. Emphasis in the original; letter from Greg Crafter to Gareth Evans, 4 May 1987, annotated by Gareth Evans, A13064 DPIE88/151, NAA.

69. R. N. Rawson, Minute, Department of Resources and Energy, 17 June 1987, A13064 DPIE88/151, NAA.

70. Letter from Gerry Hand to Greg Crafter, South Australian Minister for Aboriginal Affairs, September 1987, A13064 DPIE88/152, NAA.

71. Letter from Graham Knill to Brian Hill, Department of Resources and Energy, 8 September 1987, A13064 DPIE88/152, NAA.

72. Letter from Knill to Hill, 8 September 1987, A13064 DPIE88/152, NAA.

73. "Revised Proposal for Overseas Study Programme—Sociological Aspects of Resettlement on Land Affected by Nuclear Weapons Testing," 8 September 1987, A13064 DPIE88/152, NAA.

74. R. N. Rawson, Minute, 22 October 1987, A13064 DPIE88/152, NAA.

75. Rawson, Minute, 22 October 1987, A13064 DPIE88/152, NAA.

76. Niedenthal, *For the Good of Mankind*, 83; "Two Peoples Share an Atomic Legacy," *Land Rights News*, 1988, 41, in Brady Personal Papers.

77. Cablegram from Department of Foreign Affairs and Trade (DFAT), Adelaide, re. Study Tour: Resettlement on Land Affected by Nuclear Weapons, 15 January 1988, A13064 DPIE88/152, NAA.

78. Cablegram from DFAT Adelaide, re. Study Tour, 20 January 1988, A13064 DPIE88/152, NAA.

79. Cablegram from DFAT, Adelaide, re. Study Tour, 20 January 1988, A13064 DPIE88/152, NAA.

80. Cablegram from DFAT, Adelaide, re. Study Tour, 15 January 1988, A13064 DPIE88/152, NAA.

81. Letter from R. N. Rawson to Archie Barton, 3 June 1988, Visit from Australia by Mr Archie Barton and Mr Graham Knill, A13064 DPIE88/152, NAA.

82. Karen Powell, Minute for Department of Primary Industries and Energy, Visit to Maralinga and Oak Valley by Bikini Island Delegation, 1 July 1988, A13064 DPIE88/152, NAA.

83. Powell, Minute, A13064 DPIE88/152, NAA.

84. David Porter, "Atomic Bomb Lessons in the Desert," *Sydney Morning Herald*, 22 June 1988.

85. "N-Test Aborigines to Study Tactics," *The Advertiser*, 20 June 1988, 3.

86. "Two Peoples Share an Atomic Legacy."

87. "Two Peoples Share an Atomic Legacy."

88. Powell, Minute, A13064 DPIE88/152, NAA.

89. Stegnar, "Assessing Radiological Conditions at Bikini Atoll," 15–16.

90. Stegnar, "Assessing Radiological Conditions at Bikini Atoll," 15–17.

91. Stegnar, "Assessing Radiological Conditions at Bikini Atoll," 17.

92. Matthew Warren, "Bomb Test Victims Find Similarities in Struggles," *The Australian*, 21 June 1988.

93. "Bikini Islanders Visit Maralinga," *Department of Employment, Education and Training (DEET) Aboriginal News* (Canberra), October 1988, 8, in Brady Personal Papers.

94. "Two Peoples Share an Atomic Legacy."

95. "N-Test Aborigines to Study Tactics," 3.

96. Tony Hewett, "Aborigines Take Advice from Bikini Islanders," *Sydney Morning Herald*, 18 June 1988, 4.

97. Powell, Minute, A13064 DPIE88/152, NAA.

98. Powell, Minute, A13064 DPIE88/152, NAA.

99. Powell, Minute, A13064 DPIE88/152, NAA.

100. Niedenthal, *For the Good of Mankind*, 86.

101. Niedenthal, *For the Good of Mankind*, 86.

102. Brady, interview.

103. Brady, interview.

104. "Aborigines Put Human Face on Maralinga," *Canberra Times*, 30 October 1991, 18.

105. "Aborigines Put Human Face on Maralinga," 18.

106. "Aborigines Put Human Face on Maralinga," 18.

107. "Aborigines Put Human Face on Maralinga," 18.

108. "Sympathetic Hearing for Aborigines," *Canberra Times*, 1 November 1991, 11.

109. Brief to British Government, 28 October 1991, DEFE 13/2584 TNA.

110. Letter from John Coles, British High Commissioner to Australia, to Ministry for Defence, 30 April 1990, DEFE 19/627, TNA.

111. Brief to British Government, 28 October 1991, DEFE 13/2584, TNA.

112. Annex B of Brief, "Maralinga: Defensive Press Brief," 28 October 1991, DEFE 13/2584, TNA.

113. "Attorney General's Advice on the Legal Issues Relating to the Former British Nuclear Test Sites in Australia," December 1990, DEFE 13/2584, TNA.

114. Letter from Coles to Ministry for Defence, 30 April 1990, DEFE 19/627, TNA.

115. Annex C of Brief, "The Maralinga Aborigine Delegation: Main Facts," 28 October 1991, DEFE 13/2584, TNA.

116. Telegram from British High Commission, Canberra, 23 October 1991, DEFE 19/627, TNA. In my discussions with Collett, whose oral history interview vitally informed this research, he maintained that he has no recollection of having made this comment to British officials, who claimed the conversation took place as detailed.

117. Andrew Collett quoted in "Sympathetic Hearing for Aborigines," 11.

118. Record of Visit by Group of Maralinga Aborigines to Ministry of Defence, 7 November 1991, DEFE 19/627, TNA.

119. Collett quoted in "Sympathetic Hearing for Aborigines," 11.

120. R. N. Rawson, Minute re. Meeting with Maralinga Tjarutja, Commonwealth Department of Primary Industries and Energy, 24 June 1992, Maralinga Rehabilitation—Discussions with Maralinga Tjarutja TSMU, A13063 DPIE91/2302, NAA.

121. Rawson, Minute re. Meeting with Maralinga Tjarutja, 24 June 1992, A13063 DPIE91/2302, NAA.

122. Rawson, Minute re. Meeting with Maralinga Tjarutja, 24 June 1992, A13063 DPIE91/2302, NAA.

123. Zac Donovan and Rex Jory, "Maralinga Visit Twist: Elders in Push for Compo," *The Advertiser*, September 1992, 5, in Maralinga Rehabilitation, A13063 DPIE91/2302, NAA.

124. Letter from R. N. Rawson to Andrew Collett, 11 September 1992, A13064 DPIE91/2302, NAA.

125. Donovan and Jory, "Maralinga Visit Twist," 5.

126. "Elders 'Could Lobby' Britain," *Canberra Times*, 4 September 1991, 18.

127. Draft Itinerary, London and Salzburg Trip, 1992, A13064 DPIE91/2302, NAA.

128. Claus Biegert, "Opening Speech on the Eve of the Hearing," in *Poison Fire, Sacred Earth: Testimonies, Lectures, Conclusions; The World Uranium Hearing, Salzburg 1992* (World Uranium Hearing, 1992), accessed at https://ratical.org/radiation/WorldUraniumHearing/OpeningSpeechEve.html.

129. Archie Barton, "Speech to World Uranium Hearing, Salzburg," in *Poison Fire, Sacred Earth: Testimonies, Lectures, Conclusions; The World Uranium Hearing, Salzburg 1992* (World Uranium Hearing, 1992), accessed at https://ratical.org/radiation/WorldUraniumHearing/ArchieBarton.html.

130. Barton, "Speech to World Uranium Hearing."

131. Barton, "Speech to World Uranium Hearing."

132. "Hot Gift," *The Advertiser*, 17 October 1992, 27, in Brady Personal Papers.

133. "Hot Gift," 27.

134. "Hot Gift," 27.

135. Collett, interview.

136. See *The Times* (London), 28 October 1991, 2; *Secrets in the Sand*; Larissa Behrendt, dir., *Maralinga Tjarutja* (Australian Broadcasting Corporation, 2021).

137. Collett, interview.

138. "Hot Gift," 27.

139. Department of Education, Science and Training, "Rehabilitation of Former Nuclear Test Sites at Emu and Maralinga (Australia) 2003; Report by the Maralinga Rehabilitation Technical Advisory Committee" (Commonwealth of Australia, 2002), 175–303.

140. While an official cleanup was completed, some have speculated that it, too, was inadequate. See Parkinson, *Maralinga: Australia's Nuclear Waste Cover-Up*.

141. Nance Haxton, "Maralinga Returned to Traditional Owners," *ABC News*, 18 December 2009.

Seven Irati Wanti

1. The abbreviation AM after Eileen Kampakuta Brown's name is reflective of her status as a member of the Order of Australia.

2. These women, and other Kungka Tjuta, will be referred to with "Mrs." in front of their surname, as those associated with the Kungka Tjuta still refer to them in this manner out of respect. This was the way these women were referred to throughout my oral history interviews.

3. Goldman Environmental Prize, "2003 Goldman Environmental Prize Ceremony: Eileen Kampakuta Brown and Eileen Wani Wingfield," video via YouTube.

4. "Witness Statement of Eileen Wingfield, 2010, Environment, Resources and Development Court of South Australia, re. Mining Exploration of Lake Torrens," private collection of Wingfield family.

5. Tania Wingfield, interview with the author, March 2022.

6. Gerster, "Down the Yellowcake Road," 440.

7. Cawte, *Atomic Australia*, 170.

8. Lynette Allen, interview with the author, March 2022.

9. Women have long protested against nuclear imposition. For literature on this subject, see Junor and Howse, *Greenham Common Women's Peace Camp*; Harford and Hopkins, *Greenham Common*; Roseneil, *Disarming Patriarchy*; Eschle, "Beyond Greenham Woman?"; Eschle, "Gender and the Subject of (Anti)Nuclear Politics"; Maleta, "Australian Women's Anti-Nuclear Leadership"; Cohn, "Sex and Death in the Rational World of Defense Intellectuals"; Das, "A Post-Colonial Analysis of India–United States Nuclear Security"; Das, "Colonial Legacies, Post-Colonial (In)Securities, and Gender(ed) Representations"; Das, "Nation, Gender and Representations of (In)Securities"; Acheson, *Banning the Bomb, Smashing the Patriarchy*; Enloe and Cohn, "A Conversation with Cynthia Enloe," 1188; Choi and Eschle, "Rethinking Global Nuclear Politics, Rethinking Feminism."

10. As early as 1956, *Tharunka*, the student union newspaper of the University of Technology Sydney, was reporting on Baxter's discussions with students about the future of nuclear power in Australia. See "Prof. Baxter Speaks at Hostel," *Tharunka*, September 1956, 3. Ernest Titterton spent the majority of his career advocating for the civilian use of nuclear energy. Examples of this work are scattered throughout his archive, housed at the Adolph Basser Library, Australian Academy of Science, Canberra.

11. "Australian Relations Policy," AB 48/264, the National Archives (TNA), London.

12. Lowe, *Long Half-Life*, 5.

13. That British officials and scientists were conscious of wanting and needing to exchange some nuclear technology and knowledge with Australia for testing sites and uranium is explored in a suite of documents at the National Archives, London. See Relations with the Dominions and Colonies, Australia (3), CAB 126/292, TNA.

14. Lowe, *Long Half-Life*, 45–46, 129.

15. Broinowski, *Fact or Fission?*, 34; Reynolds, *Australia's Bid for the Atomic Bomb*, 138–61.

16. Lowe, *Long Half-Life*, 47.

17. Australian Atomic Energy Commission (AAEC), "Aptcare–Lucas Heights: A Plan to Cope with Accidents at the Research Establishment of the Australian Atomic Energy Commission, Lucas Heights, NSW" (AAEC, 1986), 18; Australian National Parks and Wildlife Service, "Lucas Heights Buffer Zone: Plan of Management" (Australian National Parks and Wildlife Service on behalf of the AAEC, 1986), 12.

18. Lowe, *Long Half-Life*, 138.

19. Taylor, "Australia: Host for a Nuclear Waste Storage Site?"; Holland, "Waste Not Want Not?"; Nagtzaam, "Pass the Parcel."

20. Slovic, Flynn, and Layman, "Perceived Risk," 1603.

21. Dee Margetts and Meg Lees, "Senate Select Committee on Uranium Mining and Milling, Minority Report" (Parliament of Australia, 1997), 8.3.

22. Holland, "Waste Not Want Not?," 283.

23. Mike Codd, "Review of Arrangements for the Recent Transportation of Radioactive Waste" (Department of Industry, Science and Technology, 1995), 4.

24. Codd, "Recent Transportation of Radioactive Waste," 4; Commonwealth of Australia, "No Time to Waste: Report of the Senate Select Committee on the Dangers of Radioactive Waste" (Senate Printing Unit, April 1996), 3–4.

25. Commonwealth of Australia, "No Time to Waste," 3–4.

26. Commonwealth Hansard, House of Representatives, 2 June 2003.

27. Commonwealth of Australia, "No Time to Waste," iv.

28. Commonwealth of Australia, "No Time to Waste," 176.

29. Commonwealth of Australia, "No Time to Waste," 176–77.

30. Commonwealth of Australia, "No Time to Waste," 7.

31. Commonwealth of Australia, "No Time to Waste," 12–13.

32. Simon Evans, "Uproar over Plan for SA Nuclear Dump," *Australian Financial Review*, 12 February 1998.

33. Daniel Voronoff, "Shallow Grave," *Chain Reaction* (Melbourne), 1 August 1999, 36.

34. South Australian Hansard, House of Assembly, 30 June 1998.

35. Department of Primary Industries and Energy (DPIE), "National Radioactive Waste Repository Site Selection Study: Phase 1: A Report on Public Comment, August 1993" (Australian Government Publishing Service, 1993); DPIE, "National Radioactive Waste Repository Site Selection Study: Phase 2: A Report on Public Comment, November 1995" (Australian Government Publishing Service, 1995).

36. South Australian Hansard, House of Assembly, 30 June 1998, 1197.

37. South Australian Hansard, House of Assembly, 30 June 1998, 1197.

38. Karina Lester, interview with the author, October 2020.

39. South Australian Hansard, House of Assembly, 30 June 1998, 1197.

40. Kupa Piti Kungka Tjuta, *Talking Straight Out*, 10–11.

41. Vincent, "Knowing the Country," 157; Vincent, "Never Mind Our Country Is the Desert," 55.

42. Michele Madigan, interview with the author, March 2022; Allen, interview.

43. Kungka Tjuta quoted in Brown and Sowerwine, "Irati Wanti," 11.

44. Junor and Howse, *Greenham Common Women's Peace Camp*; Harford and Hopkins, *Greenham Common*; Roseneil, *Disarming Patriarchy*; Eschle, "Beyond Greenham Woman?"

45. Eschle, "Gender and the Subject of (Anti)Nuclear Politics"; Maleta, "Australian Women's Anti-Nuclear Leadership."

46. Cohn, "Sex and Death in the Rational World of Defense Intellectuals"; Das, "A Post-Colonial Analysis of India–United States Nuclear Security"; Das, "Colonial Legacies, Post-Colonial (In)Securities, and Gender(ed) Representations"; Das, "Nation, Gender and Representations of (In)Securities"; Acheson, *Banning the Bomb, Smashing the Patriarchy*; Enloe and Cohn, "A Conversation with Cynthia Enloe," 1188; Choi and Eschle, "Rethinking Global Nuclear Politics, Rethinking Feminism."

47. For complementary examples of other Indigenous women and antinuclearism, see Hogue and Maurer, "Pacific Women's Anti-Nuclear Poetry"; Runyan, "Indigenous Women's Resistances"; Runyan, "Disposable Waste, Lands and Bodies"; Leddy, *Serpent River Resurgence*; Gómez, *Nuclear Nuevo México*.

48. Brock, "Aboriginal Women, Politics and Land," 12.

49. See Brock, *Words and Silences*.

50. Goodall, *Invasion to Embassy*, 9.

51. It is important to note that Indigenous women's activism of the nature described in this chapter is not isolated to nuclear impositions. There are numerous examples of Aboriginal women standing up strong against environmental imposition in Australia. See also Rose, "The Silence and Power of Women"; Bell, "The Word of a Woman."

52. Janice Wingfield, interview with the author, March 2022.

53. Bell, *Daughters of the Dreaming*, 21.

54. Bell, *Daughters of the Dreaming*, 21; Kupa Piti Kungka Tjuta, *Talking Straight Out*, 1–28.

55. For testimonies on the black mist, see chapters 2 and 5; see also Transcript of Proceedings 11 April–2 May 1985, plus pp. 7080a–7540, Royal Commission into British Nuclear Tests in Australia, A6448, 13, National Archives of Australia (NAA), Canberra.

56. Letter to the editor, *Coober Pedy Times*, 14 July 1999, 7–8.

57. For more information on MacDougall, see chapter 2; see also Gara, "Ooldea, the Spinifex People and the Bomb," 366–71.

58. Madigan, interview.

59. Kupa Piti Kungka Tjuta, *Talking Straight Out*, 11.

60. Folkers, "Disproportionate Impacts of Radiation Exposure."

61. Janice Wingfield, interview.

62. Janice Wingfield, Lynette Allen, Sonja Gaston, and Tania Wingfield, interviews with the author, March 2022; Sue Coleman-Haseldine, "My People Are Still Suffering from Australia's Secret Nuclear Testing," *Sydney Morning Herald*, 8 December 2017, https://www.smh.com.au/opinion/my-people-are-still-suffering-from-australias-secret-nuclear-testing-20171208-h01a3l.html.

63. Kupa Piti Kungka Tjuta, *Talking Straight Out*, 11.

64. Vincent, "'Through the Smoke.'"

65. Kahnawà:ke Mohawk political anthropologist Audra Simpson has written at length about the politics of refusal among the Kahnawà:ke Mohawks in southwestern Quebec. She stresses the need for scholars to consider refusal of citizenship and other settler impositions as in opposition to histories of political recognition. This is in light of scholars traditionally focusing on the struggle for political recognition—and thus integration into the nation—as being the crux of the history of Indigenous politics within settler-colonial states. Alternatively, Simpson points to "refusal" as a vital form of Indigenous politics. See Simpson, *Mohawk Interruptus*; Simpson, "On Ethnographic Refusal."

66. Madigan, interview.

67. This is not to say that urban spaces are not Aboriginal land. Rather, urban populations and rapid urbanization have largely displaced Aboriginal people from these spaces, while writing new, mostly settler, histories over them.

68. Commonwealth Hansard, *Parliamentary Debates*, Senate, no. 178, 20 June 1996, 1998–99.

69. Kupa Piti Kungka Tjuta, *Talking Straight Out*, 12.

70. Madigan, interview.

71. James and Williamson, "*Kungkarangkalpa Inma Alatjila Kuwari Palyani*," 180.

72. Handwritten note explaining the Seven Sisters Inma, date unknown, in

Papers of Sister Michele Madigan, PRG 1686, State Library of South Australia (SLSA), Adelaide.

73. Lester, interview.

74. Watson, "Kungka Tjuta and the Struggle for the Manta."

75. Janice Wingfield, interview.

76. Emily Munyungka Austin quoted in McConchie, *Elders*, 17–18.

77. Janice Wingfield, interview; Allen, interview.

78. Tania Wingfield, interview.

79. Allen, interview.

80. Janice Wingfield, interview.

81. Eileen Wani Wingfield quoted in McConchie, *Elders*, 21.

82. Eileen Unkari Crombie quoted in McConchie, *Elders*, 19.

83. Friends of the Earth Australia, *30 Years of Creative Resistance* (2004), 41, https://commonslibrary.org/wp-content/uploads/30-Years-of-Creative-Resistance.pdf.

84. Letter to Friends of the Earth Melbourne from Kupa Piti Kungka Tjuta, 3 August 1998, "Kupa Piti Kungka Tjuta Waste Dump," Madigan Papers, PRG 1686/1, SLSA.

85. Program of the Second Gathering in Solidarity with Indigenous People and the Earth, Global Survival and Indigenous Rights, International Sustainability Conference Series 1998, Kupa Piti Kungka Tjuta Waste Dump, Madigan Papers, PRG 1686/1, SLSA.

86. Madigan, interview.

87. Carolyn Webb, "Women United by a Really Hot Topic," *The Age* (Melbourne), 21 November 1998.

88. Kupa Piti Kungka Tjuta, *Talking Straight Out*, 20.

89. Kupa Piti Kungka Tjuta, *Talking Straight Out*, 22.

90. Madigan, interview; Vincent, *"Against Native Title,"* 155.

91. This point is of great discussion in environmental humanities—especially in the United States—and is perhaps best represented by contentions over wilderness rhetoric.

92. Vincent, *"Against Native Title,"* 155. See also Vincent and Neale, *Unstable Relations*.

93. Eve Vincent has referred to such tensions as "unstable relations." Perhaps the most obvious example of such tensions is offered by the wilderness movement, such that white environmentalists' preoccupation with "wilderness" has been exposed as undermining Indigenous connections to certain "wilderness" environments, discursively erasing them and reinforcing colonial structures. See Langton, "Art, Wilderness and *Terra Nullius*"; Langton, "What Do We Mean by Wilderness?"; Langton, *Boyer Lectures 2021*, 101–31; Bayet-Charlton, "Overturning the Doctrine"; Ferdinand, "Behind the Colonial Silence of Wilderness."

94. Vincent, "*Against Native Title,*" 159. See also Vincent, "Kangaroo Tails for Dinner?," 213–52.

95. Clare Brown quoted in Vincent, "*Against Native Title,*" 159.

96. Vincent, "*Against Native Title,*" 159; Vincent, "Kangaroo Tails for Dinner?," 213–52.

97. Madigan, interview.

98. Sherrill Nixon, "Roo Barbecue and Red Heart Hospitality for Kilmer; Superstar's Tribal Visit," *Sunday Mail* (Brisbane), 26 September 1999, 8.

99. Sherrill Nixon, "Fame with Heart," *The Advertiser*, 14 January 2000, 61; "Hollywood Dreaming," *The Age*, 26 September 1999, 6.

100. Nixon, "Roo Barbecue and Red Heart Hospitality," 8; "Kilmer Makes a Connection," *The Age*, 23 September 1999, 27.

101. "Hollywood Dreaming," 6.

102. "Hollywood Dreaming," 6.

103. Commonwealth of Australia, "National Radioactive Waste Repository Site Selection Study, Phase 3" (Commonwealth of Australia, 1999), 18.

104. Letter from Senator Nick Minchin, Minister for Industry, Science and Resources, to Michele Madigan, 16 April 1999, in Madigan Papers, Government re R/A Waste, PRG 1686/1, file 10, SLSA.

105. Madigan, interview.

106. Sister Michele Madigan, in private correspondence, noted the importance of recognizing the contribution of ACF Adelaide's campaigner David Noonan to the organization of this vital event.

107. In Australia, "shadow ministers" comprise a "shadow cabinet," which scrutinizes the sitting cabinet's actions from the Opposition. The reference to "shadow environment minister" indicates John Hill's position in the Opposition in 1999. When Labor was elected to the South Australian Parliament in 2002, Hill became the sitting minister for environment.

108. Madigan, interview.

109. Kupa Piti Kungka Tjuta, *Talking Straight Out*, 24.

110. Madigan, interview; Kupa Piti Kungka Tjuta, *Talking Straight Out*, 24.

111. "Long-Marchers Set to Take Fire over Harbour Bridge," *Koori Mail* (Sydney), 6 September 2000, 62.

112. Buzzacott, *Lake Eyre Is Calling*, 6.

113. Kupa Piti Kungka Tjuta, *Talking Straight Out*, 33.

114. Madigan, interview.

115. Kupa Piti Kungka Tjuta, *Talking Straight Out*, 33.

116. Todd Condie, "Women Tell of Their Plight," *Koori Mail*, 20 September 2000, 2.

117. Condie, "Women Tell of Their Plight," 2.

118. Madigan, interview.

119. Madigan, interview.

120. Lester, interview; Janice Wingfield, interview.

121. Lester, interview.

122. Goldman Environmental Prize, "Prize History," accessed 24 March 2022, https://www.goldmanprize.org/history/.

123. Tania Wingfield, interview.

124. Goldman Trip Itinerary, 9–20 April 2003, private collection of Wingfield family.

125. Goldman Environmental Prize, "2003 Goldman Environmental Prize Ceremony: Eileen Kampakuta Brown and Eileen Wani Wingfield."

126. Goldman Environmental Prize, "Eileen Kampakuta Brown and Eileen Wani Wingfield," accessed 24 March 2022, https://www.goldmanprize.org/recipient/eileen-kampakuta-brown-eileen-wani-wingfield/.

127. Goldman Environmental Prize, "Eileen Kampakuta Brown and Eileen Wani Wingfield."

128. Janice Wingfield, interview; Lester, interview.

129. Letter from Haunani Apoliona, Chairperson, Board of Trustees, Office of Hawaiian Affairs, to Eileen Wani Wingfield, 15 April 2003, private collection of Wingfield family.

130. Letter from Tex G. Hall, President of the National Congress of American Indians, to Eileen Wani Wingfield, 14 April 2003, private collection of Wingfield family.

131. Janice Wingfield, interview.

132. Amie Horner, "Aboriginal Elder Awarded World Environmental Prize," *Transcontinental* (Port Augusta), 23 April 2003, 4.

133. South Australian Hansard, Legislative Council, 28 April 2003, 2114.

134. South Australian Hansard, Legislative Council, 28 April 2003, 2114–15.

135. Cabinet papers detailing the Commonwealth government's intention to extinguish Native Title rights in the region and override South Australian legislation were released in early 2023 and can be found in "Cabinet Submission JH02/0229—Strategies for Progressing National Radioactive Waste Management Facilities—Decision JH02/0229/CAB, 19 June–16 July 2002," A14370, JH2002/229, NAA.

136. South Australian Hansard, House of Assembly, 19 July 2004.

137. Gaston, interview.

138. Green Left, "Open Letter from the Kupa Piti Kungka Tjuta," 3 August 2005, https://www.greenleft.org.au/content/open-letter-kupa-piti-kungka-tjuta.

Conclusion Fallout

1. Karina Lester, interview with the author, October 2020.
2. Lester, interview.
3. Lester, interview.
4. Lester, interview.

BIBLIOGRAPHY

Archival Sources

Australian Institute of Aboriginal and Torres Strait Islander Studies (AIATSIS), Canberra

Kath Walker (Oodgeroo Noonuccal), "Black-White Coalition Can Work," *Origin* 1, no. 4 (1969), RS 21/21

FLINDERS UNIVERSITY SPECIAL COLLECTIONS (FUSC), ADELAIDE

Maralinga—Letter to Hawke and his reply, BANN/PR/071.3

Maralinga Inquiry, BANN/065/MEU06

Olympic Dam, BANN/033/Roxby Downs

Opening Olympic Dam Operations, Roxby Downs, BANN/SP/1288

THE NATIONAL ARCHIVES (TNA), LONDON

Australia Part II (Section II), AB/312 BT 3-4

Commonwealth Defence Co-operation (Policy), CAB 21/1799

Cooperation with Australia on Uranium Enrichment, FCO 96/252

Development of Australian Resources, MH 270

"Maralinga: Meeting with the Aboriginal Delegation, Wednesday 30 October 1991," DEFE 13/2584

(Maralinga) British Nuclear Testing, DEFE 19/627

Policy Coordination of British and Australian Effort General, AB 16/750, TNA

Relations with the Dominions and Colonies, Australia (3), CAB 126/292, TNA

Report of Suffering by Australian Aborigines at Woomera, DO 35/10903

Testing of United Kingdom Atomic Weapon, CAB 126/325

Uranium Australia, AB 1 83

Uranium Australia, AB 1 667

NATIONAL ARCHIVES OF AUSTRALIA (NAA), CANBERRA

Cabinet Decision 3243—Atomic Testing at Maralinga, Possible Inquiry—Without Submission, A13979 3243

Cabinet Submission 7479—Rehabilitation of Former British Nuclear Test Sites, Technical Assessment Group (TAG) Report, Decision 14548, A14039 7479

Campaign against Uranium Mining and for Land Rights by Aboriginal Representatives in Western Europe—Aboriginal Issues at the United Nations, A432, A1979/5353

Defence Representation on Atomic Energy Research Advisory Committee, A5954 1385/7

Effects of Nuclear Radiation on Man, A5954 1385/2

French Nuclear Tests in the Kerguelen Islands, A1946 186/2/26

General Correspondence, M3596 277

Informal Commonwealth Conference on Defence Science—Notes on Items of Agenda, A1196 12/501/298

Informal Commonwealth Conference on Defence Science—Reports, A1196 12/501/295

International Control of Atomic Energy—Formation of Atomic Energy Commission, A5954 2163/3

International Court of Justice—Advisory Opinions, French Nuclear Tests, Australia vs. France, A1838 1558/1/144, Part 1

International Court of Justice—Advisory Opinions, French Nuclear Tests, Australia vs. France, A1838 1558/1/44, Part 2

Maralinga Rehabilitation—Discussions with Maralinga Tjarutja, A13064 DPIE91/2302

Maralinga Tjarutja Conditions at Oak Valley, A13064 DPIE87/1327

Minutes of Meeting of Full Cabinet, at 11 a.m., Tuesday, 4 June 1946, at Parliament House, Canberra, A2703 129

Personal Papers of Prime Minister E. G. Whitlam—French Nuclear Tests, 13 June 1972, M170, 72/80

Personal Papers of Prime Minister Malcolm Fraser, M1268, 188

Roxby Downs—Western Mining Corporation—Uranium Venture, A1209 1979/990

Royal Commission into British Nuclear Tests in Australia

Aboriginal Collation, A6455 RC 819

Aboriginals Section, A3730 1984/5108, Part 2

Documents referred to Sir E Titterton by G Eames, A6455 RC523

Final Submission of the Government of the United Kingdom, Royal Commission into British Nuclear Tests in Australia, A6455 RC865

Representation by R. A. Macaulay, A13064 DPIE86/002049

Representation by R. A. Macaulay, A13064 DPIE87/000461

Transcript of Proceedings 11 April–2 May 1985, A6448 13

Transcript of Proceedings 5 May–30 May 1985, A6448 14

UK Atomic Test, SA Aboriginal Health Inquiry, A13064 DPIE84/001697

UK Atomic Test Program, Calls for Public Inquiry, May–June 1984, A13064 DPIE84/001501

Visit from Australia by Mr Archie Barton and Mr Graham Knill, Marshall Islands, February–March 1988, to Study Effects of Nuclear Testing, A13064 DPIE88/151

Visit from Australia by Mr Archie Barton and Mr Graham Knill, Marshall Islands, February–March 1988, to Study Effects of Nuclear Testing, A13064 DPIE88/152
Welfare of Aborigines, A6456 R022/008

NATIONAL LIBRARY OF AUSTRALIA (NLA), CANBERRA

"The Olympic Dam Project: A Short Summary of the Environmental Impact Statement," October 1982, NLpf 333.8510994238

NOEL BUTLIN ARCHIVE CENTRE (NBAC), AUSTRALIAN NATIONAL UNIVERSITY, CANBERRA

Amalgamated Metal Workers' Union—Uranium Mining, Assorted Papers, N395-144
Australian Council of Trade Unions Deposit—Uranium, N147-338
Council of Australian Government Employee Organisations Deposit, N87
Federated Engine Drivers' and Firemen's Association of Australasia—Uranium, N129-2510
Richard Eves Collection, N358
Union of Australian Women—Uranium, N96-137
Waterside Workers' Federation of Australia, Federal Office Deposit, N114

ROBERT HAWKE PRIME MINISTERIAL LIBRARY (RHPML), UNIVERSITY OF ADELAIDE, ADELAIDE

Papers Relating to the Australian Labor Party (ALP)—Robert J. L. Hawke, President, Australian Council of Trade Unions (ACTU), 1970–1980, RH9
Subject Files—Robert J. L. Hawke, President, Australian Council of Trade Unions (ACTU), 1970–1980, RH10

SOUTH AUSTRALIAN MUSEUM (SAM), ADELAIDE

Aborigines Friends Association, Annual Reports, AA1/67
Delta Metal Co. (Letters), Mawson Collection, MI247
Douglas Mawson Diary, Mount Painter 1910, 1924, Mawson Collection, 30DM.3a
Mawson Correspondence re. Radioactivity (1906), Mawson Collection, MI316
Mawson Mineral Resources Correspondence, 1935–1958, Mawson Collection, 40DM
Radio Mineral Investigations—Correspondence and Related Papers, 1905–1954, Mawson Collection, 34DM

STATE LIBRARY OF SOUTH AUSTRALIA (SLSA), ADELAIDE

Greenwood Family Papers, PRG 274
Interview with Gordon (Smiler) Greenwood, ca. 1964, OH 389
Papers of Sister Michele Madigan, PRG 1686/4

STATE RECORDS OF SOUTH AUSTRALIA (SRSA), ADELAIDE

Aborigines Protection Board Reports, Minister of Health, Department of the Premier and Cabinet, RDS1466/7.1

Annual Reports—Protector of Aborigines and Successors, GRS/12387

Correspondence Files ("ME" Files)—Office of the Minister of Agriculture and Education, and Successors, 1902, GRG18/1/16

Correspondence Files, Annual Single Number Series—Department of Mines, GRG30/4

Gazette Notice Books—Department of Mines and Successors, GRS/14696

Mining Acts and Regulations, GRS/111328

Ministerial Correspondence Files, Annual Single Number Series—Minister of Mines and Energy and Predecessors, GRS/966

Miscellaneous Printed Items Relating to Australian Aborigines, GRG52/47

Office Diaries of the Secretary, Aborigines Protection Board, 1947–1954, GRG52/14

Protector of Aborigines Reports, 1901–1937, GRG52/12

Reports—Mount Painter Uranium Project, GRS/11322

Western Mining Corporation Olympic Dam Project Indenture Policy—Aboriginal Heritage, GRS/5505/14/16

Private Collections

Maggie Brady Personal Papers

Private collection of Wingfield family

Unpublished Works

Compton, Anthea. "The Function of 'Traditional Culture' in Australian Political Discourse, 1963–2007." PhD thesis, University of New South Wales, 2019.

Kerin, Sitarani. "'Doctor Do-Good'? Charles Duguid and Aboriginal Politics, 1930s–1970s." PhD thesis, Australian National University, 2004.

Shumway, Gary Lee. "A History of Uranium Mining on the Colorado Plateau." PhD diss., University of Southern California, 1970.

Vincent, Eve. "'Through the Smoke': The Kupa Piti Kungka Tjuta Remember British Atomic Tests." Honours thesis, University of Melbourne, 2002.

Oral History Interviews with the Author

Allen, Lynette, March 2022.
Brady, Maggie, January 2021.
Collett, Andrew, June 2020.
Gaston, Sonja, March 2022.
Goodall, Heather, April 2021.
Lester, Karina, October 2020.
Madigan, Michele, March 2022.
Wingfield, Janice, March 2022.
Wingfield, Tania, March 2022.

Government Reports, Publications, and Acts

Atomic Energy (Control of Materials) Act, 1946 (Commonwealth).

Australian Atomic Energy Commission (AAEC). "Aptcare–Lucas Heights: A Plan to Cope with Accidents at the Research Establishment of the Australian Atomic Energy Commission, Lucas Heights, NSW." AAEC, 1986.

Australian National Parks and Wildlife Service. "Lucas Heights Buffer Zone: Plan of Management." Australian National Parks and Wildlife Service on behalf of the AAEC, 1986.

Carter, Michael, Francis (Rob) Robotham, Keith Wise, Geoffrey A. Williams and Philip Crouch. *Australian Participants in British Nuclear Tests in Australia*. Vol. 1, *Dosimetry*. Commonwealth of Australia, Department of Veterans' Affairs, 2006.

Codd, Mike. "Review of Arrangements for the Recent Transportation of Radioactive Waste." Department of Industry, Science and Technology, 1995.

Commissioner of Crown Lands and Immigration. "South Australia: A Brief Account of Its Progress and Resources." E. Spiller Government Printer, 1882.

Commonwealth of Australia. "National Radioactive Waste Repository Site Selection Study, Phase 3." Commonwealth of Australia, 1999.

———. "No Time to Waste: Report of the Senate Select Committee on the Dangers of Radioactive Waste." Senate Printing Unit, April 1996.

Department of Climate Change, Energy, the Environment and Water (DCCEEW). "Ranger Uranium Environmental Inquiry Final Report 1977." https://www.dcceew.gov.au/science-research/supervising-scientist/publications/ranger-uranium-environmental-inquiry-report-final.

Department of Education, Science and Training (DEST). "Rehabilitation of Former Nuclear Test Sites at Emu and Maralinga (Australia) 2003; Report by the

Maralinga Rehabilitation Technical Advisory Committee." Commonwealth of Australia, 2002.

Department of External Affairs. *Current Notes on International Affairs*, March 1954.

Department of Planning, Lands and Heritage. "A Brief History of the Aboriginal Heritage Act 1972." Government of Western Australia, 2016.

Department of Primary Industries and Energy (DPIE). "National Radioactive Waste Repository Site Selection Study: Phase 1: A Report on Public Comment, August 1993." Australian Government Publishing Service, 1993.

———. "National Radioactive Waste Repository Site Selection Study: Phase 2: A Report on Public Comment, November 1995." Australian Government Publishing Service, 1995.

Dow, Coral, and John Gardiner-Garden. "Overview of Indigenous Affairs: Part 1: 1901–1991." Parliament of the Commonwealth of Australia, 2010.

Expert Committee on the Review of Data on Atmospheric Fallout Arising from British Nuclear Tests in Australia. "Report of the Expert Committee on the Review of Data on Atmospheric Fallout Arising from British Nuclear Tests in Australia, 31 May 1984." Commonwealth Government of Australia, 1984.

Fox, R. W., G. G. Kelleher, and C. B. Kerr. "Ranger Uranium Environmental Inquiry, Second Report." Australian Government Publishing Service, 1977.

Giles, M. S., J. R. Twining, A. R. Williams, R. A. Jeffree, and R. U. Domel. "Final Report to the Technical Assessment Group for the Maralinga Rehabilitation Project, Study No. 2 (Radioecology), April 1990." Australian Government Publishing Service, 1990.

Johnston, Peter N., Peter A. Burns, Malcolm B. Cooper, and Geoffrey A. Williams. "Isotopic Ratios of Actinides Used in British Nuclear Trials at Maralinga and Emu." Australian Radiation Laboratory, Department of Community Services and Health, 1988.

Maralinga Tjarutja Land Rights Act, 1984 (South Australia).

Margetts, Dee, and Meg Lees. "Senate Select Committee on Uranium Mining and Milling, Minority Report." Parliament of Australia, 1997.

McClelland, James, Jill Fitch, and William J. A. Jonas. "The Report of the Royal Commission into British Nuclear Tests in Australia: Conclusions and Recommendations." Australian Government Publishing Service, 1985.

Roxby Downs (Indenture Ratification) Act, 1982 (South Australia).

Senate Environment, Communications, Information Technology and the Arts Committees. "Report on Commonwealth Environment Powers." Senate Standing Committees on Environment and Communications, Parliament of Australia, 1999.

Senate Select Committee. "Report on Senate Select Committee on Uranium Mining and Milling." Australian Parliament, 1997.

Standing Committee on Aboriginal Affairs (SCAA). "Return to Country: The Aboriginal Homelands Movement in Australia." Australian Government Publishing Service, 1987.

Technical Assessment Group (TAG). "Rehabilitation of Former Nuclear Test Sites in Australia: Report by the Technical Assessment Group." Department of Primary Industries and Energy and Australian Government Publishing Service, 1990.

Hansard Parliamentary Debates

Commonwealth Hansard. House of Representatives. 2 June 2003.

Commonwealth Hansard. Senate. 5 June 1984.

Commonwealth Hansard. Senate. 20 June 1996.

Commonwealth Hansard. Senate. 25 August 1997.

South Australian Hansard. House of Assembly. 30 June 1998.

South Australian Hansard. House of Assembly. 19 July 2004.

South Australian Hansard. Legislative Council. 28 April 2003.

Speeches

Barton, Archie. "Speech to World Uranium Hearing, Salzburg." In *Poison Fire, Sacred Earth: Testimonies, Lectures, Conclusions; The World Uranium Hearing, Salzburg 1992*. World Uranium Hearing, 1992. Accessed at https://ratical.org/radiation/WorldUraniumHearing/ArchieBarton.html.

Biegert, Claus. "Opening Speech on the Eve of the Hearing." In *Poison Fire, Sacred Earth: Testimonies, Lectures, Conclusions; The World Uranium Hearing, Salzburg 1992*. World Uranium Hearing, 1992. Accessed at https://ratical.org/radiation/WorldUraniumHearing/OpeningSpeechEve.html.

Fraser, Malcolm. "Report to the Nation, 28 August 1977." Department of the Prime Minister and Cabinet. https://pmtranscripts.pmc.gov.au/release/transcript-4479.

———. "Uranium—Australia's Decision, Statement by the Prime Minister." Commonwealth of Australia, 1977. https://pmtranscripts.pmc.gov.au/sites/default/files/original/00006007.pdf.

Whitlam, Gough. "Election Speech Delivered in Blacktown, NSW, November 13th 1972." Museum of Australian Democracy. https://electionspeeches.moadoph.gov.au/speeches/1972-gough-whitlam.

Multimedia

Backs to the Blast, an Australian Nuclear Story. 1981. Video via National Film and Sound Archive, Canberra. https://aso.gov.au/titles/documentaries/backs-blast/clip1/.

Behrendt, Larissa, dir., *Maralinga Tjarutja*. Australian Broadcasting Corporation, 2021.

Goldman Environmental Prize. "2003 Goldman Environmental Prize Ceremony: Eileen Kampakuta Brown and Eileen Wani Wingfield." Video via YouTube, 6:37. https://www.youtube.com/watch?v=Y2yPINceAg4.

"Karina Lester Addresses the Second Meeting of States Parties to the TPNW." 2023. Video via YouTube, 13:36. https://www.youtube.com/watch?v=D22ppVlXS5k.

"Nuclear Test Survivor Sue Coleman-Haseldine." 2017. Video via YouTube, 3:52. https://www.youtube.com/watch?v=YcfmfVFH_8c.

Secrets in the Sand. British Broadcasting Corporation, 1991.

Newspapers and Print Media

ABC News (Sydney)

Adelaide Observer

Advertiser (Adelaide)

Age (Melbourne)

Argus (Melbourne)

Australian (Sydney)

Australian Financial Review (Sydney)

Ballarat Star (Victoria)

Bulletin (Sydney)

Cairns Post (Queensland)

Canberra Times

Chain Reaction (Melbourne)

Clarence and Richmond Examiner (Grafton, New South Wales)

Coober Pedy Times

Daily Telegraph (Sydney)

Department of Employment, Education and Training (DEET) Aboriginal News (Canberra)

Empire Times (Adelaide)

Evening Journal (Adelaide)

Evening News (Sydney)

Express and Telegraph (Adelaide)

Glen Innes Examiner and General Advertiser (New South Wales)
Goulburn Evening Post (New South Wales)
Koori Mail (Sydney)
Land Rights News
Mail (Adelaide)
Matilda
News (Adelaide)
North West Post (Tasmania)
Northern Argus (Rockhampton, Queensland)
Observer (Adelaide)
On Dit (Adelaide)
Papua New Guinea Post-Courier (Port Moresby)
Register (Adelaide)
Science Progress
Smith's Weekly (Sydney)
Sun News-Pictorial (Melbourne)
Sunday Mail (Brisbane)
Sydney Morning Herald
Tharunka (Sydney)
Times (London)
Transcontinental (Port Augusta)
Tribune (Sydney)
Week (Brisbane)
Western Herald (New South Wales)
Woroni (Canberra)

Online Sources

Australian Institute of Aboriginal and Torres Strait Islander Studies. "Vale Dr William Jonas AM." 3 June 2019. https://aiatsis.gov.au/whats-new/news/vale-dr-william-jonas-am.

Department of Climate Change, Energy, the Environment and Water. "Great Artesian Basin." Accessed 13 June 2024. https://www.dcceew.gov.au/water/policy/national/great-artesian-basin.

Friends of the Earth Australia. *30 Years of Creative Resistance.* 2004. https://commonslibrary.org/wp-content/uploads/30-Years-of-Creative-Resistance.pdf.

Goldman Environmental Prize. "Eileen Kampakuta Brown and Eileen Wani Wingfield." Accessed 24 March 2022. https://www.goldmanprize.org/recipient/eileen-kampakuta-brown-eileen-wani-wingfield/.

———. "Prize History." Accessed 24 March 2022. https://www.goldmanprize.org/history/.

Green Left. "Open Letter from the Kupa Piti Kungka Tjuta." 3 August 2005. https://www.greenleft.org.au/content/open-letter-kupa-piti-kungka-tjuta.

Gundjehmi Aboriginal Corporation. "'We Are Not Talking about Mining': The History of Duress and the Jabiluka Project." July 1977. https://tinyurl.com/49nsnzhz.

Jacka, F. J. "Mawson, Sir Douglas (1882–1958)." In *Australian Dictionary of Biography*. National Centre of Biography, Australian National University, 2006. https://adb.anu.edu.au/biography/mawson-sir-douglas-7531. Published first in hardcopy 1986.

Mining Technology. "Olympic Dam Copper-Uranium Mine, Adelaide, Australia." 14 November 2012. https://www.mining-technology.com/projects/olympic-dam/.

National Archives of Australia. "Gough Whitlam: Before Office." Accessed 25 July 2023. https://www.naa.gov.au/explore-collection/australias-prime-ministers/gough-whitlam/before-office#deputy-party-leader.

Parliament of Australia. "Chronology of ALP Uranium Policy 1950–1994." Accessed 15 November 2023. https://parlinfo.aph.gov.au/parlInfo/search/display/display.w3p;query=Id:%22library/rspub/8FW10%22.

Treaty on the Prohibition of Nuclear Weapons. United Nations, New York, 7 July 2017. https://documents-dds-ny.un.org/doc/UNDOC/GEN/N17/209/73/PDF/N1720973.pdf.

Published Works

Acheson, Ray. *Banning the Bomb, Smashing the Patriarchy*. Rowman and Littlefield, 2021.

Alcalay, Glenn. "The Ethnography of Destabilization: Pacific Islanders in the Nuclear Age." *Dialectical Anthropology* 13, no. 3 (1988): 243–51.

Alexis-Martin, Becky. "The Nuclear Imperialism–Necropolitics Nexus: Contextualizing Chinese-Uyghur Oppression in Our Nuclear Age." *Eurasian Geography and Economics* 60, no. 2 (2019): 152–76.

Allman, Jean. "Nuclear Imperialism and the Pan-African Struggle for Peace and Freedom: Ghana, 1959–1962." *Souls: A Critical Journal of Black Politics, Culture and Society* 10, no. 2 (2008): 83–102.

Arnold, Lorna. *A Very Special Relationship: British Atomic Weapon Trials in Australia*. Her Majesty's Stationery Office, 1987.

Arrow, Michelle. *The Seventies: The Personal, the Political and the Making of Modern Australia*. NewSouth, 2019.

Attwood, Bain, and Andrew Markus. *The 1967 Referendum: Race, Power and the Australian Constitution*. Aboriginal Studies Press, 2007.

Badash, Lawrence. *Radioactivity in America: Growth and Decay of a Science*. Johns Hopkins University Press, 1979.

———. "Radium, Radioactivity and the Popularity of Scientific Discovery." *Proceedings of the American Philosophical Society* 122, no. 3 (1978): 145–54.

Banivanua Mar, Tracey. *Decolonisation and the Pacific: Indigenous Globalisation and the Ends of Empire*. Cambridge University Press, 2016.

Bayet-Charlton, Fabienne. "Overturning the Doctrine: Indigenous Peoples and Wilderness—Being Aboriginal in the Environmental Movement." In *Blacklines: Contemporary Critical Writings by Indigenous Australians*, edited by Michelle Grossman, 154–62. Melbourne University Publishing, 2003.

Bell, Diane. *Daughters of the Dreaming*. 3rd ed. Spinifex Press, 2002.

———. "The Word of a Woman: Ngarrindjeri Stories and a Bridge to Hindmarsh Island." In *Women, Rites and Sites: Aboriginal Women's Cultural Knowledge*, edited by Peggy Brock, 117–38. Allen & Unwin, 1989.

Biswas, Shampa. *Nuclear Desire: Power and the Postcolonial Nuclear Order*. University of Minnesota Press, 2014.

Bongiorno, Frank. *Dreamers and Schemers: A Political History of Australia*. La Trobe University Press, 2022.

———. *The Eighties: The Decade that Transformed Australia*. Black Inc., 2015.

Bongiorno, Frank, and Emma Cupit. "Australia before Whitlam: A Slice of the Sixties." Whitlam Institute, Western Sydney University, 2022.

Bradshaw, Richard, and Andrew Collett. "Aboriginal Land Rights in South Australia." *Aboriginal Law Bulletin* 52, no. 1 (1991). https://classic.austlii.edu.au/au/journals/AboriginalLawB/1991/54.html.

Brady, Maggie. "The Politics of Space and Mobility: Controlling the Ooldea/Yalata Aborigines, 1952–1982." *Aboriginal History* 23 (1999): 1–14.

Bramston, Troy, ed. *The Whitlam Legacy*. Federation Press, 2013.

Brock, Peggy. "Aboriginal Women, Politics and Land." In *Words and Silences: Aboriginal Women, Politics and Land*, edited by Peggy Brock, 1–17. Allen & Unwin, 2001.

———. *Outback Ghettos: Aborigines, Institutionalisation and Survival*. Cambridge University Press, 1993.

———, ed. *Words and Silences: Aboriginal Women, Politics and Land*. Allen & Unwin, 2001.

———. *Yura and Udnyu: A History of the Adnyamathanha of the Northern Flinders Ranges*. 1985. Reprint, Wakefield Press, 2019.

Brockwell, Sally, Tom Gara, Sarah Colley, and Scott Cane. "The History and

Archaeology of Ooldea Soak and Mission." *Australian Archaeology*, no. 28 (1989): 55–78.

Broinowski, Richard. *Fact or Fission? The Truth about Australia's Nuclear Ambitions*. Scribe, 2022.

Brown, Nina, and Sam Sowerwine. "Irati Wanti: Senior Aboriginal Women Fight a Nuclear Waste Dump." *Indigenous Law Bulletin* 6, no. 1 (2004). https://www.austlii.edu.au/cgi-bin/viewdoc/au/journals/ILB/2004/23.html.

Bsumek, Erika. *The Foundations of Glen Canyon Dam: Infrastructures of Dispossession on the Colorado Plateau*. University of Texas Press, 2023.

Bullard, Robert, ed. *Confronting Environmental Racism: Voices from the Grassroots*. South End Press, 1993.

———. "Dismantling Environmental Racism in the USA." *Local Environment* 4, no. 1 (1999): 5–19.

———. *Environment and Morality: Confronting Environmental Racism in the United States*. United Nations Research Institute for Social Development, 2004.

Bullard, Robert, Paul Mohai, Robin Saha, and Beverely Wright. "Toxic Wastes and Race at Twenty: Why Race Still Matters after All of These Years." *Environmental Law* 38, no. 2 (2008): 371–411.

Buzzacott, Kevin. *Lake Eyre Is Calling: "Ankaku—For Life."* Nyiri Publications, 1999.

Carey, Jane, and Jane Lydon, eds. *Indigenous Networks: Mobility, Connections and Exchange*. Routledge, 2014.

Caufield, Catherine. *Multiple Exposures: Chronicles of the Radiation Age*. Harper & Row, 1989.

Cawte, Alice. *Atomic Australia, 1944–1990*. New South Wales University Press, 1992.

Chen, Changwei. "Shifting Interests: Whitlam, Britain and French Nuclear Tests in the South Pacific." *Australian Journal of Politics and History* 59, no. 2 (2013): 196–211.

Choi, Shine, and Catherine Eschle. "Rethinking Global Nuclear Politics, Rethinking Feminism." *International Affairs* 98, no. 4 (2022): 1129–47.

Christiansen, Samantha, and Zachary Scarlett, eds. *The Third World in the Global 1960s*. Berghahn Books, 2013.

Clarke, Michael, Stephan Frühling, and Andrew O'Neil. *Australia's Nuclear Policy: Reconciling Strategic, Economic and Normative Interests*. Ashgate, 2015.

Cohn, Carol. "Sex and Death in the Rational World of Defense Intellectuals." *Signs: Journal of Women in Culture and Society* 12, no. 4 (1987): 687–718.

Cook, Kevin, and Heather Goodall. *Making Change Happen: Black and White Activists Talk to Kevin Cook about Aboriginal, Union and Liberation Politics*. ANU Press, 2013.

Curran, James. "Australia at Empire's End: Approaches and Arguments." *History Australia* 10, no. 3 (2013): 23–35.

———. "'An Organic Part of the Whole Structure': John Curtin's Empire." *Journal of Imperial and Commonwealth History* 37, no. 1 (2009): 51–75.

Das, Runa. "Colonial Legacies, Post-Colonial (In)Securities, and Gender(ed) Representations in South Asia's Nuclear Policies." *Social Identities* 16, no. 6 (2010): 717–40.

———. "Nation, Gender and Representations of (In)Securities in Indian Politics: Secular-Modernity and Hindutva Ideology." *European Journal of Women's Studies* 15, no. 3 (2008): 203–21.

———. "A Post-Colonial Analysis of India–United States Nuclear Security: Orientalism, Discourse, and Identity in International Relations." *Journal of Asian and African Studies* (Leiden) 52, no. 6 (2017): 741–59.

de Costa, Ravi. *A Higher Authority: Indigenous Transnationalism and Australia.* NewSouth, 2006.

Doig, Jack. "New Nationalism in Australia and New Zealand: The Construction of National Identities by Two Labo(u)r Governments in the Early 1970s." *Australian Journal of Politics and History* 59, no. 4 (2013): 559–75.

Donald, Bruce G. "Aboriginal Land Council Attitudes to Mining Negotiations." *AMPLA Yearbook* 1985: 509–29.

Doyle, Timothy. *Green Power: The Environment Movement in Australia.* UNSW Press, 2000.

Duguid, Charles. *The Aborigines of Australia, Broadcasts and an Address.* Reliance Printing, 1946.

Echo-Hawk, Walter R. "Colonialism and Law in the Post-Colonial Era." In *Coming to Terms: Aboriginal Title in South Australia*, edited by Shaun Berg, 148–205. Wakefield Press, 2010.

Edmonds, Penelope, and Amanda Nettelbeck, eds. *Intimacies of Violence in the Settler Colony: Economies of Dispossession around the Pacific Rim.* Palgrave Macmillan, 2018.

Edwards, Nelta. "Nuclear Colonialism and the Social Construction of Landscape in Alaska." *Environmental Justice* 4, no. 2 (2011): 109–14.

Ellwood, Galiina (Kal). "Aboriginal Prospectors and Miners in Tropical Queensland, from Pre-contact Times to ca. 1950." *Journal of Australasian Mining History* 12 (2014): 59–80.

Ellwood, Galiina (Kal), and Janice Wegner. "Shared History Forgotten: The Neglected Stories of Aboriginal Miners, Prospectors and Ancillary Workers in the North Queensland Mining Industry." *Journal of Australasian Mining History* 17 (2019): 1–19.

Endres, Danielle. "From Wasteland to Waste Site: The Role of Discourse in

Nuclear Power's Environmental Injustices." *Local Environment* 14, no. 10 (2009): 917–37.

———. *Nuclear Decolonization: Indigenous Resistance to High-Level Nuclear Waste Siting*. Ohio State University Press, 2023.

———. "The Rhetoric of Nuclear Colonialism: Rhetorical Exclusion of American Indian Arguments in the Yucca Mountain Nuclear Waste Siting Decision." *Communication and Critical/Cultural Studies* 6, no. 1 (2009): 39–60.

Enloe, Cythia, and Carol Cohn. "A Conversation with Cynthia Enloe: Feminists Look at Masculinity and the Men Who Wage War." *Signs: Journal of Women in Culture and Society* 28, no. 4 (2003): 1187–207.

Eschle, Catherine. "Beyond Greenham Woman? Gender Identities and Anti-Nuclear Activism in Peace Camps." *International Feminist Journal of Politics* 19, no. 4 (2017): 471–90.

———. "Gender and the Subject of (Anti)Nuclear Politics: Revisiting Women's Campaigning against the Bomb." *International Studies Quarterly* 57, no. 4 (2013): 713–24.

Fan, Mei-Fang. "Nuclear Waste Facilities on Tribal Land: The Yami's Struggles for Environmental Justice." *Local Environment: The International Journal of Justice and Sustainability* 11, no. 4 (2006): 433–44.

Ferdinand, Malcom. "Behind the Colonial Silence of Wilderness." *Environmental Humanities* 14, no. 1 (2022): 182–201.

Firth, Stewart. *Nuclear Playground*. Allen & Unwin, 1987.

Fisher, Gillian. *Half-Life: The NDP; Peace, Protest and Party Politics*. State Library of NSW Press, 1995.

FitzSimons, Peter. *Mawson and the Ice Men of the Heroic Age: Scott, Shackleton and Amundsen*. Penguin, 2014.

Foley, Gary. *A Condensed History of the Australian Indigenous Resistance*. Subversion Press, 2010.

Folkers, Cynthia. "Disproportionate Impacts of Radiation Exposure on Women, Children, and Pregnancy: Taking Back Our Narrative." *Journal of the History of Biology* 54, no. 1 (2021): 31–66.

Formby, John. "The Australian Government's Experience with Environmental Impact Assessment." *Environmental Impact Assessment Review* 7, no. 3 (1987): 207–10.

Foster, Robert. "'An Ethnographical Laboratory': Science, Religion and the Origins of the North-West Reserve." *History Australia* 16, no. 2 (2019): 338–57.

———. "'His Majesty's Most Gracious and Benevolent Intentions': South Australia's Foundation, the Idea of 'Difference,' and Aboriginal Rights." *Journal of Australian Colonial History* 15 (2013): 105–20.

———. "Rations, Coexistence, and the Colonisation of Aboriginal Labour in the

South Australian Pastoral Industry, 1860–1911." *Aboriginal History* 24 (2000): 4–13.

———. "True Lies: South Australia's Foundation, the Idea of 'Difference,' and the Rights of Aboriginal People." In *Foundational Fictions in South Australian History*, edited by Carolyn Collins and Paul Sendziuk, 64–78. Wakefield Press, 2018.

Foster, Robert, Rick Hosking, and Amanda Nettelbeck. *Fatal Collisions: The South Australian Frontier and the Violence of Memory*. Wakefield Press, 2001.

Fraser, Malcolm, and Margaret Simons. *Malcolm Fraser: The Political Memoirs*. Miegunyah Press, 2010.

Gara, Tom. "Ooldea, the Spinifex People and the Bomb." In *Colonialism and Its Aftermath: A History of Aboriginal South Australia*, edited by Peggy Brock and Tom Gara, 351–71. Wakefield Press, 2017.

Gerster, Robin. "Anzac, New Mexico: Placing Australia in the Nuclear Empire." *Meanjin* 73, no. 1 (2014): 52–65.

———. "Down the Yellowcake Road: The Minefield of Australian Uranium." *Journal of Australian Studies* 37, no. 4 (2013): 438–50.

Gómez, Myrriah. *Nuclear Nuevo México: Colonialism and the Effects of the Nuclear Industrial Complex on Nuevomexicanos*. University of Arizona Press, 2022.

Goodall, Heather. "Colonialism and Catastrophe: Contested Memories of Nuclear Testing and Measles Epidemics at Ernabella." In *Memory and History in Twentieth-Century Australia*, edited by Kate Darian-Smith and Paula Hamilton, 55–76. Oxford University Press, 1994.

———. *Invasion to Embassy: Land in Aboriginal Politics in New South Wales, 1770–1972*. Allen & Unwin, 1996.

Gordon, David, and Victor Ryan, eds. *Handbook of South Australia: The British Association for the Advancement of Science, Australian Meeting, 1914*. R. E. E. Rogers, Government Printer, 1914.

Gray, Geoffrey. "Aborigines, Elkin and the Guided Projectiles Project." *Aboriginal History* 15, no. 2 (1991): 153–62.

Griffiths, Tom. *Hunters and Collectors: The Antiquarian Imagination in Australia*. Cambridge University Press, 1997.

———. "A Polar Drama: The Australasian Antarctic Expedition of 1911–14." In *Expedition into Empire: Exploratory Journeys and the Making of the Modern World*, edited by Martin Thomas, 171–93. Routledge, 2014.

Hains, Brigid. *The Ice and the Inland: Mawson, Flynn, and the Myth of the Frontier*. Melbourne University Press, 2002.

———. "Mawson of the Antarctic, Flynn of the Inland: Progressive Heroes on Australia's Ecological Frontiers." In *Ecology and Empire: Environmental History of Settler Societies*, edited by Tom Griffiths and Libby Robin, 154–68. University of Washington Press, 1997.

Halvorson, Dan. *Commonwealth Responsibility and Cold War Solidarity: Australia in Asia, 1944–74*. ANU Press, 2019.

Harford, Barbara, and Sarah Hopkins. *Greenham Common: Women at the Wire*. Women's Press, 1984.

Harvey, Kyle. "How Far Left? Negotiating Radicalism in Australian Anti-Nuclear Politics in the 1960s." In *The Far Left in Australia since 1945*, edited by Jon Piccini, Evan Smith, and Matthew Worley, 118–33. Routledge, 2018.

———. "Nuclear Migrants, Radical Protest, and the Transnational Movement against French Nuclear Testing in the 1960s: The 1967 Voyage of the *Trident*." *Labour History*, no. 111 (2016): 79–98.

Hay, Chris. "Philip Baxter: Man in Search of the Nuclear (St)age." *Journal of Australian Studies* 24, no. 1 (2021): 94–107.

Hecht, Gabrielle. *Being Nuclear: Africans and the Global Uranium Trade*. MIT Press, 2012.

———. "A Cosmogram for Nuclear Things." *Isis* 98, no. 1 (2007): 100–108.

———, ed. *Entangled Geographies: Empire and Technopolitics in the Global Cold War*. MIT Press, 2011.

———. "Globalization Meets Frankenstein? Reflections on Terrorism, Nuclearity, and Global Technopolitical Discourse." *History and Technology* 19, no. 1 (2003): 1–8.

———. "Nuclear Ontologies." *Constellations* 13, no. 3 (2006): 320–31.

———. "The Power of Nuclear Things." *Technology and Culture* 51, no. 1 (2010): 1–30.

———. *The Radiance of France: Nuclear Power and National Identity after World War II*. MIT Press, 2009.

———. *Residual Governance: How South Africa Foretells Planetary Futures*. Duke University Press, 2023.

———. "Rupture-Talk in the Nuclear Age: Conjugating Colonial Power in Africa." *Social Studies of Science* 32, no. 5–6 (2002): 691–727.

———. "2012: An Elemental Force: Uranium Production in Africa, and What It Means to Be Nuclear." *Bulletin of the Atomic Scientists* 68, no. 2 (2012): 22–33.

Henningham, Stephen. "Whitlam and Australia's Relations with France, 1972–75: Conflict and Cordiality." *History Australia* 14, no. 3 (2017): 414–28.

Hill, Christopher Robert. "Britain, West Africa and 'The New Nuclear Imperialism': Decolonisation and Development during French Tests." *Contemporary British History* 33, no. 2 (2019): 274–89.

Hirst, John. *Sense and Nonsense in Australian History*. Black Inc. Agenda, 2009.

Hiskey, Garry. *Maralinga: The Struggle for the Return of the Lands*. Wakefield Press, 2021.

Hocking, Jenny. *Gough Whitlam: His Time*. Miegunyah Press, 2014.

———. *The Palace Letters: The Queen, the Governor-General, and the Plot to Dismiss Gough Whitlam*. Scribe, 2020.

Hogan, Eleanor. *Into the Loneliness: The Unholy Alliance of Ernestine Hill and Daisy Bates*. NewSouth, 2022.

Hogan, Patrick Colm. *What Is Colonialism?* Routledge, 2023.

Hogue, Rebecca H., and Anaïs Maurer. "Pacific Women's Anti-Nuclear Poetry: Centring Indigenous Knowledges." *International Affairs* 98, no. 4 (2022): 1267–88.

Hokari, Minoru. "From Wattle Creek to Wattie Creek: An Oral Historical Approach to the Gurindji Walk-Off." *Aboriginal History* 24 (2000): 98–116.

———. *Gurindji Journey: A Japanese Historian in the Outback*. UNSW Press, 2011.

Holden, Darren. "'On the Oliphant Deign, Now to Sound the Blast': How Mark Oliphant Secretly Warned of America's Post-War Intentions of an Atomic Monopoly." *Historical Records of Australian Science* 29, no. 2 (2018): 130–37.

Holland, Ian. "Waste Not Want Not? Australia and the Politics of High-Level Nuclear Waste." *Australian Journal of Political Science* 37, no. 2 (2002): 283–301.

Horne, Donald. *Time of Hope: Australia 1966–72*. Angus & Robertson, 1980.

Horowitz, Leah S., Arn Keeling, Francis Levesque, Thierry Rodon, Stephan Schott, and Sophie Theriault. "Indigenous Peoples' Relationships to Large-Scale Mining in Post/Colonial Contexts: Toward Multidisciplinary Comparative Perspectives." *Extractive Industries and Society* 5, no. 5 (2018): 404–14.

Howitt, Richard, John Connell, and Philip Hirsch. "Resources, Nations and Indigenous Peoples." In *Resources, Nations and Indigenous Peoples: Case Studies from Australasia, Melanesia and Southeast Asia*, edited by Richard Howitt, John Connell, and Philip Hirsch, 1–31. Oxford University Press, 1996.

Humphrys, Elizabeth. *How Labour Built Neoliberalism: Australia's Accord, the Labour Movement and the Neoliberal Project*. Brill, 2018.

Hutton, Drew, and Libby Connors. *A History of the Australian Environment Movement*. Cambridge University Press, 1999.

Irving, Nick. "Anti-Conscription Protest, Liberal Individualism and the Limits of National Myths in the Global 1960s." *History Australia* 14, no. 2 (2017): 187–201.

Jacobs, Jane M. "Politics and the Cultural Landscape: The Case of Aboriginal Land Rights." *Australian Geographical Studies* 26, no. 2 (1988): 249–63.

Jacobs, Robert. "Nuclear Conquistadors: Military Colonialism in Nuclear Test Site Selection during the Cold War." *Asian Journal of Peacebuilding* 1, no. 2 (2013): 157–77.

Jacobsen, Carl G. *The Nuclear Era: Its History, Its Implications*. Spokesman, 1982.

Jago, James, and Mark Pharaoh. "Douglas Mawson's First Major Geological Expedition: The New Hebrides, 1903." *Earth Sciences History: Journal of the History of the Earth Sciences Society* 24, no. 1 (2005): 93–111.

———. "Pre-Antarctic Mawson in South Australia and Western New South Wales." *Transactions of the Royal Society of South Australia* 140, no. 1 (2016): 107–28.

James, Diana, and Inawinytji Williamson. "*Kungkarangkalpa Inma Alatjila Kuwari Palyani*: Dancing the Seven Sisters Songline Today!" *Musicology Australia* 42, no. 2 (2020): 179–95.

Johns, R. Keith. *A Mirage in the Desert? The Discovery, Evaluation and Development of the Olympic Dam Ore Body at Roxby Downs, South Australia, 1975–88*. O'Neil Historical & Editorial Services, 2010.

Johnson, Miranda. "Indigenizing Self-Determination at the United Nations: Reparative Progress in the Declaration on the Rights of Indigenous Peoples." *Journal of the History of International Law* 23, no. 1 (2021): 206–28.

Johnston, Barbara Rose, ed. *Half-Lives and Half-Truths: Confronting the Radioactive Legacies of the Cold War*. School for Advanced Research Press, 2007.

Johnston, Peter N., Geoffrey A. Williams, Peter A. Burns, and Malcolm B. Cooper. "Plutonium Resuspension and Airborne Dust Loadings in the Desert Environment of Maralinga, South Australia." *Journal of Environmental Radioactivity* 20, no. 2 (1993): 117–31.

Jones, Philip. *Ochre and Rust: Artefacts and Encounters on Australian Frontiers*. Wakefield Press, 2018.

Jordan, Matthew. "'Not on Your Life': Cabinet and the Liberalisation of the White Australia Policy, 1964–67." *Journal of Imperial and Commonwealth History* 46, no. 1 (2018): 169–201.

Junor, Beth, and Katrina Howse. *Greenham Common Women's Peace Camp: A History of Non-violent Resistance, 1984–1995*. Working Press, 1995.

Kahn, Miriam. *Tahiti beyond the Postcard: Power, Place, and Everyday Life*. University of Washington Press, 2011.

Kaye, G. W. C. "The Romance of Radium. Will England or Germany Control This Commodity after the War?" *Science Progress* 11, no. 41 (1916): 55–61.

Keeble, Kathryn M. "Frankenstein's Machine: Redressing Mark Oliphant's Scientific Reputation." *Historical Records of Australian Science* 29, no. 2 (2018): 122–29.

Keown, Michelle. "Waves of Destruction: Nuclear Imperialism and Anti-Nuclear Protest in the Indigenous Literatures of the Pacific." *Journal of Postcolonial Writing* 54, no. 5 (2018): 585–600.

Kerin, Sitarani. *Doctor Do-Good: Charles Duguid and Aboriginal Advancement, 1930s–1970s*. Australian Scholarly Publishing, 2011.

Khatun, Samia. *Australianama: The South Asian Odyssey in Australia*. Hurst, 2018.

Kirchhof, Astrid Mignon. "Spanning the Globe: West-German Support for the Australian Anti-Nuclear Movement." *Historical Social Research / Historische Sozialforschung* 39, no. 1 (2014): 254–73.

Klimke, Martin. *The Other Alliance: Student Protest in West Germany and the United States in the Global Sixties*. Princeton University Press, 2010.

Knox, Malcolm. *Boom: The Underground History of Australia, from Gold Rush to GFC*. Viking, 2013.

Krell, Jacob. "Genealogies of Technology and Prehistory in France: The 'Atomic Age.'" *Res* 69–70, no. 1 (2018): 158–72.

Kuletz, Valerie L. *The Tainted Desert: Environmental and Social Ruin in the American West*. Routledge, 1998.

Kupa Piti Kungka Tjuta. *Talking Straight Out: Stories from the Irati Wanti Campaign*. Alapalatja Press, 2005.

Langton, Marcia. "Art, Wilderness and *Terra Nullius*." In *Ecopolitics IX Conference Papers and Resolutions: Perspectives on Indigenous Peoples Management of Environment Resources*, edited by Ros Sultan, Paul Josif, Chips Mackinolty, and Judy Mackinolty, 11–24. Northern Land Council, 1996.

———. *Boyer Lectures 2021: The Quiet Revolution: Indigenous People and the Resources Boom*. HarperCollins, 2013.

———. "What Do We Mean by Wilderness? Wilderness and *Terra Nullius* in Australian Art." *Sydney Papers* 8, no. 1 (1996): 11–31.

Lavelle, Ashley. "'Conflicts of Loyalty': The Australian Labor Party and Uranium Policy, 1976–82." *Labour History*, no. 102 (2012): 177–96.

Lawrence, Herman. *Radium: How and When to Use*. Stillwell, 1911.

Leddy, Lianne. *Serpent River Resurgence: Confronting Uranium Mining at Elliot Lake*. University of Toronto Press, 2021.

Lee, David. *The Second Rush: Mining and the Transformation of Australia*. Connor Court Publishing, 2016.

Lester, Alan. "Imperial Circuits and Networks: Geographies of the British Empire." *History Compass* 4, no. 1 (2006): 124–41.

Libby, Ronald. *Hawke's Law: The Politics of Mining and Aboriginal Land Rights in Australia*. University of Western Australia Press, 1989.

Lim, Brendan. *Australia's Constitution after Whitlam*. Cambridge University Press, 2017.

Lowe, Ian. *Long Half-Life: The Nuclear Industry in Australia*. Monash University Press, 2021.

Maddock, Kenneth. *Your Land Is Our Land: Aboriginal Land Rights*. Penguin, 1983.

Maddock, Shane. *Nuclear Apartheid: The Quest for American Atomic Supremacy from World War II to the Present*. University of North Carolina Press, 2010.

Mahood, Kim. "The Seething Landscape." In *Songlines: Tracking the Seven Sisters*, edited by Margo Neale, 32–36. National Museum of Australia Press, 2017.

Maleta, Yulia. "Australian Women's Anti-Nuclear Leadership: The Framing of Peace and Social Change." *Journal of International Women's Studies* 19, no. 6 (2018): 70–86.

Malin, Stephanie. *The Price of Nuclear Power: Uranium Communities and Environmental Justice*. Rutgers University Press, 2015.

Marsh, Jillian, and Jim Green. "First Nations Rights and Colonising Practices by the Nuclear Industry: An Australian Battleground for Environmental Justice." *Extractive Industries and Society* 7, no. 3 (2020): 870–81.

Maurer, Anaïs, and Rebecca H. Hogue. "Introduction: Transnational Nuclear Imperialisms." *Journal of Transnational American Studies* 11, no. 2 (2020): 25–43.

Mawson, Douglas. "The Geology of the New Hebrides." *Proceedings of the Linnaean Society of New South Wales* 30 (1905): 400–485.

———. "The Nature and Occurrence of Uraniferous Mineral Deposits in South Australia." *Transactions of the Royal Society of South Australia* 68, no. 2 (1944): 334–57.

Mawson, Douglas, and Paul Hossfeld. "Relics of Aboriginal Occupation in the Olary District." *Transactions of the Royal Society of South Australia* 1 (1926): 17–24.

Mawson, Douglas, and Thomas Laby. "Preliminary Observations on Radio-Activity and the Occurrence of Radium in Australian Minerals." *Journal and Proceedings of the Royal Society of New South Wales* 38 (1904): 382–89.

Maynard, John. *Fight for Liberty and Freedom: The Origins of Aboriginal Activism*. Aboriginal Studies Press, 2007.

Mazel, Odette. "Returning *Parna Wiru*: Restitution of the Maralinga Lands to Traditional Owners in South Australia." In *Settling with Indigenous People*, edited by Marcia Langton, Odette Mazel, Lisa Palmer, Kathryn Shain, and Maureen Tehan, 158–81. Federation Press, 2006.

McConchie, Peter, ed. *Elders: Wisdom from Australia's Indigenous Leaders*. Cambridge University Press, 2003.

McEachern, Doug. "Mining Meaning from the Rhetoric of Nature: Australian Mining Companies and Their Attitudes to the Environment at Home and Abroad." *Policy, Organisation and Society* 10, no. 1 (1995): 48–69.

McGregor, Russell. "Another Nation: Aboriginal Activism in the Late 1960s and Early 1970s." *Australian Historical Studies* 40, no. 3 (2009): 343–60.

———. *Indifferent Inclusion: Aboriginal People and the Australian Nation*. Aboriginal Studies Press, 2011.

McGurty, Eileen Maura. "From NIMBY to Civil Rights: The Origins of the Environmental Justice Movement." *Environmental History* 2, no. 3 (1997): 301–23.

McLean, Ian. *Why Australia Prospered: The Shifting Sources of Economic Growth*. Princeton University Press, 2011.

McLisky, Claire, with Lynette Russell and Leigh Boucher. "Managing Mission Life, 1869–1886." In *Settler Colonial Governance in Nineteenth-Century Victoria*, edited by Leigh Boucher and Lynette Russell, 117–38. ANU Press, 2015.

Michel, Dieter. "Villains, Victims and Heroes: Contested Memory and the British Nuclear Tests in Australia." *Journal of Australian Studies* 27, no. 80 (2003): 221–28.

Moore, Kate. *The Radium Girls: The Dark Story of America's Shining Women*. Sourcebooks, 2017.

Moreton, Peter. *Fire across the Desert: Woomera and the Anglo-Australian Joint Project 1946–1980*. Australian Government Publishing Service, 1989.

Moreton-Robinson, Aileen. *The White Possessive: Property, Power, And Indigenous Sovereignty*. University of Minnesota Press, 2015.

Mudd, Gavin. "The Legacy of Early Uranium Efforts in Australia, 1906–1945: From Radium Hill to the Atomic Bomb and Today." *Historical Records of Australian Science* 16, no. 2 (2005): 169–98.

Müller, Simone. *The Toxic Ship: The Voyage of the Khian Sea and the Global Waste Trade*. University of Washington Press, 2023.

Myers, Fred, and Nicolas Peterson. "The Origins and History of Outstations as Aboriginal Life Projects. In *Experiments in Self-Determination: Histories of the Outstation Movement in Australia*, edited by Nicolas Peterson and Fred Myers, 1–22. ANU Press, 2016.

Nagtzaam, Gerry. "Pass the Parcel: Australia and the Vexing Issue of a Federal Nuclear Waste Repository." *Alternative Law Journal* 39, no. 4 (2014): 246–48.

Neale, Timothy, and Eve Vincent. "Mining, Indigeneity, Alterity: Or, Mining Indigenous Alterity?" *Cultural Studies* 31, no. 2–3 (2017): 417–39.

Niedenthal, Jack. *For the Good of Mankind: A History of the People of Bikini and Their Islands*. Bravo Publishers, 2001.

Norman, Heidi. *What Do We Want? A Political History of Aboriginal Land Rights in New South Wales*. Aboriginal Studies Press, 2015.

O'Shea, Darcy. "The Future Foreshadowed: Yalata Community and Maralinga Lands." *Legal Service Bulletin* (1984): 212–14.

Paisley, Fiona. "No Back Streets in the Bush: 1920s and 1930s Pro-Aboriginal White Women's Activism and the Trans-Australia Railway." *Australian Feminist Studies* 12, no. 25 (1997): 119–37.

Palmer, Kingsley. "Dealing with the Legacy of the Past: Aborigines and Atomic Testing in South Australia." *Aboriginal History* 14, no. 1–2 (1992): 197–207.

Palmer, Shannyn. *Unmaking Angas Downs: Myth and History on a Central Australian Pastoral Station*. Melbourne University Publishing, 2022.

Parkes, Rebecca. "Traces of the Cameleers: Landscape Archaeology and Landscape Perception." *Australasian Historical Archaeology* 27 (2009): 87–97.

Parkinson, Alan. *Maralinga: Australia's Nuclear Waste Cover-Up*. ABC Books, 2007.

Peel, Mark, and Christina Twomey. *A History of Australia*. 2nd ed. Palgrave, 2018.

Pellow, David Naguib. *Resisting Global Toxics: Transnational Movements for Environmental Justice*. MIT Press, 2007.

Peterson, Nicolas, and Fred Myers, eds. *Experiments in Self-Determination: Histories of the Outstation Movement in Australia*. ANU Press, 2016.

Piccini, Jon. *Transnational Protest, Australia and the 1960s: Global Radicals*. Palgrave Macmillan, 2016.

Priestley, Rebecca. *Mad on Radium: New Zealand in the Atomic Age*. Auckland University Press, 2012.

Pring, Allan, and Joël Brugger. "Mawson and the Radium and Uranium Mineralisation at Mount Painter, Northern Flinders Ranges, South Australia." *AusIMM Bulletin*, no. 6 (2012): 86–89.

Raftery, Judith. *Not Part of the Public: Non-Indigenous Policies and Practices and the Health of Indigenous South Australians, 1836–1973*. Wakefield Press, 2006.

Reynolds, Wayne. *Australia's Bid for the Atomic Bomb*. Melbourne University Press, 2000.

———. "Australia's Quest to Enrich Uranium and the Whitlam Government's Loans Affair." *Australian Journal of Politics and History* 54, no. 4 (2008): 562–78.

———. "Rethinking the Joint Project: Australia's Bid for Nuclear Weapons, 1945–1960." *Historical Journal* 41, no. 3 (1998): 853–73.

———. "'To the Brink of Manufacture': Nuclear Weapons, the Anglo-American Alliance and Australia's Approach to the Nuclear Non-Proliferation Treaty." *Australian Historical Studies* 46, no. 2 (2015): 269–84.

———. "The Yellow Cake Road: Malcolm Fraser, the Ranger Enquiry and Australia's Role in the US International Fuel Cycle Project." *Australian Journal of Politics and History* 57, no. 4 (2011): 511–25.

Reynolds, Wayne, and David Lee, eds. *Australia and the Nuclear Non-Proliferation Treaty, 1945–1974*. Australian Department of Foreign Affairs and Trade, 2013.

Riffenburgh, Beau. *Racing with Death: Douglas Mawson—Antarctic Explorer*. Bloomsbury, 2008.

Roberts, Amy L., Rachel Poelka-Filcoff, Craig Westell, and the River Murray and

Mallee Aboriginal Corporation. "Ochre, Flint and Violence: An Aboriginal History of the Ma:ko Region (Overland Corner)." *Transactions of the Royal Society of South Australia* 146, no. 2 (2022): 319–40.

Robin, Libby. *Defending the Little Desert: The Rise of Ecological Consciousness in Australia.* Melbourne University Press, 1998.

Rose, Deborah Bird. "The Silence and Power of Women." In *Women, Rites and Sites: Aboriginal Women's Cultural Knowledge*, edited by Peggy Brock, 91–116. Allen & Unwin, 1989.

Roseneil, Sasha. *Disarming Patriarchy: Feminism and Political Action at Greenham.* Open University Press, 1995.

Rowse, Tim, ed. *Contesting Assimilation.* Australia Research Institute, 2005.

———. *Indigenous and Other Australians since 1901.* UNSW Press, 2017.

———. *Rethinking Social Justice: From "Peoples" to "Populations."* Aboriginal Studies Press, 2012.

Runyan, Anne Sisson. "Disposable Waste, Lands and Bodies under Canada's Gendered Nuclear Colonialism." *International Feminist Journal of Politics* 20, no. 1 (2018): 24–38.

———. "Indigenous Women's Resistances at the Start and End of the Nuclear Fuel Chain." *International Affairs* 98, no. 4 (2022): 1149–67.

Scambary, Benedict. *My Country, Mine Country: Indigenous People, Mining and Development Contestation in Remote Australia.* ANU Press, 2013.

Sendziuk, Paul, and Robert Foster. *A History of South Australia.* Cambridge University Press, 2017.

Shiga, John. "The Nuclear Sensorium: Cold War Nuclear Imperialism and Sensory Violence." *Canadian Journal of Law and Society* 34, no. 2 (2019): 281–306.

Simpson, Audra. *Mohawk Interruptus: Political Life across the Borders of Settler States.* Duke University Press, 2014.

———. "On Ethnographic Refusal: Indigeneity, 'Voice' and Colonial Citizenship." *Junctures: The Journal for Thematic Dialogue* 9 (2007): 67–80.

Simpson, Leanne Betasamosake. "Indigenous Resurgence and Co-resistance." *Critical Ethnic Studies* 2, no. 2 (2016): 19–34.

Slovic, Paul, James H. Flynn, and Mark Layman. "Perceived Risk, Trust, and the Politics of Nuclear Waste." *Science* (American Association for the Advancement of Science) 254, no. 5038 (1991): 1603–7.

Smith, M. A. *Peopling the Cleland Hills: Aboriginal History in Western Central Australia, 1850–1980.* Aboriginal History, 2005.

Smith, Roy. *The Nuclear Free and Independent Pacific Movement: After Muroroa.* I. B. Tauris, 1997.

Southall, Ivan. *Woomera.* Angus & Robertson, 1962.

Sprigg, Reg. *Arkaroola–Mount Painter in the Northern Flinders Ranges, S.A.: The Last Billion Years*. Lutheran Publishing House, 1984.

———. *A Geologist Strikes Out: Recollections, 1954–1993*. R. Sprigg, 1993.

Stegnar, Peter. "Assessing Radiological Conditions at Bikini Atoll and the Prospects of Resettlement: Review at Bikini Atoll." *IAEA Bulletin* 14, no. 4 (1998): 15–17.

Stillwell, F. L. "Uraninite from Rum Jungle and Fergusson River, Northern Territory." In *Sir Douglas Mawson Anniversary Volume: Contributions to Geology in Honour of Sir Douglas Mawson's 70th Birthday Anniversary*, edited by M. Glaessner and E. Rudd, 161–66. University of Adelaide, 1952.

Strauss, Jonathan. "What Did We Want? Debates within the Australian Nuclear Disarmament Movement in the 1980s." *Labour History*, no. 115 (2018): 145–65.

Tame, Adrian, and Francis Robotham. *Maralinga: British A-Bomb, Australian Legacy*. Fontana, 1982.

Tatz, Colin, Alan Cass, John Condon, and George Tippett. *Aborigines and Uranium: Monitoring the Health Hazards*. Australian Institute of Aboriginal and Torres Strait Islander Studies, 2006.

Taylor, Geoffrey N. "Australia: Host for a Nuclear Waste Storage Site?" *International Journal of Environmental Studies* 63, no. 6 (2006): 873–81.

Thomas, Martin, ed. *Expedition into Empire: Exploratory Journeys and the Making of the Modern World*. Routledge, 2014.

Thomson, Donald. "The Aborigines and the Rocket Range." Rocket Range Protest Committee, May 1947.

Toyne, Phillip, and Daniel Vachon. *Growing Up the Country: The Pitjantjatjara Struggle for Their Land*. McPhee Gribble, 1984.

Trigger, David S. "Mining, Landscape and the Culture of Development Ideology in Australia." *Ecumene* 4, no. 2 (1997): 161–80.

Tynan, Elizabeth. *Atomic Thunder: The Maralinga Story*. NewSouth, 2016.

———. *The Secrets of Emu Field: Britain's Forgotten Atomic Tests in Australia*. NewSouth, 2022.

Urwin, Jessica. "'Better Active Today Than Radioactive Tomorrow': Environmentalism and the Australian Anti-Uranium Movement, 1975–1982." *International Review of Environmental History* 9, no. 2 (2023): 123–44.

———. "The British Empire's Dr Strangelove? Ernest Titterton and the Royal Commission into British Nuclear Tests in Australia." *History Australia* 18, no. 4 (2021): 714–36.

———. "'The Old Colonial Power Can Stand Proxy': The Royal Commission into British Nuclear Tests in Australia and the Politics of the 1980s." *Australian Journal of Politics and History* 68, no. 4 (2022): 525–43.

———. "The Radioactive Dr Mawson: Douglas Mawson and the Quest for Australia's Radium Riches, 1904–58." *Australian Historical Studies* 53, no. 1 (2022): 22–42.

Vaarzon-Morel, Petronella. "Camels and the Transformation of Indigenous Economic Landscapes." In *Indigenous Participation in Australian Economies II: Historical Engagements and Current Enterprises*, edited by Natasha Fijn, Ian Keen, Christopher Lloyd, and Michael Pickering, 73–96. ANU Press, 2010.

Vincent, Eve. *"Against Native Title": Conflict and Creativity in Outback Australia*. Aboriginal Studies Press, 2017.

———. "Kangaroo Tails for Dinner? Environmental Culturalists Encounter Aboriginal Greenies." In *Unstable Relations: Indigenous People and Environmentalism in Contemporary Australia*, edited by Eve Vincent and Timothy Neale, 212–51. UWA Publishing, 2017.

———. "Knowing the Country." *Cultural Studies Review* 13, no. 2 (2007): 156–65.

———. "Never Mind Our Country Is the Desert." In *Making Settler Colonial Space: Perspectives on Race, Place and Identity*, edited by Tracey Banivanua Mar and Penelope Edmonds, 53–72. Palgrave Macmillan, 2010.

Vincent, Eve, and Timothy Neale, eds. *Unstable Relations: Indigenous People and Environmentalism in Contemporary Australia*. UWA Publishing, 2017.

Voyles, Traci Brynne. "Anatomic Bombs: The Sexual Life of Nuclearism, 1945–57." *American Quarterly* 72, no. 3 (2020): 651–73.

———. *The Settler Sea: California's Salton Sea and the Consequences of Colonialism*. University of Nebraska, 2021.

———. *Wastelanding: Legacies of Uranium Mining in Navajo Country*. University of Minnesota Press, 2015.

Wakeford, Richard. "A Double Diamond Anniversary—Kyshtym and Windscale: The Nuclear Accidents of 1957." *Journal of Radiological Protection* 37 (2017): E7–E13.

Walker, Errin. "Yirrkala Bark Petitions." *Indigenous Law Bulletin* 8, no. 7 (2013): 33–34.

Walker, Frank. *Maralinga: The Chilling Exposé of Our Secret Nuclear Shame and Betrayal of Our Troops and Country*. Hachette, 2016.

Walsh, Peter. *Confessions of a Failed Finance Minister*. Random House Australia, 1995.

Ward, Charlie. *A Handful of Sand: The Gurindji Struggle, after the Walk-Off*. Monash University Publishing, 2016.

Watson, Irene. "Kungka Tjuta and the Struggle for the Manta: Interview with Rebecca Bear Wingfield." *Indigenous Law Bulletin* 5, no. 1 (2000). https://classic.austlii.edu.au/au/journals/IndigLawB/2000/50.html.

———. "Walking the Land for Our Ancient Rights: Interview with Kevin Buzzacott." *Indigenous Law Bulletin* 49 (2000). https://classic.austlii.edu.au/au/journals/IndigLawB/2000/49.html.

Weidenbach, Kristen. *Rock Star: The Story of Reg Sprigg—an Outback Legend*. East Street Publications, 2008.

Whitlam, Gough. *The Whitlam Government, 1972–1975*. Viking, Penguin Books Australia, 1985.

Woollacott, Angela. *Don Dunstan: The Visionary Politician Who Changed Australia*. Allen & Unwin, 2019.

Wright, Clare. *N̲äku Dhäruk: The Bark Petitions; How the People of Yirrkala Changed the Course of Australian Democracy*. Text Publishing, 2024.

Yalata and Oak Valley Communities and Christobel Mattingley. *Maralinga: The An̲angu Story*. Allen & Unwin, 2009.

Zelko, Frank. *Make It a Green Peace! The Rise of Countercultural Environmentalism*. Oxford University Press.

INDEX

Page numbers in *italics* refer to illustrations.

Aboriginal activism, xii–xiii, 81–84, 108, 155, 192–205, 215

Aboriginal employment/labor, 16–17, 27, 29–33, 40, 47, 51, 58–60, 110; prospectors, 26

Aboriginal Heritage Act, 111–12, 117

Aboriginal knowledge, 40, 142, 159, 183, 205–6; of Country/place, 113–14, 142, 209–10; exploitation of, xi, 17, 33

Aboriginal Land Rights Movement Incorporated, 130. *See also* land rights

Aboriginal Land Rights (Northern Territory) Act (1974), 97–98. *See also* land rights

Aboriginal Lands Trust, 97–98, 105. *See also* land rights

Aboriginal mobility/migration, 31, 42, 59, 61, 66, 148

Aboriginal nuclear survivors, 13, 56, 62, 126, 142, 146, 152–55, 166

Aboriginal political mobilization, 14, 66, 111, 123, 126, 208, 212; international, xiii, 155, 183; women, 192

Aboriginal politics: development of, 12, 111, 142, 151–53, 212, 215, 217; land rights, 83–84, 91, 107; transformations in, 81, 83, 151–52

Aboriginal "problem," 42, 147, 152

Aboriginal resistance, xiii, 2–3, 114, 186, 196, 200, 210

Aboriginal testimony, 126, 142–43, 151–53, 216

Aboriginal women, xiii, 192–94, 208–9. *See also* Kupa Piti Kungka Tjuta

Aborigines Protection Board of South Australia, 49, 59–61

activism. *See* Aboriginal activism; student activism; youth activism/rebellion

Adnyamathanha, 11–12, 27, 30, 32, 40

Alamogordo (New Mexico), 44, 138

Allen, Lynette, 197

Amos, Sydney, *109*

Aṉangu, 14, 56, 129, 160, 191, 196, 211; and MacDougall, 58–65; meaning of, xix, 12; testimony, 147

Aṉangu Pitjantjatjara Yankunytjatjara Land Rights Act (1981), 105, 107, 215. *See also* land rights

Aṉangu Pitjantjatjara Yankunytjatjara lands, *156*

Antakirinja, xii, 12, 41, 185, 195

anthropology, 19, 27, 50, 112–14, 202; and Kokatha, 112–22; and Royal Commission, 141, 147, 159, 169, 183

anti-British sentiment, 132, 135–37

antinuclear movement, 6, 11, 69, 74–81, 84–85, 128, 166; Aboriginal resistance, 210, 216; women's campaigns, 186, 192

antinuclear sentiments, 68, 89, 91, 93, 94, 104, 167, 198, 212, 215

anti–uranium mining, 92, 100, *121*

Arabunna, xii, 12, 41, 185

assimilation, 43, 50–51, 63, 83–84, 111, 151

atomic age, ix, 68–69. *See also* nuclear age

Atomic Energy (Control of Materials) Act (1946), 36
Atomic Energy Research Establishment, 5
Attlee, Clement, 43, 45
Austin, Emily Munyungka, 192, *201*, 204
Australia, New Zealand, and United States Security Treaty (ANZUS), 89–90
Australia, the United Kingdom, and the United States partnership (AUKUS), 6–7
Australia–Britain relationship, 11, 44, 91, 136–37, 178
Australian Atomic Energy Commission, 187
Australian Committee on Guided Projectiles, 49–50
Australian Conservation Foundation, 202–3
Australian Mining Industry Council, 107, 133
Australian nationalism, 33, 134, 136–37, 152
Australian Nuclear Science and Technology Organisation (ANSTO), 187–89, 204
Australian sovereignty, threats to, 87, 89, 101

ballistic missiles, 44–45, 50, 54
Banivanua Mar, Tracey, 167
Bannon, John, 117–18, 120–22, 124, 129–31: government, 122, 128
Barnett, David, 107
Barngarla, xii, 12, 41, *57*
Barton, Archie, 154, 162, 164, 168–74, 176, 179–81, 183
Baxter, Philip, 38, 187
Beavis, L. E., 46
Berndt, Ronald, 120–22
bicentenary of Anglo-European invasion of Australia (1988), 132, 152, 162
Bikini Atoll, 49, 68, 70, 171–74, 217
Billa Kalina, xiii, *4*, *156*, 184–85, 190, 191, 194–95, 208
black mist, 1, 62–63, 128, 143–44, 191, 193
Bowler, A., 35
Brady, Maggie, 141–42, *144*, 147, 159–62, *161*, 176
Bragg, William, 24
Breuer, Lyn, 190–91
British government. *See* Whitehall
British nuclear testing. *See* Expert Committee on the Review of Data on Atmospheric Fallout Arising from British Nuclear Tests in Australia; Royal Commission into British Nuclear Tests in Australia
British Petroleum (BP), 93–94, 108. *See also* Joint Venturers
Brock, Peggy, 192
Broughton, A. C., 34–35
Brown, Eileen Kampakuta, xiii, 1, 184, 203, 205, 206–8
Brown, Lucy, 205
Bryant, Barka, 154, 176, 179–81
Burtt, Alfred, 30
Butement, William, 64, 139
Buzzacott, Kevin, 119, 123, 203–4

camels, 27, 29–33, *32*
cancer, 15, 189; cure for, 22; deaths from, 87, 145, 185
Canegrass Swamp, 94, 118–23, 160, 185
carnotite, 15–16, 23–24, 39
Casey, Richard, 70–71
Castle Bravo, 70–71

Central Aboriginal Reserve, 48–51
Central Australian Aboriginal Congress, 130
central deserts, depictions of, 10, 47, 49, 66
Chifley, Ben, 44–46, 137
China, as nuclear power, 71–72, 88–89, 91
"Claypan George," 16, 26, 29–30, 33
Cold War, 14, 70, 145
Coleman-Haseldine, Sue, 2, 3
Collett, Andrew, 141–42, 147, 154, 164, 178–79, 181–82
colonialism: nuclear, concept/definition, 2–3, 7–8, 212; nuclear weapons and, 7–9, 40, 66–71, 91, 145, 167; settler, x–xii, 3, 8, 11, 39–40, 110, 213; systemic, 127
colonization: of central deserts, 31–32, 34, 54, 56, 63; forms of, 155; impact of, 9, 25, 111, 126
Combined Development Agency, 5
Committee Against Nuclear Testing (CANT), 79–80, 86
compensation: Australian government response to requests for, 179, 182; British government response to requests for, 177–79; for contamination, xiii, 13, 133, 154–55, 157–58, 162; for dispossession, xiii, 84, 122, 132–33, 153, 165–66, 174; for loss of culture, 100; international experiences in seeking, 169, 172, 174
Connor, Rex, 95, 100
contamination, nuclear, xiii, 10, 170, 206. *See also* fallout
Coober Pedy, 57, *156*, 185, 192, 1 94–95, 198–202, 205, 217
Coober Pedy Senior Women. *See* Kupa Piti Kungka Tjuta
Cook, Kevin, 133
Coombs, Herbert Cole (Nugget), 100
Country, Aboriginal concept of, x–xi, 1
Cox, Alice, 56, 58, *144*, 148, 161
Crafter, Greg, 170
Crombie, Eileen Unkari, 192, 194–95, 197, *201*, 203
Cundeelee Mission, 61
Curie, Marie and Pierre, 4, 21, 70
Curtin, John, 44, 46, 137
Cutter, Trevor, 130

Davidson, Charles Findlay, 38
Day, Mervyn, 149–50, 179, 181
decolonization, 68, 72, 76–77, 86, 168
Dey-Dey, Lake, 148
disarmament, nuclear, 128. *See also* Nuclear Disarmament Party
dislocation, 14, 130–32, 134, 141–53
displacement, 137, 141, 145, 147, 151–52, 168–69, 216; of children, 64; and colonialism, 124; as consequence of tests, 13, 126, 135, 152; and paternalism, 137
dispossession, 14, 16–17, 26, 66, 134, 141–52, 213; and colonialism, xii, 10, 36, 124–25, 141, 216–17; as common/shared experience, 166, 173, 175–76, 183; compensation for, xiii, 84, 132–33, 165, 174; as consequence of tests, 13, 126, 131, 152–53; formal acknowledgment/recognition of, 82, 132; justification of, 12, 214; logics of, 9; and MacDougall, 63; and Maralinga Tjarutja, 125, 129; and paternalism, 9; physical act of, 214; politics of, xii; systemic, 42; violent, 41
Duguid, Charles, 49–51
Dunstan, Don, 86, 97, 104, 127

Eames, Geoff, 141–43, 147–49
Eggleston, George T., 68
Elkin, A. P., 49
employment. *See* Aboriginal employment/labor
Emu Field, xii, *4*, 41–42, 52–53, 67, 97, 160, 189, 214–15; cleanup, 124, 129, 155, 157, 176; first nuclear tests, 60–61; justification of site, 47; as peopled space, 54, 61–62; questions about fallout, 71; testimony about, 152
energy, nuclear, 5, 42, 90, 92, 94, 104, 124, 180, 218. *See also* fuel, nuclear; power, nuclear
Eniwetok, 52
environmentalism, 76, 78
environmentalists, 11, *79*, 80, 94, 120; urban-based/white, 197, 199–200
environmental justice/injustice, xiv, 2, 7–8, 212
Environmental Protection (Impact of Proposals) Act (1974), 113
environmental racism, 8
Ernabella Mission, 61, 142, 144–46
Evans, Gareth, 158, 169–70
Expert Committee on the Review of Data on Atmospheric Fallout Arising from British Nuclear Tests in Australia, 129–31
explorer-scientists, 16–17, 19–20, 29

fallout, ix, 71, 74, 80–81, 87, 89, 129, 150
Federal Council for the Advancement of Aborigines and Torres Strait Islanders (FCAATSI), 83
Fitch, Jill, 135, 141–42, *144*
Flinders Ranges, 11, 15–16, 24–26, *28*, 29–36, 40
Foley, Gary, 83–84
Fourth World, 167–68
Fox, Russell, 95, 97–99
Fox Inquiry, 95, 97
Fraser, Malcolm, 97, 99–100, 102–3, 127, 158
French nuclear testing, 6, 69–73, 84, 91; environmental concerns about, 79, 81, 87–89, 127; opposition to, xii, 6, 12, 67–68, 74, *75*, 77–79, *79*, 91; and Whitlam, 69, 85–87, 89
Friends of the Earth (FOE), 74, 86, 197–98, 206
fuel, nuclear, 6, 92, 101, 103, 118; vs. fossil fuels, 218. *See also* energy, nuclear; power, nuclear

gender, 192–93
Gerard Mission, 56
Gibson, Punch, 203
global nuclear order. *See* nuclear order: global
Goldman Environmental Prize, xiii, 184, 205–8
Goldsworthy, Roger, 104–6, 108–12, 114–17, 124
Goodall, Heather, 63, 126, 141–42, 145, 193
Gorton, John, 85, 187
Great Artesian Basin, 113, 190, 203
Green Nobel. *See* Goldman Environmental Prize
Greenwood, Gordon “Smiler,” 26–27, *28*, 29–30, 36–38, 40
Greenwood, William Bentley, 26, 29–30, 33–35
guided missile range, 45, 51
guided weapons. *See* ballistic missiles

Hagen, Rod, 119
Hawke, Robert (Bob), 100–101, 130–33,

152, 216; government, 125, 130, 141, 155, 158–59, 162, 164
Hecht, Gabrielle, x, 9–10, 69
hibakusha, 168, 173, 205. *See also* nuclear survivors
"hierarchy of tragedy," 126, 152
High Flux Australian Reactor, 187
Hiroshima, 70, 101, 168
homelands, 49, 58, 142, 149–51, 168, 172–75, 207
homelands movement, 151, 216
Howard, John, 185; government, 190–91, 202, 208–9

Illie, Elizabeth, 148
Inma (ceremonial song and dance), 195–96, 199–200, 203
intergenerational trauma, 142, 192
Irati Wanti (The Poison, Leave It) campaign, 14, 186, 194–205, 209–10, 217
irradiation, 8, 180; due to French tests, 87; as focus of Royal Commission, 126, 131, 134, 137, 145–46, 152–53, 216

Jabiluka, 95, *96*
Joint Venturers, 93, 110–15, 117
Jonas, William, 135, 141–43, *144*

Kerr, Charles, 129–31
Kerr Report, 129–31
Kilmer, Val, 200–202, *201*
Knill, Graham, 168–71
knowledge, Aboriginal. *See* Aboriginal knowledge
Kokatha, xii, 12, 41; and anthropologists, 114–17; and Canegrass Swamp, 94, 118–22, 160; knowledge of Country, 113; land, *156*; and Olympic Dam, 13, 107–18, 184–85
Kokatha Peoples Committee (KPC), 111, 114–15, 119, 121–22
Koongarra, 95, *96*
Koonibba Mission, 59, 147
Kungka Tjuta. *See* Kupa Piti Kungka Tjuta
Kupa Piti Kungka Tjuta, xiii, 14, 184–86, 191–211, *201*

labor. *See* Aboriginal employment/labor
Laby, Thomas, 21
Lake Dey-Dey, 148
land rights, 82–84, 90–99, 103, 115–17, 149, 153; and Australian Labor Party, 133–34; Berndt Report on, 121–22; claims of, 83, 93, 106, 115, 122, 132; debates over, 93–94, 125, 133, 140, 151, 212, 215; Kokatha, 13, 122–23; movements, 13, 69, 83, 164, 216; opposition to, 105–7, 110–12
land use: Aboriginal, 159–61, 166, 169, 178, 183; Anglo-European, 109
Langton, Marcia, 100
Lawrence, Herman, 22
Lennon, Lallie, 62–63, 143
Lester, Karina, 1–2, 191, 196, 205, 211–12
Lester, Yami, 1, 128, 143
Liddle, John, 130
Lucas Heights (Nuclear Reactor), 5, 187–89, 204

Mabel Creek, 62, 185
MacDougall, Walter, 54, 58–64, 148, 194
Madigan, Michele, 192, 194–95, 199–200, 202, 204
malnutrition, 31, 64
mamu (bad spirits), 55, 61, 143
Manhattan Project, 36, 138
Manta (earth), 105, 195–96, 207

Maralinga, *4*, 130, 132, 142–43, 152–53, 160, 165, 169; cleanup, 124, 142, 150, 153–59, 162–65, 176–79, 182; contamination, 124–25, 127, 129, 155, 157, 182, 218; cultural significance, 178; nuclear test site, xii, 41–42, 47, 52, 63–67, 71, 97; peopled space, 54; Pitjantjatjara word meaning, 53
Maralinga Camp, *144*, 148–51, 179. *See also* Oak Valley
Maralinga Prohibited Area, 42, 56, *57*, 59–61, 65, 157, 165
Maralinga Rehabilitation Technical Advisory Committee, 182, 191
Maralinga Tjarutja: experts, 13; spokesmen visit London, 154–55, 176–81. *See also* Southern Pitjantjatjara
Maralinga Tjarutja Council, 159, 162, 164
Maralinga Tjarutja Land Rights Act (1984), 128–29, 132, *156*
Marcoo, 65, 146–47
Marla Bore, 142–44, 147
Marshallese, 49, 168, 171–76, 183, 217
Mary Kathleen, *4*
Mawson, Douglas, 15–17, 20–29, 33–40
McClelland, James (Diamond Jim), 135–36, 138–39, 141–43, *144*, 148–49, 153
McClelland Commission. *See* Royal Commission into British Nuclear Tests in Australia
measles, 144–45
Menzies, Robert, 5, 43, 46, 52, 68, 139; as Anglophile, 43, 67, 126, 136–37, 139, 216; and China, 71–72, 88; criticism of, 136–37, 152; and French testing, 73, 85–86, 91; government, 71, 140, 178, 216; and Ernest Titterton, 138–41
migration. *See* mobility/migration, Aboriginal
Milliken, Robert, 160
Milpuddie, Edie, 65, 146–48
mining, general, 93–94, 98, 105, 107
Mintabie, *57*, 61–62, 143–44
missiles, ballistic, 44–45, 50, 54
missions, 54–56, 60–61, 127, 130, 142, 151, 216; effect of, 59; as form of colonial control, 214; Lutheran, 56, 147; and measles, 144; and paternalism, 55
mist, black. *See* black mist
mobility/migration, Aboriginal, 31, 42, 59, 61, 66, 148
mobilization, political. *See* Aboriginal political mobilization
Monte Bello Islands, xi, 41, 52, 138, 140
Morgan, Hugh, 106–7
Morrison, Scott, 6
Mount Painter, 26, 35, 37–38
Mount Serle, 27, 30–32, 60
Murphy, Lionel, 87
Mururoa Atoll, 74, 76, 80. *See also* French nuclear testing

Nagasaki, 51, 101, 168
Narbalek, *96*
neoliberalism, 11, 92, 101–2, 104
New Left, 76, 106, 128
new nationalism, 66
New Right, 106
Niedenthal, Jack, 175–76
Noonuccal, Oodgeroo, 83
nuclear age, 3, 8, 9, 69–70, 76, 102, 217; dawn of, ix, 10, 11, 16, 34, 39–40, 44; and technological developments, 67
nuclear ambitions: of Australia, 7, 12, 43–44, 63, 66, 212, 214; of Britain,

xii, 12, 43–44, 213–14; of France, 69, 72
nuclear atrocities, 128, 166
nuclear colonialism, concept/definition, 2–3, 7–8, 212
nuclear contamination, xiii, 10, 170, 206. *See also* fallout
nuclear disarmament, 128
Nuclear Disarmament Party, 133. *See also* peace movement
nuclear exceptionalism, ix, x, 9, 213–14, 217
Nuclear Exposure Tour, 197–98. *See also* Friends of the Earth
Nuclear Free and Independent Pacific movement, 128, 167
nuclear imperialism, 7–8, 69; Britain, 40, 43, 72, 213–14; France, 68, 84; US, 72, 84
nuclear industry, 90–91, 97, 122, 213; Australia, 9, 12, 204, 215; global, 38, 124; opposition to, 197. *See also* antinuclear movement; antinuclear sentiments; energy, nuclear; fuel, nuclear; power; nuclear
nuclear injustice, xii, 12, 82, 84, 135, 211
nuclearity, x, 93, 94, 103, 123
Nuclear Non-Proliferation Treaty, 85
nuclear order, x–xi, 86, 90, 186, 192, 195, 197, 211; Australia, 91, 152, 217; global, 2, 43, 67, 166, 209
nuclear proliferation, 71, 90, 100–101, 103
nuclear renaissance, 2, 218
nuclear survivors, 2, 7, 13–14; Aboriginal, 13, 56, 62, 126, 142, 146, 152–55, 166; global Indigenous, 155, 166–70, 175, 183, 211, 216–17; *hibakusha,* 168, 173, 205
nuclear violence, 10, 185
Oak Valley, *144*, 148–51, *156*, 179. *See also* Maralinga Camp.
ocher, 25, 36–37
Olary, 15–16, 24–25, 34–35, 39
Oliphant, Mark, 36, 38
Olympic Dam mine, *4*, 13, 92–94, 101–23, 184–85, 188, 215, 218; Environmental Impact Statement, 112–15, 117–18, 120; protests, 119, 198; three mines policy, 133; uranium deposit at, xii, 92;
Ooldea Mission, 56, *57*, 58–59, 65, 146–48, *156*
Ooldea Soak, 56, 58–59. *See also* Yuldi
Operation Antler, 53, 127
Operation Brumby, 150, 158
Operation Buffalo, 53, 65
Operation Clean-Up, 150
Operation Hercules, 150
Operation Totem, 1, 52, 62, 191
"out of sight, out of mind" perspective, 191, 195, 209

Painter, Mount, 26, 35, 37–38
Palmer, Kingsley, 141–42, 159–60
Partial Test Ban Treaty, 73, 90
pastoralism, 9, 30, 211
paternalism (colonial), 55, 58, 60, 67, 152; policies, 41, 43, 51, 137
peace movement, 6, 75, 86, 128, 192, 215; World Peace Council, 77
Penney, William, 38, 138
Peters, Gracie, 148
Pitjantjatjara, xii, 12, 41, 53, 105, 107–8, 185; land rights, 179. *See also* Southern Pitjantjatjara
Pitjantjatjara Council, 105–6, 131, 140
Playford, Thomas, 50
plutonium, 41, 53, 127, 150, 157–59, 162
Pohnpei Charter (1978), 167

politics. *See* Aboriginal political mobilization; Aboriginal politics
power, nuclear, xiv, 7, 94, 104, 218; Australia's lack of, 3, 5, 186–88

Queama, Mabel, *144*, 148, *161*
Queama, Tommy, 148–49
radiation: as energy source, 22–23; medicinal/health applications, 17, 22–23, 34–35, 81
radium, 4, 11, 15–18, 21–25, 27–30, 35–37, 39–40, 213
Radium Extraction Company, 26, 29–30, 33–34
Radium Hill, *4*, 39
Radium Ridge, 27, 29, 34–35
Ranger Uranium Environmental Inquiry, 95, 97
Ranger Uranium Mine, *4*, 96, 98, 100–101, 103, 133, 188, 198
rations, 30–32, 41, 54–56, 60–61
red heart, xi, 19, 20, 47, 213
Referendum (1967), 82–83
Reid, Ningel, 118–19
resistance, Aboriginal, xiii, 2–3, 114, 186, 196, 200, 209–10
Roberts, Silas, 98–99
Rowse, Tim, 129
Roxby Downs, 105, 108–10, 114–16, 118. *See also* Olympic Dam mine
Roxby Downs (Indenture Ratification) Act (1982), 93, 113, 118, 120
Roxby Management Services, 119–20
Roxstop Action and Music Festival, 198
Royal Commission into British Nuclear Tests in Australia, xiii, 13, 124–27, 154, 216; irradiation as focus of, 126, 131, 134, 137, 145–46, 152–53, 216
Rum Jungle, *4*, *96*
Ryan, Susan, 130–31
sacred sites: destruction of, 59, 94, 114, 151; protection of, 107–8, 110–12, 114, 116–17, 120, 184, 217
Sandimar, Rene, *144*, 148–49, *161*
Saunders, Tina, 125
Second World War, ix, xi, 7, 17, 38, 44, 70, 138
Secrets in the Sand (documentary), 154, 161, 177
segregation, 43, 48, 50, 63
self-determination, 68, 76, 151–52, 168, 215
Serle, Mount, 27, 30–32, 60
settler colonialism, x–xii, 3, 8, 11, 39–40, 110, 213
Seven Sisters Dreaming, 119–20, 201
Small, Andrew, 80
Smith, Arthur, 15, 24, 34, 39
social consciousness, 74, 136, 140
sociology, 169–70
South Australian Mining Act (1893), 18
Southall, Ivan, 47
Southern Land Council, 105, 108, 114
Southern Pitjantjatjara, 13, 128, 147. *See also* Maralinga Tjarutja
spinifex grass, 53, 54, 55, 56, 148
Sprigg, Reg, 21, 25
stagflation, 92–93, 102–3
Stewart, Ivy Makinti, 191–92, 203
Strangeway, Terry, *109*
student activism, 12, 75, 78–79, 81, 84–86. *See also* youth activism/rebellion
systemic colonialism, 127

Taranaki, 127, 181
Technical Assessment Group (TAG), 158–66, 168–70, 176, 180, 182–83
testimony, Aboriginal, 126, 142–43, 151–53, 216
Thatcher, Margaret, 130

Thomas, Max, 120
Thomson, Donald, 49–50
three-mines policy, 133
Titterton, Ernest, 38, 137–41, 153, 187
Tizard, Henry, 45
Tjarutja, meaning of, 129
Tjukur (Dreaming), 193, 195–96
Tonkin, David, 102–3, 106
Totem I, 1, 52, 62, 191
Traditional Owners, 105, 156, 158, 160, 191; Maralinga lands, 128, *156*, 163, 165, 182
trauma, intergenerational, 142, 192
Treaty on the Prohibition of Nuclear Weapons, 2, 218

United Aborigines Mission, 58
United Mount Painter Radium Company, 35
unpeopling, of the central deserts, 41, 46–47, 51, 111, 213
uraninite, 15, 24
uranium: empire supply, xi, 36–37, 187; export, 73, 90, 94–95, 99–103, 123–24, 188; mineral, 15, 17, 21, 24, 36–39, 92–93, 214; opposition to mining, 92, 100, *121*
uranium industry, Australia, 92, 94–97, 100–101, 104, 123
uranium moratorium (ALP), 100, 133

Vietnam War, 76–78, 83
Voyles, Traci Brynne, x, 10, 47, 81

Wallatinna, *57*, 128, 142–44, 182, 193
Walsh, Peter, 130–31, 134, 141
Wangati, William, 58–59
Ward, L. Keith, 34
waste, nuclear: debates about, 11, 204; disposal of, 1, 3, 6, 10, 104, 127, 134, 188–98, 216; national repository for, 189–90, 193–94, 202, 204, 218; storage of, xiii, 6, 13, 184, 187, 207–9
wastelanding, 10, 47
Watson, Dulcie, *144*, 148
Watson, Tjunmutja, 56, 58, 147–48
weapons, nuclear: and Australian ambitions, 3, 5, 9; and colonialism, 7–9, 40, 66–71, 91, 145, 167; and Britain, xii, 5–6, 12, 42–44, 213–14; and environment, x, 9, 81, 173; and exceptionalism, x, 9, 213–14; and France, 71–74; and imperialism, xi, 5, 7, 12, 36, 40–46, 66, 69–70, 78; testing of, xi, 5, 9, 12, 41, 73, 157; Treaty on the Prohibition of Nuclear Weapons, 2, 218; and United States, 70–71. *See also* French nuclear testing; Royal Commission into British Nuclear Tests in Australia
Western Australian Chamber of Mines and Energy, 133
Western Mining Corporation (WMC), 93–94, 102, 106, 108, 133. *See also* Joint Venturers
White Australia policy, 31, 85, 111
Whitehall (British government), 5, 35–36, 42, 44–46, 51–52, 64, 140, 157; Maralinga Tjarutja delegation to, 154, 176–82
Whitlam, Gough, 69, 81–82, 85–91, 95–98, 100; government, 86, 88, 90, 98, 113, 135
Williams, Willie, 119
Windlass, Hughie, 56, 58, 148–50, 154, 176, 179, 181
Windscale disaster, 104, 241n58
Wingfield, Eileen Wani, xiii, 184–85, 197, 200, *201*, 205–8
Wingfield, Glen, *109*

Wingfield, Janice, 194, 196–97
Wingfield, Joan, 114–16, 122
Wingfield, Rebecca Bear, 184, 193, 196, *201*, 201, 203, 206
Wingfield, Stanley, *109*
women, Aboriginal, xiii, 192–94, 208–9. *See also* Kupa Piti Kungka Tjuta
Woodward Royal Commission, 98–99
Woomera, 42, *57*, 59, 64, 119, *156*, 188–89; Dharug word meaning, 46, 53, 154; establishment of site, 46–48; opposition to, 49–51; peopled space, 54
World Peace Council, 77
World War II, ix, xi, 7, 17, 38, 44, 70, 138
Worster, Donald, ix, x

Yalata Mission, *57*, 58–59, 65, 130, 146–49, 151, *156*, 169
Yankunytjatjara, xii, 12, 41, 61, 128, 185, 195, 211; land rights, 149
Yirrkala, 82
youth activism/rebellion, 73, 75–76; Aboriginal, 83. *See also* student activism
Yuldi (Ooldea Soak), 56, 58–59. *See also* Ooldea Soak

Weyerhaeuser Environmental Books

Contaminated Country: Nuclear Colonialism and Aboriginal Resistance in Australia, by Jessica Urwin
Animating Central Park: A Multispecies History, by Dawn Day Biehler
Cleaning Up the Bomb Factory: Grassroots Activism and Nuclear Waste in the Midwest, by Casey A. Huegel
Capturing Glaciers: A History of Repeat Photography and Global Warming, by Dani Inkpen
The Toxic Ship: The Voyage of the Khian Sea *and the Global Waste Trade*, by Simone M. Müller
People of the Ecotone: Environment and Indigenous Power at the Center of Early America, by Robert Michael Morrissey
Charged: A History of Batteries and Lessons for a Clean Energy Future, by James Morton Turner
Wetlands in a Dry Land: More-Than-Human Histories of Australia's Murray-Darling Basin, by Emily O'Gorman
Seeds of Control: Japan's Empire of Forestry in Colonial Korea, by David Fedman
Fir and Empire: The Transformation of Forests in Early Modern China, by Ian M. Miller
Communist Pigs: An Animal History of East Germany's Rise and Fall, by Thomas Fleischman
Footprints of War: Militarized Landscapes in Vietnam, by David Biggs
Cultivating Nature: The Conservation of a Valencian Working Landscape, by Sarah R. Hamilton
Bringing Whales Ashore: Oceans and the Environment of Early Modern Japan, by Jakobina K. Arch
The Organic Profit: Rodale and the Making of Marketplace Environmentalism, by Andrew N. Case
Seismic City: An Environmental History of San Francisco's 1906 Earthquake, by Joanna L. Dyl
Smell Detectives: An Olfactory History of Nineteenth-Century Urban America, by Melanie A. Kiechle
Defending Giants: The Redwood Wars and the Transformation of American Environmental Politics, by Darren Frederick Speece
The City Is More Than Human: An Animal History of Seattle, by Frederick L. Brown
Wilderburbs: Communities on Nature's Edge, by Lincoln Bramwell
How to Read the American West: A Field Guide, by William Wyckoff
Behind the Curve: Science and the Politics of Global Warming, by Joshua P. Howe

Whales and Nations: Environmental Diplomacy on the High Seas, by Kurkpatrick Dorsey

Loving Nature, Fearing the State: Environmentalism and Antigovernment Politics before Reagan, by Brian Allen Drake

Pests in the City: Flies, Bedbugs, Cockroaches, and Rats, by Dawn Day Biehler

Tangled Roots: The Appalachian Trail and American Environmental Politics, by Sarah Mittlefehldt

Vacationland: Tourism and Environment in the Colorado High Country, by William Philpott

Car Country: An Environmental History, by Christopher W. Wells

Nature Next Door: Cities and Trees in the American Northeast, by Ellen Stroud

Pumpkin: The Curious History of an American Icon, by Cindy Ott

The Promise of Wilderness: American Environmental Politics since 1964, by James Morton Turner

The Republic of Nature: An Environmental History of the United States, by Mark Fiege

A Storied Wilderness: Rewilding the Apostle Islands, by James W. Feldman

Iceland Imagined: Nature, Culture, and Storytelling in the North Atlantic, by Karen Oslund

Quagmire: Nation-Building and Nature in the Mekong Delta, by David Biggs

Seeking Refuge: Birds and Landscapes of the Pacific Flyway, by Robert M. Wilson

Toxic Archipelago: A History of Industrial Disease in Japan, by Brett L. Walker

Dreaming of Sheep in Navajo Country, by Marsha L. Weisiger

Shaping the Shoreline: Fisheries and Tourism on the Monterey Coast, by Connie Y. Chiang

The Fishermen's Frontier: People and Salmon in Southeast Alaska, by David F. Arnold

Making Mountains: New York City and the Catskills, by David Stradling

Plowed Under: Agriculture and Environment in the Palouse, by Andrew P. Duffin

The Country in the City: The Greening of the San Francisco Bay Area, by Richard A. Walker

Native Seattle: Histories from the Crossing-Over Place, by Coll Thrush

Drawing Lines in the Forest: Creating Wilderness Areas in the Pacific Northwest, by Kevin R. Marsh

Public Power, Private Dams: The Hells Canyon High Dam Controversy, by Karl Boyd Brooks

Windshield Wilderness: Cars, Roads, and Nature in Washington's National Parks, by David Louter

On the Road Again: Montana's Changing Landscape, by William Wyckoff

Wilderness Forever: Howard Zahniser and the Path to the Wilderness Act, by Mark W. T. Harvey
The Lost Wolves of Japan, by Brett L. Walker
Landscapes of Conflict: The Oregon Story, 1940–2000, by William G. Robbins
Faith in Nature: Environmentalism as Religious Quest, by Thomas R. Dunlap
The Nature of Gold: An Environmental History of the Klondike Gold Rush, by Kathryn Morse
Where Land and Water Meet: A Western Landscape Transformed, by Nancy Langston
The Rhine: An Eco-Biography, 1815–2000, by Mark Cioc
Driven Wild: How the Fight against Automobiles Launched the Modern Wilderness Movement, by Paul S. Sutter
George Perkins Marsh: Prophet of Conservation, by David Lowenthal
Making Salmon: An Environmental History of the Northwest Fisheries Crisis, by Joseph E. Taylor III
Irrigated Eden: The Making of an Agricultural Landscape in the American West, by Mark Fiege
The Dawn of Conservation Diplomacy: U.S.-Canadian Wildlife Protection Treaties in the Progressive Era, by Kurkpatrick Dorsey
Landscapes of Promise: The Oregon Story, 1800–1940, by William G. Robbins
Forest Dreams, Forest Nightmares: The Paradox of Old Growth in the Inland West, by Nancy Langston
The Natural History of Puget Sound Country, by Arthur R. Kruckeberg

Weyerhaeuser Environmental Classics

Debating Malthus: A Documentary Reader on Population, Resources, and the Environment, edited by Robert J. Mayhew
Environmental Justice in Postwar America: A Documentary Reader, edited by Christopher W. Wells
Making Climate Change History: Documents from Global Warming's Past, edited by Joshua P. Howe
Nuclear Reactions: Documenting American Encounters with Nuclear Energy, edited by James W. Feldman
The Wilderness Writings of Howard Zahniser, edited by Mark W. T. Harvey
The Environmental Moment: 1968–1972, edited by David Stradling
Reel Nature: America's Romance with Wildlife on Film, by Gregg Mitman
DDT, Silent Spring, and the Rise of Environmentalism, edited by Thomas R. Dunlap
Conservation in the Progressive Era: Classic Texts, edited by David Stradling
Man and Nature: Or, Physical Geography as Modified by Human Action, by George Perkins Marsh

A Symbol of Wilderness: Echo Park and the American Conservation Movement, by Mark W. T. Harvey
Tutira: The Story of a New Zealand Sheep Station, by Herbert Guthrie-Smith
Mountain Gloom and Mountain Glory: The Development of the Aesthetics of the Infinite, by Marjorie Hope Nicolson
The Great Columbia Plain: A Historical Geography, 1805–1910, by Donald W. Meinig

CYCLE OF FIRE

Fire: A Brief History, second edition, by Stephen J. Pyne
The Ice: A Journey to Antarctica, by Stephen J. Pyne
Burning Bush: A Fire History of Australia, by Stephen J. Pyne
Fire in America: A Cultural History of Wildland and Rural Fire, by Stephen J. Pyne
Vestal Fire: An Environmental History, Told through Fire, of Europe and Europe's Encounter with the World, by Stephen J. Pyne
World Fire: The Culture of Fire on Earth, by Stephen J. Pyne

ALSO AVAILABLE

Awful Splendour: A Fire History of Canada, by Stephen J. Pyne